"A WISE AND DISCERNING MIND"

Program in Judaic Studies
Brown University
Box 1826
Providence, RI 02912

BROWN JUDAIC STUDIES

Edited by
Shaye J. D. Cohen

Number 325

"A WISE AND DISCERNING MIND"
Essays in Honor of Burke O. Long

Edited by
Saul M. Olyan
Robert C. Culley

"A WISE AND DISCERNING MIND"
Essays in Honor of Burke O. Long

Edited by

Saul M. Olyan
Robert C. Culley

Brown Judaic Studies
Providence, Rhode Island

Library of Congress Cataloging-in-Publication Data
"A wise and discerning mind" : essays in honor of Burke O. Long / edited by
    Saul M. Olyan, Robert C. Culley
        p.   cm. — (Brown Judaic studies ; no. 325)
    "Selected publications of Burke O. Long": pp. xiii–xvi.
    ISBN 1-930675-01-1 (cloth : alk. paper)
    1. Bible. O.T.—Criticism, interpretation, etc. I. Long, Burke O. II. Olyan, Saul M. III. Culley, Robert C. IV. Series.

BS1188.W58 2000
221.6—dc21
                                                    00-056468
                                                    CIP

Printed in the United States of America
on acid-free paper

Contents

Burke O. Long

Preface

It is a great pleasure and, indeed, an honor to present this volume of essays to our colleague and friend Burke O. Long on the occasion of his sixtieth birthday and his retirement from teaching. The Kenan Professor of Religion and the Humanities at Bowdoin College, Burke is a biblical scholar of distinction and influence, an honored teacher, and a vital contributor to the intellectual mission of the Society of Biblical Literature over many years. As we celebrate his accomplishments on this occasion, we eagerly anticipate many more years of probing, insightful scholarship and intellectual leadership.

Burke O'Connor Long was born in Richmond, Virginia on 17 September 1938. After receiving a B.A. in philosophy from Randolph-Macon College in 1961, Burke attended Yale Divinity School, where he took a B.D. degree in 1964. Determined to pursue biblical studies on the doctoral level, he began his graduate studies in Yale's Department of Religious Studies, earning an M.A. in 1966 and a Ph.D. in 1967. His dissertation, supervised by Brevard Childs, became his first book: *The Problem of Etiological Narrative in the Old Testament* (Töpelmann, 1968). This short and insightful monograph, still frequently cited by scholars in the field thirty-two years after its publication, significantly furthered our understanding of biblical etiologies and their function. It established Burke early on as a serious young contributor to biblical research, particularly in the area of form criticism. The same year that the monograph on etiological narrative appeared in print, Burke began his teaching career at Bowdoin College in Brunswick, Maine, where he has remained ever since. From 1969, articles on such topics as divination, etiologies, and prophetic narrative genres began to appear in the major journals and in collections of essays. By the middle of the 1970s, he was publishing papers on oral literature, and the social dimensions of prophecy and prophetic narrative. An edited volume, *Canon and Authority: Essays in Old Testament Religion and Theology*, appeared in 1977; a second edited volume, entitled *Images of Man and God: Old Testament Short Stories in Literary Focus*, was published in 1981.

By the early 1980s, Burke had embarked on a major project that was to keep him occupied until the early '90s: his two-volume commentary on the Book of Kings for the Forms of the Old Testament Literature series (FOTL). In *1 Kings: With an Introduction to Historical Literature* (1984) and in *2 Kings* (1991), he produced a pair of model commentaries that have garnered much praise for their literary insight, methodological sophistication, and comprehensiveness. Going well beyond the classical categories of form criticism, Burke emphasized the literary dimensions of biblical historiographic writing in these works. Various articles focusing on historiography also appeared during the 1980s and early 1990s, as well as new essays on social history, literary criticism, literary theory, and theology. A third edited book, *Re-thinking the Place of Biblical Studies in the Academy*, was published in 1990. The period 1977–1985 saw Burke assume the editorship of the Sources for Biblical Study series (Scholars Press), and, more significantly, he founded the highly successful and useful SBL Writings from the Ancient World series in 1988, remaining editor until 1993.

During the early 1990s, Burke's interests came to focus on the history and politics of modern biblical scholarship itself. A series of essays on the work of W. F. Albright and his early students culminated in the publication of a major book-length assessment of the Albright school entitled *Planting and Reaping Albright: Politics, Ideology, and Interpreting the Bible* (1997). Combining careful mining of archival data with a moderate post-modernist analysis of the production and dissemination of knowledge, *Planting and Reaping Albright* became a subject of major controversy as well as a classic of the field from the time of its publication. Though castigated verbally and in print by some "children" and "grandchildren" of Albright for its critical and contextual portrait of the master, many other colleagues, including some with impeccable Albrightian pedigrees, regard the book as a landmark in the field, considerably advancing our historical and theoretical understanding of the practice of modern biblical scholarship. We can only expect to be further stimulated by Burke's current work on the Holy Land in the nineteenth- and twentieth-century American imagination.

Burke Long's career is not only to be characterized by innovative and daring scholarship, outstanding teaching, and distinguished leadership in the shaping of the field. He has also been a significant colleague for many of us, always willing to read and react to a manuscript, always helpful with honest, constructive criticism. Many younger scholars owe Burke a special debt of gratitude for his generous support and encouragement. In a field where many of the most accomplished senior scholars are not willing to take the time to engage the work of scholars in their first years after the Ph.D., Burke stands out for his commitment to mentoring promising people at the beginning of their careers.

The essays in this volume reflect something of the range of Burke Long's scholarly interests. There are contributions that employ the more familiar approaches of historical criticism, including form critical analysis, reflections on the historical books of the Hebrew Bible, and discussions of texts from ancient West Asia. But there are also essays that pursue less familiar paths. Some explore the different ways texts may be read by examining their literary, psychological, theological, and hermeneutical dimensions. Others consider the implications of the reading process itself, seeing that readers are themselves bound up with their own cultural and ideological contexts. The variety in the volume invites us to contemplate anew the rich and fertile field that is biblical studies.

Saul M. Olyan and Robert C. Culley

Selected Publications of Burke O. Long

Books

Author

1. *The Problem of Etiological Narrative in the Old Testament* (BZAW 108; Berlin: Töpelmann, 1968).
2. *1 Kings: With an Introduction to Historical Literature* (FOTL 9; Grand Rapids, Mich.: Eerdmans, 1984).
3. *2 Kings* (FOTL 10; Grand Rapids, Mich.: Eerdmans, 1991).
4. *Planting and Reaping Albright: Politics, Ideology, and Interpreting the Bible* (University Park, Pa.: Pennsylvania State Univ. Press, 1997).

Editor and Contributor

5. *Canon and Authority: Essays in Old Testament Religion and Theology* (with G. W. Coats; Philadelphia: Fortress, 1977).
6. *Images of Man and God: Old Testament Short Stories in Literary Focus* (Sheffield: Almond, 1981).
7. *Re-thinking the Place of Biblical Studies in the Academy* (Brunswick, Maine: Bowdoin College, 1990).

Professional Articles

Literary Studies

8. "Etymological Etiology and the DT Historian," *Catholic Biblical Quarterly* 31 (1969) 35–41.
9. "Two Question and Answer Schemata in the Prophets," *Journal of Biblical Literature* 90 (1971) 129–39.
10. "Prophetic Call Traditions and Reports of Vision," *Zeitschrift für die Alttestamentliche Wissenschaft* 84 (1972) 494–500.
11. "II Kings 3 and Genres of Prophetic Narrative," *Vetus Testamentum* 23 (1973) 337–48. Reprinted in *Prophecy in the Hebrew Bible:*

Selected Studies From Vetus Testamentum (compiled by David E. Orton; Leiden: Brill, 1999) 72–83.

12. "The Effect of Divination Upon Israelite Literature," *Journal of Biblical Literature* 92 (1973) 489–97.

13. "Divination As Model for Literary Form," in *Language in Religious Practice* (ed. W. J. Samarin; Rowley, Mass.: Newbury House, 1976) 84–100.

14. "Recent Field Studies in Oral Literature and their Bearing on OT Criticism," *Vetus Testamentum* 26 (1976) 187–98.

15. "Recent Field Studies in Oral Literature and the Question of *Sitz im Leben*," *Semeia* 5 (1976) 35–49.

16. "Reports of Vision Among the Prophets," *Journal of Biblical Literature* 95 (1976) 353–65.

17. "The Stylistic Components of Jer 3:1–5," *Zeitschrift für die Alttestamentliche Wissenschaft* 88 (1976) 386–90.

18. "A Darkness Between Brothers: Solomon and Adonijah," *Journal for the Study of the Old Testament* 19 (1981) 79–94.

19. "The Form and Significance of 1 Kings 22:1–38," in *Isac Leo Seeligmann Volume: Essays on the Bible and the Ancient World* (ed. Alexander Rofé and Yair Zakovitch; Jerusalem: E. Rubinstein, 1983) 3.193–208.

20. "Historical Narrative and the Fictionalizing Imagination," *Vetus Testamentum* 35 (1985) 405–16.

21. "Framing Repetitions in Biblical Historiography," *Journal of Biblical Literature* 106 (1987) 385–99.

22. "On Finding the Hidden Premises," *Journal for the Study of the Old Testament* 39 (1987) 10–14.

23. "Second Kings," in *Harper's Bible Commentary* (San Francisco: Harper & Row, 1988) 323–41.

24. "The Books of Kings," in *Books of the Bible* (ed. Bernhard Anderson; New York: Scribner's, 1989) 141–53.

25. "The Historical Books" (introductory articles and revised annotations to Samuel, Kings, and Chronicles) in *The New Oxford Annotated Bible* (ed. Bruce M. Metzger; New York: Oxford Univ. Press, 1991) 267–69, 340–580.

26. "The 'New' Biblical Poetics of Alter and Sternberg," *Journal for the Study of the Old Testament* 51 (1991) 71–84.

27. "The Shunammite Woman: In the Shadow of the Prophet?" *Bible Review* 7 (1991) 12–19, 42.

28. "Sacred Geography As Narrative Structure in 2 Kings 11," in *Pome-*

granates and Golden Bells (Festschrift for Jacob Milgrom; ed. David P. Wright et al.; Winona Lake, Ind.: Eisenbrauns, 1995) 231–38.

History of Criticism

29. "Mythic Trope in the Autobiography of William Foxwell Albright," *Biblical Archaeologist* 56 (1993) 36–45.

30. "W. F. Albright, G. E. Wright, and the Legacies of Christian Hebraism," in *Proceedings of the Eleventh World Congress of Jewish Studies: Division A, The Bible and Its World* (Jerusalem: World Union of Jewish Studies, 1994) 239–46.

31. "W. F. Albright As Prophet Reformer: A Theological Paradigm Inscribed in Scholarly Practice," in *Prophets and Paradigms: Essays in Honor of Gene M. Tucker* (Sheffield: Sheffield Academic Press, 1996) 152–72.

32. "Historical Imaginings, Ideological Gestures: Albright and the 'Reasoning Faculties of Man,'" in *The Archaeology of Israel: Constructing the Past, Interpreting the Present* (ed. Neil Asher Silberman et al.; Sheffield: Sheffield Academic Press, 1997) 82–94.

33. "Scenery of Eternity: William Foxwell Albright and Notions of Holy Land," in *"Ihr Völker alle, Klatscht in die Hände!" Festschrift für Erhard Gerstenberger* (Exegese in Unserer Zeit 3; ed. Rainer Kessler et al.; Münster: LIT Verlag, 1997) 317–32.

34. "Scenes of Eternity: Biblical Scholars and Notions of 'Holy Land,'" in *Proceedings of the Twelfth World Congress of Jewish Studies: Division A, The Bible and Its World* (Jerusalem: World Union of Jewish Studies, 1999) 79–93.

35. "Scholarship," in *Handbook of Post Modern Biblical Interpretation* (ed. A. K. M. Adam; St. Louis: Chalice, in press).

Biblical Culture, Religion and Theology

36. "The Social Setting for Prophetic Miracle Stories," *Semeia* 3 (1975) 46–63.

37. "Prophetic Authority as Social Reality," in *Canon and Authority: Essays in Old Testament Religion and Theology* (ed. G. W. Coats and B. O. Long; Philadelphia: Fortress, 1977) 3–20.

38. "The Social World of Ancient Israel," *Interpretation* 36 (1982) 243–55.

39. "The Figure at the Gate: Readers, Reading, and Biblical Theologians," in *Canon, Theology and Old Testament Interpretation: Essays in Honor of Brevard S. Childs* (ed. G. Tucker; Philadelphia: Fortress, 1988) 166–86.

40. "The Social Dimensions of Prophetic Conflict," *Semeia* 21 (1981) 31–53. Reprinted in *"The Place is Too Small for Us": The Israelite Prophets in Recent Scholarship* (ed. R. P. Gordon; Winona Lake, Ind.: Eisenbrauns, 1995) 308–331.

41. "Ambitions of Dissent: Biblical Theology in a Postmodern Future," *Journal of Religion* 76 (1996) 276–89.

42. "Letting Rival Gods be Rivals: Biblical Theology in a Postmodern Age," in *Problems in Biblical Theology: Essays in Honor of Rolf Knierim* (ed. Henry Sun et al.; Grand Rapids, Mich.: Eerdmans, 1997) 222–233.

Bible and Cultural Studies

43. "Reading the Land: Holy Land as Text of Witness," in *The Labour of Reading: Desire, Alienation, and Biblical Interpretation* (Festschrift for Robert C. Culley; ed. Fiona Black et al.; Atlanta: Society of Biblical Literature, 1999) 141–159.

44. "Parlor Tours of the Holy Land: Fantasy and Ideology in Stereographic Photos of Palestine," in *A Land Flowing with Milk and Honey: Visions of Israel from Biblical to Modern Times* (ed. Leonard Greenspoon; Omaha, Neb.: Creighton Univ. Press, in press).

45. "Lakeside at Chautauqua's Holy Land," *Biblicon* (forthcoming, 2000).

Works-in-Progress

46. Book: "Bringing the Holy Land Home to America: Bible Study and Contested American Identities" (a study of holy land in popular imagination, and how critically trained biblical scholars reflected, and helped shape, ideologically charged notions of holy land).

47. Book: "Holy Persuasions: The Bible in Advertising."

Contributors

Alice Bach, Case Western Reserve University

Gary Beckman, University of Michigan

Adele Berlin, University of Maryland

Marc Z. Brettler, Brandeis University

John J. Collins, Yale University

Robert C. Culley, McGill University

J. Cheryl Exum, University of Sheffield

Danna Nolan Fewell, Drew University

Erhard S. Gerstenberger, Philipps-Universität, Marburg

Edward L. Greenstein, Tel Aviv University

David M. Gunn, Texas Christian University

Douglas A. Knight, Vanderbilt University

Saul M. Olyan, Brown University

Alexander Rofé, Hebrew University of Jerusalem

Jack M. Sasson, Vanderbilt University

Mark S. Smith, New York University

Hugh C. White, Rutgers University

Marsha White, Somerville, Massachusetts

Robert R. Wilson, Yale University

Yair Zakovitch, Hebrew University of Jerusalem

Chapter 1

De-Doxifying Miriam

Alice Bach
Case Western Reserve University

My first encounter with reader-response theory occurred many years before I encountered Burke Long. Actually I was six years old—I was given a
beautiful edition of *Alice in Wonderland* with hand-tipped colored plates.
My eyes loved seeing the name Alice on every page. Of course I thought
that the book had been written for me: In my narcissistic childlike world, I
had become one of the Alices of literature. As an adult, when I wrote (and
published) a series of books about twin bears, named Ronald and Oliver, I
was really writing about two sides of myself. It is certainly not news that
writers write about themselves; most creative writing is, after all, *dreaming
on paper*. While novel writing has always been considered light years away
from scholarly writing, feminist theories have altered the timbre of scholarly writing through the acknowledgment of the shadow of the self that
imbues all writing. The power of the self has acted as a hammer that
cracked open the geode of biblical studies, revealing multifaceted crystals,
many of them gendered. Long after the literary theorists have flown, to im-
bibe the nectar of a prettier flower, feminist theory will, in my opinion, always be pivotal for its emphasis on the multiple subject positions of the
reader. In delineating and demanding our own spaces, our bodies ourselves, educated white women became the first visible Other in the academy, diffusing the spotlight of universalism and totalizing truth assumed
by the former academicians—white men. Then came demands for equal
time from blacks, chicanos, queers, transsexuals. In the past fifteen minutes reading as pornographer, reading as body builder, and reading as
salmon fisherman have become fashionable. Fortunately for the scholarly
world, Burke Long has not fallen victim to a virulent attack of the trendies,
and remains a careful scholar, who still maintains the ability to surprise

1

and inform his readers. To honor Professor Long's work in the field, I think it is appropriate to look at the category of feminist theory, particularly as it has affected scholars of the Bible, and see where such theory has taken us, and where it might be headed.

Even though some feminist scholars are committed to uncovering the ideological bias inherent in these interpretive texts, too often the blinders of race, class, and even of theology have stayed in place. Thus, to follow the canonical unit along its traditional interpretive trajectory has not resulted in an escape from the well-defended borders of class, ethnicity, and race that are common to both ancient and modern biblical scholars. As more scholars pursue the continuing discourse we have with past interpreters, we will need to cut through the tangled undergrowth of partisan antagonisms as well as the adversarial roles that may be more easily defined. In spite of the fact that half of the seminary graduates and almost half of the Ph.D. graduates in religion since the 1970s have been women, gendered readings and feminist curricular advances in the academy hardly reflect such demographics. Clarifying issues is not enough; they need to be debated, and we should refuse to grant either authors and editors or traditional commentators of biblical texts the authority they seek to control interpretation.

As a member of the feminist biblical guild, I have been surprised at what I see as a lack of engagement with philosophical and political issues among feminist scholars. In many ways feminist scholars of ancient Mediterranean texts seem blind to their own life situations, in both the everyday world and the politics of academic institutions. (As a New Yorker, I found the general aura of politeness in academia rather frustrating.) While feminists certainly differ in interpretations of specific terms or narrative units, there has been an assumption that feminist theorists working in the field possess a monolithic viewpoint, an essentialist *feminist* approach to reading the Bible. Feminists must stick together, although often we have no more in common than the languages of the ancient texts we study. While I think that the intellectual process can only become sticky as tar baby when an entire group tries to speak as one, I am continually surprised at how routine feminist discourse has become. Passion seems to have the flown the scene. Feminists are too comfortable to be effective.

There has arisen a mannerly but perfunctory nod to issues of religiosity, race, ethnicity, but as Toni Morrison has noted, "in these matters, silence and evasion have historically ruled literary discourse. Evasion has fostered another, substitute language in which the issues are encoded, foreclosing open debate."[1] Morrison is concerned with the ways in which nineteenth-

---

[1] Toni Morrison, *Playing in the Dark: Whiteness and the Literary Imagination* (Cambridge: Harvard Univ. Press, 1992) 7.

and twentieth-century Euro-American literary discourse arranges itself in relation to the African other. Biblical scholars can certainly be stimulated by her arguments in relation to our contemporary interpretive corpus relative to the silence about race in the critical writings of the guild, especially the effects of that silence upon the dominant culture. Further, the subject of ethnicity in ancient literary texts has barely been mentioned in contemporary critical work.

Every woman, scholar and activist, has multiple relationships with chosen audiences. I am mindful of Phyllis Trible's call more than twenty years ago to "Choose ye whom you will serve: the God of the fathers or the God of sisterhood." While her choice is perhaps too narrow for those of us who are wary of binary oppositions, I understand the problem of identifying one's audience. For myself, the confusion of audiences results in a feeling that I am a New Age Persephone, spending half my time within the borders of Bible and the other half within feminist studies. (I vacillate upon which world is ruled by Ceres and which by Hades.) My time in each world has convinced me that there is not one pure world of light, one land within whose borders feminist scholars can rest. In order to illustrate how differently one feminist can think about one text in less than five years, I shall offer some alternate observations on the biblical character of Miriam augmented and altered from an article that I published in 1994.[2]

Dreaming of Miriam's Well

Midrashic storytelling, revisioning the biblical narrative from one's own perspective, points toward a contrapuntal, nomadic style of reading. Such a reading eludes the borders of accepted reading conventions and makes no claims for historical truth. As a student of modern midrash, I am challenged by the power of narrative expansion—and as a student of ancient aggadic midrash I feel constrained by scholarly reliance upon the dating and provenance of each text in determining its authenticity—and value. Several years ago, for a volume of the *Feminist Companion to the Bible*, Athalya Brenner asked me to write a response to several articles on Miriam.[3] As part of that work, I wrote a narrative midrash in dialogue to illustrate what I had interpreted as Miriam's pacifist cry at the Sea,

> Sing to the Lord, for he has triumphed gloriously.
> Horse and Rider he has thrown into the sea.

---

[2] Alice Bach, "With a Song in Her Heart: Listening to Scholars Listening for Miriam," in *A Feminist Companion to Exodus to Deuteronomy* (vol. 6 of *The Feminist Companion to the Bible*, ed. Athalya Brenner; Sheffield: Sheffield Academic Press, 1994) 243–255.

[3] See previous note.

In the text of Exodus 15 the elements of warfare—the horses, the riders, their armor and their shields, the chariots—point toward a male culture. If, as Carol Meyers argues in that same volume,[4] there were communities of female performers, might they not have been rejoicing in the destruction of the dominant male culture, exemplified by and encoded within the language of warfare?

> Sing to the Lord, for he has triumphed gloriously.
> Horse and Rider he has thrown into the sea.

A classical echo of a lyric that appeals to the elements of women's culture over militaristic ideals is attributed to Sappho:

> Some say the cavalry corps
> Some infantry, some again
> Will maintain that the swift oars
> Of our fleet are the finest
> Sight on dark earth; but I say
> That whatever one loves, is.[5]

While I found support for my pacifist reading in this lyric of Sappho, I could find no classical Jewish commentary or midrash that read Miriam's song in the way that I had. Perhaps pacifism is a modern category. My search has persisted among the modern midrashim, for I believe that pacifism is an important element of feminist theory. However, if the classical midrashist holds the power to narrate, he also has the power to block other narratives from forming or emerging. Perhaps that explains the absence of expansions beyond those aggadic midrashim that award the famous Well, water to sustain Israel, to Miriam because she had first watched out for her baby brother Moses when he was rescued from the treacherous water of the Nile.

As I watch contemporary films and read novels based on the biblical book of Exodus and listen to feminist Passover Seder prayers about Miriam, I listen for Miriam's Song at the Sea, and I hear no echo of my construction of Miriam as a peacemaker, singing for the end of warfare at the edge of the Sea. Of course I know I am walking disputed territory. Like many of my generation, I was trained to halt at the border of classical aggadic midrash, the province of the *darshanim*. But doesn't that give a reading pride of place to the ancients? If texts can yield meaning only when situated in context, one's reading positions are limited. For context itself is a contrived and preferential construction. But echoes persist, and I still find myself needing to justify reading any texts against any others.

---

[4] Carol Meyers, "Miriam the Musician," in *A Feminist Companion*, 207–230.

[5] Mary Bernard, *Sappho, A New Translation* (Berkeley: Univ. of California Press, 1958) fragment 41.

The central question for this paper revolves around the Scylla of defining midrash as a formalist closed genre and the Charybdis of viewing midrash as a dynamic juggling of cultural memory that reinvents itself at each border crossing. What is the significance for the narrative critic if the midrash was collected by groups of *darshanim* during the so-called classic midrashic period ending in the ninth century CE, after an unknown period of oral circulation and transmission, or written ten years ago as a biblical expansion by Israeli writer Amos Oz, or American Cynthia Ozick? Modern aggadic midrash differs not only in its being created within the past two hundred years, but even more important, it is written by a named author. Thus, modern midrash is considered to be a creative work of a known author, as opposed to a collection, cloaked in the mystery and authority of "the rabbis." For a feminist reading, it seems imperative to use the tools of cultural criticism to dig beneath the masculine codes in which the ancient texts and their ancient expansions were written.

Certainly I am not the first scholar to wonder about the authenticity of midrash composed after the classical period. The august Shalom Spiegel, while not concerned with feminist issues, has argued against the tradition which considers the creation of authentic midrash to have been cut off before the last millennium:

> With the sacred writings of the Jews there traveled to the nations of East and West who had adopted them [pause] traditions and tales current among the Jews. Along with the Bible spread far and wide, having their imprint many a celebrated center of art and literature, gaining at times a surprising hold upon the popular imagination. [*sic*][6]

Two of Spiegel's insights are important to my own thinking: his understanding that narrative grows and remains fluid, and that it develops with a society's *current* traditions and tales. Thus, midrash reflects the time in which it is written more than some reified adherence to biblical or classical accuracy. The Exodus midrash created by Jeffrey Katzenberg and the kids at Dreamworks reflects their desire to keep current movie audiences not only entertained but also reassured that it's a small world after all. *The Prince of Egypt* was conceived, according to the Dreamworks founding trio, during the initial burst of excitement of inventing the company in 1994.[7] In a meeting at Spielberg's house, the talk turned to animation. Spielberg said he wanted to do a project with the grandeur of *The Ten Commandments*. "What a great idea," Geffen said. "Let's do it."

---

[6] Quoted in Judah Goldin, *Studies in Midrash and Related Literature* (Philadelphia: Jewish Publication Society, 1988) 395.

[7] *Time* magazine, Vol. 152, No. 24, December 14, 1998. For many further articles and reviews concerning *The Prince of Egypt*, see "In Search of Moses" on the web at <http://www.time.com/time/magazine/1998/dom/981214/cover1.html>, and follow links.

At first, Katzenberg didn't recognize the risks of treading on such literally sacred ground. Then it hit him. "The Moses story is central to three of the world's major religions," Katzenberg told an interviewer from *Time* magazine. "It is so much more complicated, so much more challenging than simply making a movie." His eye fixed firmly on audience demographics, Katzenberg illustrates perfectly Shalom Spiegel's second point about the surprising hold midrashic creations have upon the popular imagination. Here is where Spiegel speaks directly to the Dreamworks boys, masters of marketing Moses to a multicultural audience. Katzenberg continues, "Just putting together the script raised enough delicate questions to fill the Red Sea. How to portray the Egyptians as cruel slave masters without antagonizing the Arab world?" "We were very careful with skin tones to show that the slave population was multicultural, multiethnic," says Tzivia Schwartz-Getzug, an expert in interfaith relations who was hired as liaison to the religious communities. "And in the Exodus scene, you actually see some Egyptians going with the Hebrews." Spiegel expected midrash to reflect the community that has created it. Nevertheless, I consider it a blessing that he did not live to see *The Prince of Egypt*.[8]

However, there were plenty of religious experts involved in the project. A focus group of the Faithful, rabbis, evangelical Christians, and Muslim specialists convened in Hollywood to vet the film script, in our century's version of the meeting in Javneh. And these canon-makers of caution took their job very seriously. The result is not surprising: The film sometimes looks starched as a vicar's surplice, sounds stodgy as a UN fundraising pitch. What is lacking is any trace of irreverence or wit within the dialogue or narrative. The most imaginative sequence for me is the hieroglyphs that come to life. The most charitable comment I can make about the parting of the Red Sea is that it is an homage to Mr. DeMille.

And what of my major concern: the wily Miriam? One would think that Dreamworks would capitalize upon the young girl who brokers a deal with the Pharaoh's daughter to reunite her brother with his biological mother. But alas, Disneyesque casting has sent spunky Miriam to the bottom of the Sea, more little mermaid than biblical prophet. Sandra Bullock makes no attempt to camouflage her well-known voice. Even when she is telling Moses of his Hebrew heritage, her sugar-coated accent sounds too much as though she's recently returned from the mall. She is too fizzy to be completely believable as a beleaguered slave laborer in danger of getting

[8] *The Prince of Egypt*: 1998. Directed by Brenda Chapman, Steve Hickner, and Simon Wells. Written by Philip La Zebnik and Nicholas Meyer. Produced by Dreamworks, Inc. Running time: 97 minutes. Cast: Val Kilmer, Moses/God; Ralph Fiennes, Rameses; Michelle Pfeiffer, Tzipporah; Sandra Bullock, Miriam; Jeff Goldblum, Aaron; Danny Glover, Jethro; Patrick Stewart, Pharaoh Seti; Helen Mirren, The Queen; Steve Martin, Hotep; Martin Short, Huy.

lashed across the back if she takes too much time churning out the bricks. A couple of times I thought Bullock was about to ask Moses if he wanted to super-size his fries. Thus, Miriam the prophet is relegated to perky sister status, a narrative strategy meant to please a cartoon audience that expects only Moses to be super-sized. Perhaps Spiegel's prodigious imagination had not counted on the wonder that is Dreamworks. Who holds the power to narrate is in my view what is truly at issue. Surely the genre of midrash benefits from cultural readings which avoid the privileging of high art over popular culture. For midrash, like any narrative text, reflects the cultural milieu of its creators. Gap-filling activity also reflects the interests of the midrashist. There is no whole picture that waits to be filled in by midrash, since the perception and filling of a gap lead to other gaps.

While Sandra Bullock's real swell Miriam was still cluttering up my mind, I came across an ancient midrash called the *Book of Miriam.* Well trained, I looked for its provenance. Translated into English by Canadian philosopher Leonard Angel, the book had apparently never before appeared in English.[9] Indeed it had not been widely available in published form either in the original Hebrew, or in the Teutsch Miriam (a Yiddish form which appeared in Bohemia in the late fourteenth century). So it was no surprise that I had never come across this text. According to Angel, a decision had been taken over half a millennium ago, in 1472, to restrict access to the work to the few women who then possessed the physical manuscripts, to those women's daughters, to the daughters of these daughters, etc. I thought this odd since ordinary medieval women's access to literacy, much less to sacred texts, would have been doubtful. As a result of physical attacks on the few European manuscripts by the husbands of the women studying the Book, only a single German copy is extant, and is to be found in the city of Bonn. Outside of Europe there was a copy in a small town near Marrakech, and it was this Moroccan copy that was now in the hands of Miriam HaCohen, a student of the renowned Sarah al-Fasudi, the leader of the Miriamic study circle in the early twentieth century. Finally the text manuscript was shown to Professor Angel, who was authorized by the aged Miriam HaCohen to make an English translation. I had a transitory doubt that a man would be allowed the responsibility to translate this book preserved by women, but Miriam HaCohen was old and frail, and time was running out. She had no daughter to entrust the manuscript to. Might this work be an antidote to the simplistic Miriam of the Boy's Life of Moses?

From the few passages Angel had reprinted from the Hebrew I saw that the Hebrew was difficult, and according to Angel much of it had been written in an elegant Rashi script. Related in poetic form (translated by Angel)

---

[9] Leonard Angel, *The Book of Miriam* (Oakville, Ont.: Mosaic Press, 1997).

the narrative tells of several named Israelite women going to the Egyptian Pharaoh Picol to plead for the Israelites' freedom. The first is Adah, who plays a familiar role.

> Adah was wearing flowing garments, white, gold, and blue
> Sea green border, a nose ring, earrings, anklets
> A silver comb in her hair, jewelry adorning her crown,
> Her left shoulder bare. Bells that tinkled as she moved
> Among scarves of finest gauze,
> Trailing fragrance of anointing balm, myrrh, and frank
> Moving softly like a cat.
> Picol was captured. (234)

Now that she has Picol's attention, Adah warns him that his sons and daughters will be killed because the ruler "has extended his dominion at the cost of Heaven." And then she reveals the prophecy from God: Come live with us, be free in God's land, you, your children, your children's children. Picol remembers words from the Hebrew prophet:

> God gives this land to all of us
> You too will not be counted, if you're among us
> Beat your swords into ploughshares.

But Picol's heart was hardened. After consulting with the male elders, Miriam dances with timbrel and drum for Picol, first to gain his confidence, then to show him signs and wonders. On the first day,

> She seemed to him a fog
> Picol, amazed, shouted
> His fear was gone.
>
> Next day, Miriam danced, her veils flow
> Picol listened. It seemed to him Miriam was lost within a cloud of gnats.
> The gnats were buzzing him.
> Picol shouted: the gnats were gone. Picol was still afraid. (235)

The pattern is set for the days of the dance.

Next day Miriam danced, led Picol to his harem, and lo! The women fell, screamed, rocked in agonizing pain. Next day, Miriam danced upon the portico, the heavens opened. Hail.

Next day and next day and next day Miriam danced, and in her song she said:

> The fields will be bared by locusts
> The crops will be spared by none.
>
> Next day, Miriam, sang and danced and closed her eyes and Picol
>   closed his eyes.
> When she ceased to sing, he was lost in darkness, could not open them.
> Picol shouted but his mind was lost in darkness.
> Picol was still afraid.

> Next day Miriam danced and sang, Now look at me, whom—do—
>   you—see
> She bowed and darkened her face until Picol saw his son.
> Bloodied, staggered, limping, dripping red. (236)

OK, you all get the drill. But don't dismiss the power of the text that quickly. The next part of the narrative contains the midrash I had been searching for.

> When Adah and Miriam returned, Picol escorting them
> Fringe garmented and rainbow sleeved,
> a guest of the Hebrews
> The Hebrew elders, Picol, and all his retinue saw the folly of war.
> They said, "War is madness."
> Picol emptied his harem, destroyed his palace immersed in a cold and
>   bitter spring
> Became astonished, even he himself, a Hebrew
> Taking the name Lamadyah, saying because I learned of Yah
> And from Yah and from his people
> And his people, one tenth the Philistines
> Immersed that day, in the cold, bitter spring
> Taking Hebrew names, women, men, children, all of them.
> The Hebrew elders gave them gifts, cattle, flocks, and to each, a new-
>   born heifer not to be fatted, not to be killed, but for milking,
> All the days in which it would be milked. (242–243)

This is the teaching of Miriam, who came from the desert, from Sinai: *God is the womb of the world.*

Katzenberg and the Dreamworks crowd seemed to teeter on the brink of transforming Miriam into a New Age persona and used her to justify their one world theme. If only they had found the *Book of Miriam*. The scene in which Miriam becomes the plagues for the Pharaoh would have made a dynamic musical mime number, with animation crossing the boundaries of human possibility. Some of the Egyptians left Egypt with the Israelites in both these cultural productions. Lest you think that I have eclipsed the great scholars for a glitzy world of animation, I shall evoke the memory of Father Freud, who speculated that Moses was actually an Egyptian who passed single-deity worship derived from Akhenaton to the Jews.[10] More recently, German scholar Jan Assmann, author of *Moses the Egyptian*, argues that Moses and Hebrew monotheism are a memory of Akhenaton, whose name was purged from all lists of rulers when the priests of Amon retook power.[11] Perhaps Katzenberg was merely tapping into a *Zeitgeist* that renders Israel not chosen by God, but derivative of a much older

[10] Sigmund Freud, *Moses and Monotheism* (1939; reprint, New York: Random House, 1987).

[11] Jan Assmann, *Moses the Egyptian: The Memory of Egypt in Western Monotheism* (Cambridge: Harvard Univ. Press, 1997).

culture. A collective unconscious longing for the fleshpots of Egypt. And what of Leonard Angel, and his discovery of the *Book of Miriam*? I must admit that this is not a clockwise midrash. Rather it falls backwards through time, going counterclockwise. The *Book of Miriam* is an invention of Angel, the Canadian philosopher, who cast his fictive Miriam in the genre of Targum and midrashic commentary.

Angel's creation argues for accepting midrash as a hybrid strategy, heterogeneous and unmonolithic, one that intermingles midrashic versions regardless of their place in the chain of chronology. Midrash has historical roots certainly, but midrash is not an object to be described, neither is it a unified corpus of symbols and meanings that can be definitively interpreted. Midrash rides the back of culture, contested, temporal, emergent. Read together, the film and the novel reveal an interesting contrast: The film follows the subjectivity of the ancient male-centered midrashists. Indeed, even the feminist reading of Trible in creating her mosaic of Miriam does not separate the woman from the patriarchal culture of triumphal warfare. The *Book of Miriam* is a true midrash of the Other. As such it debates the historical and political construction of identities and Self/Other relations. It allows the voice of the Other to come through the level of the doxa text. This Miriam has been de-doxified, and as such she has sung a revolutionary Song of the Sea.

Chapter 2

Goddess Worship—Ancient and Modern

Gary Beckman
University of Michigan

Almost 3500 years ago a Hittite worshipper addressed a goddess:
Whatever household is hated by Ištar,
she sends those (her attendants) into that house in order to treat it.
They do the housework with groaning and anguish.
The young brides were at odds,
and (so) one always pulls the other by the head,
and they no longer weave cloth in harmony.
The brothers have become enemies,
and (so) they no longer plow the field by the acre;
they have quarreled,
and (so) grinding of grain no longer takes place.
. . . .
A man and his wife who love each other and carry their love
to fulfillment:
That has been decreed by you, Ištar.
He who seduces a woman and carries the seduction to fulfillment:
That has been decreed by you, Ištar.
. . . .
But if a woman is hated by her husband,
then you, Ištar, have caused her to be hated.

Special abbreviations employed in this essay are:
IBoT — Istanbul Arkeoloji Müzelerinde Bulunan Boğazköy Tabletlerinden Seçme Metinler
(Istanbul, 1944–88)
KBo — Keilschrifttexte aus Boghazköi (Berlin, 1916–)
KUB — Keilschrifturkunden aus Boghazköi (Leipzig, Berlin, 1921–90)

11

> But if a man is even hated by his wife,
> then you, Ištar, have heaped up misery(?) for them.[1]

These lines exalt the powers of the deity to determine interpersonal relations among humans, to render them negative as well as positive. In contrast, a neo-pagan ritual from the second half of the past century has only nice things to say about the Goddess (singular and capitalized), who is thought by her adherents to be the continuation of all female divinities recognized by past cultures of Europe and western Asia:

> The presence of the noble Goddess extends everywhere.
> Throughout the many strange, magical,
> And beautiful worlds.
> To all places of wilderness, enchantment, and freedom.
>
> The Lady is awesome.
> The Powers of death bow before Her.
>
> Our Goddess is a Lady of Joy.
> The winds are Her servants.
>
> Our Goddess is a Goddess of Love.
> At Her blessings and desire
> the sun brings forth life anew.
>
> The seas are the domains of our Serene Lady.
> The mysteries of the depths are Hers alone.
>
> The circle is sealed, and all herein
> Are totally and completely apart
> From the outside world,
> That we may glorify the Lady whom we adore.
> Blessed Be![2]

No ambivalent nature like that of the Hittite goddess is in evidence in the apostrophe to her successor. Did the ancient poet enjoy a closer acquaintance with his subject than the author of the modern text, or has the nature of female divinity become milder over the course of millennia?

My attention has been drawn to the question of gods in female form in the course of work on a Hittite ritual addressed to a goddess of Mesopotamian origin, represented in the cuneiform text by the logogram (word-sign) IŠTAR.[3] Seeking to grasp her essence—moving "toward the image of

---

[1] *KUB* 24.7 i 24–33, 38–40, 48–50. Translation by H. G. Güterbock, "A Hurro-Hittite Hymn to Ishtar," *JAOS* 103 (1984) 156–57. I have simplified the typography here by eliminating the brackets indicating restored portions, and have supplied the "misery" in the final line.

[2] E. Fitch, "Pagan Ritual for General Use," quoted in M. Adler, *Bringing Down the Moon*. Revised and Expanded Edition (New York: Penguin/Arkana, 1986) 470–71.

[3] See my "Babylonica Hethitica: The '*babilili*-Ritual' from Boğazköy," in *Recent*

Ištar"[4] as it were—I began to collect information about goddesses in Hittite religion and in other belief systems of the ancient Near East, and to peruse anthropological and religio-historical discussions of goddess worship.

Inevitably, I was confronted by the centrality of the Goddess within the twentieth century's so-called "neo-pagan revival." When in early 1999 I ran a search for the keyword "goddess" on the Amazon.com bookstore web page, I got 122 "hits," 110 of which appeared from their titles to deal with present-day beliefs about, and reverence for, a deity in female form. By now I have done a fair amount of reading in literature of this sort, tracking down many relevant essays in feminist and New Age periodicals. A fair summary of modern Goddess belief is given by *thealogian*[5] Carol Christ:

> ... the Goddess is the power of intelligent embodied love that is the ground of all being. The earth is the body of the Goddess. All beings are interdependent in the web of life. Nature is intelligent, alive and aware. As part of nature, human beings are relational, embodied, and interdependent. The basis of ethics is the feeling of deep connection to all people and all beings in the web of life. The symbols and rituals of Goddess religion bring these values to consciousness and help us build communities in which we can create a more just, peaceful, and harmonious world. . . .[6]

I find it difficult to object to the ethical viewpoint enunciated here.

However, as an historian, I have been struck by the apparent need of many authors of Goddess literature to buttress their newly-adopted faith with claims of its great antiquity and unbroken subterranean transmission, in the face of Christian persecution, to contemporary communities of belief. According to this "Goddess hypothesis," or "conviction,"[7] there existed early in the human experience "an original, uniform, peaceful, matriarchal/matrilineal society with the Goddess as deity." This Goddess herself could be described as "a single, ubiquitous, prehistoric and historic paramount deity."[8]

Developments in Hittite Archaeology and History (ed. H. G. Güterbock, H. A. Hoffner, Jr., and K. A. Yener; Winona Lake, Ind.: Eisenbrauns, forthcoming).

[4] *Homage* to the essay of Th. Jacobsen, "Toward the Image of Tammuz," *HR* 1 (1961) 189–213.

[5] This neologism is in common use among Goddess theorists and devotees.

[6] *Rebirth of the Goddess* (New York: Routledge, 1997) xv.

[7] So characterized by M. W. Conkey and R. E. Tringham, "Archaeology and the Goddess: Exploring the Contours of Feminist Archaeology," in *Feminisms in the Academy* (ed. D. C. Stanton and A. J. Stewart; Ann Arbor: Univ. of Michigan Press, 1995) 206.

[8] I have borrowed this concise summary from J. B. Townsend, "The Goddess: Fact, Fallacy and Revitalization Movement," in *Goddesses in Religions and Modern Debate* (ed. L. W. Hurtado; Atlanta: Scholars Press, 1990) 181.

Thus there is a tendency within Goddess circles to view all historically attested female divinities as full or partial manifestations of a single figure—sometimes called the "Great Mother"[9]—and to see the tracks of this Goddess also in prehistoric artifacts thought to be religious in character. The desire for historical validation is clear, for example, in the words of Carol Christ: "It makes a great deal of difference to me to know that the Goddess has a history, that feminists in the twentieth century did not make her up out of whole cloth."[10]

Here I will review some of the evidence for the flourishing of a pre-modern Goddess cult, emphasizing material from my own area of expertise, the religion of the Hittites. Of course there is no doubt that countless cultures have conceived of innumerable deities in the form of the human female.[11] What is in question, rather, is the alleged widespread or even universal worship of a unitary, supreme, and unfailingly benevolent female creator and mother, a figure such as that addressed by the modern hymnist quoted earlier.

Here I must clarify my personal approach to historical scholarship: Despite the realization that I often fail to attain my ideal due to prejudice and societal conditioning, I nonetheless strive for objectivity. While postmodernists and radical feminists have indeed demonstrated that historical—as well as other—*meaning* is constructed by each person and each group,[12] this observation does not negate the autonomous existence of historical *facts* outside of particular discourses.[13] Cleopatra either dallied with Caesar and with Anthony, or she did not. King David either ruled in Jerusalem, or he did not. Our remote ancestors either universally honored the Great Mother, or they did not.

---

[9] This designation obviously goes back to an epithet of Cybele of the pre-Classical and Classical periods, on whom see now L. E. Roller, *In Search of God the Mother: The Cult of Anatolian Cybele* (Berkeley: Univ. of California Press, 1999), but it owes its contemporary popularity to the work of E. Neumann, *The Great Mother: An Analysis of the Archetype* (Princeton: Princeton Univ. Press, 1955).

[10] *Rebirth of the Goddess*, 44.

[11] For a thoughtful discussion of the conceptual difficulties which arise when one attributes only a masculine gender to the divine, see T. Frymer-Kensky, *In the Wake of the Goddesses: Women, Culture and the Biblical Transformation of Pagan Myth* (New York: Free Press, 1992).

[12] The contentious issue of the degree of distortion inevitably introduced by historians in their reconstructions of the past is discussed at length by P. Novick, *That Noble Dream: The "Objectivity Question" and the American Historical Profession* (Cambridge: Cambridge Univ. Press, 1988).

[13] On the other hand, the recognition of particular facts as significant—as "historical facts"—is dependent upon the interests, needs, and biases of the individual historian. See E. H. Carr, "The Historian and His Facts," in *What is History?* (New York: Vintage Books, 1961) 3–35.

Whether we today possess sufficient information to establish the facts concerning an individual person, event, or belief of the past is another matter. His or her preconceptions may make an observer loath to accept evidence which threatens a worldview, but this by no means eliminates that evidence. Witness the flowering in recent decades of women's history, whose practitioners have made use of material which was available all along, although ignored by writers working in the mainstream historical tradition, who privileged records created by, for, and about "Great Men."[14]

Thus, even if we inevitably fall short in our efforts at objectivity, it is highly inadvisable to follow Professor Christ in abandoning this way of thought in favor of what she calls "embodied thinking,"[15] that is, empathetic subjectivity checked, in theory, by the opinion of the community with which one identifies. If we should adopt this approach, the world of scholarship would fragment into a babble of incommensurate and mutually unintelligible discourses. And lest one argue that it doesn't really matter anyway, that the disputes of academics are so many meaningless skirmishes in Cloudcuckooland, we must remember that ideas do have consequences. German historical and religious scholarship in the first half of the twentieth century was subjected to the disastrous influence of *völkish* thought, which rejected objectivity and approached all questions from a standpoint of ostensible empathy with an imagined "racial community."[16] The disastrous consequences of this development are well known.

To return to my topic—advocates of the Goddess hypothesis see the deity's presence in some of the earliest recovered works of human craft: in Paleolithic cave paintings and in steatopygous figurines.[17] Of course, verification or falsification of social conditions or beliefs postulated for prehistory is practically an impossible task,[18] since written documents are by

---

[14] See G. Lerner, "Why History Matters," in *Why History Matters* (New York: Oxford Univ. Press, 1997) 199–211.

[15] *Rebirth of the Goddess,* 34–40.

[16] See in general M. Weinreich, *Hitler's Professors: The Part of Scholarship in Germany's Crimes against the Jewish People* (New York: YIVO, 1946), and more to the point for the subject at hand, S. Heschel, "Deutsche Theologen für Hitler: Walter Grundmann und das Eisenacher Institut zur Erforschung und Beseitigung des jüdischen Einflusses auf das deutsche kirchliche Leben," in *"Beseitigung des jüdischen Einflusses . . .": antisemitische Forschung, Eliten und Karrieren im Nationalsozialismus* (ed. A. Hofmann; Darmstadt: Wissenschaftliche Buchgesellschaft, 1999) 147–67.

[17] E. O. James, *The Cult of the Mother-Goddess* (New York: Praeger, 1959) 13–22; G. R. Levy, *The Gate of Horn* (London: Faber and Faber, 1948) 56–63.

[18] Cf. D. H. French, "Archaeology, Prehistory and Religion," in *Studien zur Religion und Kultur Kleinasiens: Festschrift für Friedrich Karl Dörner zum 65. Geburtstag am 28. Februar 1976* (ed. S. Sahin et al.; Leiden: E. J. Brill, 1978) 375–83.

definition lacking, and the interpretation of mute artifacts is fraught with arbitrariness and uncertainty. But let us try.

Everyone is familiar with the cave paintings of France, most of which depict animals, sometimes as the quarry of hunters. While this subject matter does not immediately point to the Goddess—or to any deity at all— Goddess theorists would have it that the very placement of the art in caverns is significant. In their view, the caves themselves should be interpreted as symbolic representations of the womb of the Goddess,[19] and the beasts as her offspring. To this argument I would reply, "Kann sein, muß aber nicht," or "T'ain't necessarily so." An alternative explanation for the location of the paintings can easily be adduced: In the time before settled life and therefore before architecture, for instance, humans could have been expected to seek shelter in readily available caves. It would only be natural for early people to place illustrations which they wished to preserve on the walls of such periodic habitations. Perhaps paintings were also done elsewhere—say on exterior rock outcroppings—but they could hardly have survived for us to view today.

The evidence of the statuettes is equally problematic. Most European and west Asian prehistoric small sculpture is actually either androgynous or theriomorphic,[20] and does not overwhelmingly portray a fecund female human as maintained by advocates of the Goddess hypothesis. Furthermore, do the images which *do* depict females represent humans or deities? If the latter, do all of the figurines portray a single divinity? Their function is also obscure. Were prehistoric female statuettes intended to stimulate fertility, or perhaps to aid human mothers in giving birth? In sum, evidence for a cult of the Goddess in the Paleolithic is not probative.

Regarding Neolithic Europe, enthusiasts of the Goddess generally embrace the reconstruction of developments put forward by archaeologist Marija Gimbutas.[21] A critic has summarized this interpretation as follows:

> Originally, society was matriarchal, matrilineal, matrilocal, egalitarian and peaceful. Women held the positions of power equal to, or greater than, [those] of men. The religion of this primal stage of culture was concerned with "*the* (Mother) Goddess." A time of destruction followed. Matriarchal (or at least matrilineal) society under the Mother Goddess was usurped by the invasion of more warlike, male-dominated, pastoral societies whose deity was male.[22] . . . Following that conquest by the pastoral, patriarchal,

---

[19] Christ, *Rebirth of the Goddess,* 50–53.

[20] Conkey and Tringham, "Archaeology and the Goddess," 215.

[21] Her ideas are well summarized in the posthumous *The Living Goddesses* (edited and supplemented by M. R. Dexter; Berkeley: Univ. of California Press, 1999).

[22] This is a reference to the arrival of speakers of the Indo-European languages in Europe.

patrilineal societies, the Goddess religion was suppressed and women were subordinated to the rule of men.[23]

Matriarchy is fundamental to Gimbutas's earthly Eden. The concept of a universal stage in human cultural evolution in which women exercised political power was first formulated in 1861 by the Swiss jurist and classicist Johann Jakob Bachofen,[24] primarily on the basis of an analysis of Greek mythological tales. Rejected or ignored by contemporary classical scholars, Bachofen's ideas on what he called "mother-right" (*das Mutterrecht*) were adopted by Friedrich Engels in his *Der Ursprung der Familie, des Privateigentums und des Staats* of 1884,[25] and in this century they have been enthusiastically revived by followers of C. J. Jung.[26] Indeed, the standard— and greatly abridged—English translation of *Das Mutterrecht* was published in the Jungian Bollingen series with an introduction by Joseph Campbell. It was only in the late 1970s that feminist theorists including Mary Daly[27] and Charlene Spretnak[28] began to employ the concept of primitive matriarchy to support their (re)construction of a "Goddess religion."

In the absence of textual evidence from the Neolithic, we must turn to ethnological parallels to test the plausibility of a primeval matriarchy. It is surely telling that anthropologists have failed to identify a single living society—no matter how primitive its economic structure—in which women are dominant over men.[29] Thus we must reject the place of matriarchy as an *inevitable* phase of human social development. This conclusion poses no particular difficulties for Jungians, since they hold that "mother-right" is nonetheless valid as a stage of youthful psychological development. But considerable damage has obviously been sustained by Engels's theory of early history as a progression of stages including matriarchy. More importantly, an important prop of the Goddess hypothesis which we are considering has been knocked out.

---

[23] J. B. Townsend, "The Goddess" 180–81. See also L. Meskel, "Goddesses, Gimbutas and 'New Age' Archaeology," *Antiquity* 69 (1995) 74–86.

[24] Excerpted in *Myth, Religion and Mother Right: Selected Writings of J. J. Bachofen* (tr. R. Manheim; Princeton: Princeton Univ. Press, 1967) 69–207.

[25] Available in Friedrich Engels, *Studienausgabe* 3 (ed. H. Mehringer and G. Mergner; Reinbek bei Hamburg: Rowolt, 1973) 15–146.

[26] See R. Noll, *The Jung Cult: Origins of a Charismatic Movement* (New York: Free Press, 1997) 161–76.

[27] *Gyn-Ecology* (Boston: Beacon Press, 1978) 107–12.

[28] *Lost Goddesses of Early Greece: A Collection of Pre-Hellenic Myths* (Boston: Beacon Press, 1984).

[29] See J. F. Collier and M. Z. Rosaldo, "Politics and Gender in Simple Societies," in *Sexual Meanings: The Cultural Construction of Gender and Sexuality* (ed. S. B. Ortner and H. Whitehead; Cambridge: Cambridge Univ. Press, 1981) 275–329, and cf. G. Lerner, *The Creation of Patriarchy* (New York: Oxford Univ. Press, 1986) 15–35, esp. 31.

The argument for this theory is also marred by the selective use of evidence. Contrary to Gimbutas's claims, fortifications and other indications of warfare predating the penetration by the Indo-Europeans have in fact been recovered archaeologically in central and western Europe. Some burials from this region do present the variation in wealth usually associated with social hierarchy. And what is known from later texts about the goddesses of early Europe does not support the idea of a single, all-powerful goddess. Rather, we find a plethora of female deities, each with her own character and sphere of influence.[30]

The earliest textual documentation for religious belief and practice—and indeed for anything at all—was produced in the ancient Near East, beginning near the close of the fourth millennium in both Egypt and Mesopotamia. The religion of early Sumer, as evidenced primarily in lists of deities and registers of temple offerings, honored a great many goddesses. The most prominent female divinity was Ninḫursag,[31] whom we may describe as a Mother-goddess. Ninḫursag, however, did not subsume or even dominate the other Sumerian goddesses. Rather, each of these figures was responsible for a particular aspect of the cosmos—for example, overseeing the brewing of beer or looking out for the fortunes of a single city. Inanna of Uruk, who was named Ištar by Semitic speakers, was a particularly intriguing figure. According to the Sumerologist Thorkild Jacobsen,[32] Inanna was originally the spirit of the communal storehouse, but she soon came to embody human desires of all sorts, cupidity as well as avarice. The Hittite hymn with which I began invokes her as Ištar and celebrates her control of interpersonal relations among humans.

In a curious development, Ištar expands her sphere of influence over time, and by the late second millennium she has absorbed most other Mesopotamian goddesses.[33] The number of gods also falls, but not so radically. Why this occurred is not clear to me. But I must stress that a single Goddess was never paramount in the religions of the ancient Near East.

I come now to the area which I know best, the Hittite religion of second-millennium Anatolia. The numerous texts from the Hittite capital of Ḫattuša (the modern Turkish village of Boğazkale) allow us to establish many facts about Hittite society, including the position of women within it. Although they lived under patriarchal norms and were thereby disadvantaged in many spheres, women played an important role in religious

[30] H. E. Davidson, *Roles of the Northern Goddess* (London: Routledge, 1998) 182–90.

[31] Th. Jacobsen, *The Treasures of Darkness* (New Haven: Yale Univ. Press, 1976) 104–10.

[32] Ibid., 135–43.

[33] On Ištar among the Hittites, see my essay, "Ištar of Nineveh Reconsidered," *JCS* 50 (1998) 1–10.

affairs.[34] They were not denied access to temples in Ḫatti, and female practitioners were active in many ceremonies of the state cult. While these
women were normally present in subordinate roles, such as singers and
musicians, priestesses such as the "Mother of God" (AMA.DINGIR-*LIM*)
and "Lady/Goddess" (NIN.DINGIR) seem to have directed the rites in
which they participated.[35] It is my impression that the prominence of female officiants in official worship increased over time.

From earliest times the role of one particular woman—the queen—was
of great importance in Hittite cult. According to Hittite royal ideology,[36]
the king stood at the apex of human society by virtue of his position as
chief priest of the state gods and as administrator of Ḫatti on their behalf. A
blessing of the monarch reads:

> May the Tabarna,[37] the king, be dear to the gods! The land belongs to the
> Storm-god alone. Heaven, earth, and the people belong to the Storm-god
> alone. He has made the Labarna, the king, his administrator, and has given
> him the entire Land of Ḫatti. The Labarna shall continue to administer the
> entire land with his hand. May the Storm-god destroy whoever should ap-
> proach the person of the Labarna, [the king], and the borders of Ḫatti![38]

Although she is not expressly mentioned in this benediction, it is clear
from ritual texts that the queen joined her male counterpart at the focal
point of Hittite worship already in earliest times. This joint responsibility
for the cult is nicely illustrated by the rock relief at Firaktin near Kayseri in
south-central Turkey in which Queen Puduḫepa worships the Sun-goddess while her husband Ḫattušili III serves the Storm-god.[39]

But what can we say about the personal religious beliefs of the ordinary
Hittite? Of course, the records from the royal archives are far more infor-
mative about the state cult than concerning popular beliefs and practices,
but an important window into this latter area is provided by the compositions which Hittitologists call "rituals." Such texts frequently begin with
the identification of an "author" and the statement of the difficulty which
the procedure is intended to resolve. For example, "Thus says Uḫḫamuwa,
man of the Land of Arzawa: When there is mass death in the land—if some

---

[34] See my "From Cradle to Grave: Women's Role in Hittite Medicine and
Magic," *Journal of Ancient Civilizations* 8 (1993) 25–39.

[35] On these functionaries see S. R. Bin-Nun, *The Tawananna in the Hittite Kingdom*
(Heidelberg: Carl Winter, 1975) 189–92.

[36] I discuss this complex of ideas in my "Royal Ideology and State Administration in Hittite Anatolia," in *Civilizations of the Ancient Near East* (ed. J. Sasson et al.;
New York: Scribners, 1995) 1.529–43.

[37] *Tabarna,* or *Labarna,* is a title of the king.

[38] *IBoT* 1.30.

[39] An excellent photograph of this relief is given by K. Bittel, *Die Hethiter,*
Universum der Kunst (Munich: C. H. Beck, 1976) 176–77, Abb. 198.

god of the enemy has brought it about, then I do as follows."[40] This particular rite would have been performed on behalf of a community, but many others focused on an individual. These included *rites de passage* for birth, adolescence, and death. For instance, the Hittite tablet collections have yielded more than a dozen birth rituals,[41] and the contents of several of these are mutually incompatible. I interpret this situation as follows: Hittite royal bureaucrats set about collecting the totality of information available within the central Hittite realm concerning various problems. All of this knowledge was filed in the archives of the capital for immediate use should a member of the royal family or court be confronted by any of these crises. These documents, then, afford us just a glimpse into popular religion in Late Bronze Age Anatolia.

Now, in connection with our consideration of the position of women in Ḫatti, it is striking how many of the practitioners in Hittite ritual texts are female. Indeed, of the 71 individuals attested by name as authors of rituals in E. Laroche's *Catalogue des textes hittites*,[42] 38, or more than 50%, are women. The most common designation borne by these magicians is "Old Woman," a title which links them to the realm of birth and practical obstetrics—compare the French *sage femme*. Indeed, I have shown elsewhere that midwifery is the original locus from which there expanded the magical competence of Hittite women.[43] In sum, we may judge that in the realm of religious practice, the authority of women was approximately equal to that of men.

And so we come to the role of goddesses in Hittite religion. This is a daunting problem, since the size of the Hittite pantheon is truly overwhelming. Indeed, the ancients themselves spoke of the "Thousand Gods of Ḫatti."[44] This multiplicity arose from the Hittites' practice of taking over the worship of the deities of territories which they added to their realm, rather than simply ignoring them or perhaps identifying them with their own traditional gods—as the Romans were later to treat the Olympians. A preliminary census of the Hittite pantheon reveals that more than one-third of the deities whose gender can be ascertained are female.[45] This anal-

---

[40] *KUB* 9.31 ii 1–3.

[41] These were the subject of my dissertation, published as *Hittite Birth Rituals* (Wiesbaden: Otto Harrassowitz, 1983).

[42] Paris: Klincksieck, 1971.

[43] *Hittite Birth Rituals,* 232–35.

[44] See now Cem Karasu, "Why Did the Hittites Have a Thousand Deities?" in *Hittite Studies in Honor of Harry A. Hoffner, Jr. on the Occasion of His 65th Birthday* (ed. R. Beal, G. Beckman, and G. McMahon; Winona Lake, Ind.: Eisenbrauns, forthcoming).

[45] The raw material has been collected by B. H. L. van Gessel, *Onomasticon of the Hittite Pantheon* (Leiden: E. J. Brill, 1998).

ysis must be refined in the future, however, to determine whether there are differences in the distribution of sex among the groups of divinities contributed by the various ethnic groups making up the population of Ḫatti, and to track changes in the relative prestige enjoyed by gods and goddesses over the 500-year course of Hittite history.

Prominent among the goddesses were grandmother Ḫannaḫanna, whose intervention is crucial in restoring the equilibrium of the universe in many Anatolian myths, as well as a number of other Mother-goddesses.[46] The Fate-deities and those responsible for birth were also female. In light of what we have seen earlier about the affinity of Hittite women for magic, it should come as no surprise that goddesses such as Kamrušepa[47] and Išḫara[48] are in charge of incantations and oaths on the divine level. Finally, the closing centuries of the Hittite Empire witnessed the steady increase in importance of Ištar-figures, imported from—or at least inspired by—the Mesopotamian and Syrian pantheons. Once more we encounter not a single Goddess but numerous female deities with special duties and competencies.

At the very head of the Hittite gods stood a chthonic and solar deity called the Sun-goddess of (the city of) Arinna,[49] who was adopted by the Hittites from their Hattic predecessors, and who is said to "direct the kingship and queenship"[50] of Ḫatti. Her partner was the Storm-god of Ḫatti (or of the Heavens),[51] who developed from the common Indo-European god of the bright sky. We have already seen his relationship to the Hittite monarch. Together with their son, the Storm-god of (the city of) Nerik,[52] these divinities constituted a sort of trinity on behalf of whom the mortal royal family governed Ḫatti. This imperial ideology takes concrete form in the sanctuary of Yazılıkaya, situated just outside Ḫattuša.[53] Here two converging processions of deities have been carved onto the opposing walls of an impressive rock outcropping—approximately 30 gods on the left and around 20 goddesses on the right. At the head of the open-air chamber the

---

[46] *Hittite Birth Rituals*, 238–48.

[47] J. Klinger, *Untersuchungen zur Rekonstruktion der hattischen Kultschicht* (Wiesbaden: Harrassowitz Verlag, 1996) 155–59.

[48] D. Prechel, *Die Göttin Išḫara* (Münster: Ugarit-Verlag, 1996) 91–97.

[49] V. Haas, *Geschichte der hethitischen Religion* (Leiden: E. J. Brill, 1994) 423–26.

[50] *KBo* 1.1 rev. 35.

[51] A comprehensive recent study of this deity is P. H. J. Houwink ten Cate, "The Hittite Storm God: His Role and His Rule according to Hittite Cuneiform Sources," in *Natural Phenomena: Their Meaning, Depiction and Description in the Ancient Near East* (ed. D. J. W. Meijer; Amsterdam: Koninklijke Nederlandse Akademie van Wetenschappen, 1992) 83–148.

[52] V. Haas, *Der Kult von Nerik* (Rome: Päpstliches Bibelinstitut, 1970) 93–112.

[53] For excellent photographs, see K. Bittel, *Die Hethiter*, 203ff., Abb. 23–41.

columns meet in the persons of the imperial triad. Although far fewer than 1000 gods are depicted at Yazılıkaya, the monument nevertheless constitutes a clear statement of the "sexual politics" of Hittite religion: Male and female, god and goddess, are of symmetrical and equal importance for the proper functioning of the cosmos.

It is interesting to see that the patriarchal norms characteristic of the economy and society of the Hittites are absent from their religious life, and indeed from both the practical (cultic) and ideal (theological) levels. Feminist anthropologist Sherry Ortner has shown how useful it can be to think of a society's relative assignment of prestige by gender as hegemonic rather than absolute. This ordering, she writes, is "culturally dominant and relatively deeply embedded but nonetheless historically emergent, politically constructed, and nontotalistic." Furthermore, "every society/culture has some axes of male prestige and some of female, some of gender equality, and some (sometimes many) axes of prestige which have nothing to do with gender at all."[54]

I would judge that religious ideology was an aspect of Hittite life resistant to the patriarchal hegemony of the culture. It is easy to see how this might be so, given the anthropomorphism and polytheism of Hittite religion. Since the service which humans were thought to owe their divine masters was conceived of on analogy to that offered to mortal rulers, various aspects of worship might call for the particular qualities and talents—biologically determined or culturally defined—of both men and women. But the Hittite gods were not in fact simply human beings endowed with greater powers and immortality. As representatives of natural forces or of societal functions, deities could not be ordered hierarchically in relationship to one another in the manner of men and women within society. A Hittite might feel himself to be superior to his wife, and even receive social reinforcement in that judgement, but who could say that the fertility of the earth as embodied by the Sun-goddess of Arinna was any less crucial to all life than the fructifying rains of the Storm-god?

Having examined a variety of ancient evidence, including Hittite records, in some detail, we have noted scant support for the alleged historical underpinnings of the Goddess hypothesis. The pantheons of the documented societies of the ancient Near East featured not a single, paramount, and benevolent Goddess, but multiplicities of female figures. Each goddess had her own powers and duties and—as is clear from the Hittite hymn excerpted at the outset—could wreak havoc as well as distribute boons among humans.

---

[54] "Gender Hegemonies," in *Making Gender: The Politics and Erotics of Culture* (Boston: Beacon, 1996) 146–47.

Therefore the thealogians of the Goddess movement are not revivalists but inventors of a new tradition. But does this reduce the value of a faith which clearly fills a spiritual need for many contemporary women as well as for a considerable number of men? Not in the opinion of feminist writer Mary Jo Weaver, who recognizes that the Goddess movement rests upon a myth rather than on verifiable historical evidence. Nonetheless, she points out that

> utopias need not have connections to a real past in order to provide hope for a real future. . . . Goddess feminists use their rituals as moments of celebration, as a means of connection with the natural world, and as energy centers whence they emerge to seek the transformation of the world. Whoever she is, therefore, the Goddess appears to emerge out of a lost past with an invitation to criticize the present and to create a new future.[55]

While my scholarly inquiries are directed toward the recovery of the historical realities of the religions of the ancient Near East, the questionable historicity of the foundational myth of modern Goddess religion ought not to trouble its adherents. Nor does it seem to me particularly relevant to those investigating Goddess worship as a living faith. The truth of myth is not subject to empirical verification. On this level, argument about whether the Goddess once reigned supreme is comparable to the seemingly endless and ultimately misguided efforts to demonstrate the historical veracity of the Exodus tradition and other narratives of the Hebrew Bible.[56]

---

[55] M. J. Weaver, "Who is the Goddess and Where Does She Get Us?" *JFSR* 5 (1989) 64.

[56] See J. K. Hoffmeier, *Israel in Egypt: The Evidence for the Authenticity of the Exodus Tradition* (New York: Oxford Univ. Press, 1996).

Chapter 3

Numinous *Nomos*: On the Relationship between Narrative and Law

Adele Berlin
University of Maryland

In this essay I would like to offer some observations on the relationship between law and narrative in the Bible. My question: Is the Torah a series of
legal collections with narrative sections serving as the glue that holds them
together, or is the Torah primarily a narrative, with some blocks of legal
material inserted here and there? From the amount of energy put forth by
modern biblical scholars on the study of narrative, compared with the
study of law, one would conclude that the legal passages are incidental. In
fact, along with the genealogical lists, the legal sections are the parts that
everyone skips.

David Damrosch remarks upon the same phenomenon, making the
point even more vividly:

> Leviticus customarily receives short shrift from literary analysts. Indeed,
> faced with such an unappetizing vein of gristle in the midst of the Penta-
> teuch, the natural reaction of most readers is simply to push it quietly off
> the plate.[1]

Damrosch correctly surmises that the short shrift given to Leviticus and
other legal sections is a product of a Christian mentality, or even polemic,

---

This paper was read at the Biblical Law Section at the Annual Meeting of the Society of Biblical Literature, San Francisco, November 23, 1997. It is a pleasure to
present it in written form here, in honor of my colleague Burke Long, whose interests include the study of literary genres in the Bible and the study of biblical
narrative.
   [1] David Damrosch, *The Narrative Covenant* (San Francisco: Harper & Row,
1987) 262.

in which the value of biblical law is denigrated.[2] Burke Long makes the same observation even more explicitly in regard to one particular project planned by Albright and his students:

> [The] proposal to separate the narrative of redemption (exodus and wanderings) from the narrative of law (the reception of Torah and commandments) may have implied conventionally Protestant, and ultimately New Testament Pauline, values. This line of theological reasoning located the efficacy of God's redemptive activity primarily in historical process ("revelation in history") rather than in the stabilities of eternal Torah.[3]

I would add that in addition to this Christian mindset which unconsciously underlies much of biblical scholarship, there is also a secular mindset which finds narrative easier and more enjoyable to read than law, with its meaning more accessible. Besides, modern literary theory has given us better tools to analyze narrative, whereas it is only beginning to give us tools to analyze law.

All of this stands in contrast to the traditional Jewish approach, which values law above everything else, and which therefore begins the child's curriculum with the Book of Leviticus. In this tradition, to call the Torah "literature" would be a sacrilegious trivialization. The tradition is not absolutely one-sided, however, as we can learn from Rashi's very first comment at the beginning of Genesis:

> The Torah did not have to commence before "This month shall be unto you the first of months" (Exod 12:1), which is the first commandment given to Israel. What is the reason, then, that it commences with "In the beginning"? Because of (the idea in Ps 111:6), "The strength of his deeds He declared to his people, to give to them the heritage of nations." For should the peoples of the world say to Israel, "You are thieves because you conquered the land of the seven nations (of Canaan)," they (Israel) would say to them, "All the earth belongs to the Holy One, Blessed be He; He created it and He gave it to whomever he wished. . . ."

Rashi gives recognition to the view that the Torah is essentially a book of commandments, or laws, to Israel, but at the same time he recognizes that the Torah is more than this, for if it were not, there would be no purpose to the Book of Genesis and the first eleven chapters of Exodus. He sees that the "prologue to the commandments," if we can call it that, serves an important ideological function. We will hear more about the idea of "prologue to the laws" shortly, in connection with Codex Hammurabi.

Let us return to David Damrosch, who has a number of interesting things to say on the relationship between law and narrative:

> From a developmental point of view it can be said that the laws were added

---

[2] Ibid., 33–34.

[3] Burke O. Long, *Planting and Reaping Albright* (University Park, Pa.: Pennsylvania State Univ. Press, 1997) 62.

to the stories, but from the point of view of the people who shaped the text as we have it, it is truer to say that the stories have been preserved as a useful setting for the Law, indeed as commentary on the Law. The mixing of law and narrative was not a crude blunder by incompetent editors . . . ; rather, it was the most important generic innovation of its age. It can fairly be compared with the revolutionary mixing of prose and poetic values by the Yahwistic writers, and has had far-reaching effects on the narrative material around it.[4]

Damrosch's statement on the mixing of law and narrative as an innovation is worthy of more consideration because, much as I would like to see the Bible as an innovator in this regard, I am not convinced that it was. As we will soon see, genre-mixing pre-dates the Bible. I would go even further and question the entire notion of the modern generic distinctions that we relentlessly seek to impose on the Bible. Our assumptions about which genres were used by ancient writers and how they utilized them often prevent us from seeing important aspects of the text.

A case in point is Codex Hammurabi. If biblical scholars have ignored the legal sections and favored the literary sections of the Bible, then the reverse is true for Assyriologists in their studies of Codex Hammurabi. Assyriologists have heaped attention upon the legal sections and given little thought to the so-called "Prologue" and "Epilogue." In fact, the terms "prologue" and "epilogue" suggest that the sections so characterized are not central to the composition. Some scholars have gone further and suggested that they were composed separately and added to the laws. No matter how they came to be present, it is fair to say that most people think of Codex Hammurabi primarily as a law collection, with its non-legal sections present more or less for decoration. Even so, no one seems especially surprised by this "mixture" of legal and non-legal genres in one text. Other Mesopotamian works, for example, incantations and treaties, also employ genre-mixing, and one of the genres is historical or mythical narration, in poetic form.

Recently, Victor Hurowitz has examined the non-juridical sections of Codex Hammurabi, and his conclusions put this text in a new light, one that is very suggestive for the study of the legal sections of the Bible.[5] Hurowitz concludes that Codex Hammurabi is a fully integrated text whose parts are unified by an intricate literary structure. Although he continues to use the terms "prologue" and "epilogue" for the sake of convenience, he sees not a three-part structure but rather a two-part structure, consisting of a "divine command" section (the command to teach justice)

---

[4] *The Narrative Covenant*, 35–36.

[5] Victor Hurowitz, *Inu Anum Ṣīrum: Literary Structures in the Non-Juridical Sections of Codex Hammurabi* (Philadelphia: Occasional Publications of the Samuel Noah Kramer Fund, 1994).

and the "royal fulfillment" section. Most important, Codex Hammurabi is as much a royal inscription as it is a juridical text. Its purpose was not to promulgate laws, but to memorialize Hammurabi as a king who followed the divine command to provide justice for his people. The work is structured like a royal inscription and uses some of the same language, although it differs in its main theme, which in the Codex has to do with the justice of the king.

The legal section may, indeed, have once stood independently or been borrowed from other law collections. But in its present position in Codex Hammurabi it functions as part of the "fulfillment" section, and counterbalances the "piety register" in the command section. Thus Hurowitz has demonstrated that Codex Hammurabi is a sophisticated literary work predating the Bible that incorporates various genres, and perhaps even some pre-existing texts, in a way that completely transforms those genres and texts. In Codex Hammurabi it is not a question of the law collection vs. the narrative. Each is in service to the other. The law collection is subsumed into the larger narrative of the royal inscription, but the royal inscription, instead of being based on the theme of cultic and civic projects (as these inscriptions often are), is based on the idea of promulgating justice.

It is, of course, very tempting to apply this to the Bible, to see in Codex Hammurabi a model for the Torah. I will not go this far, although there are certainly a number of similarities between the two.[6] But I do find Hurowitz's analysis a good antidote to Damrosch's view of biblical genre-mixing, and a stimulus to re-thinking the structure of the Torah.

The Torah's literary genius was not the mixing of genres; it was the invention of long prose narrative, which surrounds and overwhelms all the other ancient literary forms (poems, legal collections, treaties, etc.) which are embedded in it. The most obvious difference between the material surrounding Hammurabi's laws and the material surrounding the biblical laws is that the former consists of short poems and the latter is a long prose narrative. There is in the Torah a generic innovation, but it is not so much a "mixing," as Damrosch would have it, as the forging of a new genre altogether. A genre that subordinates other genres for its own ends.

This is evident in Exodus 32–34, the pericope that I have selected for discussion, as it is elsewhere in Exodus. Chapters 32–34 are generally known as the story of the Golden Calf, but I notice that nowhere in the text does this phrase occur. It is, rather, the "molten calf"—made of gold of course, but never referred to as the "golden calf," a phrase used only of the "two golden calves" of Jeroboam (1 Kings 12:28 and elsewhere). There are

---

[6] Both Codex Hammurabi and the Torah begin with talk of origins—of the world or of Babylon; both link the lawgiver to God or the gods, and to sanctuaries or the tabernacle.

several fine literary treatments of Exodus 32–34, so I will just mention that the molten calf narrative provides a sharp contrast to what the surrounding chapters are trying to say about law and revelation.[7] Law and revelation are the precise topic of Exodus 34:29–35, and I would like to look at these verses more carefully. This section, like others in Exodus, lends a strong sense of the numinous to the giving of the law. The law is couched in the form of a divine revelation. The giving of the law, and hence the law after it is given, is enveloped in the concept of the divine presence. The law is numinous. And the Exodus narrative is, over and over again, concerned with whether God can be seen, how close can one get to him, what dangers there are in getting too close. The issue is presented in a concrete and immediate manner in Exodus 34:29–35:

> When Moses came down from Mount Sinai—the two tablets of the Testimony in Moses' hand when he came down from the mountain—Moses was not aware that the skin of his face had become radiant when he had spoken with Him. And Aaron and all the Israelites saw Moses, and behold the skin of his face was radiant; and they were afraid to come near him. But Moses called to them, and Aaron and all the chieftains in the assembly returned to him, and Moses spoke to them. Afterward all the Israelites came near, and he commanded them concerning all that the Lord had told him on Mount Sinai. And when Moses had finished speaking with them, he put a veil over his face. Whenever Moses went before the Lord to speak with Him, he would take the veil off until he came out; and he came out and told the Israelites what he had been commanded. And the Israelites would see how radiant the skin of Moses' face was, and Moses would (then) put the veil back over his face until he went to speak with Him.

Contact with God has made Moses' face radiant and the people are afraid, lest contact with Moses, like contact with God, be fatal. To protect the people, Moses veils his face. But notice that *his face is unveiled when he instructs them in the laws.* This happens initially, and again each time Moses goes into God's presence. Each time, Moses lets the people see the radiance of his face until *after* he has instructed them. He does not veil his face immediately upon coming out from God's presence, but only after he has conveyed God's commands. The commands, that is, the laws, partake of the numinousness of God's presence. It is not only numinous *nomos,* but also luminous *nomos.* It is true, but perhaps too simple, to say that when Moses' radiant face is visible he is acting as the spokesman for God. It is not just that Moses acts as the mediator or the conduit between God and Israel.

---

[7] For literary treatments see Herbert C. Brichto, *Toward a Grammar of Biblical Poetics: Tales of the Prophets* (New York and Oxford: Oxford Univ. Press, 1992) 88–121, and R. W. L. Moberly, *At the Mountain of God: Story and Theology in Exodus 32–34* (Sheffield: JSOT Press, 1983). See also Gary Knoppers, "Aaron's Calf and Jeroboam's Calves," in *Fortunate the Eyes that See* (ed. A. B. Beck et al.; Grand Rapids, Mich.: Eerdmans, 1995) 92–104.

Communion with God is effected through the people's experience of hearing and seeing: They see the radiance of Moses' face and they hear the laws. The laws, then, become an aural radiance. The laws are the sound of the revelation. The laws are a vehicle through which Israel apprehends God.

Exodus 34:29–35, usually ascribed to the Priestly writer, forms a neat transition to the other narrative thread that, along with the giving of the law, is woven into the second half of Exodus: that is the building of the מִשְׁכָּן, the Tabernacle.[8] Baruch Schwartz writes the following about the relationship between the Priestly law collection and narrative:

> The overall structure of the Priestly narrative is aimed at describing the gradual arrival of the immanent Presence of God to dwell upon earth in the midst of the Israelites. At the center of this tale is the construction of the divine abode and the actual arrival of the *kavod* to dwell therein. Yet, once this has been told, the bulk of the Priestly document is still to come: the laws conveyed from the tabernacle. In this way, the process of lawgiving and the laws themselves become at least a primary aim, if not indeed the supreme purpose, of the very descent of the divine Presence. As much as the law collection is a function of the tabernacle story, the tabernacle story is told in order to provide the only imaginable circumstances for the giving of the laws.[9]

Whether it is the JE author's story of Sinai and its laws or the P author's story of the Tabernacle and its laws, there is a narrative of a divine lawgiving and a set of laws, and one cannot be set above the other. For the Priestly writer, the Tabernacle is the site of the on-going revelation of God, the portable Sinai. The law and the Tabernacle are the two manifestations of God's presence. The law is a permanent record of the divine revelation and the Tabernacle is the locus of the ever-renewing revelation. In later generations, when there was no more Tabernacle and no more Temple, Jewish tradition would vest both aspects of revelation in the study of the law.

Is the narrative the background for the law or is the law a detail of the narrative? This is like asking whether in the perceptual puzzle the image is an urn or a human profile. In the Torah, there could be no set of laws without the narrative of revelation and no narrative of revelation without the laws. The laws would have no *raison d'être* without the revelation narrative and the revelation would have no content without the laws. While we need

---

[8] Victor Hurowitz has also written on the relationship between the story of the molten calf and the story of the Tabernacle in Avigdor (Victor) Hurowitz, "The Calf and the Tabernacle," *Shnaton* 7–8 (1984) 51–59 [Hebrew]. See now also A. Cohen, "Maʿaseh haʿegel—neged hammiqdaš," *Beth Mikra* 42 [150] (1997) 257–271.

[9] Baruch J. Schwartz, "The Priestly Account of the Theophany and Lawgiving at Sinai," in *Texts, Temples, and Traditions: A Tribute to Menahem Haran* (ed. M. Fox et al.; Winona Lake, Ind.: Eisenbrauns, 1996) 122–123. See also S. E. Loewenstamm, "Review of A. Toeg, *Lawgiving at Sinai*," in *From Babylon to Canaan: Studies in the Bible and its Oriental Background* (Jerusalem: Magnes, 1992) 424–442.

to continue to analyze individual laws and law collections, we also need to consider the possibilities of more profound meanings that the laws together with their narratives may evoke.[10]

---

[10] I thank Barry Eichler and Victor Hurowitz for their comments on this paper. The paper was completed during my tenure as a Fellow of the Center for Judaic Studies, University of Pennsylvania, and I am grateful to the Center for providing such a supportive research environment.

At the SBL session at which this paper was presented, Martha Roth made known to me her article "Mesopotamian Legal Traditions and the Laws of Hammurabi," *Chicago-Kent Law Review* 71 (1995) 13–39. Her discussion of the structure and literary genres in Codex Hammurabi relates to Hurowitz's observations.

Chapter 4

A "Literary Sermon" in Deuteronomy 4

Marc Z. Brettler
Brandeis University

In a recently published paper, "Predestination in Deuteronomy 30.1–10," I suggested that the initial pericope of Deuteronomy 30 should not be seen, contrary to the predominant scholarly opinion, as a sermon.[1] I also observed: "In brief, 'sermon' is a quite Protestant term that suggests an exposition of a central biblical text by a particular type of religious functionary. This situation does not fit the book of Deuteronomy very well."

Given that the label "sermon," or its German equivalent "Predigt," continues to be used widely in studies on Deuteronomy,[2] I have decided to return to this issue, to explore and defend my laconic statement. I will begin

It is a particular pleasure to dedicate this work to Burke O. Long, who has taught me so much. Like Burke's early work, this paper deals with form critical issues. I am referring, of course, to his *Problem of Etiological Narrative in the Old Testament* (BZAW 108; Berlin: Töpelmann, 1968). Like his more recent book, *Planting and Reaping Albright: Politics, Ideology, and Interpreting the Bible* (University Park, Pa.: Pennsylvania State Univ. Press, 1997), it attempts to be iconoclastic, calling into question some cherished "truths" associated with one of the giants of biblical scholarship. I would like to thank Mr. Alan Lenzi, Ms. Michelle Taylor and Ms. Sarah Shectman, who assisted me with this article; Professors Bernard Levinson and Thomas Römer, who suggested some relevant bibliography; Professor Norbert Lohfink, who commented on a draft of this essay; and various people who offered constructive criticism after a presentation of a shorter version of the article at the 1999 Annual Meeting of the Society of Biblical Literature in Boston.

[1] "Predestination in Deuteronomy 30.1–10," in *Those Elusive Deuteronomists* (ed. Linda S. Shearing and Steven L. McKenzie; JSOTSup 268; Sheffield: Sheffield Academic Press, 1999) 171–88.

[2] See Timothy A. Lenchak, *"Choose Life!": A Rhetorical-Critical Investigation of Deuteronomy 28,69–30,20* (AnBib 129; Rome: Biblical Institute Press, 1993) 2–3, esp. 2 n. 7. The following may be added to his list: Rosario Pius Merindino, *Das Deutero-*

by looking at the broadest question, the usefulness of the term "sermon" for studies of Deuteronomy. I will then turn to Deuteronomy 4, which in commentaries is often cited as a classic example of a Deuteronomic sermon, and will show that the label "sermon" is particularly problematic for that unit. The many similarities between Deuteronomy 30, the subject of my earlier study, and Deuteronomy 4,[3] make this chapter particularly suitable for study.

The precise origin of the notion that Deuteronomy contains sermons is difficult to trace. Without any question, it has become closely associated with von Rad, who first expressed the idea in 1934, in an article eventually translated as "The Levitical Sermon in *I* and *II Chronicles*,"[4] but von Rad acknowledged that he was adopting the idea from Ludwig Köhler. Köhler already in 1930–31 had stated:

> In about 700 there began in Judah a great preaching . . . The purpose of this preaching, whether we examine it in the 'framework' of the book of Judges, or in the amplifications of the book of Jeremiah, or in the introductions to Deuteronomy, is always the education of the people of Judah to zeal for the statutes of God.[5]

Though Köhler does not acknowledge earlier sources, the idea is not original to him either; it was expressed already in the first decade of the twentieth century by Baudissin and Klosterman, and hinted at still earlier by others.[6]

Phrased differently, the idea of the Deuteronomic sermon began to develop with critical biblical scholarship, though the cluster of studies of Köhler, von Rad, and the less well-known monograph of Herbert Breit, *Die Predigt des Deuteronomisten*,[7] all first published in the 1930s, certainly propelled the idea forward. The prestige of von Rad, and the way in which he repeated this idea in various forms, including in his *Studies in Deuteronomy*, throughout his Deuteronomy commentary, and in a 1961 article, "Ancient Word and Living Word" in *Interpretation*, assured that the notion had a

---

nomische Gesetz: Eine literarkritische, gattungs- und überlieferungsgeschichtliche Untersuchung zu Dt 12–26 (BBB 31; Bonn: Peter Hanstein, 1969).

[3] "Predestination in Deuteronomy 30.1–10," 185.

[4] This article is translated in Gerhard von Rad, *The Problem of the Hexateuch and Other Essays* (London: SCM, 1984) 267–80. For more detailed bibliographical information, see Rex Mason, "Some Echoes of the Preaching in the Second Temple? Tradition Elements in Zechariah 1–8," *ZAW* 96 (1984) 221, n. 2.

[5] The quotation is from Ludwig Köhler, *Hebrew Man* (London: SCM, 1956); for the publication history of this work, see Mason, "Some Echoes," 222 n. 8.

[6] See the survey in Dietmer Mathias, "'Levitische Predigt' und Deuteronomismus," *ZAW* 96 (1984) 23–24.

[7] Herbert Breit, *Die Predigt des Deuteronomisten* (Munich: Chr. Kaiser, 1933).

wide audience.[8] The adoption of von Rad's arguments in Eissfeldt's classic *Introduction* helped spread this idea.[9]

Von Rad's main thesis was:

> The whole framework (Deut. 1–11, 28–31) is exclusively paraenetic, that is, it consists of a great many sermons of various length. It would hardly be accurate to consider these sermons purely literary products. It is much more probable that they are to be considered the literary deposit of an extensive preaching activity as it had already been developing in the late period of the monarchy, perhaps by the Levites.[10]

This latter notion, that the preaching should be connected to Levites, who were also viewed by von Rad as the fundamental group responsible for the creation of Deuteronomy, has been soundly criticized.[11] Yet the more limited idea of Deuteronomic sermons, that need not be seen as specifically Levitical, has become a staple of biblical scholarship;[12] it is even found in the recent Anchor Bible commentary by Weinfeld and in the Jewish Publi-

---

[8] G. von Rad, *Studies in Deuteronomy* (SBT 9; Chicago: Henry Regnery, 1953); *Deuteronomy: A Commentary* (OTL; Philadelphia: Westminster, 1966); "Ancient Word and Living Word," *Int* 15 (1961) 3–13.

[9] Otto Eissfeldt, *The Old Testament: An Introduction* (New York: Harper & Row, 1965) 15–17.

[10] Von Rad, "Ancient Word and Living Word," 4.

[11] See Leslie J. Hoppe, "The Origins of Deuteronomy" (Ph.D. diss., Northwestern University, 1978) 155–211 ("The Priest and Levite in Deuteronomy"), and Mathias, "'Levitische Predigt' und Deuteronomismus," 23–49. For additional critics, see William M. Schniedewind, *The Word of God in Transition: From Prophet to Exegete in the Second Temple Period* (JSOTSup 197; Sheffield: Sheffield Academic Press, 1995) 32 n. 4.

[12] Scholars speak of sermons or preaching in other biblical contexts as well; see especially Rex Mason, *Preaching the Tradition: Homily and Hermeneutics After the Exile: Based on the "Addresses" in Chronicles, the "Speeches" in the Books of Ezra and Nehemiah, and the Post-Exilic Prophetic Books* (Cambridge: Cambridge Univ. Press, 1990), and many other works, such as Ernest W. Nicholson, *Preaching to the Exiles: A Study of the Prose Tradition in the Book of Jeremiah* (New York: Schocken, 1971). "Preaching" has also been used of pre-exilic prophets; see, for example, Konrad Beyer, *Spruch und Predigt bei den vorexilischen Schriftpropheten: Eine Untersuchung der Gestalt der prophetischen mündlichen Verkündigung* (Erlargen: Gutenberg-Druckerei, 1933). For the use of the term with early postbiblical works, see Robert G. Hall, *Revealed Histories: Techniques for Ancient Jewish and Christian Historiography* (JSPSup 6; Sheffield: JSOT Press, 1991) 48–60 ("Inspired Historical Sermons"). The most significant dissent from the view that large sections of Deuteronomy should be viewed as sermons has come, not coincidentally, from Catholic scholars; see especially the work of Norbert Lohfink, *Das Hauptgebot: Eine Untersuchung literarischer Einleitungsfragen zu Dtn 5–11* (ÁnBib 20; Rome: Pontifical Biblical Institute, 1963), and that of his student, Georg Braulik.

cation Society commentary by Tigay,[13] works which generally eschew form-critical perspectives.

It is a fact that the Bible contains no word that is even somewhat similar in semantics to "sermon."[14] The lack of terminology, however, does not bother me. As I have discussed elsewhere, I believe that it is appropriate to use non-native genre labels for biblical materials.[15] Genres must be seen as flexible, and are often cross-cultural and cross-generational; they can be of great help in allowing us to understand what a particular foreign or ancient work means. However, when we do impose non-native genres upon biblical material, we must define them carefully, and must be cautious not to engage in anachronisms.

With this in mind, how might we define a sermon within a biblical context? There are at least two ways to go about this: It is possible to see how a sermon is defined in modern studies, and to see the extent to which biblical texts share in those characteristics, or it is possible to examine various proposals made by modern biblical scholars concerning the definition of biblical sermons. The best results will derive from surveying both of these perspectives, especially since, as we shall see, the definition of a biblical "sermon" by modern scholars shares a great deal with typical definitions of post-biblical preached sermons.

There is obviously no single modern definition of a sermon; there are significant cross-denominational differences, and differences over time—I am reminded of this whenever I visit the nearby Sturbridge Village, and see the sticks used to keep the worshippers awake during the several-hour-long sermons that typified worship of the early nineteenth century. The editor of the recent Library of America volume *American Sermons: The Pilgrims*

---

[13] See Moshe Weinfeld, *Deuteronomy 1–11* (AB 5; New York: Doubleday, 1991), e.g. 215 and 228 (on Deut 4), and 328 (on Deut 6:4–9); and Jeffrey H. Tigay, *Deuteronomy* (The JPS Torah Commentary; Philadelphia: Jewish Publication Society, 1996) xviii, where he refers to "the exhortatory, didactic, sermonic character" of Deuteronomy.

[14] The verb דרשׁ is biblical, though it never is used in the sense of "to preach." On preaching in the Second Temple period, see Leopold Zunz, *Die Gottesdienstlichen Vorträge der Juden historisch Entwickelt* (Frankfurt a. M.: J. Kauffmann, 1892) 342–73. A more recent summary may be found in Jonah Frankel, *The Method of Aggadah and Midrash* (Israel: Masada/Yad La-Talmud, 1991) 1.11–43 (Hebrew). Several sermons are collected and analyzed in Joseph Heinemann, *Public Preaching from the Talmudic Period* (Jerusalem: Mosad Bialik, 1970; Hebrew).

[15] I do not, for example, agree with Kugel's notion that we must avoid terms like "poetry" in the Bible; see my discussion in *The Creation of History in Ancient Israel*, 85–86. The following two critiques of Kugel's objection to "biblical Poetry" are especially noteworthy: Francis Landy, "Poetics and Parallelism: Some Comments on James Kugel's *The Idea of Biblical Poetry*," *JSOT* 28 (1984) 67–71 and Wilfred G. E. Watson, "A Review of Kugel's *The Idea of Biblical Poetry*," *JSOT* 28 (1984) 93–4.

to Martin Luther King Jr.[16] also encountered the problem of definition in collecting his corpus. He introduces his section "Note on the Sermon Form" with a quotation of the following four characteristics of a proper sermon from the 1592 textbook by William Perkins, *The Art of Prophesying*:

1. To read the Text distinctly out of the Canonicall Scriptures.
2. To give the sense and understanding of it being read, by the Scripture itself.
3. To collect a few and profitable points of doctrine out of the naturall sense.
4. To apply (if he has the gift) the doctrines rightly collected, to the life and manners of men in a simple and plaine speech.[17]

Though over four hundred years old, this suggested form is recognizable to a large extent in both contemporary and much more ancient liturgical settings.

I continue to find it surprising that von Rad, the great form-critic, nowhere outlines the structure of the sermon.[18] He does make the following observations: The Deuteronomic sermon arose in response to an "urgent need" of convincing people to keep "loyal to Yahweh." It is to be connected to "the solemn reading of the law by Ezra" narrated in Neh 8:7–18, which suggests a model of reading from the text, followed by "instruction in it."[19] The characteristics outlined by von Rad fit Perkins' definition quite well; I will later examine whether they properly describe the structure of Deuteronomic texts.

As is well-known, one of the major faults of the FOTL series is that it does not contain a uniform set of definitions for the forms that it describes. In the volumes that have been published, the form "sermon" is defined so far only by de Vries in Chronicles, as "A formalized address in a liturgical setting rehearsing the past in light of present conditions and obligations."[20] This definition is quite different from that outlined by von Rad. Unlike most definitions of sermons, it does not focus on textual exposition; it replaces

---

[16] Michael Warner, ed., *American Sermons: The Pilgrims to Martin Luther King Jr.* (New York: The Library of America, 1999).

[17] *American Sermons*, 889. See Ian Breward, *The Work of William Perkins* (The Courtenay Library of Reformation Classics 3; Abingdon (Berks.): Sutton Courtenay Press, 1970) 349.

[18] The reason for this, I believe, is that there is no clear form. This, as we shall see, is part of the argument against seeing "sermons" in Deuteronomy and Chronicles as belonging to the same genre.

[19] "The Levitical Sermon in *I* and *II Chronicles*," 267–268.

[20] Simon J. de Vries, *1 and 2 Chronicles* (FOTL 11; Grand Rapids, Mich.: Eerdmans, 1989) 435. There is a cross-reference from "Sermon" to "Instruction" in Erhard S. Gerstenberger, *Psalms: Part 1: With an Introduction to Cultic Poetry* (FOTL 14; Grand Rapids, Mich.: Eerdmans, 1988) 251, but this does not discuss the genre "sermon" at any length.

that idea with reflection on the past. Perhaps this is due to the lack of certainty concerning the status of the Torah as text for the Chronicler.[21] In any case, it raises a significant issue: Given that genres are defined cross-culturally based on shared characteristics, may we speak of a sermon, which in modern times is characterized by its text-centeredness, in a period where there was not yet a central text to exposit? In other words, are "the Canonicall Scriptures" so central to the "sermon-ness" of a sermon, that we may not speak of sermons unless they focus on an authoritative text?

The definition of de Vries is also important because it makes explicit what I believe was implicit in the definitions of Perkins and von Rad: Sermons require "a liturgical setting." This setting may vary, but is necessary. In addition, it is reasonable to assume that a sermon requires a sermonizer or preacher, and we should be able to define in broadest terms who may serve in this role. This is, of course, what stands behind von Rad's suggestion of Levitical preachers. Yet, even if we reject this model for Deuteronomy, as scholars have properly suggested we must,[22] the question of who might have offered this type of "formalized address" needs to be probed.

Within the last fifteen years, the issue of preaching in the Bible has been explored most extensively by Rex Mason, first in his 1986 *ZAW* study, "Some Echoes of the Preaching in the Second Temple? Tradition Elements in Zechariah 1–8," and four years later, in his book *Preaching the Tradition: Homily and Hermeneutics after the Exile.*[23] These studies are especially useful because they do not focus on Deuteronomy, and thus their appropriateness for clarifying issues concerning that book are not suspect for circular reasoning.

Mason is very direct in admitting that "the great difficulty is to establish precise and objective criteria by which such a genre [sermon] can be defined."[24] He correctly notes that such a search depends on our ability to find a *Sitz im Leben* for these speeches and their "homiletical methods" (144), but of course, "we do not know if 'sermons' in any way akin to the form in which they are now delivered were preached in the second temple" (129). Yet, despite these problems, which seem quite severe to me, Mason does believe that a set of post-exilic texts reflects "a general pattern of preaching and teaching which was familiar from the practice of the second temple" (258).

Mason suggests three essential characteristics for the genre sermon; these overlap significantly with the suggestions of Perkins. First, "a

---

[21] On this problem, see Judson R. Shaver, *Torah and the Chronicler's History Work: An Inquiry into the Chronicler's Reference to Laws, Festivals, and Cultic Institutions in Relationship to Pentateuchal Legislation* (BJS 196; Atlanta: Scholars Press, 1989).

[22] See above, n. 11.

[23] Full publication data on these may be found above, in nn. 4 and 12.

[24] *Preaching the Tradition*, 143.

preached sermon must appeal to some agreed authority." Second, "it proclaims some theological teaching about God." Finally, it must "call for a response on the part of the hearers in light of the truth proclaimed. This call may be for penitence, trust or obedience in some specific command."[25] In addition, some "literary devices" that "maintain interest and make what is said more assimilable" often characterize sermons.[26]

The strength of these particular suggested criteria is that they do exactly what genre criteria are supposed to do: They are elastic enough to bring together a set of texts which otherwise would not have been seen together, so that they might be interpreted in a mutually enhancing fashion. The group may also be tied together as reflecting a hypothesized *Sitz im Leben*, and in this case connected to the early Second Temple sermon.

As I noted above, I am somewhat skeptical concerning this *Sitz im Leben* for Deuteronomic sermons for the simple reason that it is entirely conjectural. Although evidence from Philo, Josephus, the New Testament and rabbinic sources converges to suggest that preaching existed at the end of the Second Temple period,[27] this evidence does not allow us to reach into the exilic or early post-exilic period, nor is it sufficiently detailed to allow us to reconstruct typical Second Temple sermon types. According to the accounts in the Books of the Maccabees and Josephus' *Antiquities,* Antiochus forbade the major manifestations of the practice of Judaism; offering sermons was not one of the religious acts he prohibited. This suggests that sermons were not at that point a significant part of Jewish practice. In an earlier generation, we at least would have had the synagogue as an institution which developed in the exilic or early post-exilic period as a good home for such preaching.[28] Current scholarship, however, suggests that the earliest we may speak of the synagogue is the third or second century BCE in the Diaspora, and later for Israel.[29] Thus, if the sermon is already found in exilic and early post-exilic texts, as is typically suggested, it must predate the development of the synagogue, especially in Israel.

---

[25] "Some Echoes of the Preaching," 223–225. These three points are also summarized in *Preaching the Tradition,* 142.

[26] "Some Echoes of the Preaching," 225.

[27] See Zunz, *Die Gottesdienstlichen Vorträge der Juden,* 345–6 and Lee I. Levine, *Judaism and Hellenism in Antiquity: Conflict or Confluence?* (Seattle: Univ. of Washington Press, 1998) 166–67.

[28] See, for example, Enno Janssen, *Juda in der Exilszeit: Ein Beitrag zur Frage der Entstehung des Judentums* (Göttingen: Vandenhoeck & Ruprecht, 1956) 105–115.

[29] In addition to Lester L. Grabbe, *Judaism from Cyrus to Hadrian* (Minneapolis: Fortress, 1992) 2.541–42, see Lee Levine, "The Nature and Origin of the Palestinian Synagogue Reconsidered," *JBL* 115 (1996) 425–48; Rachel Hachlili, "The Origin of the Synagogue—A Reassessment," *JSJ* 28 (1997) 34–47; Hanswulf Bloedhorn and Gil Hüttenmeister, "The Synagogue," *CHJ* 3.267–97, esp. 270–72.

A contrast between what I take to be a particularly successful case of putative *Sitze im Leben* and the case for the sermon should make my objections to the form-critical label "sermon" clearer. Already in 1934, Joachim Begrich suggested that the change in "tense" in certain laments of the individual reflected an oracle of encouragement that the supplicant heard through a cultic prophet.[30] He supported this contention by citing Lamentations 3:57, קָרַבְתָּ בְּיוֹם אֶקְרָאֶךָּ אָמַרְתָּ אַל־תִּירָא, "You have drawn near on the day I called to you; you said, 'do not fear,'" which seems to *directly* reflect that institution. Additional support from the אַל־תִּירָא oracles in Deutero-Isaiah, along with their significant parallels in some of the prophetic oracles to Esarhaddon,[31] now strongly buttress the case. As a result of this configuration of internal biblical evidence and external evidence, most scholars accept as very likely the idea that this "confidence motif"[32] reflects the positive reaction of the supplicant to an oracle,[33] despite the fact that no such oracle is ever present in the psalms. In terms of evidence adduced, the case for sermons is quite different; the logic is much more circular, since the main reason for recreating early Second Temple period sermons is to explain a set of biblical texts. No text like Lam 3:57, in other words, no text outside of the corpus under investigation, suggests that they existed. Their existence is thus quite tenuous indeed.

Even if I felt that the similarities in form allow us to posit the genre "sermon" despite the fact that the genre's *Sitz im Leben* is most uncertain, there seems little reason to connect various texts in Deuteronomy to those studied by Mason. In a model section that deserves to be followed by others, Mason summarizes the structure of these sermon-like addresses from Chronicles, noting how prevalent each element is. The "ideal" address has eight elements. It begins with a "specific address" followed by a "call for attention"; these may be seen together, e.g., in 2 Chr 15:2: שְׁמָעוּנִי אָסָא וְכָל־יְהוּדָה וּבִנְיָמִן, "Hear me Asa and all of Judah and Benjamin." The priestly and prophetic sermons in particular are followed by "a prophetic formula"; this need not concern us, for in Deuteronomy, as in the royal addresses, no such formula is expected. The address then contains an "appeal to or cita-

---

[30] Joachim Begrich, "Das priestlicher Heilsorakel," *ZAW* 52 (1934) 81–92.

[31] *ANET*, 605; cf. the more recent study of Simo Parpola, *Assyrian Prophecies* (SAA 9; Helsinki: Helsinki Univ. Press, 1997) 1.1, 1.2, 1.4, 2.2, 2.3, 2.5.

[32] This is the technical term sometimes used to reflect the newly acquired confidence felt by the supplicant, which is typically reflected through a change in "tenses," from a request, usually in the imperative, to a perfect.

[33] This interpretation is widely, though not universally accepted. See, for example, Claus Westermann, *Praise and Lament in the Psalms* (Atlanta: John Knox, 1981) 72–73; Craig C. Broyles, *The Conflict of Faith and Experience in the Psalms: A Form-Critical and Theological Study* (JSOTSup 52; Sheffield: JSOT Press, 1989) 48; Gerstenberger, *Psalms: Part 1*, 62.

tion of 'Scripture'" and/or "illustration from history." An example of the former is 2 Chr 20:20, where King Jehoshaphat says, האמינו ביהוה אלהיכם ותאמנו האמינו בנביאיו והצליחו, "Trust firmly in YHWH your God so you will stand firm; trust firmly in His prophets so you will succeed," echoing Isa 7:9; the latter is found, for example, in Hezekiah's speech in 2 Chr 30:7: ואל־תהיו כאבותיכם וכאחיכם אשר מעלו ביהוה אלהי אבותיהם, "Do not be like your ancestors and brothers who trespassed against YHWH, the God of their fathers." Several contain an "encouragement formula," either in imperatives and/or prohibitives, as in 2 Chr 32:7: חזקו ואמצו אל־תיראו ואל־תחתו, "Be strong and courageous; do not be frightened or dismayed." Many contain "inversion[s]/play on words," as we saw above in Jehoshaphat's speech in 2 Chr 20:20, and several close with a "rhetorical question," such as הלרשע לעזר ולשנאי יהוה תאהב, "Should one help the wicked and befriend those who hate YHWH?" (2 Chr 19:2).[34]

It is difficult to know how to apply these suggested form-critical criteria to Deuteronomy since they are not all found in every single sermon-like speech in Chronicles. Thus, it is legitimate to wonder which are sufficient and which are necessary, and the number of criteria that must be present before we may state that the text under consideration should be thought of as a reflection of the sermon. I will thus focus on two texts: the שמע pericope of Deut 6:4–9, which might be considered a central short sermon, and the much longer Deuteronomy 4.

The שמע prayer opens in a promising fashion for a sermon, with the words שמע ישראל, following Mason's pattern of a "specific address" followed by a "call for attention." Yet, closer study shows that this phrase is never found in Chronicles, and indeed is unique to Deuteronomy;[35] we may only state that it is Deuteronomic, not that it is sermonic.[36] Furthermore, and more significantly, this pattern of שמע in the imperative followed by a noun is so common in such a variety of situations, that it certainly could not be characterized as a *sufficient* criterion for determining that a particular unit is sermonic.[37]

It would seem that the core of the sermon should be the "appeal to or

---

[34] See *Preaching the Tradition*, 137–42, and esp. the chart on p. 141.

[35] Deut 5:1; 9:1; 20:3; 27:9; cf. 6:3. See the analysis of this formula in Reinhard Achenbach, *Israel zwischen Verheißung und Gebot: Literarkritische Untersuchungen zu Deuteronomium 5–11* (European University Series XXIII 422; Frankfurt a. M.: Peter Lang, 1991) 70–76.

[36] In fact, this introduction using שמע followed by a noun might instead be connected to Wisdom influence, which is often posited for Deuteronomy; see e.g. Prov 1:8; 4:10.

[37] See, for example, Num 20:10; Judg 5:3; 1 Sam 22:7, 12.

citation of 'Scripture'" and/or the "illustration from history."[38] This particular passage has neither, although Deuteronomy in places certainly has
these elements. I would consider Deut 5:32, וּשְׁמַרְתֶּם לַעֲשׂוֹת כַּאֲשֶׁר צִוָּה יהוה
אֱלֹהֵיכֶם אֶתְכֶם, "Be careful to do as YHWH your God has commanded you,"
to be a type of appeal to scripture, broadly conceived, and texts such as
6:16, לֹא תְנַסּוּ אֶת־יְהוָה אֱלֹהֵיכֶם כַּאֲשֶׁר נִסִּיתֶם בַּמַּסָּה, "Do not try YHWH your God,
like you tried Him at Massah," to contain an "illustration from history."
Nothing paralleling these is found in Deut 6:4–9. Nor are the final three elements, an "encouragement formula," an "inversion/play on words," or a
"rhetorical question" found in this passage.

The fundamental dissimilarity between Deut 6:4–9 and the sermon-like
structure of Chronicles' speeches may be seen even more sharply by out-
lining the structure of the Deuteronomic pericope in comparison to those
found in Chronicles. After the "specific address" and "call for attention,"
Deuteronomy follows with what has been called a creed; I would just note
parenthetically that the final word of v. 4 is impossible, as others have come
close to admitting, and most likely should be emended to אֵין אַחֵר.[39] This is
followed by a set of five converted perfects, all used in a modal sense
which approaches the imperative.[40] Not one of the 32 addresses in Chronicles that serve as Mason's main corpus for defining sermons shares the
structure of Deut 6:4–9. Of course we can say that this particular Deutero-

---

[38] Note how this first criterion cited by Mason follows von Rad, while the second is seen as central by De Vries.

[39] See the discussions of the problematics of אֶחָד in Achenbach, *Israel zwischen
Verheißung und Gebot*, 76–82; S. Dean McBride, "The Yoke of the Kingdom: An Ex-
position of Deuteronomy 6:4–5," *Int* 27 (1973) 291–97; J. Gerald Janzen, "On the
Most Important Word in the Shema (Deuteronomy VI 4–5)," *VT* 37 (1987) 280–300;
R. W. L. Moberly, "'Yahweh is One': The Translation of the Shema," *Studies in the
Pentateuch* (ed. J. A. Emerton; SVT 41; Leiden: Brill, 1990) 209–215; Tigay, *Deuteronomy*, 438–40; Weinfeld, *Deuteronomy*, 337–38. Though various different suggestions
are proffered, none is satisfactory; אֶחָד in typical biblical Hebrew means "one," and
this makes little sense in the context. I suggest that the verse originally ended
יְהוָה אֵין אַחֵר; this suggested original text is especially suitable for scholars who see
this verse as an elaboration on the beginning of the decalogue. (Note 5:7: לֹא יִהְיֶה־לְךָ
אֱלֹהִים אֲחֵרִים עַל־פָּנַי.) אֵין dropped out by homoioarcton with the following אַחֵר which
was then changed naturally to אֶחָד to preserve some sense. (For a discussion of
these types of errors, see Emanuel Tov, *Textual Criticism of the Hebrew Bible* [Minne-
apolis: Fortress, 1992], 238, 245–46. A classic case of graphic confusion between אַחֵר
and אֶחָד is Gen 22:13; for additional suggested cases of this confusion, see Friedrich
Delitsch, *Die Lese- und Schreibfehler im Altern Testament* [Berlin: Vereinigung Wissenschaftlicher Verleger, 1920] 105–106.) This series of errors needed to have happened
before the composition of Zech 14:9, a very late biblical text, the only biblical verse
that cites Deut 6:4.

[40] IBHS § 32.2.2.

nomic pericope is *sui generis*; this would, however, ignore the fact that in general, the short Deuteronomic pieces that are often called sermons might share *some* elements with the material adduced from the Chronicler, but they are more unlike rather than like them.

Phrased differently, certain aspects of Deuteronomistic phraseology share a great deal with certain aspects of the sermon-like addresses in Chronicles. We saw this above—both have similar opening invocations, the types of appeal to traditional "law" and traditions concerning the past are found in both, and even the word plays found in Chronicles are found in sections of Deuteronomy; I can think, for example, of the plays on שוב in Deut 30:1–10.[41] As is widely recognized, Deuteronomy is very interested in persuasion,[42] and this is why it uses these devices, which are also found in sermons, which attempt to persuade. But Deuteronomy tends to use these devices in an isolated fashion, and does not string them together into the sermon-like structure suggested for Chronicles. Stated differently, I could write, in good Deuteronomic Hebrew, a sermon that would follow the pattern developed by Mason, but I would have to compose this myself, since there is no extant model in Deuteronomy.[43] As I suggested earlier, the question of *Sitz im Leben* raises serious problems for the use of the term "sermon" for Chronicles; given that the units in Deuteronomy are fundamentally different from the supposed sermon-like units in Chronicles, the use of the term for Deuteronomy is extremely problematic.

Initially, it might seem that the long and complex Deut 4:1–40,[44]

---

[41] For similar observations on this play in the speech of Solomon in 1 Kings 8, see Jon D. Levenson, "The Paronomasia of Solomon's Seventh Petition," *HAR* 6 (1982) 135–38.

[42] Much of the literature on this is cited in Lenchak, *"Choose Life!"*, which concerns the rhetoric of the end of Deuteronomy; see also the earlier important treatment of Deuteronomy as parenesis in Lohfink, *Das Hauptgebot*, esp. 271–72.

[43] Such a Deuteronomic sermon might look like this:

שמע ישראל (Address and call for attention—Deut 6:4)

כי־ירחיב יהוה אלהיך את־גבולך כאשר דבר־לך (appeal to scripture—Deut 12:20)

לא תנסו את־יהוה אלהיכם כאשר נסיתם במסה (illustration from history—Deut 6:16)

חזקו ואמצו אל־תיראו ואל־תערצו מפניהם (encouragement formula—Deut 31:6)

ושבת עד־יהוה אלהיך בכל־לבבך ובכל־נפשיך

ושב יהוה אלהיך את־שבותך ורחמך (play on words—Deut 30:2–3, selections)

ואמרת ביום ההוא הלא על כי־אין אלהי בקרבי מצאוני הרעות האלה (rhetorical questions—Deut 31:17, modified)

[44] In the continuation of the paper, I will use "Deuteronomy 4" as a shorthand for 4:1–40. The compositional unity of the unit is a serious problem. I tend toward the position of Stephen Geller, "Fiery Wisdom: The Deuteronomic Tradition," in *Sacred Enigmas: Literary Religion in the Hebrew Bible* (London: Routledge, 1996) 30–61, 203 n. 8, that it should be viewed as a compositional unity. (This chapter was originally published as "Fiery Wisdom: Logos and Lexis in Deuteronomy 4," *Prooftexts*

44   *Marc Z. Brettler*

considered to be "the theological heart of Deuteronomy,"[45] comes closer to fulfilling the criteria suggested by Mason, and that this chapter should be considered a sermon. It certainly has the three essential characteristics of a sermon:[46] It opens with an appeal "to some agreed authority"—namely הדבר אשר אנכי מצוה אתכם, "the matter which I am commanding you" (4:2). Its thesis is that YHWH must be worshipped aniconically; it thus "proclaims some theological teaching about God."[47] Finally, it concludes with a "call for response on the part of the hearers in light of the truth proclaimed"—in this particular case, ושמרת את־חקיו ואת־מצותיו אשר אנכי מצוך היום, "Observe His laws and commandments, that I am commanding you this day" (4:40). It also contains "literary devices" that "maintain interest and make what is said more assimilable," including the chiastic reference to the first creation story in vv. 16–19.[48]

In terms of form as well, chapter 4 shares much with the general pattern for sermon-like addresses noted by Mason. It opens with a "specific address" and "a call for attention": ועתה ישראל שמע, "And now, Israel, give heed" (v. 1), though in a slightly different order than what is found in 6:4. It contains several appeals to scripture. Some of these are in broad terms, as in references to אל־החקים ואל־המשפטים, "(to) the laws and rules" (v. 1; see also vv. 5, 8, 14, 40) or מצות יהוה אלהיכם, "the commandments of YHWH your God" (v. 2), as well as (ה)דברים, "(the) words" heard on Horeb (vv. 9, 12). An "illustration from history," concerning YHWH's destruction of those who followed Baal Pe'or is found at the beginning of the chapter (v. 3). Verses 32–38 offer an additional, more extensive "illustration from history." There is no encouragement using words like חזק, "be strong." The chapter is, however, typified by "play[s] on words"; in fact, it could be summarized as שמע ("hear/heed"—vv. 1, 30) ושמר ("and observe"—vv. 2, 6, 9, 15, 23, 40) פן תשמד ("lest you are destroyed"—v. 26).[49] It even contains two long rhetorical questions (vv. 7–8; 32b–34). In sum, in terms of content and struc-

---

14 [1994] 103–139.) For a detailed discussion of this problem, see Dietrich Knapp, *Deuteronomium 4: Literarische Analyse und theologische Interpretation* (Göttinger Theologishe Arbeiten 35; Göttingen: Vandenhoeck & Ruprecht, 1987) 3–20. For a recent defense of its unity, see Dennis T. Olson, *Deuteronomy and the Death of Moses: A Theological Reading* (OBT; Minneapolis: Fortress, 1994) 29 n. 5. The issue of the unity of the chapter, however, is not crucial for my argument; various suggested earlier versions of the chapter are less, rather than more sermonic in nature.

[45] Tigay, *Deuteronomy*, 41.

[46] See my earlier remarks.

[47] "Some Echoes of the Preaching," 224.

[48] This is often called Seidel's law; see the many references to this in Benjamin D. Sommer, *A Prophet Reads Scripture: Allusion in Isaiah 40–66* (Stanford: Stanford Univ. Press, 1998).

[49] See in addition the play on קרב and קרא in v. 7.

ture, Deuteronomy 4 fits Mason's criteria for sermons better than most of the passages on which Mason develops these criteria! Why, then, should we hesitate at all in calling this pericope a sermon?[50]

My previous study of Deut 30:1–10 begins to explain my hesitation. That pericope, which is closely related to ours,[51] also shares many of the characteristics noted by Mason, and others have typified it as a sermon.[52] Yet, it cannot be a sermon for various reasons, including the fact that it is deeply embedded in Deuteronomy, referring to texts in the previous chapters.[53] It is thus very difficult to conceive of Deut 30:1–10 as a transcribed version of a preached original.

Similar issues arise when we want to consider Deuteronomy 4 as a transcription of sorts of a real sermon that was preached in the exile.[54] Even if we were to overcome the basic *Sitz im Leben* issues, and could imagine with some conviction a non-synagogal, formal setting in which an individual preached,[55] I do not believe that Deuteronomy 4 would be a suitable candidate for a preserved sermon. First of all, it shares a literary conceit of Deuteronomy, that the generation about to enter the land is the addressee; how likely is it that a preacher in the exile could say (v. 3) אשר־ את הראות עיניכם עשה יהוה בבעל פעור, "You saw with your own eyes what YHWH did at Baal Pe'or"? A second major literary conceit of Deuteronomy is that Moses is the first-person speaker; does it make sense to imagine an exilic preacher speaking for Moses, saying ואתי צוה יהוה בעת ההיא ללמד אתכם חקים ומשפטים, "At

---

[50] For a similar hesitation concerning the use of "sermon" for Deuteronomy, see Lenchak, *"Choose Life!"*, who studies the style of the book within the study of rhetoric, and thus does not focus on the issue of *Sitz im Leben*. A more substantial critique of Deuteronomy 4 as a sermon is found in Georg Braulik, *Die Mittel Deuteronomische Rhetorik: Erhoben aus Deuteronomium 4,1–40* (AnBib 68; Rome: Biblical Institute Press, 1978), who adopts the term "parenesis" from his teacher, Lohfink; see esp. pp. 78–81. Braulik makes a similar observation in his "Literarkritik und die Einrahmung von Gemälden" (review of D. Knapp, *Zur literarkritischen und redaktionsgeschichtlichen Analyse von Dtn 4,1–6,3 und 29,1–30*), *RB* 96 (1989) 273–74.

[51] On the connection of Deuteronomy 4 to chs. 29–30, see Knapp, *Deuteronomium 4*, 128–63, and more recently, on Deuteronomy 4 and 30, see Norbert Lohfink, "Der Neue Bund im Buch Deuteronomium?" *ZABR* 4 (1998) 114–15.

[52] See "Predestination in Deuteronomy 30.1–10," 173.

[53] Ibid., 184–86.

[54] There is a strong consensus that this passage must be exilic (or later). This is based on the place of the chapter within the structure of Deuteronomy, the theology of the chapter, and its use of words and phrases such as סמל (v. 16) and אין עוד (vv. 35, 39); see the commentaries.

[55] Based on the evidence of Chronicles, where such speeches are attributed to a wide spectrum of individuals (contra von Rad!), it would seem inappropriate to speak of a "preacher" (later Hebrew דרשן) as an office fulfilled by a single individual.

the same time YHWH commanded me to teach you laws and rules" (v. 14)? Thus, the rhetoric underlying the chapter—the assumption that Moses is speaking to the generation about to enter the land—is simply not suitable for an exilic sermon.

In addition, it is quite likely that this chapter, like the beginning of chapter 30, is not a self-sufficient unit, but is fundamentally integrated into the book of Deuteronomy as a whole.[56] This is particularly evident in v. 8, which refers to כבל התורה הזאת אשר אנכי נתן לפניכם היום, "like all this *torah* that I am setting before you this day." Can we possibly imagine someone giving chapter 4 as the first part of a sermon, followed by a very long recitation of Deuteronomic law?[57]

Furthermore, it is likely that v. 19, ופן־תשא עיניך השמימה וראית את־השמש ואת־הירח ואת הכוכבים כל צבא השמים ונדחת והשתחוית להם ועבדתם אשר חלק יהוה אלהיך אתם לכל העמים תחת כל־השמים, "Lest you look up to the sky and behold the sun and the moon and the stars, the whole heavenly host, and you are lured into bowing down to them or serving them—these that YHWH your God allotted to other peoples everywhere under heaven," a rather unusual verse in this context, is a reflection of Deut 32:8–9, especially as it is reflected in the Septuagint and a Qumran scroll: בהנחל עליון גוים בהפרידו בני אדם יצב גבלת עמים למספר בני ישראל (אל)[58]: כי חלק יהוה עמו יעקב חבל נחלתו:, "When the Most High gave nations their inheritance, and set the divisions of man, he fixed the boundaries of peoples in relation to Israel's (read: the sons of God's) numbers. For YHWH's portion is His people, Jacob His allotment." The connections between chapter 4 and chapter 30 have already been mentioned; this additional connection between the prologue and epilogue of the book might suggest that chapter 4 is part of a balanced framework created to surround the legal material of Deuteronomy.[59] This would also

---

[56] This is true as well for Deut 30:1–10; see "Predestination in Deuteronomy 30.1–10," 182–85.

[57] The suggestion of Ronald Hals, "Is There a Genre of Preached Law?" *SBL 1973 Seminar Papers* (ed. George MacRae; Cambridge, Mass.: SBL, 1973) 1.1–12, has not been generally accepted.

[58] For this standard emendation, supported by LXX and a Qumran manuscript, see Tigay, *Deuteronomy*, 514–15.

[59] I would not, however, go as far as Duane L. Christensen, "Form and Structure in Deuteronomy 1–11," in *Das Deuteronomium: Entstehung, Gestalt und Botschaft* (ed. Norbert Lohfink; BETL 68; Leuven: Leuven Univ. Press, 1985) 135–44, or even the smaller-scale structure noted in "Deuteronomy in Modern Research: Approaches and Issues," in *A Song of Power and the Power of Song: Essays on the Book of Deuteronomy* (ed. Duane L. Christensen; Sources for Biblical and Theological Study 3; Winona Lake, Ind.: Eisenbrauns, 1993) 9 in creating various symmetries that reflect the structuring of the book. I have criticized these types of structures in a paper ("The Literary Interpretation of Biblical Historical Texts") offered at the 1999 International Meeting of the Society of Biblical Literature, held in Lahti, Finland.

explain why the chapter is *so* Deuteronomic—as a type of epitome of the book, it is trying harder than usual to use Deuteronomic phraseology throughout,[60] often quoting little snippets from elsewhere in the book.[61] Finally, it is likely that the chapter is not an independent unit, but is well-integrated into the surrounding chapters, on which it might depend.[62]

Additionally, though it is easy to initially understand the chapter as an appeal to obedience, which would be a very suitable topic for a sermon, a close look at the chapter shows that it shares the theology of predestined repentance with Deut 30:1–10.[63] Especially when read in conjunction with the closely related Deut 30:1–10, Deut 4:29–30, ובקשתם משם את־יהוה אלהיך ומצאת כי תדרשנו בכל־לבבך ובכל־נפשך: בצר לך ומצאוך כל הדברים האלה באחרית הימים ושבת עד־יהוה אלהיך ושמעת בקלו, should be translated: "You will seek from there YHWH your God and will find (him); indeed you will seek him with all of your heart and all of your being. When you are in straits, and all of these things befall you at a later time, you will return to YHWH your God, and will heed his voice." Context supports the arguments I have adduced elsewhere for this understanding of forced, God-driven repentance. The following verse emphasizes God's compassion, and his inability to forget the ancestral covenant; in other words, the covenant, which does not allow God to destroy Israel, forces God to make Israel repent, so that they will be saved. Thus, if encouraging a group to take up a particular action is a crucial aspect of the sermon, this pericope, which stresses that YHWH will ultimately force the people into repentance, might not be suitable for a sermon. Since one could in theory imagine a sermon that adheres to the idea of predestination, this factor is not decisive in suggesting that this chapter was not a sermon. However, when combined with other features that suggest that Deuteronomy 4 is not sermonic, the chapter's use of this theological conception is worth pointing out.

This notion of Deuteronomy 4 as a literary work which was composed as part of Deuteronomy, rather than as a self-standing sermon, is buttressed by additional factors both outside of and in the chapter. In most general terms, Deuteronomy is extremely bookish in nature, containing many references to written literature.[64] More broadly, it is likely that an added emphasis on studying that which is preserved in a written work,

---

[60] Note for example the extremely stereotyped Deuteronomic phraseology seen in vv. 1 and 40, the framing verses of the unit. I suspect that this extreme Deuteronomic vocabulary reflects an interest in incorporating the chapter into the larger book, rather than the Deuteronomic affiliation of a preacher.

[61] This is particularly obvious in the use of ch. 5, concerning revelation at Horeb, by ch. 4. An additional example is the reference to 13:1 in 4:2.

[62] See the discussion in Knapp, *Deuteronomium 4*, 27–29.

[63] See "Predestination in Deuteronomy 30.1–10."

[64] An extremely nuanced depiction of this bookishness is Jean-Pierre Sonnet,

developed in the Deuteronomistic exilic world. This may be seen, for example, in the addition in Joshua 1:7–8, which emphasizes the need to study the written Torah: והגית בו יומם ולילה למען תשמר לעשות ככל הכתוב בו, "you should recite it day and night, so that you may observe faithfully all that is written in it" (v. 8).[65] This study of the written word is quite possibly reflective of the exilic culture in general. Here I think of the suggestion of von Rad that Deutero-Isaiah should be understood as a literary prophet,[66] and the more recent suggestion of Ellen Davis that the eating of the scroll by Ezekiel also reflects a transition in this period from spoken to textual prophecy.[67] The exilic Deut 4:1–40 must be seen within this broader tradition.

Anthropological studies have complicated our understanding of the relationship between oral and written works, and thus have made it more difficult to suggest internal criteria that "prove" that a work has its origin in writing rather than in oral tradition.[68] Despite these warnings, I would point out, hesitantly, the extremely learned nature of Deut 4:1–40, which more likely points to its existence as a written work, rather than as a sermon. This is evident in the various ways in which the text picks up on various texts in Exodus, joins them together, reinterprets them, and in some cases, even inverts them.[69] It is difficult to see how the main argument of the chapter, that hearing, rather than seeing, is believing,[70] would have been fully appreciated through a single "listen through," as required by a

---

The Book Within the Book: Writing in Deuteronomy (Biblical Interpretation Series 14; Leiden: Brill, 1997).

[65] See Alexander Rofé, "The Piety of the Torah-disciples at the Winding-up of the Hebrew Bible: Josh 1:8; Ps 1:2; Isa 59:21," in *Bibel in jüdischer und christlicher Tradition: Festschrift für Johann Maier zum 60* (ed. H. Merklein et al.; Athenäums Monografien Theologie 88; Frankfurt a. M.: Hain, 1993) 78–85.

[66] Gerhard von Rad, *The Message of the Prophets* (New York: Harper and Row, 1965) 209–210.

[67] Ellen F. Davis, *Swallowing the Scroll: Textuality and the Dynamics of Discourse in Ezekiel's Prophecy* (JSOTSup 78; Sheffield: Sheffield Academic Press, 1989).

[68] Much of this material is summarized in Susan Niditch, *Oral World and Written Word* (Ancient Israelite Literature; Louisville, Ky.: Westminster John Knox, 1996); some of her statements should be modified in light of the suggestive new book by Alan Dundes, *Holy Writ as Oral Lit: The Bible as Folklore* (Lanham, Md.: Rowman & Littlefield, 1999).

[69] For example, Deut 4:11 integrates Exod 19:18, 16 and 20:21; קול דברים of Deut 4:12 reinterprets the קול, "thunder," of Exodus 20:16, 18–19 (see Sonnet, *The Book Within the Book*, 36). For inversion, compare Deut 4:15, כי לא ראיתם, to Exod 20:22, אתם ראיתם. For a discussion of Deuteronomic revision of earlier legal traditions, see Bernard M. Levinson, *Deuteronomy and the Hermeneutics of Legal Innovation* (New York: Oxford Univ. Press, 1997); I apply the same methodology to Deuteronomic narrative texts in *The Creation of History in Ancient Israel* (London: Routledge, 1995) 62–78.

[70] This is a central theme of Geller, "Fiery Wisdom." This is now further devel-

sermon. Even certain structural devices in the chapter seem more suitable for a written, rather than oral, world.[71] Again, I accept the notion that there is no clear ancient demarcation between what was originally written and what was originally oral; yet I am struck by the extremely learned nature of the content and structure, which almost demands that it be studied rather than heard—it simply could not have been appreciated as a popular, public sermon.[72] To my mind, this should be added to other, more decisive features that suggest a written, non-sermonic origin of the chapter.

The results of this study have been largely negative, suggesting that the term "sermon" is generally problematic in reference to texts in Deuteronomy, and is especially problematic for Deut 4:1–40.[73] I second the earlier conclusion of Lohfink, that the term "sermon" should be avoided in relation to the introduction of Deuteronomy.[74] Unfortunately, we know relatively little about the social structure of exilic life, and cannot begin to venture a guess concerning how units like Deut 6:4–9 might have originated, and which social group is responsible for their transmission. This frustrating lack of knowledge might suggest that it is wise to avoid terms like "sermons," for we simply do not know if texts found in post-exilic compositions, which have significant elements in common with later preached sermons, had their origin as preached sermons in official settings. It certainly is striking that of all the Deuteronomic texts, Deut 4:1–40 does share the most characteristics posited for ancient sermons, and thus, it is especially tempting to see this as an example of "preaching to the exiles."[75] Yet it also contains clear signs that it is a highly learned and complex unit which is not self-standing, but is deeply integrated into the structure of Deuteronomy. Thus, if we believe, even tentatively, that real

---

oped by Michael Carasik, "To See a Sound: A Deuteronomic Rereading of Exodus 20:15," *Prooftexts* 19 (1999) 257–64.

[71] Note, for example, the way in which כי is used to close and then to open adjacent sub-units in vv. 24–25 and 31–32.

[72] Some have suggested, however, that the preserved early Jewish sermons were given in the study house, rather than the synagogue, and thus had an elite audience; see Marc Hirshman, "The Preacher and his Public in Third-Century Palestine," *JJS* 42 (1991) 108–114.

[73] I am certainly not the first to note that it is problematic to view ch. 4 as a sermon. Even von Rad, who did so much to spread the idea that the framework of Deuteronomy is comprised of sermons, noted that 4:9ff. "cannot be called a sermon, although its hortatory quality is obvious"; see Gerhard von Rad, *Deuteronomy*, 21. It is ironic that von Rad's problematic label "sermon" has been adopted by others, and even applied where he recognized it as inappropriate.

[74] See esp. Lohfink, *Das Hauptgebot*, 272: "Deshalb möchten wir von Wort 'Predigt' absehen. Das Wort 'Paränese' ist für unsere Zwecke geeigneter."

[75] This is the title of Nicholson's book (see above, n. 12).

sermons did exist in the exilic period, this cannot be one of them. Instead, we must use the oxymoron "literary sermon" to describe the chapter, which shares most of the putative structures of the biblical sermon, but clearly has its origin in written form as part of Deuteronomy,[76] rather than as an oral sermon preached to the exiles.[77]

---

[76] Could the reference to Genesis 1 in Deut 4:16–19 (see above) even suggest that it was written as part of the Pentateuch?

[77] In theory, it could be suggested that the chapter was originally a sermon, which was *fundamentally* transformed when it was incorporated into the book of Deuteronomy. It is impossible to evaluate such a proposition; I would only note that the non-sermonic elements in the unit are so fundamental and numerous that this proposal seems unlikely.

Chapter 5

Models of Utopia in the Biblical Tradition

John J. Collins
Yale University

In his review of Jean Delumeau's *History of Paradise* in the *Times Literary Supplement*, Leszek Kolakowski wrote: "The Enlightenment destroyed, step by step, belief in the historical exactness of the Biblical report, but it could not destroy what formed the persistent background to the centuries-long search: human yearning for the country of eternal Spring."[1] One suspects that Kolakowski's reading of the Bible is unduly colored by the first few pages of Genesis, or perhaps it is influenced by the shape of the Christian Bible, which ends on a distinctly paradisiac note with the vision of the new Jerusalem. But in fact the motif of Paradise is not especially prominent in the Hebrew Bible. Apart from Genesis, we find an allusion to Eden in Ezek 28:11–15, and there are occasional paradisiac motifs in eschatological passages, such as Isaiah 11 and Ezekiel 40–48, but it is only in post-biblical literature that the notion of paradise as the abode of the dead is developed.[2] In short, the absence of the motif of Paradise in the Hebrew Bible is more remarkable than its persistence.

Paradise, or Eden, is the closest biblical approximation to the idea of utopia in its strict sense, *ou topos,* or "no place." The ancient Greek literature, where the genre of utopian writing was most developed, typically spoke of imaginary places such as Atlantis, or remote, unknown peoples such as the Hyperboreans.[3] Similarly, Eden is located at the mythical

---

[1] L. Kolakowski, review of J. Delumeau, *History of Paradise: The Garden of Eden in Myth and Tradition* (trans. Matthew O'Connell; New York: Continuum, 1995).

[2] J. L. Kugel, *The Bible As It Was* (Cambridge, Mass.: Belknap Press of Harvard Univ. Press, 1997) 78–80.

[3] J. Ferguson, *Utopias of the Classical World* (Ithaca, N.Y.: Cornell Univ. Press, 1975); J. S. Romm, *The Edges of the Earth in Ancient Thought* (Princeton, N.J.: Princeton Univ. Press, 1994); Unyong Sim, *Das himmlische Jerusalem in Apk 21,1–22,5 im*

source of all the major rivers of the world in Gen 2:10,[4] and at the edges of the earth in the *Book of the Watchers* from the Hellenistic period (*1 Enoch* 32).[5] But such fantastic geography is exceptional in the biblical tradition. In his influential collection of essays, *Map is Not Territory,* Jonathan Smith draws a contrast "between a *locative* vision of the world (which emphasizes place) and a *utopian* vision of the world (using the term in its strict sense: the value of being in no place)."[6] In Smith's terms, locative visions predominate in the biblical literature.

But the modern usage of "utopia" has been shaped not so much by its Greek etymology as by the work of Sir Thomas More depicting an ideal society, which made a deliberate pun on *eu-topia,* a place where all things are well.[7] So, for example, the classic work of Karl Mannheim defined the utopian state of mind as one that "is incongruous with the state of reality within which it occurs," and utopia as "that type of orientation that transcends reality and which at the same time breaks the bonds of the existing order."[8] For our purposes, then, it will be more satisfactory to recognize different kinds of utopias, different visions of an idealized or transcendent time and place. I propose to distinguish four kinds of utopia in this sense in the corpus of biblical and early Jewish writings. The first, which envisions a transformed land of Israel, may be termed agricultural. The second, which focuses on an ideal Jerusalem, has an urban character. The third is the model of an ideal community, such as we find in the Dead Sea Scrolls and in the writings of Philo. The fourth, which appears at the beginning of Genesis and again in apocalyptic visions at the end of the biblical period, is properly utopian in the sense that the place it imagines is out of this world.

I. The Transformation of the Land

In his *History of Paradise,* Delumeau comments that "there is, however, a basic element that distinguishes the paradise of Eden from the gardens of Mesopotamia and Persia: the presence of 'the tree of the knowledge of

Kontext biblisch-jüdischer Tradition und antiken Städtebaus (Trier: Wissenschaftlicher Verlag, 1996) 50–59.

[4] C. Westermann, *Genesis 1–11* (Minneapolis: Augsburg, 1984) 216, comments: "This being the case, all attempts to explain or locate the sources of the four rivers geographically are ruled out."

[5] Enoch reaches "the garden of righteousness" by going over the summits of mountains, far away to the east, over the Red Sea and far from it.

[6] J. Z. Smith, *Map is Not Territory* (Chicago: Univ. of Chicago Press, 1978) 101.

[7] See B. de Jouvenel, "Utopia for Practical Purposes," in *Utopias and Utopian Thought* (ed. F. E. Manuel; Boston: Houghton Miflin, 1966) 219: "Eutopie it shall be, if and when brought into being: till then Utopie."

[8] K. Mannheim, *Ideology and Utopia* (New York: Harcourt, Brace & Co., 1936) 173.

good and evil.' Obedience to God's command regarding it was necessary for immortality, while disobedience led to death."[9] This conditional, covenantal quality is indeed an important factor in much of the Hebrew Bible. It is neither the only nor the most consistent factor that qualifies biblical notions of utopia, but it is true that visions of a transformed land of Israel are often embedded in a covenantal context.

The law-codes of the Pentateuch hover, in the phrase of Menaham Haran, "between utopia and historical reality."[10] This is especially true of the Priestly Code, with its provision for Levitical cities and a jubilee year when all people should return to their ancestral property. The goal of this legislation might be described as an agricultural utopia. According to Leviticus 26:

> If you follow my statutes and keep my commandments and observe them faithfully, I will give you your rains in their season, and the land shall yield its produce, and the trees of the field shall yield their fruit. Your threshing shall overtake the vintage, and the vintage shall overtake the sowing; you shall eat your bread to the full, and live securely in your land. And I will grant peace in the land, and you shall lie down, and no one shall make you afraid; I will remove dangerous animals from the land and no sword shall go through your land. You shall give chase to your enemies, and they shall fall before you by the sword. . . . I will make you fruitful and multiply you, and I will maintain my covenant with you. (Lev 26:3–9)

Despite the relatively sober language, we should recognize that this is a utopian vision, which was itself rooted in ancient Near Eastern myth. In the Ugaritic myth of Baal, when Baal is rescued from Death, the heavens rain fat and the wadies flow with honey.[11] In the Israelite context, the same concerns are evident in the period of the monarchies, when most of the population of Israel, north and south, lived on the land. For the eighth-century prophet Hosea, the divine blessings were manifested in fertility, by the gift of "the grain, the wine and the oil" (Hos 2:8), just as they were for Israel's Canaanite neighbors. The point of difference was the identity of the god who gave these gifts, and the demands that he made in return.

Both the Deuteronomic authors and the Priestly school, who together were the chief editors of the Torah and the Prophets, explained the failure of Israel to achieve utopia by neglect of some aspects of covenant law, with the implication that the ideal society can in principle be brought about by appropriate human behavior.

After the Babylonian exile, however, in the later prophetic and apocalyptic writings, we increasingly find the belief that God will impose a new

---

[9] Delumeau, *History of Paradise*, 5.

[10] M. Haran, *Temples and Temple-Service in Ancient Israel* (Oxford: Clarendon, 1978) 122.

[11] H. L. Ginsberg, "Ugaritic Myths, Epics, and Legends," in *ANET*, 140.

order regardless of human failings. According to Jeremiah 31, God would make a new covenant in which the law would be written on the people's hearts so that they could not ignore it (Jer 31:31–4). Ezekiel 36 goes further: "I will remove from your body the heart of stone and give you a heart of flesh. I will put my spirit within you, and make you follow my statutes" (Ezek 36:26–7). For Ezekiel, the new order would be tantamount to a revivification of dry bones, although he did not actually anticipate a resurrection of the dead (Ezek 37:1–14). The covenantal model, with its admirable emphasis on human responsibility, was never entirely abandoned, but it was not found to be an adequate basis for utopian hope.

II. Urban Utopia

The vision of agricultural utopia survived in the Second Temple period. Obviously, it was embedded in the law codes of the Torah, as we have seen in Leviticus 26. The "new creation" described in Isaiah 65 provides that the people shall plant vineyards and eat their fruit (Isa 65:21). It is significant, however, that the people was now defined as that of Jerusalem. The restored territory of Judah was greatly reduced from that of biblical Israel, and the utopian dreams of the Second Temple period focused increasingly on the transformation of the city rather than on the fertility of the land.

Jerusalem, of course, had its own utopian traditions, which also involved cosmic transformation.[12] One of the more obviously utopian passages in the Hebrew Bible is found in the famous messianic oracle of Isaiah 11, which dreams of a time when "the wolf shall live with the lamb, the leopard shall lie down with the kid, the calf and the lion and the fatling together, and a little child shall lead them." In this kinder, gentler world "the nursing child shall play over the hole of the asp, and the weaned child shall put its hand on the adder's den. They will not hurt or destroy on all my holy mountain" (cf. Isa 65:25). The holy mountain, of course, is Mount Zion. The special status of Jerusalem was especially bound up with the temple. Because of the presence of God in the temple, Mt. Zion was the navel of the earth. The temple precincts were qualitatively radically different from other space. "Better a day in your courts than a thousand elsewhere" (Ps 84:10). Significantly for our theme, the holy mountain of God is equated with the garden of Eden in Ezekiel 28 ("You were in Eden, the garden of God . . . you were on the holy mountain of God"). The temple, in effect, was a Paradise which one might visit on pilgrimage at festival times.

---

[12] See R. J. Clifford, S. J., *The Cosmic Mountain in Canaan and the Old Testament* (Cambridge, Mass.: Harvard Univ. Press, 1972); J. D. Levenson, *Sinai and Zion* (Minneapolis: Winston, 1985) 89–184. On the traditions of Jerusalem through the ages see L. I. Levine, *Jerusalem: Its Sanctity and Centrality to Judaism, Christianity and Islam* (New York: Continuum, 1999).

This idealized vision of the temple city is found in Mesopotamia as early as the late third and early second millennium BCE. The Sumerian Hymn to Enlil speaks of Nippur just as the biblical psalmists speak of Jerusalem: "The city endowed with truth, where righteousness (and) justice are perpetuated, where clean garments are worn . . . in the city, the holy seat of Enlil, in Nippur, the beloved shrine of the father, the Great Mountain . . ."[13]

Restoration and the Temple

The restoration of the Judean community after the Babylonian exile was primarily the restoration of Jerusalem and a small surrounding territory. The people exiled to Babylon were primarily the urban elite, and included a large number of priests. The actual restoration under the Persians was first of all the restoration of Jerusalem as a temple city. The community that grew up around the temple has been described as a "citizen-temple community" (*Tempel-Bürger Gemeinde*) and for much of the Second Temple period they were ruled by the High Priest.[14] Greek ethnographers[15] and even Jewish Hellenistic writers[16] typically identify the Jews as the people who live around the temple in Jerusalem. Consequently we should not be surprised to find that priestly concerns often dominate the Jewish literature of this period.

In fact, the closest thing to utopian writing, in the sense of a blueprint for an ideal as distinct from actual society in the Hebrew Bible is the vision of the new Jerusalem and its environs in Ezekiel chapters 40–48. The prophet Ezekiel had claimed that the Lord was driven far from the sanctuary by the "abominations" practiced in the temple. The solution was to make sure that the purity of the sanctuary was safeguarded in the future.

---

[13] Trans. S. N. Kramer, in *ANET*, 573–4. See Moshe Weinfeld, "Zion and Jerusalem as Religious and Political Capital: Ideology and Utopia," in *The Poet and the Historian: Essays in Literary and Historical Biblical Criticism* (ed. R. E. Friedman; Chico, Calif.: Scholars Press, 1983) 75–115, esp. 104–114; idem, "Jerusalem—A Political and Spiritual Capital," in *Capital Cities: Urban Planning and Spiritual Dimensions* (ed. Joan Goodnick Westenholz; Jerusalem: Bible Lands Museum, 1996) 15–40, esp. 32–35. On the historical role of the temple city in Sumerian culture see Adam Falkenstein, *The Sumerian Temple City* (Introduction and translation by Maria deJ. Ellis; Los Angeles: Undena, 1974). A similar ideology is attested in Babylon in the Neo-Babylonian period. Cf. S. Langdon, *Die Neubabylonischen Königsinschriften* (Leipzig: J. C. Hinrichs, 1912) 118, 138.

[14] J. Weinberg, *The Citizen-Temple Community* (JSOTSup 151; Sheffield: Sheffield Academic Press, 1992). See also J. Blenkinsopp, "Temple and Society in Achaemenid Judah," in *Second Temple Studies 1: Persian Period* (ed. P. R. Davies; JSOTSup 117; Sheffield: Sheffield Academic Press, 1991) 22–53.

[15] Hecataeus, in Josephus, *Ag. Ap.* 1.197–199.

[16] *Sib. Or.* 3:573–80; 702–31.

At the end of the book, in chapters 40–48, we find an extensive blueprint for the restoration. In this new and utopian dispensation, Jerusalem is not mentioned by name, but is referred to as "the city." It is subsumed into the consecrated area, or תרומה, which is a strip of land that extends from the Jordan to the sea, separating the territories of Judah to the south and Benjamin to the north. Within this area, strips of land are set aside for the priests, the Levites, the city and the prince. The temple is located in the middle of the territory of the priests. The area of the city proper is declared profane (חל הוא, 48:15), and the territory of the city is only half the area of that of the priests. The city of Jerusalem becomes virtually an appendage of the temple precinct under the control of the Zadokite priests.[17]

In Ezekiel's view, the disaster that befell Israel was caused by the failure to protect the sanctity of the temple. In future, "no foreigner, uncircumcised in heart and flesh" would enter the sanctuary (44:9). Levites and ordinary Israelites were restricted to the outer court. Such restrictions were not peculiarly Jewish. An instruction to the gate-keepers of a temple of Isis at Philae in Egypt in the Ptolemaic period similarly warned that the uncircumcised, the foreigner, and the lawbreaker should not be admitted to the temple precincts.[18] Ezekiel's preoccupation with purity, however, was intensified by violation of Jerusalem by the Babylonians, in every sense of the word. That sense of violation would be revived on a number of occasions in the Second Temple period.

Pride of place in Ezekiel's new cultic order was given to the descendants of Zadok, who were credited with preserving the sanctuary when the rest of the people sinned, and who alone would be allowed to enter the inner court. They were to teach the people the difference between the sacred and the profane. If impurity was the cause of disaster, purity must henceforth be of paramount importance. Other traditional attributes of Jerusalem, such as the association with the monarchy, were of lesser importance. The Davidic prince retains a role, and is given his own allotment of land in the תרומה, but he is, in the words of Jon Levenson, an apolitical messiah,[19] charged with providing the offerings for the sacrificial cult (48:17; 22–25).

---

[17] On Ezekiel's vision see Zimmerli, *Ezekiel 2*, 325–553; also J. D. Levenson, *The Theology of the Program of Restoration of Ezekiel 40–49* (Missoula, Mont.: Scholars Press, 1976). I am indebted to the essay of Adela Yarbro Collins on "The Dream of the New Jerusalem at Qumran," presented at the Princeton Conference on the Dead Sea Scrolls in November, 1997, and forthcoming in the proceedings of that conference under the editorship of J. H. Charlesworth.

[18] M. Weinfeld, *Social Justice in Ancient Israel and in the Ancient Near East* (Jerusalem: Magnes, and Minneapolis: Fortress, 1995) 100; H. Junker, "Vorschriften für den Tempelkult in Philae," *AnBib* 12, III (1956) 152–3.

[19] Levenson, *The Theology of the Program of Restoration*, 75.

Ezekiel's vision was eschatological; it was not a pragmatic program for renewal, and it was never realized, although it remained an influential text throughout the Second Temple period.[20] Other prophets of the exilic period also spoke of Jerusalem in utopian terms. A prophecy in the Book of Isaiah predicted that the glory of Lebanon, the cypress, the plane and the pine, would be brought to Jerusalem to glorify the place of the sanctuary (Isa 60:13). Measured against such expectations, the actual temple that was built in the Persian period was a considerable disappointment. The Book of Ezra reports that the old men who remembered Solomon's temple wept at the sight of its replacement (Ezra 3:12). The prophet Haggai asked those who remembered the first temple, "How do you see it now? Is it not in your sight as nothing?" But Haggai went on to prophesy that the Lord would, "in a little while, shake the heavens and the earth and the sea and the dry land, and shake all nations so that the treasures of all nations would come in and fill this house with splendor" (Hag 2:6–7). The final glory would be greater than the former. But this prophecy too was not fulfilled.

It is no wonder, then, that another prophet expressed skepticism and disillusionment about this promised temple: "Heaven is my throne and earth is my footstool? What is the house that you would build for me?" (Isa 66:1). This question had been raised before by the Deuteronomistic historians, in Solomon's prayer at the consecration of the first temple in 1 Kings 8, and less directly in Nathan's oracle to David in 2 Samuel 7. In those passages the objection was overcome. The prophet whose oracles are preserved in the last chapters of Isaiah was more radical. His question at least seriously relativizes the importance of the temple.[21] It is unlikely, however, that he rejected it entirely. Other passages in Isaiah 56–66 speak of the wealth of the nations pouring in to beautify the temple (60:13) and speak of priests and Levites in the final transformation of Jerusalem. The vision of the future that we find in the last chapters of the Book of Isaiah is quite different from that of Ezekiel or Haggai. Ezekiel would build walls and gates to keep the Gentiles out. The Isaianic prophet would have the gates of Jerusalem be always open so that the wealth of the nations would flow into it (Isa 60:11). But neither is dreaming of isles of the blessed, or of exotic places

---

[20] S. S. Tuell, "Ezekiel 40–42 as Verbal Icon," *CBQ* 58 (1996) 649–64, goes farther and proposes that Ezekiel's vision concerns the heavenly temple, but this is difficult to maintain in view of the location of the temple within the land of Israel. Full bibliography on the debate about the meaning of Ezekiel's vision may be found in Tuell's article.

[21] Brooks Schramm, *The Opponents of Third Isaiah: Reconstructing the Cultic History of the Restoration* (JSOTSup 193; Sheffield: Sheffield Academic Press, 1995) 164, contends that Isa 66:1 is "far from any kind of 'anti-temple' polemic," and translates instead "where is the temple that you would build for me." But the context clearly implies a critique of the proposed temple.

far away. Both are focused on the city of Jerusalem, even if they anticipate a transformation without precedent in human experience.

We have then two distinct kinds of utopian expectation in the period of the Judean restoration after the exile, both of them locative, in the sense that they are this-worldly and rooted specifically in Jerusalem. One is focused on the temple and has an intense concern for purity. The other favors an open Jerusalem and finds a place for Gentiles in the new dispensation, even if only in a subordinate role. ("Strangers shall stand and feed your flocks, foreigners shall till your land and dress your vines . . . You shall enjoy the wealth of the nations and in their riches you shall glory," Isa 61:5–6.) Both of these visions recur in the later literature of the Second Temple period.

The View from the Diaspora

Throughout this period, the greater part of the Jewish people actually lived outside the land of Israel, in Diasporas from Babylon to Alexandria, and later to Rome. The prophet Jeremiah, or one of his redactors, had written to the Jews of Babylon: "Build houses and live in them; plant gardens and eat what they produce. Take wives and have sons and daughters; take wives for your sons, and give your daughters in marriage" (Jer 29:5–6). So the exiles had done, and they prospered in exile, at least down until the Roman period. But we never find a diasporic utopia, a vision of an ideal Jewish community outside the land of Israel, at least not before Philo in the first century of the common era. Instead, the eschatological literature of the Diaspora continues the inclusive strand of post-exilic prophecy, which saw Jerusalem as a cosmic center to which people of all races would flock. The tradition of the open Jerusalem, which would serve as a center of pilgrimage for the Gentiles is found especially in the third book of Sibylline Oracles, written in Egypt, beginning in the second century BCE. There we read that in the end-time peoples from all over the world will send their gifts to the Jerusalem temple. Then

> the all-bearing earth will give the most excellent unlimited fruit to mortals,
> of grain, wine, and oil, and a delightful drink of sweet honey from heaven,
> trees, fruit of the top branches and rich flocks and herds and lambs of sheep
> and kids of goats. And it will break forth sweet fountains of white milk. The
> cities will be full of good things and the fields will be rich. There will be no
> sword on earth, or din of battle . . . but there will be great peace throughout
> the whole earth. King will be friend to king to the end of the age. The Im-
> mortal in the starry heaven will put in effect a common law for men
> throughout the whole earth. (*Sib. Or.* 3:744–61)[22]

---

[22] Trans. J. J. Collins, "The Sibylline Oracles," in *OTP*, 1.378. Later, after the destruction of the temple, the fifth book of Sibylline Oracles envisions a restoration of Jerusalem with a wall that extends as far as Joppa (*Sib. Or.* 5:252). In contrast, *Sib.*

The sibyl goes on to echo the prophecy of Isaiah: "Wolves and lambs will eat grass together in the mountains. Leopards will feed together with kids. Roving bears will spend the night with calves. The flesh-eating lion will eat husks at the manger like an ox, and mere infant children will lead them with ropes. For he will make the beasts on earth harmless" (788–95). This utopian vision has a remarkable parallel in Virgil's fourth eclogue, which also invokes a sibyl, of Cumae.[23] Whether Virgil was acquainted with Isaiah or with the Jewish sibyl has long been disputed, but never conclusively shown.[24]

Utopia and Purity

The purist strand in Jewish utopian thought is more prominent than the inclusive one in the literature of the Second Temple period. It is represented most fully by two writings found among the Dead Sea Scrolls, although neither is necessarily a product of the Dead Sea sect. These are the Temple Scroll and an Aramaic text known as The Vision of the New Jerusalem. The latter text is preserved in several manuscripts but in very fragmentary condition.[25] Clearly modeled on the vision of Ezekiel, the text is narrated in the first person by a visionary who is given a guided tour by an angel. In contrast to Ezekiel's vision, the temple is located within the city, which is envisioned as an immense rectangle. It is divided by six large avenues linking the twelve gates and forming sixteen big blocks of houses. One of these avenues runs through the center of the city, and so the temple is slightly off-center. It is likely that the New Jerusalem text was influenced

---

Or. 4:8 appears to reject the idea of a temple, although the oracle goes on to mourn the destruction of the Jerusalem temple (vss. 115–29). For a range of attitudes toward Jerusalem in the Hellenistic Diaspora see Daniel R. Schwartz, "Temple or City: What did Hellenistic Jews see in Jerusalem?" in *The Centrality of Jerusalem: Historical Perspectives* (ed. M. Poorthuis and Ch. Safrai; Kampen: Kok Pharos, 1996) 114–27.

[23] Weinfeld, "Jerusalem—A Political and Spiritual Capital," 29.

[24] See J. J. Collins, "The Jewish Transformation of Sibylline Oracles," in *Seers, Sibyls and Sages in Hellenistic-Roman Judaism* (Leiden: Brill, 1997) 181–98 (especially 192–97). For an argument in favor of such acquaintance see R. G. M. Nisbet, "Virgil's Fourth Eclogue: Easterners and Westerners," *Bulletin of the Institute for Classical Studies* 25 (1978) 59–78.

[25] F. García Martínez, "The 'New Jerusalem' and the Future Temple of the Manuscripts from Qumran," in *Qumran and Apocalyptic* (ed. idem; Leiden: Brill, 1992) 180–213; idem, "The Temple Scroll and the New Jerusalem," in *The Dead Sea Scrolls after Fifty Years* (ed. P. W. Flint and J. C. VanderKam; Leiden: Brill, 1999) 2.431–60; M. Chyutin, "The New Jerusalem: Ideal City," *DSD* 1 (1994) 71–97; E. Puech, "À propos de la Jérusalem nouvelle d'après les manuscrits de la Mer Morte," *Sem* 43–44 (1995) 64–73.

by Hellenistic city planning, even at the expense of the perfect symmetry that we find in the Temple Scroll.[26]

The buildings in the New Jerusalem are built with precious stones, reminiscent of Ezekiel's description of the garden of Eden: "And all the buildings in it are of sapphire and rubies, and the windows (?) of gold . . ." (4Q554 frag. 2, col. 2:14–16).[27] Mention of "living waters" in another fragment (11Q18 frag. 24:1, 3) evokes Ezekiel 47, which describes waters flowing from below the threshold of the temple and making the Dead Sea fresh. These parallels suggest that the temple of the New Jerusalem text is an eschatological temple, created miraculously by God.[28]

The Temple Scroll, which is written in Hebrew and much more fully preserved, is a synthetic edition of laws from Leviticus and Deuteronomy, and may reasonably be considered a utopian document in the sense that it is a blueprint for an ideal society. It is presented as the revelation of God to Moses, but it is very unlikely that it was intended to replace the traditional Torah. Rather it was a guide to the Torah, which emphasized some things, omitted others and advanced a particular line of interpretation. About two thirds of the sixty six chapters of the scroll are taken up with matters relating to the temple (columns 3:1–13:7), the cult (13:8–29:10) and the city (columns 30:1–47:18). The temple envisioned is about three times the size of the Herodian enclosure,[29] and is distinguished by the strictness of its purity laws and ritual observances. The attention to the architectural design of the temple and courtyards is reminiscent of Ezekiel 40–48, but the Temple Scroll differs from the biblical model in several respects.[30] The most important of these is the relation of the city to the temple. In Ezekiel's vision they were separated, and the city was declared profane, although it too was located in the תרומה, or strip of land set aside for the Lord. In the Temple Scroll, however, the city is identified as "the city of the sanctuary" and shares in its sanctity:

> The city which I will sanctify, causing my name and [my] sanctuar[y] to abide [in it], shall be holy and pure of all impurity with which they can become impure. Whatever is in it shall be pure. Whatever enters it shall be

---

[26] M. Broshi, "Visionary Architecture and Town Planning in the Dead Sea Scrolls," in *Time to Prepare the Way in the Wilderness: Papers on the Dead Sea Scrolls* (ed. D. Dimant and L. H. Schiffman; Leiden: Brill, 1995) 9–22.

[27] Cf. also Isa 54:11–12.

[28] See Yarbro Collins, "The Dream of a New Jerusalem."

[29] M. Broshi, "The Gigantic Dimensions of the Visionary Temple in the Temple Scroll," *BARev* 13 (1987) 36–7.

[30] L. H. Schiffman, "Sacred Space: The Land of Israel in the Temple Scroll," *Biblical Archaeology Today, 1990: Proceedings of the Second International Congress on Biblical Archaeology* (Jerusalem: Israel Exploration Society, 1993) 398–410; Yarbro Collins, "The Dream of a New Jerusalem."

pure: wine, oil, all food and all moistened (food) shall be clean. No skin of clean animals slaughtered in their cities shall be brought there (to the city of the sanctuary) . . . You shall not profane the city where I cause my name and my sanctuary to abide." (47:3–11)[31]

The concern for the purity of the city is such that the latrine (one for the entire city!) must be located at least three thousand cubits outside it (46:13–16), and a man who has intercourse with his wife may not enter any part of the city of the sanctuary for three days (45:11–12).[32] So unrealistic do these regulations appear that some scholars have argued that "the city of the sanctuary" refers only to the *temenos,* or temple mount.[33] But there is no clear instance where the *temenos* is called "city."[34] Rather, as Jacob Milgrom has argued, the sanctuary (מקדש) is the sacred compound and the city is Jerusalem, while the temple building would be "the house of the sanctuary" (בית המקדש).[35] The scroll refers to "the city in which I established my name and my sanctuary" (47:9–11). Similarly, in 4QMMT "Jerusalem is the holy camp and it is the place which he chose from all the tribes of Israel" (B 59–62).

While this concern for the purity of the city was extreme, it was not without precedent. Josephus tells us that when Antiochus III of Syria captured Jerusalem he passed an edict, presumably at the request of the High Priest, that

It is unlawful for any foreigner to enter the enclosure of the temple which is forbidden to the Jews, except to those of them who are accustomed to enter after purifying themselves in accordance with the law of the country. Nor shall anyone bring into the city the flesh of horses or of mules or of wild or tame asses, or of leopards, foxes or hares or, in general, of any animals forbidden to the Jews. Nor is it lawful to bring in their skins or even to breed any of these animals in the city. But only the sacrificial animals known to

---

[31] Translations of the Dead Sea Scrolls are those of Geza Vermes, *The Complete Dead Sea Scrolls in English* (New York: Allen Lane/Penguin, 1997), with minor modifications.

[32] Sexual relations in the city of the sanctuary are also prohibited in CD 12:1–2.

[33] This was originally suggested, with reference to the Damascus Document, by L. Ginzberg, *An Unknown Jewish Sect* (New York: Jewish Theological Seminary, 1976) 73–4. In recent years it has been defended by B. A. Levine, "The Temple Scroll: Aspects of its Historical Provenance and Literary Character," *BASOR* 232 (1978) 5–23 and L. H. Schiffman, "*Ir Ha-Miqdash* and Its Meaning in the Temple Scroll and Other Qumran Texts," in *Sanctity of Time and Space in Tradition and Modernity* (ed. A. Houtman, M. Poorthuis and J. Schwartz; Leiden: Brill, 1998) 95–109.

[34] The suggested parallel with the City of David is not conclusive, since the latter name refers to an older stage of the city's development.

[35] J. Milgrom, "The City of the Temple: A Response to Lawrence H. Schiffman," *JQR* 85 (1984) 125–8.

their ancestors and necessary for the propitiation of God shall they be permitted to use. (*Ant.* 12.145–6)

The Temple Scroll similarly forbids the bringing of skins into "the city of the sanctuary" (47:11–14). If such a concern for the purity of the city was at one time enacted as the law of the land, we should not be surprised to find the concern intensified in a utopian text like the Temple Scroll. But the degree of concern for purity in such texts should probably be attributed to the threat of defilement that Jewish traditionalists felt to be omnipresent in the Hellenistic age.

For the Temple Scroll, the Temple City was at the center of the land and the temple was at the center of the city. Ezekiel had distinguished an outer court and an inner court. The Temple Scroll provides for three concentric courtyards surrounding the temple, one reserved for the priests, the second for the men of Israel over the age of twenty and the third for the women of Israel and for foreigners who were born in the land of Israel (40:6).[36] Ezekiel makes no allowance for foreigners.

The plan of the temple in the Temple Scroll does not conform to any biblical model. Larry Schiffman has suggested that it represents the layout of the Tabernacle and the desert camp combined.[37] The territories of the tribes are arranged around the holy city so that each has equal access to it. Most fundamentally, it seems to be an attempt to take the commandment, "have them make me a sanctuary so that I may dwell in the midst of them" (Exod 25:8) quite literally, by giving geographical expression to the centrality of the dwelling of God.

We have noted already that the size of the temple was unrealistic. It would have required major alterations of the terrain of Jerusalem to allow for its construction. Nonetheless, it is not strictly an eschatological temple. At the end of the discussion of the festivals in column 29 we are told: "I will dwell with them forever and ever and will sanctify my [sa]nctuary by my glory. I will cause my glory to rest on it until the day of creation on which I shall create my sanctuary, establishing it for myself for all time according to the covenant which I have made with Jacob at Bethel." From this it appears that this temple is an interim one, and that it will be replaced by a divinely constructed temple in the new creation.[38] This would be the "gate of

---

[36] See the edition of E. Qimron, *The Temple Scroll: A Critical Edition with Extensive Reconstructions* (Jerusalem: Israel Exploration Society, 1996) 57. J. Maier, *The Temple Scroll: An Introduction, Translation and Commentary* (Sheffield: JSOT Press, 1985) 37, translates "proselytes born in . . ." but the reference is clearly to non-Jews.

[37] Schiffman, "Sacred Space," 402.

[38] The idea that God would build an eschatological temple in the new creation is also found in Jub 1:17, 27, 29. See J. C. VanderKam, "The Temple Scroll and the Book of Jubilees," in *Temple Scroll Studies* (ed. G. Brooke; Sheffield: JSOT Press, 1989) 232, 236.

heaven," like Bethel in the story of Jacob. Contrary to what is often asserted, the Temple Scroll is not designed for the messianic age.[39] The king in the Scroll is not said to fulfill messianic prophecy and his rule is conditional. The Scroll is certainly utopian in character, in the sense that it is incongruous with the state of reality in which it occurs, but it stops short of the definitive claims characteristic of apocalyptic visions.

The Temple Scroll may be seen as the culmination of a trajectory initiated by Ezekiel, which envisions utopia in terms of the sanctity of the temple and the temple city. It is of course significant that this text was found among the writings of the purist, sectarian community of Qumran. But the ideal of a pure Jerusalem was by no means peculiar to sectarian circles. The *Psalms of Solomon*, which are often thought to be Pharisaic and are conspicuously absent from the Dead Sea Scrolls, pray for a messianic king who will "purify Jerusalem of the nations which trample her down in destruction" (*Pss. Sol.* 17:22) and "purify Jerusalem, making it holy as of old, so that nations shall come from the ends of the earth to see his glory" (*Pss. Sol.* 17:30–31). Even the Sibylline Oracles, written in Greek in the Egyptian Diaspora, look forward to a time when "the unclean foot of the Greeks" will no longer revel in the land of Judea (*Sib. Or.* 5:264–5) and when the wall of Jerusalem will extend as far as Joppa (*Sib. Or.* 5:248–52). It is not clear whether the Temple Scroll was actually composed within the Dead Sea sect or was simply preserved there because the community found its theology congenial.

III. Utopian Communities

In fact, the relationship of the Dead Sea sect to the temple of Jerusalem was problematic. Their vision of the ideal Israel was centered on the temple, but they refused to worship in the actual temple of their day, because they regarded it as polluted. Consequently, they had to find a way to pursue perfect holiness without a temple or a sacrificial system. So they envisioned a community that would be

> an everlasting plantation, a house of holiness for Israel, an assembly of supreme holiness for Aaron . . . It shall be a Most Holy Dwelling for Aaron, with everlasting knowledge of the covenant of justice, and it shall offer up sweet fragrance . . . And they shall be an agreeable offering, atoning for the Land and determining the judgement of wickedness, and there shall be no more iniquity. (1QS 8:5–10)[40]

---

[39] J. J. Collins, *The Scepter and the Star: The Messiahs of the Dead Sea Scrolls and Other Ancient Literature* (New York: Doubleday, 1995) 109–11.

[40] For analogies between this community and Hellenistic Utopias, see D. Mendels, "Hellenistic Utopias and the Essenes," *HTR* 72 (1979) 207–22.

These people should "separate from the habitation of unjust men and go into the wilderness to prepare there the way of Him, as it is written, *Prepare in the wilderness the way of . . . , make straight in the desert a path for our God*" (1QS 8:13–14). There can be little doubt that this passage was the charter or "manifesto" of the Qumran community,[41] which represented the spiritual elite of the Dead Sea sect and constituted itself as a surrogate, spiritual, temple in the wilderness.[42]

The notion of a spiritual temple was forced on the Dead Sea sect because of its schism with the actual temple in Jerusalem. Many Jews in the Diaspora, who were geographically remote from Jerusalem, were also led to a spiritualizing reinterpretation of the temple. Philo describes a community called Therapeutae, located near Lake Mareotis in Egypt, which is reminiscent of the Essenes although the relationship between the two groups remains obscure.[43] These people, we are told, divest themselves of their possessions and enter upon a common life. In each house they have "a consecrated room which is called a sanctuary" into which they take only laws, prophecies and psalms—in short, the scriptures.[44] For these people, location is evidently of little consequence. In a similar vein, Philo interprets the migration Abraham from Ur of the Chaldees not as a journey to the land of Israel but as the migration of the soul from the things of the body to spiritual realities.[45] Here we come close to Jonathan Smith's strict use of utopia, the value of being in no place. At one point Philo even contrasts "those who clung to the homeland" with those who "migrated to Egypt," with the clear implication that the latter are superior.[46] The ostensible refer-

---

[41] J. Murphy-O'Connor, "La genèse littéraire de la Règle de la Communauté," *RB* 76 (1969) 531.

[42] It is possible that 4QFlorilegium, which says that God ordered that a מקדש אדם (a temple of men?) be built for him, should be understood to refer to the community. (So M. Knibb, *The Qumran Community* [Cambridge: Cambridge Univ. Press, 1987] 258–62; D. Dimant, "4QFlorilegium and the Idea of the Community as Temple," in *Hellenica et Judaica: Hommage à Valentin Nikiprowetzky* [ed. A. Caquot et al.; Paris/Leuven: Peeters, 1986] 165–89.) But the reference could also be to an interim eschatological temple as in the Temple Scroll.

[43] Philo, *On the Contemplative Life*. See D. M. Hay, "Things Philo Said and Did Not Say about the Therapeutae," *SBL 1992 Seminar Papers* (Atlanta: Scholars Press, 1992) 673–83; J. E. Taylor and P. R. Davies, "The So-Called Therapeutae of De Vita Contemplativa: Identity and Character," *HTR* 91 (1998) 3–24. For a radically skeptical assessment see T. Engberg-Pedersen, "Philo's De Vita Contemplativa as a Philosopher's Dream," *JSJ* 30 (1999) 40–64.

[44] *On the Contemplative Life*, 25.

[45] Philo, *On the Migration of Abraham*. On Philo's utopian ideals see also Sim, *Das himmlische Jerusalem*, 59–61.

[46] *Life of Moses* 1.240. This passage was brought to my attention by Maren Niehoff.

ence is to the inhabitants of trans-Jordan and the Israelites of the Exodus, but the passage surely had implications for Philo's own time.

IV. A Heavenly Paradise

There was one other model of utopia in Jewish tradition that looked beyond the land of Israel for a blessed place. In the *Book of the Watchers*, which has come down to us as the opening section of *1 Enoch* and dates to the early second century BCE, Enoch is taken by an angel on a tour of places beyond normal human experience. In the course of this journey he is taken to a place where there are seven magnificent mountains:

> And there was among them a tree such as I have never smelt, and none of them nor any others were like it . . . And I said, "Behold this beautiful tree! Beautiful to look at and pleasant are its leaves, and its fruit very delightful in appearance." And then Michael, one of the holy and honored angels . . . answered me . . . "This high mountain which you saw, whose summit is like the throne of the Lord, is the throne where the Holy and Great One, the Lord of Glory, the Eternal King, will sit when he comes down to visit the earth for good. And this beautiful fragrant tree—and no creature of flesh has authority to touch it until the great judgement when he will take vengeance on all and bring everything to a consummation forever— . . . from its fruit life will be given to the chosen . . . they will each draw the fragrance of it into their bones, and they will live a long life on earth, as your fathers lived." (*1 Enoch* 24–25)[47]

Here at last we have the prospect of a return to Paradise, after the final judgment. In some later apocalypses, Paradise is located in the third heaven (*2 Enoch* 8; *3 Baruch* 4), a location also known to St. Paul in 2 Corinthians 11.[48] The desire for a heavenly Paradise was born originally out of disillusionment with the actual temple, but is found especially in texts from the Diaspora, where bonds with the land of Israel were not so close. This heavenly Paradise is seldom the sole focus of Jewish eschatology, however. Most of the apocalyptic writings of the Hellenistic and Roman periods still provide for a restoration on earth in the land of Israel, often, though not always, presided over by a messiah. Sometimes this results in a double climax of history. In *4 Ezra*, written towards the end of the first century CE, the messiah reigns on earth for 400 years, and then dies. There follows seven days of primeval silence, then the new creation and the resurrection of the dead. The contemporary *2 Baruch* describes the messianic

---

[47] A variant of this vision is found in *1 Enoch* 33, where Enoch again sees seven mountains, and again to the east of these the Garden of Righteousness with the tree of wisdom, from which Adam ate.

[48] See further A. Yarbro Collins, "The Seven Heavens in Jewish and Christian Apocalypses," in *Cosmology and Eschatology in Jewish and Christian Apocalypticism* (Leiden: Brill, 1996) 21–54; Kugel, *The Bible As It Was*, 80–82.

age in idyllic terms. Behemoth and Leviathan will be served as food to all that survive. "The earth also shall yield its fruit ten thousandfold; and on each vine there shall be a thousand branches, and each branch shall produce a thousand clusters, and each cluster produce a thousand grapes, and each grape produce a cor of wine . . . and at that time the storehouses of heaven shall descend from on high again" (*2 Bar* 29:4–8). But this is still not the final age, for "the time of the presence of the messiah will have run its course, and he will return in glory (to heaven)" (*2 Bar* 30:1). Then follows the resurrection and a more otherworldly form of fulfillment. We find a similar double fulfillment in the Book of Revelation, where the thousand-year reign provides a finale to the history of this world, but is followed by a new creation. The new creation is a renewed paradise, with the river of life, and a tree of life on either side. But this river flows through the middle street of the new Jerusalem. Even in the new creation, the specificity of place persists.

The Broken Center

When the Book of Revelation was written, the old Jerusalem had already lain in ruins for some twenty years. A few decades later the emperor Hadrian re-founded the city as Aelia Capitolina, and built a temple of Jupiter Capitolinus there. After the suppression of the Bar Kochba revolt Jews were forbidden to live there, or even to visit the city. Christianity rapidly moved away and became a religion of the Gentiles. The Judaism of the Mishnah is remarkably silent on the subject of eschatological and utopian dreams.

Jonathan Smith has suggested that "if the Temple had not been destroyed, it would have had to be neglected. For it represented a locative type of religious activity no longer perceived as effective in a new, utopian [place-less] religious situation with a concomitant shift from a cosmological to an anthropological view-point."[49] It is surely true that the spread of Christianity was facilitated by the fact that it was no longer tied to the ethnic and geographical specificity of Judaism. But Judaism itself retained its locative character long after its physical center had been destroyed. The symbolic power of Jerusalem and the land of Israel did not depend on their physical well-being, but on the mythic structure in which they were integrated. In the words of *2 Baruch,* commenting on the destruction of the temple: "Do you think that this is the city about which I said, *On the palms of my hands have I engraved you?* This building, which now stands in your midst, is not the one that is to be revealed, that is with me now, that was prepared beforehand here at the time when I determined to make Paradise, and showed it to Adam before he sinned" (*2 Bar* 4:2–3). The ideal Jerusa-

---

[49] Smith, *Map is Not Territory,* 128.

lem, like Paradise, was immune to the vicissitudes of history.[50] Centuries later the midrash could still affirm that Israel was the center of the world, Jerusalem the center of Israel and the temple the center of Jerusalem.[51] The rabbis evidently did not see the need to neglect the temple, even when it had been long destroyed. Locative religion survived quite nicely. In fact, Christianity quickly went on to develop its own sacred places and to incorporate locative aspects in its own worldview.[52]

Conclusion

What we find then in the biblical tradition is not primarily a search for a Utopia that is no-place, although such an idea appears occasionally in writers like Philo in the Hellenistic and Roman periods. To speak, as Kolakowski does, of a yearning for the country of eternal Spring is only partially correct, since it misses the most distinctive aspect of the tradition. The yearning is not for the isles of the blessed, somewhere beyond the ocean, nor, with few exceptions, for a return to the garden of Eden. Rather, it is the yearning for a very specific place, hallowed by ancestral associations that may be partly legendary but in part are all too well documented.

In his famous definition, Clifford Geertz spoke of religion as a system of symbols clothed with an aura of factuality that makes its moods and motivations seem uniquely realistic.[53] As Kolakowski noted, the biblical system has lost much, though not all, of its aura of factuality in the matter of history. In the matter of geography, however, that aura is unassailable. Much of the abiding power of the Bible surely lies in the fact that its vision of utopia is so concretely embodied in a specific land.

---

[50] See further J. J. Collins, *Jerusalem and the Temple in Jewish Apocalyptic Literature of the Second Temple Period* (International Rennert Guest Lecture Series 1; [Ramat Gan]: Bar Ilan University, 1998).

[51] Midrash Tanḥuma Kedoshim 10. See Smith, *Map is Not Territory*, 112.

[52] On the place of the land of Israel in this worldview see R. L. Wilken, *The Land Called Holy: Palestine in Christian History and Thought* (New Haven: Yale Univ. Press, 1992).

[53] C. Geertz, "Religion as a Cultural System," in *The Interpretation of Cultures* (New York: Basic Books, 1973) 88–125.

Chapter 6

The Confessions of Jeremiah and Traditional Discourse

Robert C. Culley
McGill University

In Jeremiah's confessions two kinds of discourse have been brought together. One derives from prophetic tradition, as would be expected in a
prophetic book, but the other comes from the tradition of the complaints of
the individual in the Book of Psalms. We recognize these two forms of discourse simply because we are familiar with the prophetic writings and
complaint psalms. We know the language used in each, and we can quite
easily distinguish one from the other. What interests me in this essay is
what occurs when prophetic speakers introduce another kind of conventional language into their discourse, and this is what is going on in the confessions. Since this phenomenon of recognizable modes of discourse
mingled together is not uncommon in biblical texts, this particular study of
texts from Jeremiah, where there is an interplay between complaint and
prophetic poetry, may also contribute to an understanding of the complex
nature of biblical texts as a whole.

 The confessions of Jeremiah raise many problems, and these have received ample discussion in scholarly literature. Here, I will be limiting myself to the one aspect of the confessions that I have just mentioned, the
mixing of the two traditions. The confessions of Jeremiah will be taken to
be the five sections of the Book of Jeremiah commonly identified by scholars: 11:18–12:6, 15:10–21, 17:14–18, 18:18–23, and 20:7–18, although opin-

---

It is a particular pleasure for me to participate in a volume for Burke Long, a friend
of many years. Burke holds to the comic vision of life, in the classic sense of this
term, rather than the tragic, and we need this because as biblical scholars we are all
inclined to take ourselves too seriously.

ions vary on this list. While I shall accept these as a basis for discussion and shall work within their boundaries, I am not assuming that these sections are discrete, well-formed poems or that they have no connections with the material that surrounds them.

The Book of Jeremiah is a composite, and is so in more ways than one. One can imagine that some material from the prophet Jeremiah has been put together either by himself or others. Then, other material not from Jeremiah has probably been added to and placed in and around the earlier material. Beyond this, any or all of these elements of the book may have been revised and restated over time. Readers can sense the composite nature of the book because, as we read, we experience the shifts and changes in the language. Still, it is less clear exactly how the book is composite because it is not easy to make precise divisions in the material and identify with exactitude the sources, although many valuable and interesting suggestions have been made about what the different elements of the book are and how they came together. Rather than pursuing the question of how the text is composite, it might be equally interesting and important to turn things around and ask: How does one read a composite text like Jeremiah and the other prophetic books? How does one develop a way of reading composite texts from the Bible that is able to take account of and give appropriate weight to the shifts and changes, sometimes sudden and abrupt, in the varieties of discourse, language, themes, and perspectives that meet us?

There are, of course, many ways of dealing with composite material. For example, it is commonly taken for granted that the most appropriate way of dealing with composite texts such as the Book of Jeremiah is to try to identify the historical stages in their development as a way of relating the shifting perspectives of the book. This method of drawing like to like uses chronology, a schema of historical periods, as the key to organizing the material. On the other hand, one might take the book as we have received it and follow it through from beginning to end, trying at the same time to adjust to the shifts and discontinuities in the text as they are met. Such a strategy would yield a view of the text as a whole while at the same time giving some weight to its complexity. If this is done, overriding significance is then given to the linear order of the book, which is a widely accepted convention for reading books. On the other hand, would it be possible to simply take the book as a collection of material of different kinds from different authors and times and read it not in a linear way from beginning to end but, adjusting to its nature as a composite, begin reading at various places within the book and move back and forth? I suspect that most readers over the centuries have read the book this way and that many people continue to follow this habit. By pursuing this course, the diverse material in the book can be associated by readers in various ways, say according to similarities and antitheses. Essentially, this would mean deciding to give priority to how the book is held together by the complex relationships of its imagery, themes and language. Treating the text in this way would encourage readers to explore the richness and complexity of the poetry, while at the same time still allow for some sense of the historical depth and linear organization.

The confessions could be called composites as well, although perhaps in a different sense. As I mentioned at the start, what is interesting about these brief sections of poetry is that we can hear two distinct voices, quite familiar to us and easily recognizable as the prophetic tradition and the tradition of the complaint psalms. By tradition, I do not mean much more than the fact that we can identify these two voices by their conventions, which we know and have become aware of through reading biblical material. For simplicity's sake, the main speaker throughout these sections will be called Jeremiah, whether the words have come from the prophet, or someone speaking as the prophet, or a combination of both. It is not essential to be able to make such distinctions here. What counts is that in the confessions we hear the speaker talking sometimes like a prophet, as we would expect him to, but sometimes like the sufferer in complaint psalms, and that the voices, the prophetic and the sufferer's, represent different kinds of conventional discourse that have been brought together and interwoven. What is important here in the confessions is that a prophetic speaker has introduced another kind of conventional language into his discourse, namely, the language of the complaints, which is a highly traditional language.

The study of the confessions and their relationship to the complaint psalms as a genre or literary type goes back to a study done in 1917 by Walter Baumgartner, *Die Klagegedichte des Jeremia*.[1] He argued that Jeremiah did not borrow bits and pieces from individual psalms, since the identity of phrases is not that close, but adopted the psalm style of the complaints. This was a good start. But for him the value of this observation was that he could subtract the known style of the complaint psalms, the traditional material, and in what was left identify Jeremiah's original contribution. From this remainder, he thought he could describe the individuality of the prophet. A more recent trend in the studies of the confessions accepts the connection with the complaint psalms but is more interested in reading the confessions in the context of the Book of Jeremiah. This can be seen in the titles of recent works, for example: A. R. Diamond, *The Confessions of Jeremiah in Context*,[2] Kathleen O'Connor, *The Confessions of Jeremiah: Their Interpreta-*

---

[1] W. Baumgartner, *Die Klagegedichte des Jeremia* (BZAW 32; Giessen: Töpelmann, 1917).

[2] A. Diamond, *The Confessions of Jeremiah in Context: Scenes of Prophetic Drama* (JSOTSup 45; Sheffield: JSOT Press, 1987).

tion and Role in Chapters 1–25,[3] and Mark S. Smith, *The Laments of Jeremiah and Their Contexts.*[4] The commentaries by R. Carroll, W. Holladay, and W. McKane run along similar lines.[5]

The location of the confessions in the context of the Book of Jeremiah is, of course, an important consideration, but I am restricting myself to a prior question, the combining of traditional voices, which may affect how we understand composition and context. Here we have the use of already-known language and imagery to develop a particular line of prophetic discourse in Jeremiah. In effect, the figure of traditional sufferer in the complaint psalms is drawn into and merged with prophetic discourse on the figure of the prophet. In other words, the depiction of the prophet's role, or at least his dilemma, is produced by juxtaposing the two givens of the figure of the prophet and the figure of the sufferer, and this produces a combined picture that offers new possibilities for understanding the figure of the prophet.

Before turning to the confessions of Jeremiah, more has to be said about the individual complaint psalms. In using this term, I am not wholly adopting the particular description of *Gattungsforshung*, or form criticism, developed by Gunkel, but I am taking his interest in literary types seriously. Put very simply, Gunkel noticed that many of the psalms could be grouped into *Gattungen*, or types, on the basis of the forms in which they were expressed and common language shared by the group.[6] Once the psalms were looked at in this way, some groups immediately became obvious: individual complaints, communal complaints, thanksgivings of the individual, and hymns. Gunkel and his successors claimed that other groups could be identified as well, but I am content to stick with the obvious groups. Gunkel went beyond simply identifying groups or types of psalms. In order to account for their existence at all and explain their traditional forms of expression and language, he suggested that these types arose in cultic settings within communities where there was a need for repeated prayers such as complaint, thanksgiving, and praise. Therefore, his concept of type included three required elements in which language and setting are held together. First, one must be able to conceive of an occasion or place in ancient ritual where the type of poem would fit or from which it

---

[3] K. M. O'Connor, *The Confessions of Jeremiah: Their Interpretation and Role in Chapters 1–25* (SBLDS 94; Atlanta: Scholars Press, 1988).

[4] M. S. Smith, *The Laments of Jeremiah and Their Contexts: A Literary and Redactional Study of Jeremiah 11–20* (SBLMS 42; Atlanta: Scholars Press, 1990).

[5] R. P. Carroll, *Jeremiah* (OTL; Philadelphia: Fortress, 1986); W. L. Holladay, *Jeremiah 1: A Commentary on the Book of the Prophet Jeremiah* (Hermeneia; Philadelphia: Fortress, 1986); W. McKane, *Jeremiah* (ICC; Edinburgh: T. & T. Clark, 1986).

[6] H. Gunkel, *Einleitung in die Psalmen* (Göttingen: Vandenhoeck & Ruprecht, 1966) 22–31.

could be derived, that is, the *Sitz im Leben*. Then, one must be able to see a shared fund of common thoughts and moods, derived from the ritual situation, or setting in the life of the community. Finally, a language characteristic of the form must also be apparent, and this would include sentence types, verb forms, and vocabulary characteristic of the type. In my work, I am setting aside the difficult and tangled question of *Sitz im Leben*, and focusing only on textual features and assuming that the presence of common language is sufficient to draw attention to groupings of psalms such as complaints and hymns. The complaint psalms make up about a third of the Psalter and form the best example of a type since they are very similar and use the same elements, motifs, and phrases over and over again. The following comments will fill out a little more the approach I am taking to the complaints as a group within the Psalter.

The first feature is the literary type, which I will call "genre," although the precise terminology is not an issue. For my purposes, I want to define genre as simply as possible. The complaints are rather easy to identify as a group of similar poems because they share a number of fairly obvious features. They are prayers. The speakers are individuals, an "I," who address their prayer to the deity, appealing for help about something that threatens their well-being or even their existence. There are a number of elements that are characteristic of the complaints, such as appeals for a hearing, appeals for help, assurances, and wishes, and these are frequently marked linguistically by their verbal forms; not all of these must be present, however, and there is considerable variation with regard to the elements selected and the order in which they occur. In this respect, there is no fixed pattern to which complaints conform, and so this is not the key to understanding the group. Consequently, it may be useful to think of the group of complaint psalms as a cluster of similar poems related to each other in various ways and in different degrees, although the "I" appealing to the deity for help is a constant. The cluster needs to be pictured as dense in the middle, where the poems most similar to each other would find themselves, but scattered on the edges, where poems less similar to the others would be. The edges would not form clear boundaries, since merging and blending with other types would occur. For my purposes, genre is primarily a rhetorical or literary phenomenon. It is true that genres are related to life and have historical and social dimensions, but how this is so and how best to work it out is, I think, more complicated than Gunkel and subsequent form critics have suggested. For example, one needs to consider to what extent language may influence how the experiences of life are pictured and described as well as how these experiences and circumstances of life directly shape language. For instance, when the poetic language is traditional, as in the case of the psalms, this kind of language may guide, if not govern substantially, how the activities and situations of life are understood and explained as much as settings influence the shape of the language. If the relationship between poetry and context is in some way and to some degree reciprocal, then we would have to consider the extent to which traditional discourse provides the language for describing and therefore interpreting contexts.

The second thing is that the complaint psalms are expressed in language and imagery common to their group or genre. It is virtually impossible to discern the shapes of particular individuals behind this language, people suffering from specific forms of adversity such as illness or hostility from other people. The sufferer, an "I," may complain about enemies, physical deterioration, isolation, and death, all of which may or may not have been due to Yahweh's punishment for sin. I explored some of this repeated and varied language years ago and suggested that it may represent traces of oral traditional language.[7] Even if one cannot show clearly that this language is oral in origin, it does appear to be traditional, that is, used over and over again by poets as they composed, whether this was during a period of oral composition or a period of scribal composition when oral style still had influence.[8] Traditional language has been seen as a handicap, as the drag of the past on the poets, as a sign of their inability to break free from stereotyped expressions. Yet studies of oral traditional composition suggest that the use of traditional language is very important and integral to the process.[9] Even the best poets chose to work within the stream of traditional language, yet took advantage of the fluidity and change of oral composition to express their creativity. Furthermore, this may have continued in scribal composition. In other words, traditional language, known both to poets and their audiences, may have existed for complaints. This language would have been available for use in prayers to deal with certain crises in life. Poets seemed quite happy to use the traditional discourse, and listeners wanted to hear it. As modern readers of the complaint psalms, we are in a somewhat similar situation, at least to the extent that we recognize common language in the complaints, the traces of traditional language left to us. When we encounter familiar phrases, images, or themes in psalms we happen to be reading, these call to mind similar occurrences in other psalms we know. As readers we are aware of the common language and make the connections among the complaints so that we

---

[7] R. C. Culley, *Oral Formulaic Language in the Biblical Psalms* (Near and Middle East Series 4; Toronto: Univ. of Toronto Press, 1967).

[8] Idem, "Orality and Writtenness in Prophetic Texts," in *Writings and Speech in Israelite and Ancient Near Eastern Prophecy* (Symposium Series; Atlanta: Society of Biblical Literature, in press) 45–66.

[9] See, for example, J. M. Foley, "Traditional Signs and Homeric Art," in *Written Voices, Spoken Signs: Tradition, Performance, and the Epic Text* (ed. E. Bakker and A. Kahane; Cambridge, Mass.: Harvard Univ. Press, 1997) 56–82.

might say that, when we are reading one complaint psalm, we automatically draw others into the process.

What the genre of the individual complaint with its traditional language offered was a figure of a sufferer, a kind of composite image within the symbol system of the religion of ancient Israel. Thus, when prayers were offered, instead of describing the situation of specific persons and giving the actual details of what was wrong, the language of the prayers drew the suffering individual up into the traditional discourse of the complaint psalms that already defined their situation in terms of enemies, physical deterioration, and death. This traditional language was important because it offered an identity for sufferers in the larger religious perspective. Even if their problems were not solved, and one must assume that this was often the case, the prayers with their traditional figure of a sufferer gave some meaning to the petitioners' situation by locating their problem in a larger poetic or symbolic picture of reality.

This description of the complaints is a bit too simple and needs some important qualifications. The complaint psalms, as I said earlier, are not all the same, and I used the notion of cluster to allow for a complex relationship among the psalms. They share the common form of the "I" addressing the deity but they employ various combinations of traditional language, imagery, and elements, playing with these features differently. This freedom to select and highlight the various traditional images and themes in individual psalms allowed for the exploration of themes such as enemies, physical deterioration, death, and punishment for sin, from different angles, different points of view, and in different combinations, so that different takes on the problem of suffering emerge. For example, enemies show up in most of the complaint psalms but physical deterioration or sickness occur in a smaller number. Suffering can be seen as punishment for sin, as in Psalms 6 and 38, or not related to sin, as in Psalm 22. Enemies may threaten persons who may swear their innocence and call on Yahweh to judge and affirm innocence and take vengeance on the enemies. The speaker in Psalm 88 contemplates death at the hands of Yahweh. These smaller groupings of psalms within the larger cluster of complaint psalms have long been recognized, and, as noted earlier, sometimes even considered as sub-genres. Since I am not particularly interested in identifying sub-genres, it is still valuable to identify and recognize these smaller clusters of psalms within the larger group of complaints. They reflect explorations of different aspects of the problem of suffering in terms of the traditional themes.

We may now turn to the complaint language in the confessions. Since the work of identifying most of the parallels with the complaint psalms has been done by Baumgartner and others, I would like to try to look at the parallels in another way, along the lines of what has just been said about the complaint psalms.

One particular phrase comes up three times in the confessions. Yahweh is described as one who examines the righteous person, testing the heart, or the heart and kidneys (11:20, 12:3, and 20:12, where 11:20 and 20:12 are almost identical). This kind of language also occurs in Pss 7:10, 17:3 and 26:2. These psalms, along with Psalm 5, have a lot in common and form a little cluster within the complaints (Gunkel's *Unschuldslieder*[10]). Once again, by "smaller grouping" I mean only that the psalms in the group are sufficiently similar that it is useful rhetorically to look at them together. In this grouping of psalms (5, 7, 17, and 26), enemies emerge clearly as the main problem, although the speaker is preoccupied with his innocence, and therefore the talk of testing. It may be useful to briefly review Psalms 7, 17, and 26 to try to illustrate what has just been said. In this brief survey, only details relevant to the present discussion will be noted; the many problems treated, usually quite adequately, by the commentators will be left aside. The main purpose will be to notice how the relationships between the speaker and the opponents are pictured with the confessions of Jeremiah in mind. This still leaves important issues in the poems that will not be discussed.

Psalm 7 opens with an appeal by the petitioner for rescue and for deliverance from pursuers (v. 2), from someone who will tear him[11] apart like a lion (v. 3). This description of the opponents as wild animals, later as an enemy in pursuit (v. 6) or as hunters digging a pit (v. 16), suggests a raw, physical danger from which rescue is essential, some physical intervention against the hostile force. Yahweh is called upon to arise in anger (v. 7). Yet mixed with this image is another issue, a declaration of innocence: "I have not done this" (v. 5). Yahweh is asked to judge the petitioner (v. 9) according to his innocence and his blamelessness, for Yahweh is the one who tests the heart and kidneys (vv. 9, 10). He appeals to Yahweh who is the God of the righteous, or innocent, person, and who judges him (v. 12). The sufferer affirms that the God who rescues the upright is indeed his protector (v. 11). The psalm closes with some words on the fate of the petitioner's opponents. The one who conceives wrong will fall into the pit he dug; his actions will fall back upon his own head (vv. 16, 17). The image of hunters brings us back again to raw danger as the problem, but one in which the resolution is a form of poetic justice. The relationships between the speaker and the opponents is clearly complex. Psalm 7 clearly distinguishes, as do the other psalms in the group we are considering, two types or classes of

---

[10] Gunkel, *Einleitung*, 251–54.

[11] In the discussion of the psalms I have assumed, perhaps wrongly, that the speakers are male and so have retained the masculine pronouns.

persons—the victim and his attackers according to some of the imagery, and the innocent and guilty according to other imagery. Yet, if the innocent and the guilty are sharply distinguished, why do the speakers in these psalms work so hard at making the distinction clear and establishing the fact that they are on the side favorable to Yahweh? Part of the problem, and this is the painful dilemma of the sufferer raised by these psalms, seems to be that the distinction may not be as generally obvious as it should be, nor is the status of the speaker as an innocent party obvious to all observers, whether opponents or friends.

In Psalm 17, the speaker again introduces the language of testing along with the assurance that nothing will be found that is amiss (v. 3). He affirms his innocence. His lips have not transgressed and his feet have not strayed from the path (vv. 4, 5). Yet his enemies, the wicked, track him down and surround him, again like a lion (vv. 9–12), again the danger as a display of raw hostility. His wish is not only that he may be protected but that Yahweh will deal harshly with his opponents. The genuine threat of the enemies provokes an appeal for Yahweh to rise and deal with the opponents. They and their children are cursed.

The last poem, Psalm 26, opens with the cry of the psalmist to Yahweh to judge him because he is blameless (v. 1). Yahweh is called upon to test his heart and kidneys (v. 2). He further proclaims his innocence in a negative confession in which he affirms, among other things: I did not sit with false men, the wicked, and I hate the pack of wrongdoers (vv. 4, 5). He will wash his hands in innocency and go around the altar. His appeal to Yahweh is that the deity should not carry him off with the sinners and the blood-thirsty for, as he asserts again at the close of the psalm, he is blameless. There are no enemies or pursuers who threaten the psalmist directly, but a group of wrongdoers is unambiguously identified and it is made clear that the psalmist is not among them. One of his worries seems to be that he will be identified with them, even though he is their opposite.

Now I do not want to suggest that these psalms fall nicely together and offer a seamless, unitary view of the figure of the sufferer, as they are each different. Nor do I wish to set these psalms apart unduly from other complaints. Yet Psalms 7, 17 and 26 (Psalm 5 could be added) do share similar language and imagery and do seem to be working from a similar perception of the dilemma that confronts the sufferer and the consequent anxiety that has seized his being. While there is the fear that the opponents will do him in, another concern seems to lie with the status of the speaker. As far as he is concerned, he is among the innocent, the blameless, the righteous, and not among the wicked. He wants to be sure that the deity understands this, although he appears to be confident that Yahweh, who tests and judges, will get it right. Yet he feels the need to make his case and shows no small degree of anxiety in his concern to be vindicated and have his status confirmed, and perhaps this includes a vindication of his perception of Yahweh and the world that supports and frames his own understanding of himself.

It is time now to return to the confessions. I began by pointing out that the references to testing that appear three times in the confessions led us to the group of psalms just discussed. In considering the confessions, attention will be given mainly to those verses that seem to be drawing on complaint language, and they will only be discussed to the extent necessary to make the point about the nature of the similarities.

In Jer 11:19–20 we find that opponents are alluded to, although apparently their schemes were revealed to the prophet by Yahweh. In response to their plans against him the prophet affirms two things: Yahweh who judges righteously will test his heart and kidneys (v. 20; see Pss 7:10; 17:3; 26:2), implying his confidence that he will be vindicated and that he will see Yahweh's vengeance wrought on the opponents. His case, as he claims, has been entrusted to Yahweh.

In 12:1–3 the prophet offers a similar expression of confidence that he has been tested, and couples this with a strong appeal that the opponents be dealt with, be set apart like sheep for the slaughter (v. 3). Yet in what precedes (v. 2) the prophet pushes beyond what the psalms say explicitly to challenge Yahweh, claiming that he was responsible for the wrongdoers, by planting them, and allowing them to take root and produce fruit. These people, warns the prophet, are near to Yahweh in terms of what they say but inwardly are far from Yahweh. In other words, the opponents are outwardly religious but in Jeremiah's judgment this only touches the surface.

Jer 15:15–18 opens with an appeal for vengeance on the prophet's pursuers but adds that it is Yahweh who is responsible for the abuse that he is receiving (v. 15). Because of Yahweh's hand, he says, he sits alone and filled with rage (v. 17). But he also mentions a positive side (v. 16). The prophet relates how he had found Yahweh's words and eaten them. They became a joy and a delight. Yahweh had made him his possession. Yet this positive experience just seems to make the problem worse. At this point the prophet turns to language not found in the complaints we looked at above. He asks why his pain continues, why his calamitous wound refuses to heal (v. 18). This recalls a different strand of the complaint tradition, where physical suffering is understood as Yahweh's punishment for sin (see, for example, Pss 6, 38, and 88). It is almost as though Yahweh has been beating him. This terse and enigmatic speech of the prophet closes with the charge that Yahweh has been false, like waters that cannot be relied on. The opponents are not the main issue here. Yahweh is. Even though a Yahweh speech follows (vv. 19–21), it does not directly meet the basic question that has been raised but only urges that in the end the prophet will prevail and Yahweh will rescue him from his enemies.

The next section, 17:14–18, resumes the notion of the wound by appealing to Yahweh, in language reminiscent of the complaints: heal me (Pss 6:3; 41:5) and save me (e.g. Pss 3:8; 6:5; 7:2). Yet attention turns again to the opponents who seem to be challenging his status as a prophet (v. 15), a role from which he has not run. The prophet complains that Yahweh should not be a terror to him, when he is supposed to be his protection in bad times (v. 17). The section closes with a wish against the enemies similar to the language against enemies found in complaints (Pss 35:4, 26; 40:15; 71:13).

Jer 18:19–23 returns to the opponents. The prophet complains about them and uses an image from the complaint psalms. They have dug a pit and set traps for him (vv. 20, 22; see, for example, Pss 7:16; 31:5; 35:7, 12; 38:21; 109:5; 142:4), even though he has interceded with Yahweh on their behalf for good. In response, the prophet utters a curse against them, their wives, and their children (see the curses in Pss 69:23–29 and 109:6–15). Their sins must not be forgiven. Yahweh must deal with them in his anger.

Jer 20:7, 10–13, opens by returning to Yahweh's role in the prophet's dilemma. Yahweh has deceived, or even seduced, the prophet so that he has become a laughing stock (v. 7). The opponents are still there. The prophet hears rumors or whisperings urging that he be denounced (v. 10). This seems to involve a close friend. The opponents seek to trick him and so exact their vengeance. But at this point the mood shifts. Most of verses 11–12 are statements similar to the certainty of hearing that appears frequently in the complaint psalms, and Jer 20:12 is almost identical to Jer 11:20. It is in this affirmative mood that the third instance of Yahweh as the one who tests the heart and kidneys is repeated. Confident of his vindication, he expects to see Yahweh's vengeance on his opponents. Again in this section there is the move from a serious charge against the deity to an assertion that everything will be fine. Therefore, he can call upon all to sing and praise the deity for the life of the poor one, in this case the prophet, who has been delivered, or is as good as delivered, from the wrongdoers (Pss 35:10; 40:18). Jeremiah 20:14–18 shifts to a theme which is not in the complaints: the prophet asks why was he born.

After this brief survey of the confessions from the point of view of language from the complaint psalms, it is clear that the confessions are not complaints. But there is a significant amount of language, themes, and imagery from the complaint tradition, and especially from one particular strand in the tradition, where a central theme is the sufferer who sees himself as an innocent victim threatened by opponents seeking to discredit him. This person relies on Yahweh for vindication, which he is confident will happen. Through the complaint language this perspective has been worked into the prophetic discourse, and the relationships among the three participants (speaker, opponents, Yahweh) characteristic of the complaints form a major component of the confessions. The introduction of this view of the sufferer into the prophetic discourse of Jeremiah gives the prophet figure a framework of thought that defines his situation and gives him a starting point for shaping an understanding of his dilemma which he can begin to articulate.

In Psalms 7, 17, and 26, the fundamental tension lies between the psalmist and the opponents. These psalms juxtaposed two aspects of the opponents. On the one hand, they were described as wild animals or hunters, and therefore posed the threat of physical danger and death. On the other hand, opponents appeared to challenge the psalmist's standing before the deity, and by implication his standing in the religious community. The key issue is vindication by Yahweh, whose role is seen in a positive light, as rescuer and vindicator.

In the confessions, the relationships among speaker, opponents, and Yahweh found in the complaints form a basic framework. While the opponents are never described as animals and only once as hunters (18:20), they are seen as plotting to kill the prophet (11:19). But this hostility seems to be in response to Jeremiah's role as a prophet (17:15). The opponents are also described, from Jeremiah's point of view, as persons who are close to Yahweh in their words but distant in their thoughts. That is, they *seem* to be religious people, but are not truly so. They spread rumors, even though they appear to be friends (20:10). Hence Jeremiah's desperate and fundamental need for Yahweh to test and vindicate him and condemn his opponents.

Yet, while using complaint language and imagery, especially the tension between psalmist and opponents, the prophet extends and complicates the traditional relationships by explicitly implicating Yahweh in the situation. While Yahweh continues to be portrayed as the vindicator and rescuer, an opponent role is developed for the deity. The prophet charges that Yahweh has brought the enemies into being (12:2). Yahweh has created his pain and is like an unreliable watercourse (15:18). Finally, it is charged that the deity has seduced him (20:7). This is not language characteristic of the complaints. Still, there is a possible starting point for this kind of thinking in the complaint psalms. I am thinking of psalms in which Yahweh punishes the sufferer for his sin, although Yahweh's attacks are considered justified (except possibly in Psalm 88).[12] It was noted above that some of this language can be found in the confessions, even though the question is not about Jeremiah's sin, only that he is wounded and needs healing. This line of thought, in which Yahweh is seen as opponent, goes beyond anything implied in the complaints. While the language of the complaints has helped Jeremiah identify and articulate his situation as a prophet who suffers, this same language does not seem sufficient to ac-

---

[12] R. C. Culley, "Psalm 88 Among the Complaints," in *Ascribe to the Lord: Biblical and Other Studies in Memory of Peter C. Craigie* (JSOTSup 67; ed. L. Eslinger and G. Taylor; Sheffield, Eng.: JSOT Press, 1988) 289–302.

count for the prophet's dilemma. Yet, having opened this door with all its ramifications, Jeremiah does not enter it. His charge with all its disturbing implications is interspersed with traditional statements of assurance and certainty from the complaint psalms, based as they are upon a rescue pattern which always suggests that the sufferer will be rescued and proven right in the end. The interspersed Yahweh speeches avoid the challenges and reinforce the language of assurance so that the tension between the fundamental challenge to Yahweh and the deep-seated trust in Yahweh is neither acknowledged nor resolved. And perhaps it could not be. Without the vision of rescue, how could hope be imagined? Without the challenge to the deity, how could a critique substantial enough to lend hope a measure of credibility be possible?

Still, the prophet's critique is curious. He blames his opponents and challenges Yahweh but does not seem to allow for the fact that he may not have gotten it completely right himself. He cannot, or perhaps does not wish to, question or reconsider his own prophetic word, the one that burns inside him so that he cannot contain it. Jeremiah's vision of Yahweh's punishment of Judah and Jerusalem is one shared with the other prophets, and he assumes much of the traditional prophetic language and imagery. While the fall of Jerusalem has been understood as a vindication of the prophetic vision, the prophetic model of destruction as punishment did not in the end stand up as a useful key to understanding historical events. What Jeremiah saw as the deceptiveness and unreliability of Yahweh perhaps invites another interpretation, a sign of the impossibility of identifying vindication and punishment in human history.

What I have been trying to suggest here is the way complex texts may bring together and set off against one another different voices, perspectives, and strands of tradition without resolving the tensions and contradictions they present. This happens not only in the weaving together of different documents and editorial comments, our usual notion of composite text, but occurs also within those elements where traditional perspectives are already blended and in tension. In the example considered here, the confessions of Jeremiah, traditional features from the complaint tradition have been introduced into prophetic discourse in order to help the prophet express in language the complicated nature of his quandary. On one level, the issue is authentication. Not only is the prophet's word not accepted, it stirs up deadly hostility. At the more fundamental level, the prophet sees hostility coming from the deity who is supposed to be vindicator and rescuer. Texts such as this, which embrace an unresolved tension, can never be considered closed because they contain within themselves a claim to reopen the question, and so foster and encourage further reflection.

Chapter 7

Desire Distorted and Exhibited: Lot and His Daughters in Psychoanalysis, Painting, and Film

J. Cheryl Exum
University of Sheffield

> *But in cases where the wish-fulfillment is unrecognizable, where it has been disguised, there must have existed some inclination to put up a defence against the wish; and owing to this defence the wish was unable to express itself except in a distorted shape.*
> Sigmund Freud, *The Interpretation of Dreams*

> *Even in the few mythological passages in which the loving passion seems to be presented from the viewpoint of the daughter, one has the impression that this is only a justification of the father's shocking desires; an attempt is made to shift the blame for the seduction onto her.*
> Otto Rank, *The Incest Theme in Literature and Legend*

Commentators are generally fairly reserved in their treatment of the account of the incestuous relations between Lot and his daughters in Gen 19:30–38, though rather less tolerant than about Lot's offer of his daughters to the Sodomites earlier in the chapter.[1] Doubtless the story functions on

---

[1] To offer only a sample: Claus Westermann (*Genesis 12–36* [trans. John J. Scullion; Minneapolis: Augsburg, 1985] 314–15) observes, "This text is particularly open to misinterpretation. When one makes evaluations such as 'incestuous' or 'incest' in its title or says at the very beginning, 'this revolting story' (A. Dillmann), then one is unable to understand what it intends to say. One can do justice to the text only by taking account of the history of its growth. It goes back into a distant past on which we cannot impose our criteria." Walter Brueggemann (*Genesis* [Inter-

many levels. As an etiology, if it ever in some mythological version portrayed the origins of Moab and Ammon positively by demonstrating the purity of their blood,[2] in its present context it reads more like a folktale designed to disparage Israel's neighbors by suggesting their depraved origins. But is treating Gen 19:30–38 as a folktale with mythological antecedents the best way to account for its strange character?[3] Does recourse to a

---

pretation; Atlanta: John Knox, 1982]) has little to say about vv. 30–38, but does point out that "no stigma is attached to the action of the mothers in the narrative" (176) and concludes, "Lot and his daughters are clearly treated as members of the family of promise. In an odd way, this is one more evidence of the inclusive attitude of Genesis toward other peoples" (176–77). Gerhard von Rad (*Genesis* [trans. John H. Marks; Philadelphia: Westminster, 1961] 214, 219) stresses the sympathetic portrayal of Lot, but observes, "Without doubt the narrative now contains *indirectly* a severe judgment on the incest in Lot's house . . ." (219, italics mine). Sharon Pace Jeansonne (*The Women of Genesis: From Sarah to Potiphar's Wife* [Minneapolis: Fortress, 1990] 36–42) carefully withholds judgment on the daughters while condemning Lot's behavior in Genesis 19. Bruce Vawter (*On Genesis: A New Reading* [Garden City, NY: Doubleday, 1977] 236) comments that "Really, there is no need to make excuses for [Lot], as far as the biblical perspective is concerned"; however, he is not so generous in speaking of the "unholy and forbidden relationships (cf. Leviticus 18:6–18) accomplished on [Lot] by voracious daughters whose dignity he had earlier disregarded" (242). Gordon J. Wenham (*Genesis 16–50* [WBC 2; Dallas, TX: Word Books, 1994] 56) says of Lot in the first incident, "Putting their [the angels'] welfare above his daughters' may have been questionable, but it shows just how committed he was to being a good host." He does, however, think the daughters' behavior "suggest[s] they shared the warped morality of the city from which they had all escaped" (64); however, "[b]ecause of his readers' moral assumptions, the narrator did not feel it necessary to excoriate Lot's daughters' behavior" (62). Lyn M. Bechtel ("A Feminist Reading of Genesis 19.1–11," in *A Feminist Companion to Reading the Bible: Approaches, Methods and Strategies* [ed. Athalya Brenner and Carole Fontaine; Sheffield: Sheffield Academic Press, 1997] 108–28) argues that Lot's offer of his daughters to the Sodomites is made "with confidence that its incongruity and inappropriateness will stop the action and prevent further aggression" (124); cf. B. Jacob, *Das erste Buch der Tora: Genesis* (Berlin: Schocken, 1934) 455–56. For a more critical assessment of Lot, see Laurence A. Turner, "Lot as Jekyll and Hyde: A Reading of Genesis 18–19," in *The Bible in Three Dimensions* (eds. David J. A. Clines, Stephen E. Fowl, and Stanley E. Porter; JSOTSup 87; Sheffield: Sheffield Academic Press, 1990) 85–101.

    [2] Hermann Gunkel, *Genesis* (6th ed.; Göttingen: Vandenhoeck & Ruprecht, 1964) 218; John Skinner, *Genesis* (ICC; 2d ed.; Edinburgh: T. & T. Clark, 1930) 312–14; von Rad, *Genesis,* 219; J. R. Porter, "The Daughters of Lot," *Folklore* 89 (1978) 128; Seth Daniel Kunin, *The Logic of Incest: A Structuralist Analysis of Hebrew Mythology* (JSOTSup 185; Sheffield: Sheffield Academic Press, 1995) 192.

    [3] So Porter, "The Daughters of Lot," 127–41. Most commentators mention the possible original intentions of earlier forms of the story as an explanation of its character; for a critique of the notion that the pre-Israelite history of the themes in

presumed mythic background simply make it easier to explain away difficulties that are otherwise disturbing? Or can it help us understand them?
Among the curious features of the tale, for example, is the daughters' notion that, apart from their father, there is no other man on the earth to have
sex with them. So is their simple resort to incest with their father as a
means of repopulating the earth, assuming this is their goal.[4] Have they
forgotten the men of Zoar? Were there no men in Zoar? It may have been a
small city (v. 20), but surely not that small! If they and their old father managed to get to the hills from Zoar, they can surely manage to get back there,
if, indeed, the situation is so critical. The daughters' curious logic points to
the story's most curious detail, that incest is the elder daughter's idea,
which is unquestioningly accepted by the younger daughter, and carried
out by each of them seemingly without scruple or ill after-effects.

The difficulties do not stop with the daughters' irrational responses. If
Lot is so drunk when his daughters have sex with him that he does not
know, on either occasion, when his daughter lay down or got up, could he
perform at all sexually? Not just one but both of the daughters become
pregnant, on successive nights; moreover, they appear to know immediately that they have successfully conceived, for apparently they do not feel
the same kind of urgency to try this technique again. The consequences are
also ignored: The daughters bear sons, but how are the sons going to have
children? And what of Lot? If either the possible end of the human race or
the lack of husbands for his daughters *is* the problem, why has Lot not
done anything about it? Does he, too, suffer from the illusion that there are
no men available? Why does Lot not discuss the problem with his daughters (who certainly seem to be in need of practical as well as sex educa-
tion)? Why did Lot not stay with his daughters in Zoar? What was he
afraid of (v. 30)? Has Lot, too, forgotten the men of Zoar? Or is it simply
that he would like to? There appears to be more going on here than meets
the typical commentatorial eye.

Elke Seifert exposes a more plausible, and scandalous, scenario behind
the events narrated in Gen 19:30–38. She constructs a reading of the story
according to which it is the father who commits incest with his daughters.
Basing her observations on clinical evidence about father-daughter incest
and on hints in the narrative, she treats the story as though it were an abusive father's version; in other words, a lie, a version whose function it is to

---

Genesis 19 can be reconstructed, see John Van Seters, *Abraham in History and Tradition* (New Haven: Yale Univ. Press, 1975) 209–221.

[4] Gunkel, *Genesis*, 218–19; Jacob, *Genesis*, 464–65; Skinner, *Genesis*, 313; E. A.
Speiser, *Genesis* (AB 1; Garden City, NY: Doubleday, 1964) 145; Westermann, *Genesis
12–36*, 313; the way the daughters put it is that their father's seed may live (see
below).

hide his guilt.[5] Like the abusive father in actual cases of father-daughter incest, this one shifts the blame to his daughters, and appeals as well to the effects of alcohol. But he leaves clues that point to his responsibility and his guilt. Ilona Rashkow, in a psychoanalytic-literary reading, treats the story in much the same way. Noting similarities to clinical reports of father-daughter incest and adopting a Freudian approach to the text, Rashkow argues that Lot acts out his repressed fantasies under the influence of alcohol. She also appeals to Freud's theory about the function of mythology to raise the possibility that the narrator might be expressing the unconscious desire of the society that created this tale.[6] In this essay, I shall be applying a psychoanalytic-literary approach not only to Gen 19:30–38, which I read somewhat differently in terms of its narrative symptoms, but also to the narrative about Lot's offer of his daughters to the Sodomites earlier in the chapter, where I propose that the same incestuous fantasy is entertained, but abandoned—until, that is, vv. 30–38, where it is finally played out. For confirmation, I look to some artistic examples where the father's incestuous fantasies are exposed.[7] Finally, I consider briefly what happens to the relationship between Lot and his daughters in what must surely be one of Hollywood's freest adaptations of a biblical story, *The Last Days of Sodom and Gomorrah*.

---

[5] Elke Seifert, "Lot und seine Töchter: Eine Hermeneutik des Verdachts," in *Feministische Hermeneutik und Erstes Testament* (ed. Hedwig-Jahnow-Forschungsprojekt; Stuttgart: Kohlhammer, 1994) 48–66; Seifert, *Tochter und Vater im Alten Testament: Eine ideologiekritische Untersuchung zur Verfügungsgewalt von Vätern über ihre Töchter* (Neukirchen-Vluyn: Neukirchener Verlag, 1997), esp. 82–86, 118–19, 175–78, 184–85. Seifert's important and insightful studies grew out of her work with women who were victims of sexual abuse. She draws attention to other pertinent German studies that investigate incest in Genesis 19 from this perspective; of particular importance is Josephine Rijnaarts, *Lots Töchter: Über den Vater-Tochter-Inzest* (trans. Barbara Heller; Düsseldorf: Claassen, 1988). Unfortunately these works appear not to have received the attention of recent English-speaking commentators on Genesis 19.

[6] Ilona N. Rashkow, "Daddy-Dearest and the 'Invisible Spirit of Wine,'" in *Genesis: A Feminist Companion to the Bible (Second Series)* (ed. Athalya Brenner; Sheffield: Sheffield Academic Press, 1998) 82–107 (98–107 deal with Lot).

[7] Both Seifert ("Lot und seine Töchter," 60) and Rashkow ("Daddy-Dearest," 105–106) remark on the way artistic representations of Gen 19:30–38 acknowledge the father's incestuous desire, but neither pursues the analysis of paintings. Seifert mentions Lucas van Leyden and Hendrick Goltzius; Rashkow mentions works by Rembrandt and Carraci and offers a brief description of a painting by Bonifazio de' Pitati, based on Richard Mühlberger, *The Bible in Art: The Old Testament* (New York: Portland House, 1991) 42. A painting by Alessandro Turchi inspired Rijnaarts to entitle the Dutch original of her book *Dochters van Lot* (*Lots Töchter*, 25).

The Narrative Unconscious

A psychoanalytic-literary reading does not offer a solution to the curious elements of the story, where other interpretations have failed, but aims rather to shed a different light on it by concentrating on another dimension, the narrative unconscious. As Freud himself pointed out, texts, like dreams, are plurisignificant and require over-interpretation in order to be fully understood.[8] The text/dream analogy is important for my reading, because I intend to approach the text as a fantasy that operates much the same way as a dream does. In what follows I am not endorsing Freudian theory or offering a strictly Freudian reading. In particular, I do not follow Freud in seeing father–daughter incest as representing the daughter's desire.[9] I draw on Freud for some, though not all, of my concepts both because, in analyzing a patriarchal text like this one, Freudian psychoanalytic theory is a useful tool since it pursues the same patriarchal logic[10] and because I seek below to clarify the manifold impulses of the text by relating them to the positions occupied in Freudian theory by the super-ego, ego, and id.

   In this reading I am not psychoanalyzing either the author, who is not available to me, or the characters, in particular the character Lot (the focus of Seifert's and Rashkow's studies). Rather than treat any of the characters in Genesis 19 as if they were people, I want to examine the cultural or collective unconscious that finds its expression in such literary creations as these. I assume, with most biblical scholars, that this text is a communal product. Since symbolic production has historically been controlled by men,[11] I attribute the text's origins to a kind of collective androcentric unconscious, whose spokesperson I will refer to simply as "the narrator,"[12]

---

   [8] Sigmund Freud, *The Interpretation of Dreams* (trans. and ed. James Strachey; New York: Avon Books, 1965) 299.

   [9] In a famous letter to Fliess, Freud described his change of mind about hysteria stemming from the memory of a seduction of the patient by her father. The accusation against the father, when further analyzed, revealed the patient's accusation of herself as desiring to have a child by her father; see Suzanne Gearhart, "The Scene of Psychoanalysis: The Unanswered Questions of Dora," in *In Dora's Case: Freud—Hysteria—Feminism* (ed. Charles Bernheimer and Claire Kahane; New York: Columbia Univ. Press, 1985) 105–27 (106–107). For a critique and analysis of Freud's change of mind, see Rijnaarts, *Lots Töchter*, 81–124.

   [10] Laura Mulvey, *Visual and Other Pleasures* (Houndmills: Macmillan, 1989) 15.

   [11] Gerda Lerner, *The Creation of Patriarchy* (New York: Oxford Univ. Press, 1986) 4–6, 199–211.

   [12] I adopt a similar psychoanalytic-literary approach to the "wife/sister" stories of Genesis 12, 20, and 26 in Exum, *Fragmented Women: Feminist (Sub)versions of Biblical Narratives* (JSOTSup, 163; Sheffield: JSOT Press/Valley Forge, PA: Trinity Press International, 1993) 148–69.

or, to indicate its overarching presence as distinct from the position occupied by the father-character Lot, "the Father."

Taking a cue from psychoanalytical theory and building upon the similarities between interpreting dreams and interpreting texts, I shall consider all the characters in the story as split-off parts of the narrator. The characters who appear in our dreams are the creations of our unconscious mind, even when they are based on people we know, and our unconscious determines the way they behave in our dreams. They represent not so much the people we know as our own fears, desires, wishes, and so on, that are in some way tied up with them. The characters in a text are the author's constructions, and, in the (collective) author's fantasy in Genesis 19, the characters may therefore be viewed as representing various parts of the cultural male psyche. This is the way I shall approach the text, and, since neither the author of Genesis 19 nor the culture in which it arose nor the text can contribute actively to the psychoanalytical process, I shall be both asking questions (the analyst's role) and offering answers (the analysand's role). Like psychoanalysis, such a psychoanalytic-literary approach as this is neither verifiable nor falsifiable. We can only follow it, as Freud said about psychoanalysis, to see where it will lead,[13] and the proof of the analysis will be in the light it can shed on the narrative symptoms, the textual curiosities.

Leaving aside its other, perhaps more intentional functions, let us concentrate on Genesis 19 as a literary production that allows the collective male narrative unconscious to engage in its forbidden fantasies. The forbidden fantasy is the Father's wish (that is, the desire of the spokesperson for the collective cultural unconscious) to have sex with his daughters.[14] Psychoanalysis tells us that this must be the unconscious desire because this is what the narrator sets up to happen, not once but twice in vv. 30–38, and each time with the details repeated as though they were being relished. But because the desire is unacceptable, because he would recoil from

---

[13] Sigmund Freud, *Beyond the Pleasure Principle* (trans. and ed. James Strachey; New York: W. W. Norton & Company, 1961) 4.

[14] As Rank suggests about such myths; see *The Incest Theme in Literature and Legend: Fundamentals of a Psychology of Literary Creation* [trans. G. C. Richter; Baltimore: Johns Hopkins Univ. Press, 1992) 300–301. For general treatments of incest in the Bible, see Calum M. Carmichael, *Law, Legend, and Incest in the Bible: Leviticus 18–20* (Ithaca: Cornell Univ. Press, 1997), who sees the incest laws of Leviticus 18 as responses to sexual incidents in the patriarchal traditions (on Genesis 19, see, especially, 23–24, 42–43, 58–60); Athalya Brenner, "On Incest," in *A Feminist Companion to Exodus to Deuteronomy* (vol. 6 of *The Feminist Companion to the Bible*, ed. Athalya Brenner; Sheffield: Sheffield Academic Press, 1994) 113–38; Kunin, *The Logic of Incest*.

it in horror if he acknowledged it, it appears in a distorted form.[15] He displaces his desire onto his daughters. Unable to face the fact that he desires them sexually, he imagines instead their desire for him and their desire to have his child. It is important to keep in mind that the daughters are also the creations of the collective androcentric unconscious that desires the incestuous relations. The fantasy—and the story—is not about the daughters, except insofar as they are the object of the Father's incestuous desire.

This is, moreover, a compulsive fantasy. Not only is the incest fantasy repeated twice in vv. 30–38, it also, as I argue below, appears earlier, in an even more distorted form, in the story of Lot's offer of his daughters to the men of Sodom. In this earlier version (vv. 1–11), however, the narrator abandons the fantasy and punishes himself for it. As a textual working-out of unconscious fantasies, Genesis 19 attempts to manage forbidden desires within an ordered discourse, but the symbolic enactment of the fantasy in the text, unlike, for example, the wife-sister stories of Genesis 12, 20, and 26, does not clearly effect a semiotic cure.[16] The text serves rather as a kind of confession, but full of distortion because the narrator cannot face the truth. Nevertheless, he has left the traces of the deed that betray a kind of cultural guilt and suggest a need to be caught in the fantasy, and a few commentators have caught him in vv. 30–38.[17] Both the fantasy and the distortions there provide a clue that a similar fantasy about incest may lie behind vv. 1–11.

Desire Distorted: The Incest Fantasy Entertained but Abandoned (Gen 19:1–11)

It would be a mistake to read vv. 30–38 without reference to vv. 1–29, for they form a continuous narrative in which the destruction of Sodom, the elimination of Lot's would-be sons-in-law, and the death of his wife are all important preparations for what happens between Lot and his daughters in the cave in the hills.[18] Some see in the second story a reversal of the first,

---

[15] This is how Freud describes Oedipus's desire in a letter to Wilhelm Fliess of Oct. 15, 1897, cited by Shoshana Felman, "Beyond Oedipus: The Specimen Story of Psychoanalysis," in *Lacan and Narration: The Psychoanalytic Difference in Narrative Theory* (ed. R. Con Davis; Baltimore: Johns Hopkins Univ. Press, 1983), 1021–53 (1022); see also Freud, *The Interpretation of Dreams*, 175–78, 193–94.

[16] In Genesis 12, 20, and 26, in contrast, we can observe how the intra-psychic conflict is worked out, the neurosis is cured, and the cure believed; see Exum, *Fragmented Women*, 148–69.

[17] Seifert; Rijnaarts, *Lots Töchter*, 26–27; Rashkow; Elga Sorge, *Kuckuck* 1988, 115, cited by Seifert, "Lot und seine Töchter," 56; Rita Burrichter, "Lots Töchter lesen einen biblischen Kommentar," *Schlangenbrut* 25 (1989) 22–24, cited by Seifert, "Lot und seine Töchter," 54.

[18] See, further, Van Seters, *Abraham in History and Tradition*, 219.

with the daughters now the actors and Lot the sexual object.[19] From a psy-choanalytic-literary perspective, I see it as a variation, a first attempt to fan-tasize sexual relations with his daughters, a prelude to the version in vv. 30–38, in which the fantasy is narratively realized.

In Gen 19:4–5, the men of Sodom surround Lot's house and demand that Lot's visitors be handed over to them for homosexual rape.[20] In their place, Lot offers his two virgin daughters to the townsmen to do with as they please (vv. 6–8). The offer shows the father's control of his daughter's sexuality, even though (and this is another curious feature of Genesis 19) they are betrothed and thus are not, strictly speaking, Lot's "property" to dispose of (cf. Deut 22:23–27). The narrator fixes in v. 8 on their status as virgins because incest with the daughters can happen only before they are given to other men, the sons-in-law-to-be first mentioned in v. 14. For the daughters to belong to other men would remove them as the object of his fantasy, so Lot's would-be sons-in-law are effectively absent from the pic-ture now, in Lot's offer, although their successful elimination takes place only later, in the destruction of Sodom.[21]

Lot's attempt to protect his guests by proffering his daughters angers the townsmen, who threaten Lot and attempt to break down the door (v. 9). Nothing happens to either the guests or the daughters, however, because the divine visitors intervene (vv. 10–11). The usual explanation that Lot up-

---

[19] E.g., Jeansonne, *The Women of Genesis*, 41; George W. Coats, *Genesis, with an In-troduction to Narrative Literature* (FOTL 1; Grand Rapids: Eerdmans, 1983) 147; Rob-ert Ignatius Letellier, *Day in Mamre, Night in Sodom: Abraham and Lot in Genesis 18 and 19* (BibInt Series, 10; Leiden: E. J. Brill, 1995) 187; Carol Smith, "Challenged by the Text: Interpreting Two Stories of Incest in the Hebrew Bible," in Brenner and Fontaine (eds.), *A Feminist Companion to Reading the Bible*, 114–35 (127). Weston W. Fields (*Sodom and Gomorrah: History and Motif in Biblical Narrative* [JSOTSup 231; Sheffield: Sheffield Academic Press, 1997] 124) sees Lot as later "punished measure for measure," but also suggests (n. 22) that Lot may be portrayed as "a good-na-tured but unblessed simpleton."

[20] Recent studies have emphasized that the point here is not sexual orientation but rather the desire to humiliate the men by placing them in the position of women; see, e.g., Mieke Bal, "The Rape of Narrative and the Narrative of Rape: Speech Acts and Body Language in Judges," in *Literature and the Body: Essays on Populations and Persons* (ed. Elaine Scarry; Baltimore: Johns Hopkins Univ. Press, 1988) 20–21; similarly, Bechtel ("Feminist Reading," 117–26), who sees in the ambi-guity of "to know" the possibility that the Sodomites might only want to know what the strangers are doing in the city. The desire to dominate is common to incest fantasy (Seifert, *Tochter und Vater*, 185).

[21] Rather than being willing to hand the daughters over to other men, as looks to be the case on the surface, conscious level of the text, the opposite seems to be the unconscious wish: He rejects the idea that any man other than himself should have them.

holds the ancient rules of hospitality in offering his daughters to the men of Sodom in place of his guests is not entirely satisfying. Certainly, from a psychoanalytic point of view, a narrator on the couch confessing, "I offered my daughters because I could not violate the laws of hospitality," ought to be regarded with suspicion.

Assuming that the characters in this scenario represent split-off parts of the narrator ("my brothers," v. 7), all the men of Sodom, both young and old, who act in exceptional unison, could be viewed as a cipher for the narrator's id, his libidinous forbidden desires. If the collective androcentric desire is for the daughters, why fantasize the demand for the men? I suggest that the desire for the male visitors is a further distortion that provides the narrator, as spokesperson for the collective unconscious, with an excuse to make his incest fantasy imaginable: In order to allow himself to entertain a fantasy of incest with his daughters, he imagines something even more abhorrent to him—homosexual sex. This, too, is a desire that he is unable to acknowledge,[22] an unacceptable wish that must be rejected, and it is thus dismissed in favor of another one—what for him is the lesser of the two evils, the wish for sex with his daughters. But he is unable to carry the incest fantasy through, presumably because his guilt is so great. The solution to his conflicting impulses is a temporary narrative resolution. He punishes himself with castration, which is symbolically represented in the text by blindness, so that he cannot act out his forbidden sexual fantasies in his narrative.[23] Instead he gropes in vain for "the opening" (הפתח, v. 11), possibly, through the distortions of fantasy, an allusion to his frustrated desire for sexual intercourse with his daughters.[24]

The number of distortions indicate how great the narrative defenses are. Indeed, a part of the self, the part played by Lot, has reservations. Lot, functioning as the ego in a self-regulating capacity, wants to resist. The unconscious libido, the id, in fact, accuses the reluctant part of the self of setting itself up to "judge" (וישפט שפוט, v. 9), and threatens to do it harm if not allowed to do what it wants—a sign of deep inner-psychic conflict. The visitors, who provided an excuse for the Father to entertain his incestuous

---

[22] "Die 'Männer' werden als blühende Jünglinge vorgestellt, deren frische Schönheit die böse Lust der Sodomiten reizt" (Gunkel, *Genesis*, 208).

[23] On blindness as symbolic castration, see Freud, *The Interpretation of Dreams*, 433–434 n.

[24] There are many sexual double meanings in this fantasy (see below); cf. the use of פתח in Song of Songs 5:2–6. Wenham (*Genesis 16–50*, 56) observes that "it is unexpected that no one in the large mob, even if blind, found his way to the door and summoned others there." Naturalizing the story this way leads him to explain their behavior by attributing it to "supernatural agency"; it makes sense, however, when we recall that the Sodomites act in perfect unison as though they were one (a cipher for the id), though apparently not including Lot's future sons-in-law.

fantasy, now function, on another level, as the ego's appeal to external, divinely guaranteed moral law to keep the self in check.[25] Just how welcome are these guests, anyway? Lot "presses" them to stay with him (v. 3); the ego needs the enforcing, prohibiting authority of the super-ego for support against powerful and threatening libidinal impulses. The id (the townsmen) finds the appeal to standards of moral rectitude very unwelcome.

Both the ego and the Father's propped-up super-ego are threatened by the id ("This one came to sojourn, and he would indeed judge! Now we will deal worse with you than with them," v. 9), but, unlike the ego, the super-ego is not subject to the id. It (the divine visitors) passes the judgment that the ego (Lot), because it was not strong enough, was unable to achieve on its own. For Freud, all dreams, including punishment dreams, are wish-fulfillment dreams, and the same might be said for narrative fantasies. As in a punishment dream, the text "replace[s] the forbidden wish-fulfillment by the appropriate punishment for it":[26] symbolic castration in the form of blindness. As a result, the fantasies (sex with other men, sex with his daughters) are abandoned; however, the narrative neurosis is not thereby semiotically cured. The collective male psyche has neither successfully rid itself of its incestuous desire nor finished punishing itself for it.

Conflict within the Narrative Unconscious (Gen 19:12–29)

I mentioned above that psychoanalysis alerts us to the fact that incest with his daughters is the unconscious desire within the fantasy that is Genesis 19 because that is precisely what the narrator sets up to happen.[27] It takes him time to get to the scene of the crime, for there are still too many impediments for the incest wish to be narratively fulfilled (a domineering super-ego in the form of divine authority, potential sons-in-law, and a wife). In vv. 12–29 we see the narrator's final struggle with(in) himself, even as he begins to set things up for the incest scene. The conflict within him is first played out between Lot and his would-be sons-in-law. Part of him needs them, because their possession of his daughters would prevent him from realizing his incestuous desires, so Lot urges them to leave Sodom with him and his family. But part of him does not really want them around; Lot is, so to speak, jesting (v. 14). The word מצחק, like פתח earlier, is one of a

---

[25] A fantasy, like a dream, has its own kind of logic, in which elements can have multiple significance, and here the visitors can have more than one function; see Freud, *The Interpretation of Dreams*, 182. For basic distinctions between the ego, the id, and the super-ego, see Sigmund Freud, *The Ego and the Id* (trans. Joan Riviere; rev. and ed. James Strachey; New York: W. W. Norton & Company, 1960). Freud used these terms differently and sometimes indiscriminately, and he changed his usage over time.

[26] Freud, *Beyond the Pleasure Principle*, 37.

[27] As noticed by Seifert, *Tochter und Vater*, 185.

number of overdetermined terms in this fantasy that suggest the unconscious sexual obsession (compare, e.g., its sexual connotation in Gen 26:8).
By leaving the daughters' potential husbands behind in Sodom, the narrator rids himself of one of his defense mechanisms.

Lot's lingering (v. 16), his unwillingness to flee to the hills, and his bar-
gaining to go to Zoar instead (vv. 18–23) function as further narrative defenses against incestuous desire. Of v. 19, Gordon Wenham observes,
"Lot's plea is somewhat involved syntactically, suggesting perhaps his inner confusion and bewilderment."[28] Flight to the hills is both desired and
feared: desired because that is where the narrator will entertain (in a distorted form) his forbidden desires (v. 30); feared because the desire is repul-
sive to him and merits punishment: "I cannot flee to the hills, lest the
wickedness cling to me, and I die" (v. 19). If he goes to the hills, he will commit the crime; the wickedness will, indeed, cling to him (דבק, another sexually loaded term; cf. Gen 2:24); and he will experience again the need for
discipline. He seeks to punish further his irrepressible libidinal desire (still
represented as the men of Sodom) by calling down fire and brimstone
upon it, but his efforts to repress it prove futile. After this, the divine messengers, and God, cease to function in the narrative fantasy as a regulating,
morality-enforcing agency. The mother, the final obstacle to—and final defense against—the wish fulfillment, is also removed from the picture. She
looks back, or, as Rashkow puts it, she "look[s] away" from what the father
does to his daughters.[29] The mother's absence is an important feature of the
typical father–daughter incest scenario. In the distortions of the wish-fulfillment in the next scene, we encounter others: the abuse of alcohol, the
daughters' provocative behavior, the involvement of more than one
daughter, the seemingly weak father, and an erotically charged atmosphere.[30]

Desire Distorted: The Incest Fantasy Played Out (Gen 19:30–38)

Ridding himself first of the would-be sons-in-law and then of the wife
clears the way for the Father to imagine having sex with his daughters in
the fantasy. With his daughters, Lot leaves Zoar for the hills, and specifically for a cave (literally "the cave," and another sexual innuendo). He and
his daughters cannot stay in Zoar, since in order for him to realize the
Father's incest fantasy, he needs privacy.[31] Is this the reason for Lot's fear in

---

[28] Wenham, *Genesis 16–50*, 58.

[29] Rashkow, "Daddy-Dearest," 105.

[30] Seifert, *Tochter und Vater*, 84; Seifert, "Lot und seine Töchter," 56 n. 34, following Ursula Wirtz, *Seelenmord: Inzest und Therapie* (Zürich, 1989) 51, and Rijnaarts,
Lots Töchter, 25–26; Rashkow, "Daddy-Dearest," 105.

[31] Seifert, "Lot und seine Töchter," 57.

v. 30? Is the narrator afraid of being caught? Is he afraid of having his fantasy frustrated in Zoar by the same kind of obstacles he put up against it in
Sodom? Lot must be alone with his daughters because the narrator needs
to come up with some kind of motivation, however unreasonable, for the
daughters—whom he will cast in the active role in his fantasy—to commit
incest.

The curious features of the story noted above are explicable as his
defenses against the forbidden wish, defenses that cause him to imagine
the scene in a distorted form. "The intoxication of Lot shows that the revolting nature of the proposal was felt by the Hebrew conscience," observes John Skinner.[32] Not only does the Father fantasize his daughters
as the ones who instigate sexual relations with him, he also imagines
himself in the totally passive role of the father Lot, as a victim who has
no knowledge of having sexual intercourse on two successive nights,
first with his elder daughter and then with the younger. So guiltless is
he that he is not even responsible for being drunk. That, too, is his
daughters' doing; they "caused him to drink" (*Hiphil*), as though he had
no will of his own. In his first fantasy (vv. 1–11) the narrator entertained
the wish for homosexual sex in a distorted form, within a scenario of homosexual rape; here he imagines himself as molested by his daughters.
Perhaps there is some part of the collective male unconscious in Genesis
19 that takes pleasure in imagining being the object of sexual abuse, as
well as the abuser.

The narrator obviously enjoys replaying the scene in his mind, for it is
hardly necessary for him to repeat, almost verbatim and in detail, both the
proposal and the act in such detail.[33]

> "Come, *let us make our father drink wine,*
>> and **we will lie with him,**
>>> that we may make seed live for our father" (v. 32).
> *So they made their father drink wine that night,*
>> and **the first-born went in and lay with her father.**
>>> He did not know when she lay down or when she arose (v. 33).
> On the next day, the first-born said to the younger,
>> "See, **I lay yesterday with my father;**
> *let us make him drink wine tonight also.*
>> Then **you go in and lie with him,**
>>> so that we may make seed live for our father" (v. 34).
> *So they made their father drink wine that night also,*
>> and **the younger arose and lay with him.**
>>> He did not know when she lay down or when she arose (v. 35).

---

[32] Skinner, *Genesis*, 313.

[33] As readers, we are placed in the position of voyeurs; our complicity is invited; cf. Seifert, "Lot und seine Töchter," 51: "Ihr Reiz für den Erzähler und Leser
liegt offenbar in ihrem Inhalt und dessen Wiederholung."

Making him drink wine is mentioned four times; having sex with him (אֶת/עִם שָׁכַב), five. Both encounters end with the narrative assurance of the father's innocence (vv. 33, 35).[34] The only other detail provided, and stated each time, is the daughters' motive, "that we may make seed live for our father." To an extent the fantasy seeks to absolve the daughters also: Their purpose is not sex for pleasure but continuation of the patriarchal line.[35] Whereas the narrator concentrates on the incestuous encounters, he is careful to deny pleasure to himself in the form of any of the characters; that would bring him too close to facing his forbidden desire. Nevertheless, even while protesting his innocence, he indulges in a fantasy of sexual potency in which, in a fully drunken condition, he could father a child and could do it twice.[36]

Seifert has recognized all the symptoms here not only as typical of incestuous fathers but also as narrative symptoms, and I therefore quote her at length:

> In Gen 19, 30–38 ist jedenfalls die Lust des Erzählers an intimen Beziehungen geweckt: Er bringt zunächst Vater und Töchter in der Abgeschiedenheit einer Höhle ganz eng zusammen (V 30), läßt dann die Töchter schlau und entschlossen auf Geschlechtsverkehr sinnen (V 31f) und schildert schließlich die "Verführung" des Vaters detailliert (V 33–35). Was die Breite der Erzählung und den Blick des Erzählers betrifft, so liegt das Interesse eindeutig nicht bei den Kindern, deren Zeugung schließlich als Ziel und Zweck der Erzählung erscheinen, sondern bei dem Erotik beinhaltenden "Verführungsakt" (den Vater berauschen—sich zu ihm legen—seinen Samen lebendig machen). Die gewählten Worte halten fest, daß dem Geschlechtsakt etwas Gewaltsames innewohnt. Auffälligerweise läßt ihn der Erzähler durch Lots Tochter zunächst wie einen Überfall auf ihre Person beschreiben (V 31), während er dann in Planung und Ausführung letzlich erzält wird als "Überfall" auf Lot, der nichts mehr "erkennen" kann (V 32–35). Dieser Widerspruch ließe sich dadurch erklären, daß hier sexuelle Gewalt gegen die Tochter als sexuelle "Überwältigung" des Vater

---

[34] "To be seduced by one's own daughters into an incestuous relationship with pregnancy following is bad enough. Not to know that the seduction had occurred is worse. To fall prey to the whole plot a second time is worse than ever," comments Coats (*Genesis*, 147). As Gunkel (*Genesis*, 219) observes, "Der Erzähler betont, daß Lot nichts merkt: er will Lot entlassen."

[35] Jacob, *Genesis*, 464–65; this is Letellier's reading of their motivation in the story, though he adds, "Whatever the motivation the plan is devious and morally unsettling" (81).

[36] "Das kann doch nur so gewesen sein, daß der schon alte Vater seinen Töchtern Wein gab und sie vergewaltigt hat . . . Daß die Töchter ihren Vater betrunken gemacht haben und daß ein alter, betrunkener Mann zwei Frauen schwängert, halte ich mit Shakespeare für ausgeschlossen ('alcohol provoques [*sic*] the desire but disturbs the performance')"; Sorge, *Kuckuck*, 115, cited by Seifert, "Lot und seine Töchter," 56, and Seifert, *Tochter und Vater*, 84 n. 123.

durch die Tochter dargestellt wird. Dies ist bis heute gängige Strategie in-
zestuöser Väter und einer um Verständnis für Vergewaltiger werbenden
Literatur.[37]

The close surroundings of the cave, with the father and daughters alone in
intimate proximity, creates an evocative atmosphere for the collective unconscious to play out its forbidden fantasies. Seifert rightly identifies the
narrative interest here in incestuous sex and not its outcome.

A literary creation that allows the collective male unconscious to engage in its forbidden fantasies, Genesis 19 is also a narrative symptom
of cultural guilt. The traces of the crime that the narrator fails to get rid
of are evidence of a collective wish to be caught, and the narrative serves
the collective need for confession. Freud emphasizes the importance of
puns and verbal clues in dreams as keys to their hidden meanings.[38] We
find them functioning in this part of the fantasy, vv. 30–38, as indications of the narrator's unconscious preoccupation with incestuous sex.
The expression בוא על ("come upon"), instead of the more common בוא אל
("come unto"), in the first-born's proposal in v. 31 hints at a forcible as-
sault, as Seifert notes in the citation above.[39] The cave, in which the Father's fantasized incestuous encounters with his daughters take place
(מערה, v. 30), would be readily identified in psychoanalysis as a female
symbol; in addition, it puns on several sexually suggestive terms: מערה,
"bare, naked place," from ערה, "be naked, bare"; מעור, "nakedness" or
"genitals"; ערוה, "genitals"; עריה, "nakedness"; and related forms.[40] The
repeated denial, "he did not know when she lay down or when she
arose" (vv. 33, 35), hints at the Father's wish to "know" his daughters in
the sexual sense of ידע. Similarly, in v. 36, instead of the more usual הרה
ל, the expression הרה מן points to the Father's guilt, as do the names of the
children:[41] "from the father"[42] and "son of my people."[43] How these sons

---

[37] Seifert, "Lot und seine Töchter," 59–60.

[38] Freud, *The Interpretation of Dreams*, 131, 237–40, 247–49, 311–18, 441–42, 502–
503, 557–60, *et passim*.

[39] See, further, Seifert, "Lot und seine Töchter," 50 and n. 11; Jacob, *Genesis*, 465.

[40] Rashkow, "Daddy-Dearest," 102; Letellier, *Day in Mamre*, 179.

[41] Seifert, "Lot und seine Töchter," 52, 63; cf. Jacob, *Genesis*, 466, who takes the
unusual expression as a sign that the pregnancy was without Lot's consent or
knowledge, as well as a link to the etymology that follows.

[42] Or, possibly, father's water (i.e. semen) from מי אב; so translated by Everett
Fox, *In the Beginning: An English Rendition of the Book of Genesis* (*Response* 14 [1972])
50; Vawter (*On Genesis*, 243) proposes *mu abi*, "the seed of my father," as a more hidden meaning of the name.

[43] Jacob (*Genesis*, 466) proposes that עם has here, as in many compound proper
names, the same meaning as אב; Skinner (*Genesis*, 314) also gives it the more specific
meaning, "son of my (paternal) kinsman"; similarly, Gunkel, *Genesis*, 220; von Rad,
Genesis, 218.

become fathers themselves—fathers of whole peoples—is left to our imagination.

The children, Moab and Ammon, who provide the Father with a justification for incest, also represent the desire to perpetuate the paternal line in a way that insures the greatest possible ethnic purity. The wish displaced onto the daughters in vv. 32 and 34 is expressed in unusual, and distinctly patriarchal, terms: to make the seed (offspring, but also semen) of the father live. At the beginning of the fantasy that lies behind Genesis 19, the Father's forbidden desire for incest with his daughters was entertained, in a distorted shape, but abandoned (vv. 1–11). By the end of the fantasy (vv. 30–38), the wish is fulfilled, also with distortions aimed at censoring its unacceptable content: The eponymous ancestor has incestuous relations with his daughters and he continues the family line through them. Giving birth to a literary creation in which the father's own daughters bear his sons is the closest this collective patriarchal unconscious wish can come to displacing the universal mother, Eve, with a father of all living.

Desire Exhibited: Lot and His Daughters in Painting

Art frequently sheds light on biblical stories because of the way artists fill in textual gaps and deal with ambiguities in representing visually what for them are critical moments. Lot's "seduction" by his daughters provided artists with an opportunity to paint naked women, and probably for this reason it became the most frequently painted scene from Genesis 19.[44] But in numerous paintings something else is exhibited as well: the father's incestuous desire. Whereas the Father's incest wish is expressed in distorted form in the fantasy as it is played out in Gen 19:30–38, in the iconographic tradition we find the father's complicity and active involvement openly acknowledged.

In Jan Steen's *Lot und seine Töchter*, painted in 1665, Lot, looking like a jolly middle-class country landowner, is the central figure, with what appears to be his elder daughter on his left and his younger daughter on his right. The warm, soft tones of the painting lend an erotic atmosphere and suggest the intimacy of the cave, as if it were dimly lit by a fire. We might view this scene as the beginning of the "seduction," for Lot is still sitting up and all the figures are clothed. But because the areas in the painting where the light falls are the younger daughter's neck and breasts, her sister's shoulder, and Lot's chest, our attention is drawn to the flesh that is exposed. There is already a palpable sense of the illicit: The younger daughter's breast is bared, and with her left hand she is delicately unfastening

---

[44] Netty van de Kamp, in *Im Lichte Rembrandts: Das Alte Testament im Goldenen Zeitalter der niederländischen Kunst* (ed. Christian Tümpel; Zwolle: Waanders, n.d.) 232.

her father's belt in a provocative gesture that seems calculated to titillate the viewer. Lot has kicked off one of his shoes, his long red robe is already open, and his chest and one leg are exposed. How much of this is his daughters' doing and how much he has "allowed" to happen (like kicking off his shoe) is open to conjecture.

Lot is clearly in a frolicsome mood, already feeling the effects of the wine. He appears to have drained the goblet in his right hand but his older daughter holds another glass ready for him. His attention is fixed on the

Jan Steen, *Lot und seine Töchter*, Wessenberg-Galerie, Konstanz

older daughter, at whom he looks lustfully, and his left arm is stretched out behind her, though we cannot tell if he is grasping her. She is clearly holding on to him, supporting his arm as if to keep him from toppling over, for he is sitting rather precariously, with one leg in the air. He grins at her bawdily, as though chuckling with anticipation, and she looks down at him with a faint, impenetrable smile on her lips (suggesting, perhaps, that she is the author of this plan?). The other daughter looks somewhat apprehensive, perhaps concerned lest her father notice that she is undressing him and call a halt to the unwholesome proceedings. It is difficult to imagine that, even in his wine-induced merry mood, Lot is completely unaware of what he and his daughters are doing. By portraying him as drunk but not, as in the biblical fantasy, insensible, and as so thoroughly enjoying himself, the artist reveals the father's complicity and his incestuous desire, for this Lot conceivably still could, if he wanted to, come to his senses before things go any farther.

The situation is quite different in the painting of Lot and his daughters by Francesco Furini (c. 1600–1646; the illustration appears on the following page).[45] Instead of the warm amber shades of Steen's cave scene, here we have cold blues and pale flesh tones, giving us a rather chilly atmosphere. The setting itself receives no attention, except that it is dark. The three figures fill the canvas. Lot is in the center, in the shadows, flanked by the naked torsos of his daughters, bathed in light. The daughters are facing their father; one has her back to the viewer, but the other is twisted around so that her body faces more toward the viewer, although she is looking at her father. The one holds a wine flask in one hand and offers her father a cup of wine with the other; the other daughter seems to be tugging at his garment. It is difficult to make out Lot's expression; he is looking at the daughter whose face we partially see. The daughter with her back to us is completely naked, except for the most translucent of cloths barely draped around her buttocks and thighs; the one turned toward us has a dark cloth covering her genitals, while her left arm conceals one of her breasts from the viewer but not from Lot, with the other only dimly visible. Since we are dealing with a painting by a man presumably done for a male patron and male spectators, we can reasonably assume that the women's nakedness is for the pleasure of the male spectator-owner.[46] But their nakedness also accuses their father, for in addition to signaling their guilt, it also communicates and explains Lot's desire.

[45] A full-page color reproduction of this painting can be found in Dorothée Sölle, Joe H. Kirchberger, and Herbert Haag, *Great Women of the Bible in Art and Literature* (Grand Rapids, Mich.: Eerdmans, 1994) 57.

[46] See the discussion in John Berger, *Ways of Seeing* (London: Penguin, 1972) 52–63.

Lot cannot fail to have noticed—even if he has already drunk some of the wine being offered to him—that both daughters are naked. Yet he is not resisting. His right hand is on one daughter's shoulder, while his left arm is around the other's back, with his hand resting just above her waist. Even if we imagine he is holding on to them to prop himself up, he is not pushing them away. He is more complicit, his incestuous desire more in evidence, than in Steen's painting. That Steen portrays both daughters is understandable, since in the biblical text they jointly get their father drunk ("let *us* make our father drink wine") before one of them has sex with him. But if we follow the biblical version, there is no reason for them to be naked, especially at the same time, before their father has lain down (passed out?).

Francesco Furini, *Lot and His Daughters,* Museo del Prado, Madrid

Central to the biblical fantasy is Lot's lack of knowledge of his daughters' sexual intentions toward him. Furini, in contrast, has chosen to show them enticing their father with their nakedness, as if they were both inviting him to have sex with either or both of them. Through compression the artist expresses what the biblical version suggests by lingering over the details of two separate, yet virtually identical, occasions: the incestuous desire for both daughters. The painting emphasizes not Lot's drunkenness but the temptation itself. The temptation is for the benefit of the male viewer (constructed as heterosexual), for whom the women are naked. Despite the appearance it may give of being about the women's desire, it is actually about women's desirability and male desire—the male viewer's desire, which can be attributed to Lot's desire.

The cave, with its cozy atmosphere conveyed by rich, warm hues is again the setting in a painting of the scene by Hendrick Goltzius (1558–1617; the illustration appears on the following page). In the background Sodom and Gomorrah burn, which suggests the sinful nature of the scene before us, and we can see very faintly the figure of Lot's wife who has been turned into a pillar of salt (and cannot therefore "look" to prevent or accuse). These recent calamities, still in evidence, seem to have been forgotten by this cozy threesome. As in Furini's painting, the nakedness of both of the daughters accuses the father as much as it blames the daughters. Lot is even more guilty here, because he is naked, too, apart from a red cloth that hides his genitals. Typically, he appears in the middle of the scene, between his daughters. The one on the right, who seems to be the older, leans intimately on Lot's leg with her elbow nestled provocatively between his legs. She has her back to us, but her head is twisted so that we see part of her face. She is looking at her sister, who is looking at their father. The younger daughter's body is displayed to the viewer and only the traditional bit of cloth covers her genitals. Lot's attention is divided between the women. He returns his younger daughter's gaze with a lecherous smile on his face, and his knee is pressed against her thigh, while his left hand rests on the other daughter's shoulder. In his right hand he holds the wine the younger daughter has given him, and his ruddy cheeks suggest this may not be his first cup (or is he flushed with excitement?). He is sitting up, hardly overcome by wine, and clearly having a good time. The display of female sexuality and the old man's lecherous posture toward the young women in this painting seem designed to titillate. By making Lot an active participant whose delectation is obvious, Goltzius conspicuously exhibits the incestuous desire that, owing to the Father's defenses in Gen 19:30–38, was unable to express itself except in a distorted shape.

Hendrick Goltzius, *Lot en zijn dochters*, Rijksmuseum, Amsterdam

Like Steen and Goltzius, Simon Vouet (1590–1649) also uses warm col-
ors to suggest the cave setting. His painting is striking for its bold portrayal
of Lot's incestuous impulses. Lot may not be naked, but he is actively fondling his daughter. She seems to be naked underneath the loose cloths
draped around her both to conceal and to attract the viewer's attention. Lot
is embracing her, with his left arm around her shoulders, and fondling her
breast with his right hand. Her leg is provocatively hooked over his knees,

Simon Vouet, *Loth et ses filles*, Musée des Beaux-Arts de Strasbourg

and he presses it between his thigh and arm as he draws her toward him (and he appears to be pressing his knees into her other leg). He gazes lecherously at her, and she returns his gaze, suggesting her complicity in what looks rather like something he has initiated. Were it not for the presence of the other daughter, holding a large wine jar and goblet, we might imagine that Lot has aroused this woman from sleep by molesting her. Interestingly, his legs are crossed, while hers are suggestively spread apart. It would seem, then, that the artist defends Lot even while accusing him, which calls to mind the way the biblical Father put up defenses against his unconscious incest wish in Genesis 19.

The other daughter, whose breast is somewhat exposed, looks on. Lot pays her no attention, so wrapped up is he in caressing her sister. In Steen's painting, both daughters are involved in getting Lot drunk and undressed, whereas in Furini and Goltzius, both entice their father with their naked bodies. Vouet's painting is more like the biblical account, which concentrates on sex with one daughter at a time. The second daughter, who is not doing anything but watching, becomes a voyeur, whose presence reminds us of our own status as voyeurs. All the paintings of the scene, of course, invite us to be voyeurs spying on a private and illicit moment, even as they—and Vouet especially—exhibit, for our judgment, the father's forbidden desire.[47]

The Distortions of Hollywood

The only similarities between *The Last Days of Sodom and Gomorrah*, directed by Robert Aldrich, and the story of Lot in the Bible are the beginning, when Lot separates from Abraham and journeys with his people to Sodom, and the end, when Lot's wife is turned into a pillar of salt. Everything in between in this joint Italian-French effort, is sheer fantasy (which perhaps justifies its comparison to a biblical fantasy). Lot (Stuart Granger) leads the Hebrews into the Jordan Valley, where they intend to live separately from the evil Sodomites. But the Hebrews get caught up in the

---

[47] Of the seven paintings of this scene reproduced in Sölle, Kirchberger, and Haag, *Great Women of the Bible in Art and Literature*, 48–57, the father's incestuous desire is arguably exhibited in six of them: Lucas Cranach the Elder, Jan Massys, Albrecht Altdorfer, David Teniers the Younger, Jan Breughel the Elder, Francesco Furini; the exception is Francesco Guercine. In all but one, both daughters are pictured in the foreground with Lot. In that one (Altdorfer), a seriously lecherous Lot is fondling one of his daughters, while the other, who looks already pregnant, is in the distant background. All three are naked. Though space does not permit discussion, the artists' use of the scene to indulge their own fantasies and desires, the way the paintings invite the viewer's collusion, the viewer's sexual orientation, and the ways that male and female viewers respond (differently) are topics that merit consideration.

struggle between the queen of Sodom (Anouk Aimée, pictured here with Granger), who sees them as valuable allies, and her evil brother, who is plotting a coup d'état. They end up living in Sodom, where gradually, instead of converting the Sodomites to the ways of Jehovah, the chosen people become Sodomites: Lot, now the prosperous leader of a nation of shopkeepers, lives with his family in a nice house; they have nice clothes; and they seem to enjoy going to parties, where people eat, drink, dance, and—it is suggested but not shown—end up having sex (the scene of bodies piled on top of each other pictured here in the foreground is what we see during the film's opening credits).

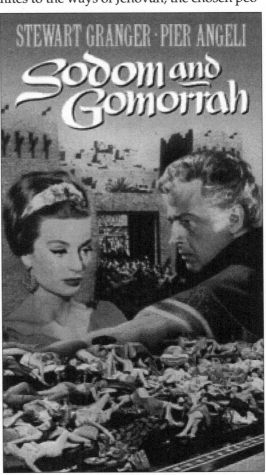

So what is really so evil about Sodom? For the Sodomites, "nothing is evil. Everything that gives pleasure is good." Like all biblical films, *The Last Days of Sodom and Gomorrah* has difficulties portraying sin of such proportions that it justifies total destruction. There are the usual suggestions of sexual immorality, and, in a distortion worthy of Hollywood, hints of lesbianism (especially in the way the queen, who is al-

The Last Days of Sodom and Gomorrah

ways attended by women, leers at her dancing body slaves) rather than male homosexuality (the popular notion of the sin of Sodom).[48] In addition, the Sodomites enjoy torturing and killing, and, worst of all, they keep slaves. Whereas the palace slaves seem quite content, the mine slaves are

---

[48] Bruce Babington and Peter William Evans, *Biblical Epics: Sacred Narrative in the Hollywood Cinema* (Manchester: Manchester Univ. Press, 1993) 59, 67.

brutally mistreated, and, in the end, escape with the Hebrews, in a *Ten Commandments*-style exodus, before the city is destroyed.

It is not surprising that a 1962 film would not include incest between Lot and his daughters, and, besides, Lot is the hero. *Sodom and Gomorrah* does, however, faintly hint at brother-sister incest between the queen and the prince sometime in the past ("It doesn't give you any longer pleasure?"). The closest the film comes to the unconscious incest fantasy of Genesis 19 is to have Lot marry a woman as young as his daughters. Stuart Granger as Lot is a gray-haired, mature, attractive widower with adult daughters who are clearly the sexiest women among the shabby-looking Hebrews. Lot describes himself as "dull, gray, old, [and] boring," but also as a man with sexual appetites. "Should I deny myself what other people take as naturally as bread and salt?" he says to Pier Angeli, in the role of Ildith, the queen's former slave, whom he wants for his wife.

Ildith, who had been "chief of the queen's body slaves," is initially a source of contention between Lot and his daughter Shuah. For Lot, the problem is Shuah's display of her sexuality; for Shuah, it is Lot's obvious sexual interest in the beautiful, young Sodomite. When Ildith is first brought to his tent, having been given to Lot by the queen to seal their friendship, she has, at Lot's command, been dressed in what looks like a sack. She says she prefers being a slave with fine clothes to freedom, which entails doing work "no slave of my class has ever done before." At that moment Shuah (the first of the Hebrews to succumb to the ways of Sodom) enters the tent. She wears the skimpy silk outfit that had belonged to Ildith, and says she would prefer to be a Sodomite slave, too, "if it means perfumes and silks like these." To Lot's incensed reply, "How dare you appear in clothes like that! What would your mother have said?!" she retorts angrily, "And what would she have said to see the woman who owned these clothes in our tent? We all know why you took her in. No need for a man who's lost his wife to be ashamed of that." For her impudence (the truth about *his desire* that he, like the biblical Father, does not want to admit), Lot slaps her.

The distortions of the film script resonate with the distortions of the biblical text: the sexual reproaches, with the sexual preoccupations of the biblical fantasy; the reference to the mother's disapproval of the *daughter's* behavior, with the absence (or looking away) of the mother and the distortion that makes incest the daughters' idea; and the daughter's counterclaim that Lot's sexual desire is just as worthy of censure by the mother, with the forbidden incest wish the Father could not express except in a distorted shape and his need to be found out.

Lot's two daughters are important for their role in bringing events to a crisis in the screenplay by Hugo Butler. In the biblical fantasy, the responsibility for committing incest is displaced onto the daughters. In a similar vein, the film blames the daughters, and in particular their sexual activities, for getting Lot into trouble. Shuah and Maleb are attracted to some of the principal Sodomite diversions: prancing around in nice clothes, wearing makeup, and having sex with the prince. Is it coincidental that Shuah, whose prominence in the family and larger role suggest she is the older daughter, is the first to have sex with the prince (she has been attracted to him from the beginning), while the other daughter simply follows suit and has sex with him too?[49] Or was Butler influenced by the roles of the daughters in Gen 19:31–35? The daughters' virtue, their loss of "innocence," is the issue that turns Lot into a murderer and thereby into, in the queen's words, "a true Sodomite."[50] The cinematic Lot shows as keen an interest in his daughters' virginity as the biblical Father; he has threatened to kill the man who violates their honor. When the prince provokes him by telling him he has had sexual relations with not one, but both of Lot's daughters, Lot kills him in a fight, even though the prince begs for mercy in the name of Lot's god and Shuah pleads for his life for her sake.[51] The same man has sex with the two virgin daughters; we could see this as a displacement of the biblical Father's desire onto the prince, for this is precisely what Lot does in the biblical story. Although the daughters are held responsible for what happens, in the cinematic version, as in the biblical account, they are not pictured as wicked.

By making so much of Lot's outraged defense of his daughters' virginity, the film provides an evaluative commentary on the incest fantasy of Genesis 19 and its distortions without ever addressing it directly. Whereas the biblical Father's fantasy discloses, in its distortions, his need to be found out, in the film Lot is held accountable for his crime by his daughter (here, of course, not incest but still a crime against her she cannot forgive, the murder of the prince). Moreover, she wants him punished for it ("I pray Jehovah to hear you cry out as I cried, to see you struck to earth to crawl on your hands and knees"), and her presence by his side will be an everlasting witness against him: "Until I see that happen, I won't leave you ever,

---

[49] And, interestingly, when compared to Lot's not "knowing" his daughters in his bed, when the prince first grabs and forces his attentions upon Maleb, he thinks she is her sister.

[50] The first step, as the queen recognizes, was his marriage to a Sodomite woman.

[51] For those curious about how it all turns out: Lot condemns himself to prison; two angels (cf. Gen 19:1–23) appear and set him free, instructing him to lead his people out of the city before Jehovah destroys it (cf. Acts 5:19–21). He gets them to agree that Jehovah will spare the city if ten righteous men can be found in it. His face shines, and, like a prophet, he urges the city to repentance. The Hebrews leave in a large exodus with the slaves and are warned not to look back.

Father."[52] Lot's punishment comes in the form of the death of his new wife Ildith, the former Sodomite slave. As the cardboard set collapses in flame and smoke, she looks back and is turned into a pillar of salt. In the typical incest scenario, the mother's absence or refusal to believe it (to see, to look) is a significant factor. In the film, Lot's wife looks back precisely because she does not *believe*.[53] And the sight kills her. The film ends with Lot's two daughters leading him away to the hills, though without setting the stage for the incest scenario, since the mixed multitude with whom they left Sodom is with them. Perhaps the family has had enough sex for one movie, since all three have had sexual relations with Sodomites.*

---

[52] There is a pause before the word "father," and the emphasis is hers.

[53] Lot urges Ildith to believe so that she will not look back, but she says: "I don't believe"; "I can't"; and "I tried but I just can't." Just before she turns to look back, she thinks, "He [Lot] is responsible for everything good that has happened. There is no such thing as Jehovah."

* I gratefully acknowledge the British Academy for a travel grant enabling me to read a version of this essay at the 2000 Annual Meeting of the Society of Biblical Literature.

Chapter 8

The Gift:
World Alteration and Obligation
in 2 Kings 4:8–37

Danna Nolan Fewell
Drew University

He will have obligated.
　　Jacques Derrida, "At This Very Moment in This Work Here I Am"

Reciprocity is a structure founded on an original inequality. For equality to make its entry into the world, beings must be able to demand more of themselves than of the Other, feel responsibilities on which the fate of humanity hangs. . . .
　　Emmanuel Levinas, *Difficult Freedom: Essays on Judaism*

I seek to complicate what may have seemed to have been a straightforward consensus, rooted in objective truth, on how to read this story as basically an Elisha story. I would like to see the day when biblical scholars practice a form of criticism that goes against the grain of such a constructed consensus. By long cultural habit such agreed upon interpretation may seem naturally true, even harmless, but that for those excluded from its protection, can be destructive.
　　Burke Long, "The Shunammite Woman: In the Shadow of the
　　Prophet?"

For what is at issue with respect to the Scriptures is not what lies behind the text in the form of an original meaning but what lies in front of it where the interpreter stands. The Bible always addresses itself to the time of interpretation; one cannot understand it except by appropriating it anew. Revelation is never something over and done with or gone for good

> *or in danger of slipping away into the past; it is ongoing, and its medium is*
> *midrash. . . .*
>
> Gerald L. Bruns, "Midrash and Allegory: The Beginnings of
> Scriptural Interpretation"[1]

She had not asked for the child.

In her mind the child was a gift that she had neither requested nor expected. Every day with that child had been a gift.

Now he was dead.

The woman[2] spurred her donkey on toward Mt. Carmel. She was on a

---

[1] Bruns goes on to describe midrash in the following way: "Midrash is a dialogue between text and history in which the task of giving an account—giving a midrash—does not involve merely construing a meaning; it also involves showing how the text still bears upon us, still speaks to us and exerts its claim upon us even though our situation is different from anything that has gone before. The task of midrash is to keep open the mutual belonging of the text and those who hear it" (ibid., in *The Literary Guide to the Bible* [ed. Robert Alter and Frank Kermode; Cambridge, Mass.: Belknap Press of Harvard Univ. Press, 1987] 634).

[2] The woman is not given a name in the story and, while it has become a common practice in feminist criticism to name unnamed women characters, I find such naming usually reduces the characters to only one particular character trait or to a social or familial connection or to an event that may have happened to them. Rather than trying to correct what is usually seen to be an androcentric narrative strategy, I would like to honor what Adam Zachary Newton (following Iris Murdoch) calls "contextual privacy." By not restricting her signification to a name, the woman is granted "an interior and unrepresentable space" (*Narrative Ethics* [Cambridge: Harvard Univ. Press, 1995] 157; 316 n. 45) which opens up rather than closes down possibilities of interpretation. (For a different understanding of the narrative functions of the anonymity of the Shunammite woman, see Adele Reinhartz, "Anonymous Women and the Collapse of the Monarchy: A Study in Narrative Technique," in *A Feminist Companion to Samuel and Kings* [ed. Athalya Brenner; Sheffield: Sheffield Academic Press, 1994] 43–65.)

One might also compare this phenomenon of namelessness with Derrida's observations on pseudonymity (in reference to Kierkegaard):

> This pseudonym . . . reminds us that a meditation linking the question of secrecy to that of responsibility immediately raises the question of the name and of the signature. One often thinks that responsibility consists of acting and signing *in one's name*. A responsible reflection on responsibility is interested in advance in whatever happens to the name in the event of pseudonymity, metonymy, homonymy, in the matter of what constitutes *a real name*. Sometimes one says or wishes it more effectively, more authentically, in the secret name by which *one calls oneself*, that *one gives oneself or affects to give oneself*, the name that is more *naming* and *named* in the pseudonym than in the official legality of the public patronym. (*The Gift of Death* [trans. David Wills; Chicago: Univ. of Chicago Press, 1995] 58)

The woman of Shunem is, of course, not the author (pseudonymically or otherwise) of her own story, but this particular secrecy, this "contextual privacy," sug-

singular quest to find the man of God.[3] He was the one responsible for all of this. He was the only one who could do anything about it.

She had met the man of God long ago. He had wandered through her village and she had insisted[4] that he share a meal in her home. He did not tell her he was a man of God, but she sensed that it was so and she always made an effort to provide him with food whenever he passed through. He passed through quite often.

At one point she had suggested to her husband that they build an additional room onto their house to accommodate this traveler. He could have been homeless for all she knew. She supervised the household addition herself: It was a second-floor chamber with everything he might need—a bed, a chair, a table, a lampstand. She quite enjoyed constructing this space for him—it was something she could afford to do (and no one else in her village could) and it gave the man a place to rest and recover his strength in the midst of his wanderings.[5] She rather liked the idea of making room in her home, making room in her life for this traveler. The very materiality of the newly created space—the cool stones in the walls, the warm wood of

---

gests that her determined attempt to save her son's life is spontaneous, uncalculated, and not motivated by a concern for recognition. She acts, not in her own name, but on behalf of her son. She acts before she thinks (cf. Levinas) about her own identity, her subjectivity, or about whether or not her action is reasonable in the eyes of others.

She is, in the words of Edmond Jabès describing Jewish identity, a "maze of signs," and his poetic dialogue (*The Book of Questions, Volume VI* [Middletown, Conn.: Wesleyan Univ. Press, 1983] 249) could easily apply to her:

> "What is your name?"
> "Look at my face."
>
> "What is your name?"
> "Look at my hands."
>
> "What is your name?"
> "Look at the road."

[3] While the man of God is named (Elisha) in the narrative, the woman herself never calls him by this name. She refers to him and perceives him only as "the man of God." He refers to her as "the Shunammite."

[4] The Hebrew root used here (חזק) suggests a kind of overpowering: she "prevailed upon him."

[5] The woman's construction hints at the depth of her perception and empathy. The structure is from beginning to end designed to protect the man and to alleviate his discomfort: The walls recognize physical vulnerability in the face of the natural elements; the bed and chair mitigate the weight of a fatigued body; the table provides the place for sustenance; and the lampstand fights off the darkness. Cf. Elaine Scarry's discussion of imagination and material making (*The Body in Pain: The Making and Unmaking of the World* [New York/Oxford: Oxford Univ. Press, 1985] 288–290). Scarry describes the relationship between the perception of another's

the lintels and in the furniture—made her feel as though she had made a difference in the world.[6] The room was her gift, her gift to God and to the man she believed spoke on behalf of God.[7]

The man of God began to stay there whenever he passed her way. She imagined that room might give him some sense of place, of belonging, some sense of connectedness to a home and to a family. Somehow a man of

---

vulnerability and the creative act to alleviate the other's discomfort as follows:

> If one imagines . . . one human being perceiving in another discomfort and in the same moment wishing the other to be relieved of the discomfort, something in that fraction of a second is occurring inside the first person's brain . . . , not just a perception of an actuality (the second person's pain) but an alteration of that actuality (for embedded in the perception is the sorrow that it is so, the wish that it were otherwise). Though this interior event must be expressed as a conjunctive duality, "seeing the pain and wishing it gone," it is a single percipient event in which the reality of pain and unreality of imagining are already conflated. Neither can occur without the other: if the person does not perceive the distress, neither will he wish it gone; conversely, if he does not wish it gone, he cannot have perceived the pain itself. . . . If this complex, mysterious, invisible percipient event, happening somewhere between the eyes and the brain and engaging the entire psyche, could be made visible, could be lifted out of the body and endowed with an external shape, that shape would be the shape of a chair. . . . (Scarry, 289–90)

or, in the case of our story, the shape of a room or a bed or a table. The Shunammite's concern for the protection and sustenance of the body is contrasted to the man of God's lack of concern for either the woman's body (manifested by his blithe assignment of a pregnancy) or her son's (manifested by his obliviousness to the child's welfare).

[6] The woman's gesture involves imagination, work, and artifice, the significance of which is often overlooked. Scarry writes:

> While imagining may entail a revolution of the entire order of things, the eclipse of the given by a *total reinvention of the world*, an artifact (a relocated piece of coal, a sentence, a cup, a piece of lace) is *a fragment of world alteration*. Imagining a city, the human being "makes" a house; imagining a political utopia, he or she instead helps to build a country; imagining the elimination of suffering from the world, the person instead nurses a friend back to health. Although, however, artifice is more modest and fragmentary than imagining, its objects have the immense advantage over imagined objects of being real, and because real, sharable; and because the objects are sharable, in the end artifice has a scale as large as that in imagining because its outcome is for the first time collective. (171)

We don't know if the woman of Shunem was inspired by a larger vision of change, but her ability to see and to transform her imagining into artifice allows the man of God to share in the benefits of her world-altering act and encourages him to live a different kind of life (namely, one more connected to the people around her) and to enter into a different kind of relationship with her. "The making of an artifact is a social act," continues Scarry, "for the object (whether an art work or instead an object of everyday use) is intended as something that will both enter into and itself elicit human responsiveness" (175).

[7] Contrast the motivation assigned by John Gray. According to Gray, Elisha did "not actually need the Shunammite lady's hospitality," but she pressed him, "ob-

God who knew of such things would be, in her mind, better able to do what he had been called to do.

One day when the man of God was there, his servant summoned her to the second-floor chamber. As she entered the room, the man of God was lying on his back staring at the ceiling. Not turning to look at her, he spoke to his servant. "Say to the woman," he said, "'You have gone to all this trouble for us[8]—you have rearranged your life for us—what can I do for you? Shall I speak to the king on your behalf, perhaps? Or to the commander of the army?'"

She had been amused at the time at the man's self-importance. She never would have taken him to be such a political name-dropper. And why he couldn't even look her in the face or speak to her directly, she didn't know.[9] She hadn't waited for the servant to repeat the speech to her. (She didn't take to such games of pretentious mediation.) "I'm quite content," she had replied as she turned to go back downstairs, "right where I am, liv-

---

serving the ancient Semitic convention of hospitality to sustain her own credit and bringing herself within the range of the 'blessing' which a man of God enjoyed" (*I & II Kings: A Commentary* [OTL; Philadelphia: Westminster, 1964/1970] 495).

[8] The Hebrew word חרד (often translated "to tremble") connotes here a pronounced disturbance, an intense attentiveness.

[9] Burke O. Long argues ("A Figure at the Gate: Readers, Reading and Biblical Theologians," in *Canon, Theology, and Old Testament Interpretation: Essays in Honor of Brevard S. Childs* [ed. Gene M. Tucker, David L. Petersen, and Robert R. Wilson; Philadelphia: Fortress, 1988] 166–86) that this protocol that separates the woman from the man of God is designed to amplify the importance of Elisha, but the fact that, in the course of the story, the protocol breaks down invites a double reading of the tale:

> [F]rom the beginning the Shunammite seems to have refused the agendas set by others. It was her initiative that established the wayside room for Elisha; she asked nothing when it was confidently suggested by the men that she must have some sort of need; and she pursued justice against thoughtless obstacles of convention thrown in her path by her husband and the prophets.
>
> On the other hand, throughout the narrative Elisha is a man of power. This is his and the narrator's view, at least most of the time. Yet on this occasion Elisha is left without second sight, resists a moral claim, and finally turns the magic trick without confessing any shortcoming to his public. The reader shares a private knowledge of the prophet's vulnerability and thus perceives matters in ways that subvert other tendencies in the narration. (174)

However, the double-edged nature of the tale that Long exposes so expertly, makes it difficult to claim that only one reading represents "the narrator's view" (even qualified with "at least most of the time"). Rather, it seems that the story is rife with irony regarding the prophet's sense of self-importance. Cf. the reading of Mary E. Shields ("Subverting a Man of God, Elevating a Woman: Role and Power Reversals in 2 Kings 4" *JSOT* 58 [1993] 59–69) and her final assessment:

> [I]n this text we find a unique blend of the two perspectives—neither canceling the other out. . . . The fact that the patriarchal gender roles are restored at the end does

ing among my own people. There's nothing I need from you or the king or the commander of the army."

She had returned to her work frustrated by the man's words. The man of God clearly wanted to pay her back for the room and for her hospitality. But this was not a matter of economic exchange and she was somewhat offended that her gift had been reduced to that.[10] It was, in her mind, just that, a gift. She had chosen to rearrange her life to accommodate this man. Whatever "trouble" she had gone to was her business, not his.

It wasn't long before she was summoned upstairs again. This time she didn't bother to enter the room. She stood in the doorway unwilling to be pulled into this silly conversation about compensation. This time the man spoke directly to her. "This time next year," he said, "you will be holding a son in your arms."

The abrupt announcement had caught the woman off guard and had greatly annoyed her. The thought of two men, guests in her own home, making reproductive plans for her really annoyed her. They hadn't asked her if she wanted a child. They had merely assumed. They assumed that that was what every woman wanted, what every woman needed to make

---

not negate the fact that a woman is elevated at the expense of the man of God. . . . [I]t is no accident that a woman . . . does the subverting. The subversion is all the more effective because it is one whose gender would normally marginalize her who challenges the structure of sacred authority. If the patriarchal or androcentric view wins out in the end, there is nevertheless a gynocentric emphasis that cannot be completely hidden. (68)

Long later returns to this text to examine more critically the tradition of "Elisha-centered" interpretation ("The Shunammite Woman: In the Shadow of the Prophet?" *Bible Review* 7 [1991] 12–19, 42):

Multiple strategies diminish [the Shunammite's] place in the tale. The writer encloses her with protocols that protect a lionized Elisha. The editor of Kings includes her as a minor character in a larger collection of stories about the prophet Elisha that reinforce expectations about Elisha's greatness and miracle working. A long procession of commentators read each other's works, but more importantly, share a socially formed way of reading that fixes on Elisha and diminishes the Shunammite.

On the other hand, one may refuse the premises that lead to this regime and, like the Shunammite, break with protocol. She can be a model of sorts for readers in a new world. The great lady from Shunem might inspire us to counteract the weight of consensus interpretation, but in a way that does not deny Elisha's place or the voice of commentators who guard a privilege for Elisha. This might be a way that allows both Elisha and the Shunammite power and independence in the story. It might even provide for new religious insights. (42)

[10] On the problem of the gift, Derrida writes (*The Gift of Death*, 112):

The moment the gift, however generous it be, is infected with the slightest hint of calculation, the moment it takes account of knowledge [connaissance] or recognition [reconnaissance], it falls within the ambit of an economy; it exchanges, in short it gives counterfeit money, since it gives in exchange for payment. Even if it gives "true" money, the alteration of the gift into a form of calculation immediately destroys the value of the very thing that is given; it destroys it as if from the inside.

her life complete.[11] They assumed that a child would more than repay for their frequent lodging. And they assumed that bringing a child into the world required no careful thought, no preparation, no responsibility on their parts. They assumed that she would be delighted.

She was not.

"No," she said to the man of God. "Do not toy with me."[12] She turned and left the room.

She had spent the rest of the day distracted and irritable. Children were not to be taken so lightly. They were not to be plopped thoughtlessly into the world for any reason. Certainly not simply as symbols of a prophet's miracle-working virility. Certainly not simply as some sort of reimbursement to keep him from feeling obligated.[13] It was this last thing that irritated her the most. The offer of a child was really more about him and his feeling of indebtedness than it was about her, her desires, or the quality of her life.

Her brusque retort had not deterred the man of God, however. The woman became pregnant in the course of that year. And while the child had grown inside her, she lived everyday torn between hope and fear. She had had to reorient her thinking completely. After many years of marriage without children, she had no longer expected ever to be a mother. Not only did she have to reenvision herself and her responsibilities, she had to think realistically about providing for this child. Her husband was much older than she. She had to prepare herself to be, at some point, her child's only parent. But she also had to prepare for the possibility that her husband, old as he was, might turn out to be her child's only parent. And, of course, she constantly worried that her child would grow up without parents at all.

---

[11] In her critique of how a patriarchal perspective has dominated traditional commentary on this story, Shields writes, "No one thinks to ask whether a child is really the woman of Shunem's greatest desire" (67). Cf. also Esther Fuch's similar critique in her work on the annunciation type-scene ("The Literary Characterization of Mothers and Sexual Politics in the Hebrew Bible," in *Feminist Perspectives on Biblical Scholarship* [ed. Adele Yarbro Collins; Chico, Calif.: Scholars Press, 1985]).

[12] The root of the verb here is כזב, usually translated "to lie" or "to deceive." I'm pressing for the more basic understanding of "to say something which has no substance or basis in reality."

[13] David Jobling argues that it is the concern of the Deuteronomistic narrator to eliminate any obligation the prophet may have to the woman. See "A Bettered Woman: Elisha and the Shunammite in the Deuteronomic Work," in *The Labour of Reading: Desire, Alienation, and Biblical Interpretation* (Semeia Studies; ed. Fiona Black, Roland Boer, and Erin Runions; Atlanta: Scholars Press, 1999).

She had watched many of her friends die giving birth and she knew that her own age was a complicating factor.[14]

She often thought that any other woman would rely on the man of God's promise and would trust that everything would work out fine, but the fact that the child had been promised by the man of God never gave her any sense of security—not even for a moment. She was convinced that the man of God never really understood the magnitude of his impulsive offer.[15] To him, the child existed only as a word on his lips. Its presence in the world would make no difference to him. It was simply a way of canceling his debt.

For her, however, the presence of the child was making all the difference in the world. It was changing her body; it was changing her perception of everything—including herself.[16] Its transforming power exceeded the protective walls of any room. It could not be contained in any kind of simple economy of exchange. She knew that nothing would ever be the same again and she found herself rearranging her life (as she had done for the man of God), making room for, accommodating the fragile body who, in the course of time, came to dwell in her home. The child was not, could not be, a payment for anything. He was a gift—an extraordinary gift from

---

[14] One would assume that the mother and infant mortality rate in the ancient world would be comparable to that in an "undeveloped" country: One in every four pregnancies would have ended in death for either the mother or the child or both. See Carol Meyers, *Discovering Eve: Ancient Israelite Women in Context* (New York: Oxford Univ. Press, 1991) 112–13, 167. With that kind of mortality rate, the dangers of giving birth would be uppermost on any woman's mind.

[15] Shields writes,

Perhaps the gift he offered her was one he had no right offer except when instructed by YHWH. In this case, the reference to YHWH's hiding knowledge from Elisha (and Elisha's preliminary failure as well) could be YHWH's judgment on the prophet's hubris, which the woman sensed in some way when she resisted the gift. (65-66)

This is not the first time that Elisha has abused his power as a man of God in relation to children. In 2 Kings 2:23–24 he curses in the name of YHWH a group of children who mock him. On account of his curse, forty-two children are mangled by bears. As Wesley Bergen remarks, "[T]here is no doubt as to his power. The question is rather of the source of the power, the use to which it is put, and its dispersal after his death. . . . The transfer of power from God to Elisha alters the reader's perception of the power, for once it has lost its connection to the divine it loses credibility" (*Elisha and the End of Prophetism* [JSOTSup 286; Sheffield: Sheffield Academic Press, 1999]).

[16] "[T]o be barren is not just to be without child but to be unalterable, unable to change from the state of without child to with child: barrenness is absolute because it means 'unalterable' except by the most radical means, unalterable except by divine intervention. . . . God in changing the body from barren to fertile is not simply changing it from being unpregnant to pregnant but changing it from being 'unchangeable' to both changed and pregnant" (Scarry, 194).

an Imagination far greater than that of the man of God. He was a gift who deserved more love and care and attention than even she could possibly give him.

Everyday with her son was a gift. He taught her things she had never known. She had never known she could love so much. She had never known how differently the world looks through the eyes of a child. She had never known such fear, such delight, such hope.

And until today she had never known such pain or such rage.

The servant had brought her son to her this morning from the fields where he had been helping his father. The child, clearly in terrible pain, was complaining about his head. She had held him all morning, trying to comfort him as best she could, applying cool cloths and caressing his forehead. She had no idea what was wrong and she had never felt so helpless in all her life. At midday he died in her arms.

At first, her pain was almost paralyzing. She sat there unable to breathe, unable to move. She looked at her lifeless son there in her lap and she remembered the words of the man of God, "This time next year you will be holding a son in your arms." Suddenly she was so angry she could hardly see. She made her way with the boy up to the room she had prepared for the man of God, the room designed to sustain and protect and provide comfort. She laid her son on the bed and closed the door.

She sent a message to her husband, telling him to send a servant and donkey, telling him that she was going to find the man of God. She said nothing to him about the boy.

"Why are you going to see the man of God today?" her husband had demanded to know. "It is neither New Moon nor Sabbath."

"Shalom. Good-bye" was her curt response.[17]

---

[17] Her response, "shalom," is loaded, as is evidenced by the various ways it has been translated and interpreted: "peace," "good-bye," "it will be well," "it is well." This response and the interchange with Gehazi that follows, in which she repeats "shalom" in response to all his questions, is parallel to a similar interchange in the Jehu story (2 Kings 9:15–28). In that story, as Jehu rides madly toward Jezreel to seize the throne, he is repeatedly asked, "Is it peace?" Clearly, peace is the last thing on Jehu's mind. So, too, for the Shunammite woman: Her mission is not one of "peace" toward the man of God. She is anything but at "peace." (A further irony implicit in this intertextual connection is that it is Elisha's abuse of power that is responsible for both moments of chaos.)

On the other hand, the response "peace" allows the Shunammite woman both to follow and to break through the protocol that separates her from the man of God. One might also see here a comparison with Abraham's response to Isaac in Genesis 22. When Isaac asks, "Where is the lamb for the burnt offering?" Abraham's response is "God will provide." On this passage Derrida (in dialogue with

She saddled the donkey herself.[18] The servant was too slow. She set out at such a pace, the servant could hardly keep up.

"This time next year you will be holding a son in your arms." The prophet's words echoed in her head, crescendoing into a scream. The promise had become a cruel joke. The arrogant attempt to "fulfill" her and to repay her had become a wound that throbbed with every breath she took.

"How could you know," she asked the absent man of God, "what it means to hold a son in your arms? How could you possibly know what this entails?"

She prodded the donkey again. "Children are such fragile gifts. How could you possibly know what it means to hold in your arms such a fragile gift and to know that your arms cannot ultimately protect it?"

She thought of all the children she had known who had not lived to see adulthood. She thought of their parents. She thought of a story she had heard once about Abraham and Sarah and Isaac, the child of promise. Abraham and Sarah had waited so long for Isaac, they had almost given up hope. But finally he came, a gift from God. Then one day Abraham began to hear voices, the voice of God he believed, demanding Isaac back. Abraham was willing to let his son die. How could that be, the woman wondered incredulously. Sarah would surely not have been so willing. How could anyone receive such a gift and not be willing to take care of him, to fight for him, to ensure that he lived no matter what the cost?[19]

Kierkegaard) explains, "Abraham thus keeps his secret at the same time as he replies to Isaac. . . . He speaks in order not to say anything about the essential thing that he must keep secret. . . . He says something that is not a non-truth, something moreover that, although he doesn't know it yet, will turn out to be true" (*The Gift of Death*, 59). The Shunammite woman uses "peace" when formality requires that she speak, and although she doesn't know it yet, "peace" will be the outcome of her passionate determination.

[18] Despite the attempts of some translations to make use of the servant's presence (e.g., NJPS: "she had the ass saddled"; NEB: "When the ass was saddled"), the text clearly says that she saddles ("binds" or "bridles") the donkey herself. Rather than understanding this to indicate her urgency, John Gray assumes this indicates her size: "The 'great lady' of Shunem personally harnesses the ass. She is a substantial peasant" (498).

[19] Derrida, too, wonders what might have happened if Sarah had been included in this story:

It is difficult not to be struck by the absence of woman. . . . It is the story of father and son, of masculine figures, of hierarchies among men (God the father, Abraham, Isaac; the woman, Sarah, is she to whom nothing is said . . .). Would the logic of sacrificial responsibility within the implacable universality of the law, of its law, be altered, inflected, attenuated, or displaced, if a woman were to intervene in some consequential manner? Does the system of this sacrificial responsibility of the double "gift of death" imply at its very basis an exclusion or sacrifice of woman? A woman's sacri-

She could see Mt. Carmel. She thought again of Mt. Moriah, of Abraham keeping his secret about what he was going to do. Abraham had to keep the secret. Otherwise, someone would have stopped him. Anyone would have thought he was crazy, trying to sacrifice his son.[20] (And he had to have been, as far as she was concerned.) She, too, was keeping a secret for much the same reason. How could she explain what she was doing? Who would possibly understand? If she were to speak the truth, she would surely be deterred from her mission.[21] No one was going to tell her she was

---

fice or a sacrifice of woman, according to one sense of the genitive or the other? Let us leave the question in suspense. (*The Gift of Death*, 76)

Later, Derrida quotes Hegel's identification of woman as "the eternal irony of the community." One might say that the story of the Shunammite woman is a case in which "the logic of sacrificial responsibility" is clearly "altered," perhaps even "displaced." Her action on behalf of her son renders ironic the traditional honoring of Abraham's repeated willingness to sacrifice members of his family.

[20] Derrida writes of Abraham's secret in Genesis 22:

Kierkegaard reflects on this double secret: that between God and Abraham but also that between the latter and his family. Abraham doesn't speak of what God has ordered him alone to do, he doesn't speak of it to Sarah, or to Eliezer, or to Isaac. He must keep the secret (that is his duty), but it is also a secret that he *must* keep as a double necessity because in the end he *can only* keep it: he doesn't know it, he is unaware of its ultimate rhyme and reason. He is sworn to secrecy because he is in secret.

Because, in this way, he doesn't speak, Abraham transgresses the ethical order. According to Kierkegaard, the highest expression of the ethical is in terms of what binds us to our own and to our fellows (that can be the family but also the actual community of friends or the nation). By keeping the secret, Abraham betrays ethics. His silence, or at least the fact that he doesn't divulge the secret of the sacrifice he has been asked to make, is certainly not designed to save Isaac. (Ibid., 59)

By contrast, the Shunammite's secret betrays rationality. She has ethical expectations beyond what is normally considered to be reasonable. And her silence is most certainly designed to save her son.

[21] Derrida writes,

To the extent that, in not saying the essential thing, namely, the secret between God and him, Abraham doesn't speak, he assumes the responsibility that consists in always being alone, entrenched in one's own singularity at the moment of decision. . . . But as soon as one speaks, as soon as one enters the medium of language, one loses that very singularity. One therefore loses the possibility of deciding or the right to decide. Thus every decision would, fundamentally, remain at the same time solitary, secret, and silent. Speaking relieves us, Kierkegaard notes, for it "translates" into the general. . . .

The first effect or first destination of language therefore involves depriving me of, or delivering me from, my singularity. By suspending my absolute singularity in speaking, I renounce at the same time my liberty and my responsibility. Once I speak I am never and no longer myself, alone and unique. It is a very strange contract—both paradoxical and terrifying—that binds infinite responsibility to silence and secrecy. (Ibid., 59–60)

crazy for thinking she might save a child who was already dead. In spite of the shared secrecy, however, she was no Abraham. She would not give up such a gift so easily.[22]

She saw a figure coming to meet her. It was the man of God's servant. He greeted her. "My master saw you in the distance. He sent me to ask you, 'Are you well?'"

"Shalom. I'm fine," she said, not slowing her pace. She was not about to disclose her secret to some surrogate.

"Is your husband well?" he asked, stepping in the donkey's path.

"Shalom. He's fine," she said, reining the animal around him.

"Is the boy well?" he persisted.

"Shalom. He's fine. Now get out of my way!" Prophetic protocol be damned! she thought.

The woman continued the relentless pace until she came to the man of God. She dismounted, ran to him, and clutched his feet. His servant who, by that time, had caught up with her, tried to push her away, but she was immovable.

"Let her alone," said the man of God. "Can't you see how upset she is?[23] Something is wrong and God has hidden it from me."[24]

Yes, the woman thought bitterly, God has hidden a lot of things from

---

[22] The figure of the Shunammite woman represents the way in which Kierkegaard's apology for Abraham's responsibility to the Wholly Other has been countered by Levinas. Derrida points out the implication of Kierkegaard's argument: ". . . God, as the wholly other, is to be found everywhere there is something of the wholly other" and cites Levinas's counter-reading (Ibid., 78 n. 6):

> In invoking Abraham [Kierkegaard] describes the meeting with God as occurring where subjectivity is raised to the level of the religious, that is to say above ethics. But one can posit the contrary: the attention Abraham pays to the voice that brings him back to the ethical order by forbidding him to carry out the human sacrifice, is the most intense moment of the drama. . . . It is there, in the ethical, that there is an appeal to the uniqueness of the subject and sense is given to life in defiance of death. (Levinas, *Noms propres,* 113)

(On this reading of Genesis 22, cf. Danna Nolan Fewell and David M. Gunn, "Keeping the Promise" in *Gender, Power, and Promise: The Subject of the Bible's First Story* [Nashville: Abingdon, 1993] 39–55, esp. 52–55.) The Shunamite woman, in contrast to Abraham, is moved by the wholly otherness of her son and demands "life in defiance of death."

[23] Literally, "her soul is bitter to her."

[24] The woman's secret is hidden from the man of God who, by virtue of who he is, should be privy to knowledge of God. But the man of God cannot graciously accept a gift—how can he be trusted with a secret? As in the case of the gift, the man of God has, in the language of Levinas, failed "to identify the particular interhuman events that open towards transcendence and reveal the traces where God has passed" ("Dialogue with Emmanuel Levinas," Emmanuel Levinas and Richard

you. If you had been present to the child you so glibly pronounced into being, you would know much more than you know now. She found her
voice.

"Did I ask you for a son? Did I not say to you, 'Don't treat me thoughtlessly?'"

The man of God could not sustain her glare. He turned to his servant.

"Here. Take my staff.[25] Hurry to the boy. Don't stop for anything. Place
my staff on the face of the boy."

The servant hurried away, but the woman refused to let go of the man.

"Don't think for one minute that a substitute will do," she said. "You
brought this boy into the world. You are responsible for his well-being.[26] I

Kearney, in *Face-to-Face with Levinas* [ed. Richard Cohen; New York: State Univ. of
New York Press, 1986] 32).

Derrida writes,

> [God] is made manifest, he manifests his nonmanifestation when, in the structures of
> the living or the entity, there appears in the course of phylo- and ontogenetic history,
> the possibility of secrecy, however differentiated, complex, plural, and overdeter-
> mined it be; that is, when there appears the desire and power to render absolutely in-
> visible and to constitute within oneself a witness of that invisibility. That is the
> history of God and of the name of God as the history of secrecy, a history that is at the
> same time secret and without any secrets. (*The Gift of Death*, 109)

To return to the issue of the woman's namelessness, or as we might at this point say,
secret identity, we have here an invitation to view differently the woman's anonymity. The secrecy that surrounds her reveals "traces where God has passed."

[25] Fokkelien van Dijk-Hemmes has noticed the phallic significance of the staff
("The Great Woman of Shunem and the Man of God: A Dual Interpretation of 2
Kings 4:8–37," in *A Feminist Companion to Samuel and Kings* [ed. Athalya Brenner;
Sheffield: Sheffield Academic Press, 1994] 218–230; 227). The man of God, as far as
the symbolism of the narrative is concerned, is the "father" of the child. The (impotent) phallus-like staff meant to bring the child back to life, is the male counterpart to
the womb-like room provided by the woman. The balance of the created and creative
artifacts suggests that the woman has helped/is helping to create/construct the man
of God in a way that is parallel to the man of God's bringing the child into being.

[26] Consider Levinas's thoughts on paternity:

> The fact of seeing the possibilities of the other as your own possibilities, of being able
> to escape the closure of your identity and what is bestowed on you, toward some-
> thing which is not bestowed on you and which nevertheless is yours—this is pater-
> nity. This future beyond my own being, this dimension constitutive of time, takes on
> a concrete content in paternity. It is not necessary that those who have no children see
> in this fact any depreciation whatever; biological filiality is only the first shape
> filiality takes; but one can very well conceive filiality as a relationship between hu-
> man beings without the tie of biological kinship. One can have a paternal attitude
> with regard to the Other. To consider the Other as a son is precisely to establish with
> him those relations I call "beyond the possible." (*Ethics and Infinity* [Pittsburgh:
> Duquesne Univ. Press, 1985] 70–71)

The Shunammite woman is urging the man of God to establish with her son relations "beyond the possible."

swear by God and by your very life, I am not leaving here without you!"[27]

There was nothing the man of God could say. He followed her back in silence. On the way they met his servant returning.

"I did as you said," he reported. "The boy will not wake up."

When the man of God arrived he went upstairs into the room where the boy was lying and he closed the door, leaving the servant to stand as sentry. The woman could hear the muffled tones of the man of God's prayer.

"It will take more than prayer," she said, even though he could not hear. "It's not like speaking to the king in exchange for a room. It takes more than prayer to make a child live and grow. It takes your presence and your proximity.[28] And sometimes—" she felt the ache of watching her child die in her arms—"sometimes, even that is not enough."

She heard other noises through the door—the creaking of the bed, footsteps pacing back and forth. She peered through a crack in the boards of the door. She saw the man of God lying on top of her son, trying to warm his lifeless body. Face to face, hand to hand, the man of God breathed into his mouth again and again. After some time—she had almost given up hope—she heard the boy exhale and gasp for breath again. The door opened.

"Call the Shunammite," the man of God was saying as she pushed past him to reach her son. His eyes were open. He was alive. She put her cheek against his, feeling his breath against her ear, feeling as though she, too, had just come back to life.

"Pick up your son," said the man of God.

She bowed in gratitude and relief that her persistence had not been in vain, that the man of God had indeed been capable of doing what needed

---

[27] Concerning this interchange Fokkelien van Dijk-Hemmes observes:

Only after the woman says to him (v. 30) the words he himself has spoken three times to Elijah (2 Kings 2:2, 4, 6), "As YHWH lives, and as your soul lives, I will not leave you," does Elisha recall his vocation, recognize that he cannot shake off his responsibilities any longer, and follow her. . . . Thanks to the persistence and actions of the "Great Woman," Elisha proves to be a man of God and the child is brought back to life. (229)

[28] In describing "proximity" Levinas says,

The tie with the Other is knotted only as responsibility, this moreover, whether accepted or refused, whether knowing or not knowing how to assume it, whether able or unable to do something concrete for the Other. To say: here I am [*me voici*: the French translation of the Hebrew *hineni*, an allusion to Genesis 22 and Isaiah 6]. To do something for the Other. To give. To be human spirit, that's it. The incarnation of human subjectivity guarantees its spirituality. . . . I analyze the inter-human relationship as if, in proximity with the Other—beyond the image I myself make of the other man (sic)—his face, the expressive in the Other (and the whole human body is in this sense more or less face), were what ordains me to serve him. . . . The face orders and ordains me. (*Ethics and Infinity*, 97)

to be done, that her son had been returned to life, to her. She picked up her son, holding him in her arms gently yet tightly—as if he were the most precious, fragile gift in the world—and she took him away to care for him, leaving the man of God standing there, alone, in the room she had built for him to stay in whenever he passed through.[29]

---

[29] Bergen narrates:

> She then takes her son and removes herself from the sphere of his power (v. 37). In the end, we are left with a picture of a prophet whose claim to power/status arises from his ability to do unnecessary miracles. It is only the supervision of the powerful which constrains him to be responsible for his activities, and to clean up the mess he has created. (p.n. not available)

However, not only does she take the initiative to remove herself from his presence (and power), but she leaves him in the material space that she herself created. Despite his attempts to erase her initial gift through reciprocity, even over-payment, he is, in the end, physically surrounded by and forced to bear witness to her ability to alter the world for him.

Chapter 9

Contextual Theologies in the Old Testament?

Erhard S. Gerstenberger
Philipps-Universität, Marburg

One Fixed Point in Exegesis

It is a commonplace in historical-critical research: Texts are rooted in specific situations, they are conditioned by contemporary values and outlooks, and every possible sort of interpretation likewise bears the stamp of
the interpreter's context. Lip-service to historical change and conditioning,
however, in much of Western theology seems to be paired with unflinching
convictions to be able, in biblical studies, to catch glimpses of the un-
changeability of God. The warnings of Exod 19:21–25; 33:18–20; Deuteronomy 4 and other passages, which imply the incompatibility of Holy and
Profane, are little heeded. In effect, most historical-critical scholars to this
day neatly split their attention into opposing directions. They admit out-
ward or formal historical changes of texts, ideas, and institutions which,
however, leave intact or do not impair an eternal nucleus of substance and
meaning. Or, more directly, for example: Concepts of God in the Scriptures
may vary, but the very core of all theological discourse, the "One God" remains "the Same" forever and ever. Israel, the people of one, exclusive
God, and her institutions are unique and incomparable to any other human group. The land of God and the place of his dwelling are sacrosanct,
escaping historical relativity. Some such Archimedean point seems to loom
large behind much of alleged Old Testament historical criticism. Burke
Long, friend from olden days at Yale Divinity School, has brought among
other items these facts to our attention, principally in his sensitive scrutiny
of William Albright's work and in his own exegetical research as well.[1]

---

[1] Burke O. Long, *Planting and Reaping Albright* (University Park, Pa.: Pennsylvania State Univ. Press, 1997): The underlying rationale of bringing together Old
Testament scholars in an influential, normative "Biblical Colloquium" under Al-

It is my intention here to reflect briefly on some aspects and scholars of the German scene, supposedly, at least in the eyes of W. F. Albright and his pupils, so critical in regard to historical facts and so negligent of the "eternal" values of the Bible. Looking at Albrecht Alt, Martin Noth and others, or, for that matter, at some more recent scholars like Werner H. Schmidt, Frank Crüsemann, and Rainer Albertz, one has to ask whether they really mean it when they speak of historical changes and contextuality, social-historical criticism and gender-specific visions of the biblical world. Careful reading of modern OT-exegetical or theological works reveals an astounding degree of very traditional, almost dogmatic lines of thinking when it comes down to some incomparable "essentials" of faith. Contextuality, with all its relativity, quickly vanishes. Almost every one of the large group of historical critics in Europe (including some of the most radical disbelievers?) professes deep allegiance to some underlying, basic, and unchangeable truth to be heeded rather than to be questioned. The oneness and exclusiveness of God is only one example. Concomitantly, the claim is made that fundamental insights into the nature of God, world, and mankind can in fact be copied directly from the Bible, without needing transformatory reflection and re-adaptation because of changing times and circumstances. Basic biblical affirmations are declared or assumed to be exempt from otherwise all-encompassing laws of time and space, cultural diversity and historical change. They simply must not wither or yield to any modifications. If these positions really are behind most of German and European criticism since the eighteenth century, then perhaps the fear of Albright and his pupils with respect to the supposed destructive historians on the continent was entirely unfounded. After this review I want to reflect a little bit on the dimensions and implications of contextuality in biblical studies.

Fathers and Sons in German Old Testament Research

To exemplify my point I offer a few concrete considerations on particular works and ideas of prominent OT historians and theologians.

Albrecht Alt (1883–1956) and one of his most famous pupils, Martin Noth (1902–1968), were both first-class historians, brought up in the true tradition of historical criticism. They certainly knew how to read ancient

---

bright's leadership certainly included the search for and the defense of a uniform Biblical Truth; cf. 78–98 and passim. Cf. also B. O. Long, "Ambitions of Dissent: Biblical Theology in a Postmodern Future," *JR* 76 (1996) 276–289: "For theologians, this meant that despite disclaimers and qualifications, precise descriptions of biblical concepts pointed to essential verities of God visible in and through, but different from, the historical circumstances of biblical writers and even postbiblical scholar-theologians themselves" (276). See also especially his studies in anthropological topics and situations as manifest in Old Testament literature.

documents in their contexts. They proposed new, inspiring hypotheses about the early history of Israel, the formation of the tribes, and the emergence of statehood, on the basis of or in closest contact with ancient Near Eastern and Egyptian history as well as within the horizons of intercultural comparison. Indeed, their historical research opened up new horizons for Old Testament research and related fields of study. Notions of historical change and historical development, of documentary facticity or authenticity, and legendary tradition history were deeply ingrained in these scholars and informed their work, and no small merit is due them for having forged and sharpened the historical and linguistic tools of biblical research. How is it possible that these great scholars, seemingly against their better knowledge, tried to pinpoint areas or aspects of Israelite faith and life that were purportedly exempt from the rules of transitoriness in thinking and theology?

Albrecht Alt, in his famous study *Der Gott der Väter* (1929), presupposed that Israel became a political unit only because of her faith in Yahweh, and tried to look beyond that crucial event of covenant-making into the prehistory of Yahwism.[2] What he discovered has stimulated the discussion of Israel's religious history ever since. There is, he claimed, a clearly visible pre-stage of that normative faith in Israel's God, namely the religion of the Fathers(!),[3] that pertained to the wandering clan-groups of pre-Israelites. Interestingly, Alt's main concern was not with the *different* type of religion he had elaborated, but primarily with the compatibility of clan and tribal religion with subsequent national faith. The God who appeared to Abraham, Isaac, and Jacob, in his opinion, by his activity in the realm of personality and history (in contrast to nature-oriented divinities of Canaan) mustered a great affinity in regard to Yahweh, thus preparing the way for the superior and unique God of the Covenant.[4] Consequently, historians of

---

[2] Albrecht Alt, *Der Gott der Väter; ein Beitrag zur Vorgeschichte der israelitischen Religion* (BWANT 3/12; Stuttgart: W. Kohlhammer, 1929). Reprinted in idem, *Kleine Schriften zur Geschichte des Volkes Israels* (München: C. H. Beck, 1953) 1.1–78.

[3] Feminist exegetes point with good reason to the patriarchal attitude of modern OT scholars who tend to ignore the fact that the Genesis stories of the "fathers" in reality talk about couples who master their lives in unknown and hostile territories, cf. Irmtraud Fischer, *Die Erzeltern Israels: feministisch-theologische Studien zu Genesis 12–36* (BZAW 222, Berlin/New York: de Gruyter, 1994).

[4] Cf. Albrecht Alt, *Kleine Schriften*, 1.62–63: "If the religion of the Fathers, as we suppose, has been an ancient heritage of Israel's tribes, then we may take it as that sought-for historical model [of Yahwism—Translator] . . . in the sense that it demonstrates in action the same fundamental relationship between God and humans which afterwards—when Yahwism subjugated to itself the whole nation—became dominant. . . . The Gods of the Fathers were the 'educators' [orig. παιδαγωγοι— Translator] preparing the way for the greater God, who later on completely took their place" (63; my translation).

religion recognize developments in time (they cannot help it, since biblical texts give the story), but they are eager to arrive at a definitive stage, when faith-history ceases, giving way to permanent concepts of the one, exclusive deity for all days to come.

This same theological perspective is behind Alt's effort to secure a bit more of the unchanging world. In 1934 he published his essay, still debated today, on "Die Ursprünge des israelitischen Rechts." The main point for our purposes is this: Alt maintains a double rootage of social and ethical norms in the Old Testament, and one would have to dig up the roots of this dichotomy more carefully than has been done in scholarship.[5] One part of Israel's behavioral orientation simply comes from "Canaanite," i.e. environmental, sources. The so-called "casuistic law" is secular in character and reveals a deep concern for settling social problems by judicial processes in a case-oriented, democratic way. Quite different is what Alt called the "apodictic" law. This "law" is formulated in various ways, predominantly in absolute interdictions: "Thou shalt not . . . ." He considered this type of law to be totally unconditioned by any historical factors (that is, immune to and incompatible with its social and cultural context), divine, everlasting, universal (but not according to human determinants).[6] The well-known quotation is: The apodictic series of norms "do not show the minimum trace of Canaanite origin. . . . Everything in them, on the contrary, is tied to the Israelite people and to their faith in Yahweh."[7] Considering the work of Albrecht Alt, it is here that his deepest ambition to break away from historical analysis and changing affirmations about God comes to the fore.

In the same vein Martin Noth, author of the epochal *Geschichte Israels* and many other historical and exegetical works, takes into account the

---

[5] Is it Luther's doctrine of the Two Kingdoms which inspires the exegete? Notably, there are other theories of origins in regard to biblical law, e.g., Alfred Jepsen, *Untersuchungen zum Bundesbuch* (BWANT 3/41; Stuttgart: Kohlhammer, 1927); Ludger Schwienhorst-Schönberger, *Das Bundesbuch: (Ex 20,22–23,33): Studien zu seiner Entstehung und Theologie* (BZAW 188; Berlin/New York: de Gruyter, 1990).

[6] The very term "apodictic" is alien to legal thinking; it does have its setting in philosophical discourse, denoting an *a priori* state of affairs which may not be questioned; cf. Erhard S. Gerstenberger, "'Apodiktisches' Recht? 'Todes' Recht?" in *Gottes Recht als Lebensraum: Festschrift für Hans Jochen Boecker* (ed. Peter Mommer et al.; Neukirchen-Vluyn: Neukirchener Verlag, 1993) 7–20; idem, "Life-Preserving Divine Threats in Old Testament Law," *Ex Auditu* 11 (1995) 43–61.

[7] Albrecht Alt, *Kleine Schriften*, 1.323. Unfortunately, the ideas of propinquity to the people and of relentless, unmitigated criminal law were rampant at the time of growing Nazism in Germany. There was a hot debate going on over judicial law reforms in regard to greater or lesser stringency and individual evaluation of criminal cases, denounced as un-German leniency by right-wing lawyers. Albrecht Alt's designation of "apodictic" law must be seen against this background; cf. Erhard S. Gerstenberger, "'Todes' Recht."

whole breadth of ancient Near Eastern history. He is a great critic of the historical trustworthiness of biblical records. Much-debated was his thesis that, historically speaking, the man Moses could hardly be recovered from texts, molded by tradition, that hand down fanciful tales about their hero and contain very little authentic information. The history of Israel, according to Noth, was a normal history like that of any other people, ancient or modern. Only at certain points does the student of Israelite history encounter phenomena "which are simply incomparable, not because materials for comparative purposes have been lacking so far, but because—according to all we know—such things do not happen at all in the normal history of nations."[8] Specifically, Noth discovered that the absolute uniqueness of Israel was embedded in her tribal alliance (which still had some remote affinity to Greek city leagues, the so-called "amphictyonies"), the office of a covenant-speaker, the ritual patterns of yearly covenant festivals, and, of course, in the quality of Israelite law, which in itself represented and promoted Yahweh's and Israel's complete and radical exclusiveness.[9]

The younger generation of Old Testament scholars in Germany by and large follows the patterns laid out by the post-war "Fathers" in the field. Werner H. Schmidt in his influential textbook *Alttestamentlicher Glaube in seiner Geschichte* adduces overwhelming evidence for historical, so-to-speak "syncretistic"[10] developments in Israelite conceptions of Yahweh. The God of Israel, through the various phases of social and faith history, integrated within himself characteristics of ancient Near Eastern deities, e.g. El, Baal, Hadad, Mot, and who knows, even Ishtar and Asherah. Schmidt does rely on an almost infinite, absorbent capacity of Israelite theological reflection. But there is a quasi-miraculous dimension to this process of theological development: Deep inside, God stays the same. Accretions and modifications of theological concepts do not touch the very essence of Yahweh and the truth of fundamental formulations of faith, such as "I am Yahweh, and there is no other; besides me there is no god" (Isa 45:5). The

---

[8] Martin Noth, *Geschichte Israels* (2d ed.; Göttingen: Vandenhoeck & Ruprecht, 1954) 11; my translation.

[9] Cf. Martin Noth, "Die Gesetze im Pentateuch" (1940), in *Gesammelte Studien zum Alten Testament* (3rd ed.; München: Chr. Kaiser, 1966), esp. 70–81: "The particularity [of Israelite law—Translator] may be subsumed under one heading: that of an exclusive relationship between God and people . . ." (70). All the more astonishing is the fact that Noth supervised and accepted this author's doctoral dissertation, though it was very critical of him (*Wesen und Herkunft des 'apodiktischen' Rechts* [WMANT 20; Neukirchen-Vluyn: Neukirchener Verlag, 1965]).

[10] "Syncretism" is still a very bad word in German biblical studies. To hear it being used positively almost made some German theologians leave the lecture hall; this still happened within the last decade of the twentieth century, as I am able to testify.

oneness, sameness, uniqueness, exclusiveness of Israel's God makes him superior to all powers there are and exempt from all historical changes, in spite of seeming incursions or shaping by alien concepts of the divine.[11] He argues that the first and second commandments of the Decalogue cannot be derived from Israel's cultural environment. "Exclusiveness of confession to one God does pertain to Israel alone." He further argues that "perhaps faith in a God of the Fathers, who revealed himself alone . . . already constituted a certain model for a unique and aniconic veneration of a deity . . . In any case, the faith of the fathers . . . does full justice to the first commandment. This commandment in essence already determined the relation to God in a period, when it had not yet been known verbatim."[12]

Similarly, Frank Crüsemann pursues the idea of oneness and exclusiveness. He exhaustively unfolds the history of Israelite law, giving due consideration to changing social and historical conditions. The Covenant Code (Exod 20:22–23:33) reflects the conditions of late eighth-century BC Judah after the disappearance of the northern kingdom. Deuteronomy is an offspring of all-too-late efforts on the part of Yahweh-oriented rural nobility (עם הארץ) to steer away from national apostasy (cf. the revolt against Amon, 2 Kgs 21:23), and the Priestly writings clearly go to the emerging communities during and after the exile. A host of valuable details is piled up in the discussion of these law-collections. Crüsemann, a qualified social-historian among biblical exegetes, has his eyes on social and political structures and movements. The wealth of his observations must not obscure, however, that he is seeking the one and unchangeable theological grounds from the beginning of his study. Instead of choosing a diachronic method, advancing from more indefinite beginnings to the final form of Israelite law, the Torah, he inverts historical research, postulating Torah as the ultimate goal, recognizable already at each preliminary stage of law-promulgation. He argues that "the question is Israel's pilgrimage towards Torah."[13] He adds that "the real issue of Torah is how the exclusive God and Creator of all humankind communicates his singular intentions to one particular people, namely his people of Israel" (10). He starts from the unity of an unchangeable will of that unmistakable "One and the Same God," everlasting, as if the concepts of oneness, sameness, everlastingness

---

[11] Cf. Werner H. Schmidt, "The Characteristics of Faith in Yahweh," §6 in *Alttestamentlicher Glaube in seiner Geschichte* (1st ed. 1968; 6th ed.; Neukirchen-Vluyn: Neukirchener Verlag, 1987) 63–114; Engl. trans. *The Faith of the Old Testament: A History* (trans. John Sturdy; Philadelphia: Westminster, 1983).

[12] Werner H. Schmidt, *Glaube*, 84.

[13] Frank Crüsemann, *Die Tora: Theologie und Sozialgeschichte des alttestamentlichen Gesetzes* (München: Chr. Kaiser, 1992) 7; my translation. For the volume in English, see *The Torah: Theology and Social History of Old Testament Law* (trans. Allan W. Mahnke; Minneapolis: Fortress, 1996).

were not part and parcel of our own transitory existence but fragments of eternity itself.

Rainer Albertz, for his part, follows suite, in line with those who strongly profess to adhere to historical-critical and social-historical orientations. On the surface, in one of his earlier works he even ventured a step further, speaking of different religions within Israel as conditioned by social structures.[14] These different types of faith, oriented, as it were, to the necessities of those social groups (family; village; tribe; nation; diaspora-communities, etc.) do not easily harmonize, but are in tension among themselves. They simply obey different interests, and, by necessity, collide in certain situations, e.g. whenever state and family loyalties are heading in opposing directions. So far, Albertz takes full account of contextuality of theological concepts. All of a sudden, however, Yahweh, the absolute God, appears in his *Religionsgeschichte*. At one time a Southern or Midianite mountain-deity, Yahweh liberates the captive Israelites in Egypt and becomes the exclusive God of the "liberated larger social unit."[15] From this point forward, faith in the exclusive, unique God of Israel becomes the hidden center of all religious history, down to our own days, submerging and surfacing again in the course of events. No longer do we find neutral descriptions of faith, cult, ethics, but only partisan judgments about those who adhere to or reject that God of Liberation. To be sure, according to biblical witnesses Albertz's diagnosis of Israelite/Judean history is quite often negative. State syncretism supersedes true Yahwism, family paganism turns into staunch orthodoxy, capable of saving Yahweh-faith through the bad years of monarchic apostasies. The exilic community is plagued by religious tensions and rifts, and the righteous are often the victims of the godless. In all these tumultuous developments the confession of Yahweh, the sole God and Liberator, remains the absolutely dependable red thread. Unity and oneness, exclusiveness and distinctions are placed against historical diversity and uncertainty.

Dimensions of Contextuality

What are we to learn from such an urgent search for a normative unity in the Scriptures? Obviously, the exegetical maxim "texts should be allowed to speak for themselves," often quoted of the Canon, can hardly make

---

[14] Cf. Rainer Albertz, *Persönliche Frömmigkeit und offizielle Religion* (Stuttgart: Calwer, 1979). The term he uses is "religionsinterner Pluralismus" (religious plurality within a given society; see also his *Religionsgeschichte Israels in alttestamentlicher Zeit* [2 vols. in one; Göttingen: Vandenhoeck & Ruprecht, 1992] 1.43; for the volume in English, see *A History of Israelite Religion in the Old Testament* [trans. John Bowden; Louisville, Ky.: Westminster/John Knox, 1994]).

[15] Idem, *Religionsgeschichte*, 1.68–104.

these texts responsible to offer, all by themselves, unified concepts or a red thread of meaning, unchangeable and steadfastly immutable through the ups and downs of history. The voices identifiable in the Scriptures are very diverse indeed. They interact with, modify and contradict each other, or they simply stand side by side with quite different outlooks on matters divine and mundane. The Canon as a whole simply does not offer itself as a systematic handbook of theology, much to the distress of modern theologians. On the contrary, as Ernst Käsemann put it many years ago: "The canon cannot be the basis for one unified church but for a plurality of confessions."[16] That means that we should first of all recognize the enormous theological diversity of this marvelous collection of testimonies to our God-talk instead of leveling out these invaluable distinctions (e.g. the many names and functions of God).[17] Unbiased readers of the Bible will quickly recognize the pluriform theological stratification of the Scriptures, while theologians and preachers, concerned—very legitimately so—with the present-day significance of the texts, will tend to condense all that diversity into one absolute affirmation, such as "there is only one God," or "the Supreme Being is eternally the same," or "God is pure Spirit, Love, Peace," etc. Theologically minded readers apparently are not discouraged by the fact that myriads of such statements are being considered the absolute cornerstones of all types of faith. They are not alerted to the problem by all the recognizable failures in the history of dogma to pinpoint absolute truth in very transient wording. They do not feel hampered or ashamed by their own limitations. They really and seriously believe in the unlikely possibility of expressing in limited human words what the unchanging reality could be like (oneness; sameness; eternity, etc.), disregarding the plain fact that we, as beings subject to time and space, do not have adequate means of knowing the absolute.[18] More precisely, they actually hold that such oneness and sameness is scientifically demonstrable within texts, historical events, and formulated ideas.

---

[16] Freely adapted from Ernst Käsemann's essay, "Begründet der neutestamentliche Kanon die Einheit der Kirche?" in *Exegetische Versuche und Besinnungen* (3rd ed.; Göttingen: Vandenhoeck & Ruprecht, 1964) 214–223, esp. 221: "The New Testament canon [because of its variable kerygmas, differing theological positions transcending the boundaries of the New Testament, and their at least partial incompatibility—Translator's addition from the preceding phrases] as it presents itself to the historian is the foundation for the plurality of confessional churches."

[17] Walter Brueggemann is, to my knowledge, the first to really acknowledge the diversity of witnesses in the Hebrew Canon; see his *Theology of the Old Testament: Testimony, Dispute, Advocacy* (Minneapolis: Fortress, 1997).

[18] There are a good number of Old Testament scholars who seem to pursue a more "neutral" and "objective" scientific path, looking soberly at the panoply of biblical theologies; cf. e.g. Niels Peter Lemche, "Kann von einer 'israelitischen Reli-

But, on the other hand, we have excellent reasons, even obligations, for trying to find firm orientations in this transient world. Everyone of us badly wants to stand on reliable ground when making decisions as to how to arrange our lives. There are too many opinions, creeds, and claims in the world; they all cannot possibly be correct and legitimate. Do we need, however, comprehensive, absolute bases, verifiable in a past which we are unable to reconstruct, anyway? Are universal affirmations about God the only legitimate answer to our need for certitude? Or is our desire for an ultimate anchorage of our selves in the one and everlasting God evidence of human insanity, preposterous self-delusion and exaggeration? The underlying motives for aspiring to the absolute may come out, unwillingly, whenever we formulate "absolute" truths about God in an exclusive way. Some people in ancient Israel appear to have fallen into this theological trap already, when describing the supreme, universal deity as being dedicated exclusively to one particular group, namely one's own. Christians all through their history have eagerly adopted this kind of thinking, refusing, as it were, access to God to everybody outside their own little sphere of interest. Naturally, this kind of insistence on having special and unique claims to be close to the Absolute, denouncing all other aspirants as non-elect and traitors, does produce strife and, in the long run, intransigence, hatred, and fanaticism, starting in Genesis 4 (Cain and Abel) and continuing through all so-called "holy" wars into the fanatic conflicts of our present days.

Still, we should ask what the legitimate shape of our search for certainty could be like. Acknowledging our own existence and thinking to be conditioned by time, space, history, culture, and all the opportunities and limitations established within this temporality, we should simply refrain from seeking ultimate, unchanging theological affirmations outside of our own time, society, and global conditioning. Inside our own times and experiences, however, and in dialogue with witnesses from the past, we need to look for the elusive presence of God. Our "Archimedean" point is hidden in present-day challenges and truths, and we can approach it only by intensive, ecumenical discussion. We can no longer afford "eternal" truisms, neither in politics nor in theology, because all alleged absolute truths have proven to be contextually conditioned and far from eternal. Within our own limited sphere of experience we should enter into debate for the right answers to burning questions, admitting different solutions by contempo-

gion' noch weiterhin die Rede sein?" in *Ein Gott allein?: JHWH-Verehrung und biblischer Monotheismus im Kontext der israelitischen und altorientalischen Religionsgeschichte* (ed. Walter Dietrich and Martin A. Klopfenstein; Freiburg, Schweiz: Universitätsverlag; Göttingen: Vandenhoeck & Ruprecht, 1994) 59–75.

rary people, groups, and religions. Plurality is the issue of our time, pluralism which has to procure survival of humankind. Absolutisms of any sort are detrimental for our present-day situation. The quest for the right definition of the one and exclusive God has to be abandoned, for the sake of the survival of this planet. But, within the limits of our time and space and within the limits of our small, globalized world, we must nevertheless look for valid orientation. This orientation cannot be expected to come from absolutist systems, be they political and economic, or spiritual and religious. Most urgent, for the occidental, Christian world, is recognition of its own limitations, precluding all kinds of hegemonies in this world. To construe a "One God-One World" pattern in pursuance of one's own desire for world domination is, frankly, anachronistic. All these constructions of past history, outmoded as they are, cannot be supported by historical facts. History as such is always pluriform and ambivalent, a *post-festum* construction, never a factual datum. It never simply is "there," but has to be imagined and built up from the viewer's vantage point. We should frankly admit, therefore, the hypothetical nature also of our affirmations about God. By necessity they are relative to absolute truth. And they remain relative, no matter how much eternal silicon we may pump into them.

Plural Theologies

What, then, really are "contextual theologies" in the Scriptures and in our times? We noted already, that the large collection of biblical texts does not lend itself to doctrinal systematization. Redactional processes in all parts of the canon, harmonizing as they were, never did smooth out the discrepancies of group-oriented and history-bound theological thinking. From our present vantage point of an occidental, pluralistic society we realize that biblical witnesses were indeed tied up in quite different modes of existence and thinking. Socially, we can easily determine ancient family and clan structures, village, town, and tribal organizations, parochial and diaspora setups, and all of these social groupings may have subdivisions and special modifications of standard models. The customs and norms reigning in each of these associations visibly influenced theological conceptualizations on their respective levels.[19] Thus, family and clan concerns and face-to-face life in more or less stable interrelationships is reflected in intimate, personal experiences with a family deity.[20] Clan, village, and city ex-

---

[19] Cf. Erhard S. Gerstenberger, "Gott in unserer Zeit," *Die Zeichen der Zeit* 52 (1998) 2–8.

[20] Cf. idem, *Yahweh, the Patriarch: Ancient Images of God and Feminist Theology* (trans. Frederick J. Gaiser; Minneapolis: Fortress, 1996); Karel van der Toorn, *Family Religion in Babylonia, Syria, and Israel: Continuity and Changes in the Forms of Religious Life* (Leiden/New York: Brill, 1996).

periences are characterized by lessening solidarity bonds and growing communal challenges. Therefore, the God of these widening, social organizations takes on qualities of common welfare and rule of law and order, and is seen as a provider of a more general welfare and protection. State religion, at least in monarchic times, becomes more authoritarian, centering on dynasty, royal administration, and firmly institutionalized temple service (controlled by the king), and fostering nationalistic overtones in theology. After the breakdown of the Judean monarchy in 597 BC, a full reconstruction of social and religious identity took place among the Israelites residing in Palestine or in the lands of their sojourn. The new and unheard-of situation challenged the community of Yahweh to rally around religious rites, traditions and values, to adopt a new identity as a purely religious congregation (as far as we know, a first confessional entity), and—in order to secure survival as an ethnic or semi-ethnic group—to practice seclusion from the surrounding nations. The uniqueness and exclusiveness of Yahweh was a necessary corollary to living conditions in an alien empire. To attribute to Israel's God supreme authority over all the rest of divine beings, to make him the sole Creator of heaven and earth and the only one to be able to right that confused and power-stricken world, was the astonishing reaction of Judeans to defeat, humiliation, deportation, and that arrogance of power so well attested in many national configurations. Yahweh became—he had not always been that way—the only and exclusive God for Israel under the pressures of foreign domination.

It would be too tiring and time-consuming to go into the details of Israel's pluralistic society that endured for more than six centuries in her ancient homeland. Suffice it to say that the theological study of social and cultural layers in the biblical period has barely begun. The influence of those times and cultures on images of Yahweh has certainly been underestimated so far. When interpreting the texts of the Bible we have to be aware of the specific contextual conditions under which they took shape and have been transmitted. No absolute affirmations about God or world are to be expected. Each single passage, beautiful and convincing as it may seem, has to be evaluated on the basis of its social and historical horizon. This is one distinct step of exegesis (Latin American interpreters teach us that it is not necessarily the first one), and must be complemented by a thorough analysis of our own time, social structures, prejudices and expectations. Knowing full well that neither ancient nor modern contexts may stand for the eternal, absolute state of affairs, a dialogue between witnesses of old and preachers of today, looking for reliable orientation within a turbulent world, must begin. Our goal must be to achieve truth and justice, as they are imperative now, in responsibility to God, in our restricted spheres of experience, i.e. in those contemporary networks of human existence in which we participate.

Such spheres of life and responsibility did vary over time, although some anthropological constants are readily discernible in the history of humankind. Changing social structures over the centuries include, most of all, the shape, size, and function of families in the larger societal organizations; the legitimations of statehood (change from monarchic to democratic constitutions); the rise of individualistic ideologies unheard of in antiquity; and the globalization of economies around the world on the basis of modern technical revolutions. Our world has grown immensely in comparison to biblical conceptions, and at the same time it has shrunk to atomistic individual existences and incredibly reduced geographic dimensions. In no way can we claim to speak for the whole universe, because our infinitely tiny planet may be just one among hundreds of millions of like celestial bodies carrying life or semblances of life. Do we really need to make cosmic affirmations about God in order to achieve certainty in our lives? Can we afford to do so? We cannot, I am sure. Our spatial limitations are obvious, and universal theological discourse can be speculative at best.

What might our theology be like, after all? It has to move to find answers for our lives and our survival, ranging from the individual and his or her rather autistic world to that global conglomeration of billions of people today constituting one coherent and conflicting mass of beings under a common destiny. The globalized economy and society requires solutions for survival perhaps more urgently than the many forlorn individuals searching for subsistence and happiness. An ecumenical theology is universal in its limitations to the present, limited world. Individual theology has to take account of all the individuals in existence. This, too, is a universal aspect, limited by present-day circumstances and outlooks. Theology in either realm occurs in that transitory space available to us. It ventures affirmations in regard to God, the ground of being, and the final destination, seeking to relate to the whole and unknown in which we find ourselves embedded. But theology, while being done in our time and space, cannot yet move out of the boundaries, and cannot march into transcendence to put up habitation there. Quite often it is exactly this that theologians pretend to do, however. Both Plato and Kant, and many other wise people, warned against human presumption in claiming to know ultimate reality.

Contextual theologies in the Bible and today, in consequence, refrain from making absolute statements on the basis of historical events, transmitted ideas, canonized texts. They take fully into account the "absolute" limitation of all human discourse, and the "absolute" certainty that everything on earth is subject to change, even concepts of the divine. Within their temporal and spatial restriction, however, contextual theologians seek truth and orientation for their respective environment and—together with an ecumenical fellowship—global ways of cooperation and survival. Justice, peace, and the preservation of creation are paramount objectives in this contextual strategy under the eyes of an "eternal" God, who, according to biblical witnesses, ever so often battled for the sake of oppressed, discriminated-against, and forlorn people.

Chapter 10

The Role of the Reader in Ugaritic Narrative

Edward L. Greenstein
Tel Aviv University

In the late 1950s and 1960s there emerged a trend within literary theory whose interest was focussed on the role of the reader in making textual meaning.[1] The emergent approaches, grouped under the names of reception theory, reader response criticism, and sometimes the phenomenological approach, were and have remained diverse. Reception theory examines the ways that texts have been read and understood, while reader response criticism lays emphasis on the ways that readers respond to and make sense of texts. The significance of the distinction between the approaches can be seen in the fact that the publisher Methuen, in its "New Accents" series of introductions to and surveys of literary theories and topics, published two separate volumes in order to present the two overall perspectives.[2] In biblical studies, there is a long and rich history of interpretation reaching back

---

This study is based on presentations I made to the Ugaritic Studies Group of the Society of Biblical Literature in 1984, 1992, and 1998.

[1] For the development of this approach and its diverse forms, see, e.g., Jane P. Tompkins, "An Introduction to Reader-Response Criticism," in *Reader-Response Criticism: From Formalism to Post-Structuralism* (ed. Jane P. Tompkins; Baltimore and London: Johns Hopkins Univ. Press, 1980) ix–xxvi; Vincent B. Leitch, *American Literary Criticism from the Thirties to the Eighties* (New York: Columbia Univ. Press, 1988) 211–37.

[2] Robert C. Holub, *Reception Theory: A Critical Introduction* (London and New York: Methuen, 1984); Elizabeth Freund, *The Return of the Reader: Reader-Response Criticism* (London and New York: Methuen, 1987). A classic theoretical presentation of the former is: Hans Robert Jauss, *Toward an Aesthetic of Reception* (trans. Timothy Bahti; Theory and History of Literature 2; Minneapolis: Univ. of Minnesota Press, 1982).

to the earliest post-biblical times[3] and even to the "inner-biblical exegesis" within the Hebrew Scriptures themselves.[4] The reception of the biblical text is a subject that can be, and has been, studied both broadly and deeply.[5] By contrast, the literature of ancient Ugarit, like most literature from the ancient Near East, has virtually no known history of reception.[6] One is, however, in a position to investigate the ways in which a reader of Ugaritic literature, like a reader of biblical literature, can and indeed must perform interpretive acts of various sorts in order to make sense of the texts. It will be the purpose of the present study to indicate and illustrate some of those readerly practices or strategies. I hope to show as well that a careful reading of Ugaritic narrative makes the same kinds of literary demands that reading biblical narrative does.

Within reader theory itself, there are two alternate emphases. Some reader response approaches lay stress on (what they perceive to be) the mechanisms by which the reader is controlled by a text to react to stylistic devices and interpret in certain directions.[7] Other reader-oriented approaches stress the initiative of readers to select and apply certain interpretive strategies by which they will make sense of texts.[8]

---

[3] See now James L. Kugel, *The Bible As It Was* (Cambridge, Mass.: Belknap Press of Harvard Univ. Press, 1997).

[4] See, e.g., Michael Fishbane, *Biblical Interpretation in Ancient Israel* (Oxford: Clarendon, 1985).

[5] For a discussion of diverse readings of a biblical text in relatively recent scholarship, see, e.g., Willem S. Forster, "Readings, Readers, and the Succession Narrative: An Essay on Reception," in *Beyond Form Criticism: Essays in Old Testament Literary Criticism* (ed. Paul R. House; Sources for Biblical and Theological Study; Winona Lake, Ind.: Eisenbrauns, 1992) 395–407.

[6] There are numerous points at which one can imagine an intertextual relationship between certain Ugaritic literary texts. There is far too little evidence to adopt the curious theory of Korpel that the similarities among the major literary texts reflect a common authorship; so Marjo C. A. Korpel, "Exegesis in the Work of Ilimilku of Ugarit," in *Intertextuality in Ugarit and Israel* (ed. Johannes C. de Moor; OTS 40; Leiden, Boston: Brill, 1998) 86–111, who admits that the textual corpus is very limited but proposes the above theory nonetheless. Among Korpel's arguments is to view what are generally taken to be poetic formulas as the "style" of a single poet.

[7] See, e.g., Wolfgang Iser, *The Implied Reader: Patterns of Communication in Prose Fiction from Bunyan to Beckett* (Baltimore and London: Johns Hopkins Univ. Press, 1974); *The Act of Reading: A Theory of Aesthetic Response* (Baltimore and London: Johns Hopkins Univ. Press, 1978); Michael Riffaterre, *Text Production* (trans. Terese Lyons; New York: Columbia Univ. Press, 1983), esp. 1–25; Norman N. Holland, *The Dynamics of Literary Response* (New York: Columbia Univ. Press, 1989).

[8] See, e.g., Stanley Fish, *Is There a Text in This Class? The Authority of Interpretive Communities* (Cambridge, Mass., and London: Harvard Univ. Press, 1980); Steven Mailloux, *Interpretive Conventions: The Reader in the Study of American Fiction*

Thanks to the precocious work of Menakhem Perry and Meir Sternberg, whose article, "The King Through Ironic Eyes: The Narrator's Devices in the Story of David and Bathsheba," appeared in Hebrew in 1968, biblical studies entered the realm of reader theory on the ground floor.[9] It is the tendency of Perry and Sternberg, and of Sternberg alone in his monumental book *The Poetics of Biblical Narrative*, as Burke Long, among others, has pointed out, to reify the moves the reader makes as little more than conventional responses to the structure and rhetoric of the biblical text.[10] It is possible nonetheless to speak of the interaction of reader and text such that one need not commit oneself either to a more text-based or to a more reader-based theory. One can speak of what the text "does" as a mirror image of what the reader does, allowing one's own reader to make any necessary rhetorical conversions from text to reader or reader to text along the way.[11]

In Ugaritic studies, there have been very few explicit treatments of Ugaritic texts from a readerly point of view.[12] There are, however, numerous interpretive comments on Ugaritic literature that, were they formulated more clearly with the role of the reader in mind, could appropriately be classified as reader response criticism. For the sake of illustration, let this simple example suffice. When King Pabuli of Udum seeks to get King Kirta of Ḫubur to lift the siege of Udum and retreat, he repeatedly offers him *šlmm šlmm*, "offerings of peace, offerings of peace."[13] On this redoubled language Gina Hens-Piazza remarks: "Repetitive rhetoric . . . connotes the semantic sense of surplus."[14] From a more readerly perspective one could say that the reader interprets the repetition to indicate the abun-

---

(Ithaca and London: Cornell Univ. Press, 1982); Peter J. Rabinowitz, *Before Reading: Narrative Conventions and the Politics of Interpretation* (Ithaca and London: Cornell Univ. Press, 1987). For a metacritical discussion, see, e.g., Robert M. Fowler, "Who is 'The Reader' in Reader Response Criticism?" in *Beyond Form Criticism* (n. 5, above) 376–94.

[9] Menakhem Perry and Meir Sternberg, ‏"המלך במבט אירוני: על תחבולותיו של המספר‎ ‏בסיפור דוד ובת-שבע ושתי הפלגות לתיאוריה של הפרוזה"‎, *Hasifrut* 1/2 (Summer 1968) 263–92; an English version appears in Meir Sternberg, *The Poetics of Biblical Narrative: Ideological Literature and the Drama of Reading* (Indiana Literary Biblical Series; Bloomington: Indiana Univ. Press, 1985) 186–229.

[10] Burke O. Long, "Some Difficulties in the New Poetics of Biblical Narrative," *Proceedings of the Tenth World Congress of Jewish Studies: Division A, The Bible and Its World* (Jerusalem: World Union of Jewish Studies, 1990) 59–66.

[11] Cf. Stanley Fish's remarks on the pedagogical value of continuing to ask what the text "does" even after one has ceased to posit the text's autonomy; Fish, *Is There a Text*, 21–22.

[12] Some notable exceptions will be cited below.

[13] CAT 1.14 v 39–40; vi 9–10; cf. iii 26–27.

[14] Gina Hens-Piazza, "Repetition and Rhetoric in Canaanite Epic: A Close Reading of KTU 1.14.III 2–49," *UF* 24 (1992) 103–12, at 107.

dant resources and/or largesse of Pabuli.[15] Alternatively, one could suggest that Pabuli's discourse reflects the pressure under which he is responding and the urgency of his appeal.

In the following pages I shall endeavor to delineate two general ways in which reader theory has been and can be applied in the reading of Ugaritic narrative poetry, pointing out several specific examples in brief and developing two or three examples in greater detail. It should be borne in mind throughout the discussion that my use of the term "reader" does not mean to imply that Ugaritic literature was quietly read rather than orally performed. On the other hand, it is worth reminding ourselves that the existing texts are scribal in character,[16] and that, although they contain a few directions to the reader,[17] there are, so far as I can recall, no addresses or asides to an audience, such as we find in some classical poetry[18] as well as in a number of biblical texts.[19]

---

[15] For this vocalization of the name, more commonly rendered "Pabil," compare the Hurrian name *Papuli* attested at Alalaḫ (AT 170: rev. 9): Donald J. Wiseman, *The Alalakh Tablets* (Occasional Publications of the British Institute of Archaeology at Ankara 2; London: The British Institute of Archaeology at Ankara, 1953) 144. The name is composed of *pap/ba/u* "mountain" and the familiar onomastic suffix *li/u*; see Frauke Gröndahl, *Die Personennamen der Texte aus Ugarit* (Studia Pohl 1; Rome: Pontifical Biblical Institute, 1967) 240, 243–44.

[16] See the cautions of Jack M. Sasson, "Literary Criticism, Folklore Scholarship, and Ugaritic Literature," in *Ugarit in Retrospect: Fifty Years of Ugarit and Ugaritic* (ed. Gordon D. Young; Winona Lake, Ind.: Eisenbrauns, 1981) 81–98.

[17] E.g., CAT 1.19 iv edge *whndt . ytb . lmspr*, "And here one returns to the story"; Simon B. Parker, "Aqhat," in *Ugaritic Narrative Poety* (ed. S. B. Parker; SBL Writings from the Ancient World; Atlanta: Scholars Press, 1997) 49–80, at 78; cf. CAT 1 v 42–43 (see, e.g., H. L. Ginsberg, in *ANET,* 134 n. 24); CAT 1.40.35 ("Now repeat the liturgy for puri[fication]"; N. Wyatt, *Religious Texts from Ugarit: The Words of Ilimilku and His Colleagues* [The Biblical Seminar 53; Sheffield: Sheffield Academic Press, 1998] 346).

[18] See, e.g., Richard P. Martin, *The Language of Heroes: Speech and Performance in the Iliad* (Ithaca and London: Cornell Univ. Press, 1989) 231–33; see more generally, e.g., Bruno Gentili, *Poetry and Its Public in Ancient Greece: From Homer to the Fifth Century* (trans. A. Thomas Cole; Baltimore and London: Johns Hopkins Univ. Press, 1988) 3–49; Rosalind Thomas, *Literacy and Orality in Ancient Greece* (Cambridge: Cambridge Univ. Press, 1992) 101–27.

[19] Not only do speakers frequently address an audience, the biblical prose narrator also occasionally "breaks frame"; see, e.g., Sternberg, *Poetics* (n. 9, above), 119–22; Frank Polak, *Biblical Narrative: Aspects of Art and Design* (2nd ed.; Biblical Encyclopaedia Library; Jerusalem: Mosad Bialik, 1999) 315–16 (Hebrew); Robert Polzin, *Moses and the Deuteronomist: A Literary Study of the Deuteronomic History, Part One* (New York: Seabury, 1980) 29–36. By contrast, Ugaritic narrators do not break frame; see Simon B. Parker, "The Literatures of Canaan, Ancient Israel, and Phoeni-

One broad category of reader theory deals with the drama of reading with respect to the emotional or non-cognitive effects of reading, or hearing, a text in the way it is constructed or presented. Readers are influenced by rhetorical devices and literary style and structure in ways that can shape meaning no less than, if not more than, plot and characterization. At times the affective aspects of a text may reinforce the themes conveyed by the semantics of a text; at times the affective and semantic sides of a text may be in tension with each other.[20]

Consider, for example, the episode in the Ugaritic epic of Aqhat in which we read, or hear, of the protagonist Danaʾil's search for the remains of his son, who we the audience know was slain by the goddess Anat and her human henchman (CAT 1.19 iii).[21] Danaʾil has learned from messengers that Aqhat is dead. He may already have deduced from the presence of vultures circling overhead that they have come to the scene in order to eat a carcass. Might it be the corpse of his son? With no carcass in sight, we must suppose,[22] Danaʾil surmises that he must seek Aqhat's remains in the bellies of the birds. The search is narrated in three stages. In each Danaʾil invokes the weather-god Baʿal to break the vultures' wings, in each the downing of the vultures is related, in each Danaʾil inspects the gizzards of the birds, and in each he draws a conclusion.[23] The virtually verbatim repe-

---

cia: An Overview," in *Civilizations of the Ancient Near East* (ed. Jack M. Sasson; New York: Charles Scribner's Sons, 1995) 4.2402.

On the problematics of distinguishing ancient Semitic written literature from the oral character of its performance, see, e.g., Shlomo Izreʾel, "The Study of Oral Poetry: Reflections of a Neophyte: Can We Learn Anything on Orality from the Study of Akkadian Poetry, Especially in Akhetaton?" in *Mesopotamian Epic Literature: Oral or Aural?* (ed. Marianna E. Vogelzang & Herman L. J. Vanstiphout; Lewiston: Edwin Mellen, 1992) 155–225; Susan Niditch, *Oral World and Written Word: Ancient Israelite Literature* (Library of Ancient Israel; Louisville: Westminster John Knox, 1996).

[20] Cf., e.g., Fish, *Is There a Text*, 21–67 (reprinted in *Reader-Response Criticism* [ed. Tompkins] 70–100), 112–35. Cf. also: Susan Sontag, *Against Interpretation and Other Essays* (New York: Delta, 1966) 3–36; Roland Barthes, *The Pleasure of the Text* (trans. Richard Miller; New York: Hill & Wang, 1975); Edward L. Greenstein, "Against Interpreting the Bible," *Ikka D'Amrei* [Jewish Theological Seminary] 4 (1982) 27–39.

[21] For the text and translation, see conveniently Parker, "Aqhat" (see n. 17, above), 72–74.

[22] The readerly gap-filling that is entailed will be discussed more explicitly below.

[23] Cf. Murray H. Lichtenstein, "Rite and Writ in an Ugaritic Legend: Ritual and Literary Elements in the Curing of King Keret" (unpublished ms., 1987) 32–33. Lichtenstein compares the repeated verbatim calls of Il to the gods for a volunteer to cure Kirta. When, upon the seventh call, no one steps forward, it becomes clear that only the wise father-god Il will be able to do it.

tition of Dana°il's search for Aqhat in one vulture after another produces tension and suspense by playing with the audience's expectations, which are manipulated through a game strategy we know as process of elimination. The suspense results not from changes in the content of what is told but from the very fact that the search is presented in a series of three identical steps at a steady, one might even say relentless, pace from one vulture to the next.

Let us consider another example, this from the Epic of Kirta.[24] It will be recalled that Kirta had departed from the instructions of the father-god Il by interrupting the seven-day journey to Udum in order to stop at the shrine of Athirat (Asherah) at Tyre or Sidon (the poetic parallelism does not render such details precisely).[25] There he vowed that, if he were successful on his mission to attain Huraya, the princess of Udum, he would donate a statue in her image to Athirat's temple.[26] Though Kirta has not only married but received eight children through his union with Huraya, he has still not paid his vow to the goddess. The effect of Kirta's fateful forgetting of his vow to Athirat is enhanced by the fact that the narrator relates a number of episodes amounting to a few hundred lines between Kirta's making the vow and Athirat's remembering it. During the years of narrated time in which Kirta should have but did not remember his vow, many minutes of narrative time have elapsed during which we have been sufficiently distracted—by a march, a siege, a negotiation, a party, a blessing—to forget the vow as well. Athirat's attention to the vow follows, then, a double forgetting, Kirta's and ours, and the dramatic effect is magnified thereby. What happens within the audience is as crucial to the sense and impact of the story as what happens, so to speak, on stage.

Consider as well the fourfold repetition, near the beginning of the Aqhat narrative, of the famous duties of the son passage. In its full form it is fourteen lines long.[27] It is recited almost consecutively by Ba'al, by Il, by a messenger to Dana°il, and by Dana°il himself. In the last repetition the list of duties takes on a cheery tone, as Dana°il recites it in a state of happiness: "Dan-

---

[24] For the text and translation, see conveniently Edward L. Greenstein, "Kirta," in *Ugaritic Narrative Poetry* (see n. 17, above) 9–48.

[25] For a different interpretation, see Jack M. Sasson, "The Vow of Mutiya, King of Shekhna," in *Crossing Boundaries and Linking Horizons: Studies in Honor of Michael C. Astour* (ed. Gordon D. Young, Mark W. Chavalas, Richard E. Averback; Bethesda, Md.: CDL, 1997) 483 n. 18.

[26] CAT 1.14 iv 38–43; for the text and translation see Greenstein, "Kirta," 20. For the interpretation, compare the vow of Puduhepa (trans. Albrecht Goetze in *ANET*, 393–394, at 394a top); and cf. Tony W. Cartledge, *Vows in the Hebrew Bible and the Ancient Near East* (JSOTSup 147; Sheffield: Sheffield Academic Press, 1992) 111.

[27] E.g., CAT 1.17 i 25–33.

iel's face beams, / His brow above lights up; / He breaks out into laughter. . . ."[28] The passage is followed by Dana'il's return home from the temple, his entertainment of the birth-goddesses, and, of course, the birth of Aqhat. The joy will eventually be turned to grief, but the extent of the grief, and the audience's sympathy toward it, is affected almost imperceptibly but at the same time immeasurably by the fourfold recitation of the filial duties passage. The expectation of a son by Dana'il and by the reader, which is protracted by the repetition, is greatly enhanced, and the importance of the boy is strongly underscored by the multiple recitations. The repetition is not a mere epic convention; it is a critically placed feature whose dramatic significance is, again, not so much in what it "says" but in the fact that the audience hears it four times through.

The reader, of course, is not simply affected by the sequence, pace, and organization of the presentation. The audience is expected to apply its background and habits of thinking toward a fuller understanding of the narrated text. The work of the reader is not limited to following the plot, fleshing out the characters, and formulating hypotheses concerning motives and consequences. I posit as a principle that there is potential significance in every aspect of an Ugaritic narrative, even a seemingly trivial one, just as readers of the Bible have come to appreciate the odd details of a biblical narrative.[29] Think, for example, of the special coat that Jacob made for Joseph (Genesis 37) or of the fact that the judge Ehud was left-handed (Judges 3). I do not always find significance in every feature and detail, but I assume, as a working hypothesis, that there is meaning in the particulars, even if we lack the means to interpret them adequately. Take, for example, the conversation, which is unfortunately almost entirely broken, between King Pabuli and his wife, when he awakens to find his town Udum under siege by Kirta.[30] Later Pabuli will summon messengers to communicate his negotiating position to Kirta. So why does the narrator see fit to tell us that Pabuli's first response is to speak to his wife?[31] Is it mere mimesis, an imitation of reality, where the king looks out his window in the morning, sees Kirta's army of 300,000 and gets the shock of his life, and then shares his reaction with his spouse?

---

[28] Parker, "Aqhat," 55.

[29] See my article "Biblical Prose Narrative and Early Canaanite Narrative," in *Mikra Le'Avraham* (Avraham Holtz Festschrift; ed. Zvia Ginor and David G. Roskies (forthcoming; in Hebrew).

[30] CAT 1.14 v 6ff. (Greenstein, "Kirta," 20–21).

[31] For a limited attempt at an answer, see Frank Polak, "Some Aspects of Literary Design in the Ancient Near Eastern Epic," in *kinattūtu ša dārâti* (Raphael Kutscher Memorial Volume; Tel Aviv Occasional Publications 1; ed. Anson F. Rainey; Tel Aviv: Tel Aviv Univ. Institute of Archaeology, 1992) 135–46 at 136.

Ugaritic narrative tends to be laconic,[32] like its literary successor in the Bible; and, as I have maintained elsewhere, it does not abound in description for its own sake, in the manner of Homeric epic.[33] From a semantic point of view, the significance of Pabuli's words to his wife necessarily escapes us, for lack of textual remains. But from a readerly perspective, some meaning is preserved. Kirta has marched to Udum in order to obtain a bride, Pabuli's daughter. When Pabuli offers Kirta silver and gold and the rest, Kirta replies:

> What is not in my house you must give me:
> You must give me Lady Huraya,
> The Fair One, your firstborn child![34]

Kirta has no children, and Pabuli has some. But Kirta also has no wife, and Pabuli has one. The preceding scene of dialogue between Pabuli and his wife has the effect of reminding the reader, subtly perhaps but no less surely, of Kirta's lack, the one that set the story off in the first place. Our contrast, as readers, between Pabuli's married state and Kirta's widowed one, renders even more ironic the typical offer of silver and gold that Pabuli will make to Kirta.[35]

Dramatic irony is produced as a result of Pabuli doing what is expected of him by diplomatic norm and our knowing that he has missed the boat. We may become aggravated by Pabuli's wasting of Kirta's time, and ours, by making the wrong offer. We may become tense as the alternatives of resolution narrow. Our responses are clearly an integral part of the story's meaning: our responses are the story's effects. In any event, Pabuli's conversation with his wife is not an incidental detail but, at least in retrospect, a scene of dramatic consequence.

Although some readers have failed to see the significance of certain details in Ugaritic narrative,[36] such details can often, like their counterparts in

---

[32] Cf., e.g., Klaas Spronk, "The Legend of Kirtu (KTU 1.14–16): A Study of the Structure and Its Consequences for Interpretation," in *The Structural Analysis of Biblical and Canaanite Poetry* (JSOTSup 74; ed. Willem van der Meer & Johannes C. de Moor; Sheffield: Sheffield Academic Press, 1988) 62–82, at 70.

[33] "Biblical Prose Narrative and Early Canaanite Narrative" (n. 29, above).

[34] CAT 1.14 vi 22–25 (Greenstein, "Kirta," 23); cf. 1.14 iii 38–40.

[35] For another irony in Pabuli's discourse, see Hens-Piazza, "Repetition and Rhetoric" (n. 14, above), 107–9, who nicely contrasts Pabuli's reference to Udum as "a gift of Il" (*ytnt il*; CAT 1.14 iii 31–32; cf. v 42–43 [restored]; vi 12–13) with Kirta's perception of Huraya as his gift from Il (*d...il ytn*; 1.14 iii 46–47; vi 31–32).

[36] E.g., Kenneth T. Aitken, *The Aqhat Narrative: A Study in the Narrative Structure and Composition of an Ugaritic Tale* (JSS Monograph 13; Manchester: Univ. of Manchester, 1990) 191–92, who enumerates five details that he characterizes as unnecessary to the story itself.

biblical narrative,[37] be found to be crucial for another major area of reader involvement in making literary meaning—gap-filling. Reader theorists, like Wolfgang Iser and like Perry and Sternberg, have analyzed the ways that readers must make deductions, draw inferences, complete a train of thought, and, even more basically, flesh out characters and plot in the course of reading a text.[38] Controversy has surrounded critics' claims that some gaps must be filled in certain ways and not in others.[39] But the process of gap-filling has become a well-recognized component of the act of reading.

A case in point is the vendetta that Pughat, Aqhat's sister, carries out against Yatpan, the henchman of Anat who had murdered her brother.[40] Pughat puts on a warrior's outfit and a lady's garb over that[41] and sets out, with her father's blessing, to find and slay Yatpan. Parker has asked a question that ought to exercise any reader: How does Pughat know "who and where her target was"?[42] Parker proposes, on the basis of comparative evidence, like the story of Yael and Sisera in Judges 4–5 and that of Judith and Holofernes in Judith 10–14, that Pughat simply knew. But there may be clues to how she knew within the Aqhat text.

Pughat is repeatedly characterized in this section of the narrative by the epithet *yādiʿtu halaka kabkabīma*, "The One Who Knows the Path of the Stars."[43] Pughat's esoteric knowledge permits her both to divine and to navigate. All she needs is divine favor. This she enjoys by virtue of her

---

[37] See, e.g., Robert Alter, "Narrative Specification and the Power of the Literal," in *The World of Biblical Literature* (New York: BasicBooks, 1992) 85–106.

[38] For references to Iser and Perry & Sternberg, see nn. 7 and 9, above. For an excellent illustration of the readerly filling out of character, see Alice Bach, *Women, Seduction, and Betrayal in Biblical Narrative* (Cambridge: Cambridge Univ. Press, 1997). For a concise discussion, see David M. Gunn & Danna Nolan Fewell, *Narrative in the Hebrew Bible* (Oxford: Oxford Univ. Press, 1993) 46–52.

[39] See, e.g., Danna Nolan Fewell and David M. Gunn, "Tipping the Balance: Sternberg's Reader and the Rape of Dinah," *JBL* 110 (1991) 193–211; Meir Sternberg, "Biblical Poetics and Sexual Politics: From Reading to Counter-Reading," *JBL* 111 (1992) 463–88.

[40] CAT 1.19 iv 28ff. (Parker, "Aqhat," 76–78).

[41] Whether the female dress is meant to disguise Pughat as the goddess Anat, as some have suggested, or as a hired prostitute, as others have suggested, may not be decidable given our present state of knowledge; for a summary of the philological ambiguity, see, e.g., Dennis Pardee, "The 'Aqhatu Legend," in *The Context of Scripture 1: Canonical Compositions from the Biblical World* (ed. William W. Hallo and K. Lawson Younger, Jr.; Leiden: Brill, 1997) 355 n. 135.

[42] Simon B. Parker, *The Pre-Biblical Narrative Tradition* (SBL Resources for Biblical Study 24; Atlanta: Scholars Press, 1989) 130.

[43] E.g., CAT 1.19 ii 2–3, 7; iv 38.

father's offerings to the gods (*dabḫu, dagašu*, "evening sacrifice"[?]),[44] which he made just prior to blessing her.[45] Aitken ascribes Pughat's request for blessing to "cultural convention,"[46] but Pughat's prayer would rather seem crucial to the logic by which a reader must fill in this gap in the plot. Pughat's success is dependent, as Gaster had seen,[47] on both her talent to track the stars and the support of her mission by the gods. She literally divined the way to her destination. And if Pughat has any doubts she has reached the right address, those doubts are allayed when Yatpan, his tongue loosened by drink, makes a boastful reference to his dastardly deed: "May the hand that slew Valiant Aqhat/ Slay enemies by the thousand!"[48]

For a somewhat subtler and more complex passage demanding readerly gap-filling, we turn to the scene in the Kirta Epic where Kirta's younger son Ilhaʾu must find his youngest sister, Thitmanit, and, without letting on that their father is ill, persuade her to go offer up a song and make a vow of silver and gold for the king.[49] Kirta is concerned that if Thitmanit realizes he is sick, out of her strong love for him and her emotional nature, she will be too broken up to make the necessary appeals to the gods. She must save her strength for the prayer and not waste her energies in sobbing.[50] So Ilhaʾu, who is himself in tears,[51] must approach his sister coolly and put up a front.

Kirta carefully cautions his son: "Wait, then, till Lady Sun sets/ And Lady Lamp [= the moon] starts to shine."[52] Why, the reader must wonder, need Ilhaʾu arrive only at night? Another item that may spark curiosity is the fact that Ilhaʾu made a point of taking his lance (*mrḥ, grgr*) with him on his run (*trẓẓ*) to his sister's house. Even if Ilhaʾu would never leave home without his lance, why would our laconic narrator bother to tell us that he

---

[44] Cf. Arabic *dagaš*, "dusk"; see Joseph Aistleitner, *Wörterbuch der ugaritischen Sprache* (4th ed.; Berlin: Akademie, 1974) 81.

[45] CAT 1.19 iv 22–40.

[46] Aitken, *The Aqhat Narrative* (n. 36, above), 160.

[47] Theodor H. Gaster, *The Oldest Stories in the World* (Boston: Beacon, 1958) 184; cf. Francis Landy, *The Tale of Aqhat* (London: Menard, 1981) 14–15.

[48] CAT 1.19 iv 58–59 (my translation).

[49] CAT 1.16 i 24–62; for the reading of lines 41–42 and 44–45 see my article "New Readings in the Kirta Epic," *IOS* 18 (1998) 105–23.

[50] Contrast, e.g., Baruch Margalit, "K-R-T Studies," *UF* 27 (1995) 269.

[51] See CAT 1.16 i 12–14, 24–28.

[52] Greenstein, "Kirta," 32; cf. Andrée Herdner, "La légende de Keret," in André Caquot, Maurice Sznycer, and Andrée Herdner, *Textes ougaritiques 1: Mythes et légendes* (Paris: Cerf, 1974) 546; W. G. E. Watson, "A Suppliant Surprised (CTA 16 I 41b–53a)," *JANES* 8 (1976) 105–11, at 110. Compare the moon god Yarikh's epithet *nyr šmm*, "lamp of the sky," in CAT 1.24.16, 31 (text and translation in David Marcus, "The Betrothal of Yarikh and Nikkal-Ib," in *Ugaritic Narrative Poetry* [see n. 17, above] 215–18).

took it?[53] Both the nocturnal timing of the visit and the lance are necessary elements for the reader who would understand the plot. There is an array of gaps to be filled, and they may be understood in line with the same logic. They are bound up with the motive that Kirta expressed in wanting to hide his illness from his devoted daughter, and they stem from the fact that Ilhaʾu has himself been crying.

The reader may infer that Ilhaʾu has been told to see his sister at night so that his tears would be covered by darkness. One look at her brother's weeping, and she would realize that their father was ill. It is for a narratological purpose we are told that Ilhaʾu takes his lance with him: because the lance is a necessary prop in the next stage of the plot. When Ilhaʾu arrives his sister has not yet come back from drawing the evening's water; so he stands outside waiting, hiding his tears in the dark. But he makes one innocent mistake—he rests his lance in the doorway, where its metallic blade catches and reflects light from inside the house or perhaps from the shining moon.[54]

> *mrḥh . ltl [.] yṣb // pnh . t̲ǵr / yṣu*
> His lance he stands up on the threshold;
> Its radiance shines in the doorway.[55]

---

[53] John Gray (*The Krt Text in the Literature of Ras Shamra: A Social Myth of Ancient Canaan* [Leiden: Brill, 1955] 52) suggests that the lance merely signifies the manhood or royalty of Ilhaʾu, comparing 1 Sam 26:7ff. Watson ("A Suppliant Surprised" [see n. 52, above]) interprets Ilhaʾu's actions as a ritual gesture of entreaty; cf. Wyatt, *Religious Texts* 227 n. 232. Watson's interpretation is based on a misreading of the preceding passage (see the reference in n. 49, above), as well as on a faulty parallel to the Mesopotamian *labān appi* gesture, which one would hardly perform with a spear (which is the only meaning of West Sem. *mrḥ/rmḥ*).

[54] Others interpret the phrase to refer to the face of Pughat coming out of the door; see recently, e.g., Dennis Pardee, "The Kirta Epic," in *The Context of Scripture 1* (see n. 41, above) 340. Wyatt (*Religious Texts*, 227) takes the phrase to refer to Ilhaʾu himself looking out toward the gate. Pardee's translation makes little sense in context because, as Pardee—and Wyatt—translate, Thitmanit had already gone out to fetch water. The *QTL* verb form *yṣat* has here the pluperfect usage, rendering time that precedes the present; see my review essay "On a New Grammar of Ugaritic," *IOS* 18 (1998) 397–420, at 411–13. More important, neither Pardee, nor Wyatt, nor other interpreters explain how Pughat comes to realize that her father is direly ill.

[55] CAT 1.16 i 51–53 (Greenstein, "Kirta," 33). For *pnm*, "face" in the sense of "radiance," compare Akk. *zīmu*, Aram. זיו, "brightness, countenance." For *yṣu* in the sense of "shine," cf. H. L. Ginsberg, *The Legend of King Keret* (BASORSup 2–3; New Haven: American Schools of Oriental Research, 1946) 45, who compares Arab. *ḍāʾa*, "shine, be bright," and the nuances of Heb. יצא in Isa 62:1b and Hos 6:5 (end); note too that the Ugaritic equivalent of Heb. מזרח שמש, lit. "shining of the sun," i.e., "east," is *ṣat špš*, "the going out/shining of the sun." There is, of course, a similar semantic nexus between "going out" and "shining" in the Heb. verb הופיע, "appear, shine"; cf. Ugar. *ypʿ*, "appear," Akk. *(w)apū*, "appear, shine (in the Št form)."

Unbeknown to Ilhaʾu, the glint of the blade illumines his face, so that when Thitmanit approaches, she immediately perceives that something is gravely wrong.

> Just as her brother she sees,
> Her [tend]ons go lax, she collapses;[56]
> On her brother's [neck] she falls crying.[57]

What brought on her tears? Margalit maintains that these "are tears of joy at seeing her brother after a presumably lengthy separation."[58] But from the continuation of the scene it is clear that Thitmanit is upset by the evidence that her father is unwell. She immediately asks Ilhaʾu:

> Is the king, then, direly sick?
> Is Kirta, your father, then, [ill]?[59]

When Ilhaʾu tries to conceal the truth, as he was bidden by Kirta to do, Thitmanit will not permit the charade. The reader may reasonably surmise, then, that the tears on Ilhaʾu's face, which were revealed by the gleam of the lance—together with the unexpected nocturnal visit itself—indicated to the doting daughter that their father's condition was grave. Now just as Thitmanit had to deduce from her brother's tears that their father was ill, so does the reader need to deduce from Thitmanit's dismay that her brother's tears became visible. It is a simple inference, drawn from details that, I would contend, would not likely be there were they not to be interpreted.

As our final example, let us consider what may be the most curious gap in all Ugaritic narrative.[60] Kirta, on march with his army to get his princess bride, follows the instructions he received from his god Il down to every detail. But for some reason he deviates from course and stops at the shrine of Athirat, where he makes his nearly fatal vow of a statue in the image of his future wife (see above).[61] The fatefulness of the vow, and of his forgetting to fulfill it, exacerbate the reader's need to know why Kirta departed

---

[56] That we have here an abbreviated version of the formula for reacting to bad news is recognized, e.g., by Parker, *The Pre-Biblical Narrative Tradition*, 182; contrast, e.g., Johannes C. de Moor and Klaas Spronk, "Problematic Passages in the Legend of Kirtu (II)," *UF* 14 (1982) 184; Margalit, "K-R-T Studies" (see n. 50, above), 268–69.

[57] CAT 1.16 i 53–55 (Greenstein, "Kirta" 33). For the conventional behavior of crying on a family member's neck (e.g., Gen 33:4; 45:14; 46:29), cf. Margalit, "K-R-T Studies," 270.

[58] Margalit, "K-R-T Studies," 269.

[59] CAT 1.16 i 56–57 (trans. Greenstein, "Kirta," 33).

[60] Cf. my "Biblical Prose Narrative and Early Canaanite Narrative" (see n. 29, above).

[61] Cf. Samuel E. Loewenstamm, "On the Theology of the Keret-Epic," in *From Babylon to Canaan: Studies in the Bible and Its Oriental Background* (Jerusalem: Magnes, 1992) 185–200.

from his instructions in this particular case and took the precarious initiative of making the vow. It is possible, as some have suggested, that Kirta wanted to hedge his bets, so to speak, and not rely on the old god Il alone.[62] Or perhaps Kirta, out of uncommon piety, simply could not pass by a shrine without honoring its deity.

In light of the way Kirta's bride was first presented to him in his dream, Gaster filled the gap quite suggestively.[63] In the shrine of Athirat there surely stood an image of the goddess.[64] The goddess's statue was in all likelihood made of stone or wood, plated with precious metal, and its eyes made of precious stones. When Kirta arrived at the shrine at daybreak, (*špšm*, lit., "with the sun"), the eyes of the statue must have glistened as they received the stream of sunlight entering the temple.[65] The eyes of the goddess must have recalled the vision of his bride-to-be. Il described her to Kirta as follows:

> Who's as fair as the goddess Anath,
> Who's as comely as Astarte;
> Whose eyes are lapis lazuli,
> Eyeballs, gleaming alabaster.[66]

The narrator chose to have Il speak of Lady Huraya as if she were the statue of a goddess. The full significance of the description becomes clear only later, when the reader makes use of what one knows about the shrines of goddesses and connects Kirta's encounter with the image of Athirat with his enthusiasm for and apparent obsession with the image of Huraya, which found expression in his vow.

The role of the reader of Ugaritic texts, like all other literature, is to become involved in the making of meaning. Our use of induction and imagination is as essential to reading Ugaritic narrative as it is in the reading of biblical or any other narrative literature.

---

[62] E.g., Parker, *The Pre-Biblical Narrative Tradition*, 159.

[63] Gaster, "The King Who Forgot" (see n. 47, above), 194.

[64] See Ivan Engnell, *A Rigid Scrutiny: Critical Essays on the Old Testament* (trans. and ed. John T. Willis with Helmer Ringgren; Nashville: Vanderbilt Univ. Press, 1969) 254.

[65] Although West Asian temples were not always constructed, like the Solomonic Temple described in 1 Kings, with an entrance or opening to the East or Southeast, it may be pertinent to note that in the Mesopotamian ritual of animating a divine statue, the idol is placed on a mat facing East in the morning, such that its eyes are illuminated by the sun; see C. Walker & M. B. Dick, "The Induction of the Cult Image in Ancient Mesopotamia: The Mesopotamian *mīs pî* Ritual," in *Born in Heaven, Made on Earth: The Making of the Cult Image in the Ancient Near East* (ed. Michael B. Dick; Winona Lake, Ind.: Eisenbrauns, 1999) 55–121, esp. 78–81, lines 37–53; 90–93, lines 94–145; 99–100, lines 58–62.

[66] CAT 1.14 iii 41–44 (trans. Greenstein, "Kirta," 17); cf. vi 26–30.

Chapter 11

Entertainment, Ideology, and the Reception of "History": "David's Jerusalem" As a Question of Space

David M. Gunn
Texas Christian University

It is a privilege to contribute to a volume in honor of Burke Long. We have often shared the same paths over the past few decades, from our beginning collaboration in the publication of Burke's collection of essays on biblical "short stories in literary focus" to current common interests in the ideological dimensions of biblical criticism, the morphology of the Bible in Western culture, and the reception history of the "Holy Land." Admired friend and colleague, you have my heartfelt gratitude for insight, encouragement, and many a shared smile. Which latter brings me, after a fashion, to the beginning of my topic.

The term "entertainment" evokes at the same time a genre label, a social performance, a mode of communication, and a reader/viewer/hearer response which Philip Davies characterizes as no less than "pleasure."[1] Recently he was kind enough to revive my characterization of the King David story in 2 Samuel and 1 Kings as "serious entertainment," borrowing from Matthew Arnold's use of the phrase "high seriousness" to describe the artistry of the finest poets, which has "an ability to tap significant veins of truth about humanity" (my paraphrase of Arnold). This is entertainment "which demands the active engagement of those being entertained, which

---

[1] Philip R. Davies, *Scribes and Schools: The Canonization of the Hebrew Scriptures* (Louisville, Ky.: Westminster John Knox, 1998) 142.

challenges their intellect, their emotions, their understanding of people, of society and of themselves."[2]

The possible relationships between entertainment and history are many and various, depending on whether by "history" we are understanding something like "what actually happened," on one end of a simplistic scale, or a critical construction of the "past" (as in "history writing," as opposed to "fiction"), on the other. Clearly the designation of the King David story as "serious entertainment" does not in itself obviate all possibility that the artistic production could yield data pertinent to an historical reconstruction of the "past" that it purports to recount. In fact, both entertainer and audience might well believe that the genre disclosed the past as what we might call "historical" truth in the sense of "what actually happened," though as audience/readership changed that perception could also change. But a history writer today would obviously be well advised to treat the data in such a work with great circumspection, absent corroborating external evidence. In short, we might expect the burden of proof to lie with the historian to show the historical reliability of the story.

Of course, in the last analysis it is always the historian's obligation to shoulder the burden of proof, but in practice genre decisions will often play into the question of what counts as evidence. For example, it has generally been assumed by students of ancient history (though this assumption has been problematized) that Thucydides's *History of the Peloponnesian War* may be relied upon to a qualitatively different degree than the plays of Sophocles or Euripides. And despite the difficulties (which start with Thucydides's speeches and the danger of arguing in circles) that still seems to me to be a reasonable point of departure. As it happens, I believe that probably the closest literary productions in the ancient world to the King David story are not the "histories" of Herodotus or Thucydides (cf. John van Seters, Sarah Mandell and David Noel Freedman, Flemming Nielsen),[3] with their authorial self-consciousness and concern with sources, but the late fifth century plays of Euripides, Thucydides's contemporary, with their engaging plots and characters, their intricate ironies and ambiguities, and their splendid potential for subversive readings of the established order.

In speaking of the King David story (let me call it the David family story; including most of 2 Samuel 2–20 and 1 Kings 1–2), Davies accepts

---

[2] David M. Gunn, *The Story of King David: Genre and Interpretation* (Sheffield: JSOT Press, 1978) 61.

[3] John Van Seters, *In Search of History: Historiography in the Ancient World and the Origins of Biblical History* (New Haven and London: Yale Univ. Press, 1983); Sarah Mandell and David Noel Freedman, *The Relationship between Herodotus' History and the Primary History* (Atlanta: Scholars Press, 1993); Flemming Nielsen, *The Tragedy in History: Herodotus and the Deuteronomistic History* (Sheffield: Sheffield Academic Press, 1997).

with Van Seters and Graeme Auld that it is "a late addition [to Samuel and Kings] and not deliberately left out by the Chronicler."[4] While I am not persuaded that either Van Seters or Auld have entirely succeeded in making that case, for present purposes this judgment does not matter much (and here is not the place to review it). Whether the story had an independent existence in the fifth or fourth centuries (or later?), or was circulating as part of a larger composite narrative akin to our Samuel and Kings, it was still presumably being read (and perhaps edited). If so, what do we suppose people were reading from it that gave the story traction in the emerging canon? Davies writes:

> In what circumstances do such writings [of serious entertainment] move on the path toward canonization? How is a hitherto scribal canon open to such works? Is it simply that they are widely read? There are two possibilities: one is that these works were used very widely in the school curriculum. Indeed, Jonah, Ruth, and Esther are still used as college texts to teach classical Hebrew, because they are short and grammatically simple. Another factor may be a concern deliberately to loosen the control of one class on the canon and to sanction a wider range of literature held in the temple libraries.[5]

Let me consider the David family story in light of this line of inquiry. Whether or not the Chronicler had it before him, it is not difficult to understand why, if he had, he would have dropped it from his account of the national story. The Chronicler's account is saccharine and its monologic propensities would have been seriously overwhelmed by such a swathe of the savory (or unsavory!) in dialogical mode as the David family story. The Chronicler's main ideological dispositions (or political programs) are relatively clear. He is earnest to a fault about good order, national unity, and the indispensability to both of the temple and its functionaries (of whom he is presumably one). The family story, on the other hand, is so replete with ambivalence that readers for centuries have swung to and fro in their estimates of the "message" of this account. At present sardonic readings are in vogue, but it has not always been so, and is not likely to remain so. After all, this quality of openness to contextual readings is part of what makes this entertaining narrative serious.

So, indeed, in Davies's terms, the inclusion of this story in an emerging body of text on the path towards canon must represent "a concern deliberately to loosen the control of one class on the canon and to sanction a wider range of literature held in the temple libraries" (assuming that is where this literature was held). Whatever "class" this text represents—and there's a conundrum, given all we do not know about the Second Temple, especially

---

[4] Davies, *Scribes and Schools*, 149. See Van Seters, *In Search of History*; A. Graeme Auld, *Kings Without Privilege: David and Moses in the Story of the Bible's Kings* (Edinburgh: T. & T. Clark, 1994).

[5] Davies, *Scribes and Schools*, 150–51.

Persian, period—it is likely not the class that the Chronicler represents, namely the bureaucrats who "run" things and keep institutional order. At least that narrows the field,a little, if rather obviously. Nor is it obviously a "pro-" or "anti-" monarchic group (if that's a very meaningful notion for much of this period) given that it does such a mealy-mouthed job of either boosting or denigrating the "monarchy," let alone David. What else can we tell about where this text is coming from or who is appreciating it?

We could, at this point, try finding a Second Temple provenance for our text, and along with that its received meaning, the meaning propelling it towards canonical authorization. In days gone by (when I started thinking about this text) the received wisdom generally went something along these lines: This text is about the succession to the throne of David; therefore it is located in the court of Solomon; therefore the purpose of this text is political propaganda for the House of Solomon; and now that its purpose is known it is possible to establish that this text is about the succession to the throne of David. Today, if I were to seek a "late date" location to provide me with the purpose/meaning of the text, I should need to turn away from literalism towards what Bob Becking calls the lock-and-key method of determining provenance,[6] what I call socio-political allegory. One "matches" a socio-political context or even an historical event or set of events (context A—target) to a biblical text which is ostensibly treating some quite other context or event(s) (context B—source). One then "discovers" the true intent of the text, namely to disclose an understanding or rendering of context A.

Thus Thomas Thompson in his most recent book, *The Mythic Past*, comments on the story in Kings of the breakup of the united monarchy: "The pattern for this story is the break-up of the Hellenistic empire, which had separated into two integral parts: the southern Ptolemies of Egypt ruling from Alexandria, and the Seleucids of the north ruling from Antioch and Babylon. Seleucid Syria and the hated religious syncretism of Antiochus IV is reflected in II Kings' descriptions of Samaria, whose king goes to war with Solomon's successor."[7] John Hyrcanus is a focal point of the allegory: "Many have found both David and Josiah reflected in the image of John Hyrcanus, one of the Hasmonean kings of this period. Surely our philosopher-king Solomon is a Hebrew-speaking Alexander. The stories of the golden age of the United Monarchy reflect the fantasy and ambitions of Jerusalem of the Maccabees."[8] Parallels are to be observed between the stories in Kings of Hezekiah's and especially Josiah's reforms and Josephus's

---

[6] Bob Becking, "The Hellenistic Period and Ancient Israel: Three Preliminary Statements" (unpublished paper, European Seminar on Methodology in Israel's History, Lahti, 19 July, 1999).

[7] Thomas L. Thompson, *The Mythic Past: Biblical Archaeology and the Myth of Israel* ([New York]: Basic Books, 1999) 97.

[8] Ibid., 207.

account of John Hyrcanus.[9] The implication seems to be that in this figure we have an anchor point, our target context A.

The procedure is more complex than this, involving the buttressing of allegories of "events" with more abstract allegories of ideas, ideologies, thought-forms, political agendas and emotions. Nor is there anything improbable about such a function of literature, including literature of the David family story's subtlety. A famous example that springs to mind is Jean Anouilh's play, *Antigone*, written and performed in German-occupied Paris during the Second World War, ostensibly dealing with classical antiquity but open to be interpreted as an account of the occupation. So I do not question that Thompson's target context may provide a plausible provenance for some biblical texts, including the David family story (though he does not, I think, argue that). The problem I see is that, given the large number of "events" recounted in Kings (let alone Genesis–Kings) from which to choose as the matching points of the allegory, Thompson's chosen context has to be but one of many that a competent scholar could construct.

In short, before I venture on such a task myself I need to be reminded that determining the provenance of biblical texts, and arguing from there to their meaning and import, is a process of some dubiety.

Here is another possibility to consider in asking why the David family story might come to gain, as I put it, traction on the path to canon. This has to do with space, critical spatiality, that is, in particular, "Thirdspace." Edward Soja has argued that space is an articulation of three spaces: Firstspace (geophysical realities as perceived), Secondspace (mapped realities as represented), and Thirdspace (lived realities as practiced).[10] We are

---

[9] Ibid., 273; cf. 265, 296.

[10] Edward W. Soja, *Postmodern Geographies: The Reassertion of Space in Critical Social Theory* (Chicago: Univ. of Chicago Press, 1987); *Thirdspace: Journeys to Los Angeles and Other Real-and-Imagined Places* (Cambridge, Mass., and Oxford: Blackwell Publishers, 1996). For a sustained critique—and appreciation—of Soja's *Postmodern Geographies*, see Derek Gregory's delightfully written *Geographical Imaginations* (Cambridge, Mass., and Oxford: Blackwell Publishers, 1994). My introduction to the work of Soja and other critical spatiality theorists has come initially from James Flanagan's several papers mediating this work for a "biblical studies" audience (though he is not responsible for my use, or misuse, of Soja's categories here). See James W. Flanagan, "Postmodern Perspectives on Premodern Space" (*Semeia*, forthcoming); "Constructs of Space, Place, and Territoriality in Ancient Southwest Asia" (paper for the Constructs of the Social and Cultural Worlds of Antiquity Group, Orlando, 1998); "Mapping the Biblical World: Perceptions of Space in Ancient Southwestern Asia" (paper for the Humanities Research Group, University of Windsor, 1999); see http://www.cwru.edu/affil/GAIR, go to Library, Reading Room. For a helpful survey see also Jon Berquist, "Theories of Space and Construction of the Ancient World" (paper for the Constructs of the Social and Cultural Worlds of Antiquity Group, Boston, 1999; http://www.cwru.edu/affil/GAIR, go

accustomed to thinking (and writing) of biblical space in terms of the first two categories, the measurable geophysical and architectural features of Jerusalem, for example, or the innumerable Secondspace maps, that "represent" that Firstspace reality and often collapse mental representation into geophysical reality. James Flanagan has written of Thirdspace:

> [Thirdspace] is lived space. It is created by social practice. And it is known by experience. We cannot help but recall Marvin Harris' classical schema that outlines emic and etic knowledge intersecting with behavioral and mental realms. Here as there and in biblical studies, etic mental knowledge of emic behavioral experience is problematic. Has anyone ever learned to ride a bicycle by watching someone else ride? Can anyone understand the lived space of someone whose experiences are genuinely different? I do not know the answer, but Soja apparently thinks the quest or openness to the quest is worthwhile. For our use, I propose that social world studies that include concern for spatiality and are conscious of lived- or Thirdspace can offer different, if not better, readings of the past.[11]

So my proposal is that one significant reason for receptiveness to the David family story is that it creates David's Jerusalem as ancient or foundational "lived space." However small Jerusalem may have been in the Persian period (Charles Carter suggests no more than 1,500 inhabitants at any given time),[12] it seems likely from textual evidence that it was a focal point of communal identity throughout this period and later. Jerusalem stands in for Yehud, but, more importantly (and for whatever reasons—whether economic, political, cultic) it functions as a microcosm of "Israel" for many Second Temple readers (including diaspora readers). Chronicles demonstrates this point clearly, as do Ezra and Nehemiah. But what kind of a space is Jerusalem? Chronicles maps one kind of political and cultic space, one kind of, largely institutional, identity centered on the temple and its functions/functionaries. The Samuel–Kings family story invites a much wider array of readers to participate in this identity-shaping, mythic, lived space. Its readers conjure with the raw stuff of life—a gamut of experiences embedded in the political, the familial, the personal. David's Jerusalem is foundational, both stories say. David's Jerusalem, the family story says, had real people! It comes as no surprise that critics in the modern period seeking to receive "history" have urged that the family story is an "eye witness" account (which it patently cannot be). (By contrast, the silence re-

---

to Constructs Group, 1999 papers). As will be glaringly obvious to my reader, my use of Soja's categories in this paper is at best sketchy and at worst possibly misinformed. But the categories seemed to me to offer some explanatory value in an exploratory proposal which, on further examination, may or may not prove viable.

[11] Flanagan, "Constructs of Space." For Harris, see *Cultural Materialism* (New York: Random House, 1979) 38.

[12] Charles E. Carter, *The Emergence of Yehud in the Persian Period: A Social and Demographic Study* (Sheffield: Sheffield Academic Press, 1999) 199–205.

garding Chronicles on this score is deafening.) Such critics have simply found themselves sucked into the "lived space" of this story.

So I suggest that a Second Temple reader/editor/collector bent on endorsing this extraordinary story that so risks being a Soap without ever quite succumbing, such a canon-shaper may not have been interested in consciously endorsing a particular social, political, or religious institution or ideological program (by means of allegory) so much as in seeking to change what is (thought to be) a "known" Firstspace piece of real estate, "David's Jerusalem," into an intensely experienced (if only by proxy, by way of the imagination) Thirdspace.

The result, of course, is hardly innocent of social, political, religious, or ideological implications. For one thing, the more David's Jerusalem is imaginatively experienced as lived, the more it becomes entrenched in the dialectic of social symbolic order and communal identity. Such imaginative experience readily produces "belonging." David's space is (re)lived as "our" space; if David belongs to "us" then so does his "space." The imaginative "Thirdspacing" of "David's Jerusalem" overlays our own Jerusalem, even if we do not live there, and reinforces any imaginative sense we already have of Jerusalem as Thirdspace, rather than simply Firstspace, by constructing Jerusalem as foundational Thirdspace.

This investment of Jerusalem as geophysical entity with Davidic Thirdspace is not simply a matter of antiquarian inquiry. Precisely its "canonical" incorporation has lent it staying power, so that it has had long-term social and political import reaching to present times. Today an Israeli Foreign Ministry web site offers this account of Jerusalem:

> Throughout the millennia of its existence, Jerusalem has never been the capital of any other sovereign nation. Jerusalem has stood at the center of the Jewish people's national and spiritual life since King David made it the capital of his kingdom in 1003 BCE. The city remained the capital of the Davidic dynasty for 400 years, until the kingdom was conquered by the Babylonians. Following the return from the Babylonian exile in 538 BCE, Jerusalem again served as the capital of the Jewish people in its land for the next five and a half centuries.[13]

Such a statement is, of course, part of the rhetoric of possession, belonging. The Thirdspace term "capital" provides the keyword which incorporates city, land, and people, and the keyword takes its point of origin in "David's Jerusalem." And David's Jerusalem is, itself—for web readers who are Bible readers (or inherit a Bible-reading tradition)—already Thirdspace; that is, imaginatively (re)lived space. The web rhetoric has no need to retell the family story—that lies behind or between the words and lines, helping to authorize this capsule story which lays claim to Firstspace, real estate, "Jerusalem." The family story has already lent its imaginative power to

---

[13] Go to http://www.Israel.org/mfa/go.asp?MFAH01y10.

constructing "history," and "history" is what is being appealed to here. Jews, it is argued, are the rightful "owners" of Jerusalem by virtue of an "historic" connection to it and the land of which it is "capital" (an argument that played a significant role, for example, in the influential evidence and findings of the Peel Commission in 1937).

And so we find that questions of "serious entertainment" and Thirdspace may quickly become issues of "history" and claims to Firstspace.

Flanagan has argued that

> Those who are arguing for strict historicity of biblical claims are consciously or unconsciously presuming that biblical territorial claims are claims made for Firstspace, the material, physical world and its territory in Southwestern Asia. Those who have been labelled as favoring theological or mythological interpretations, may be in fact suggesting—perhaps without knowing it—that biblical territorial claims are claims for Thirdspace, the lived space that is often denied marginalized and disenfranchised minorities.[14]

Berquist has remarked how the practice of spatial labeling, "the gesture to geography" as he terms it, can often displace the people involved.[15] In short, constructions of space, especially "lived" space, can be potent forces in human lives, and no more so than in the case of "David's Jerusalem."

Which brings me, by way of a closing illustration, to a story that haunts my pondering of David's family story, canon formation, Thirdspace, and the construction of Jerusalem. In 1967 Amos Oz, born and raised as a child in Jerusalem, found himself walking through the newly captured streets of the city:

> Their eyes hate me. They wish me dead. Accursed stranger . . .
>
> I tried my hardest to feel in East Jerusalem like a man who had driven out his enemies and returned to his ancestral inheritance. The Bible came back to life for me: kings, prophets, the Temple Mount, Absalom's Pillar, the Mount of Olives. And also the Jerusalem of Abraham Mapu and Agnon's book Tmol Shilshom. I wanted to belong, I wanted to share in the general celebrations.
>
> But I couldn't, because of the people.
>
> I saw resentment and hostility, hypocrisy, bewilderment, obsequiousness, fear, humiliation and new plots being hatched. I walked the streets of East Jerusalem like a man who has broken into a forbidden city. City of my birth. City of my dreams. City of aspirations of my ancestors and my people. And here I was, stalking its streets clutching a sub-machine-gun, like a figure in one of my childhood nightmares: an alien man in an alien city.[16]

---

[14] Flanagan, "Mapping the Biblical World."

[15] Berquist, "Theories of Space."

[16] Amos Oz, "An Alien City," *Ariel* 102 (1996); http://www.Israel.org/mfa/ariel/102Oz.html.

Amos Oz, armed with his Bible, his tradition, his identity and an Uzi, had realized his people's ancient yearning, had returned and taken possession of David's Jerusalem. But Oz's Thirdspace had run slap-bang into the Thirdspace of another. And his Thirdspace was turned into a nightmare.

Chapter 12

Village Law and the Book of the Covenant

Douglas A. Knight
Vanderbilt University

The settings in which by far the greatest population of ancient Israel was located are also the contexts about which we are least informed. That gap in our knowledge is being closed somewhat as archaeologists and historians attend increasingly to life in the numerous small villages, but too little remains from most of such settlements to cast significant light on their inhabitants' lives, circumstances, perspectives, and ideologies.[1] Their relative poverty meant that they could generally not afford to build with the durable materials employed in monumental urban structures or in the houses of the elite. As evidence of village layout, housing, everyday pottery pieces, tools, storage areas, and more comes to light, our picture fills out with details that provide us with a better sense of their terms of living than we might have expected. Nonetheless, there will always be distinct limits to the extent and depth of how much we can know about these

---

[1] Among recent studies describing how details of daily living can be drawn from the archaeological record and other sources, see Paula M. McNutt, *Reconstructing the Society of Ancient Israel* (Library of Ancient Israel; Louisville: Westminster John Knox; London: SPCK, 1999); S. Bendor, *The Social Structure of Ancient Israel: The Institution of the Family* (beit 'ab) *from the Settlement to the End of the Monarchy* (Jerusalem Biblical Studies 7; Jerusalem: Simor, 1996); Victor H. Matthews and Don C. Benjamin, *Social World of Ancient Israel 1250–587 BCE* (Peabody, Mass.: Hendrickson, 1993). For comparable recent portrayals of social life in Mesopotamia, see Karen Rhea Nemet-Nejat, *Daily Life in Ancient Mesopotamia* (Westport, Conn., and London: Greenwood, 1998); Daniel C. Snell, *Life in the Ancient Near East, 3100–332 B.C.E.* (New Haven and London: Yale Univ. Press, 1997); D. T. Potts, *Mesopotamian Civilization: The Material Foundations* (London: Athlone, 1997); and Marc van de Mieroop, *The Ancient Mesopotamian City* (Oxford: Clarendon; New York: Oxford Univ. Press, 1997).

villagers, especially because much of their everyday lives left little or no trace in the material record.

The Hebrew Bible is, in its own way, extremely problematic as a reliable resource for understanding customs in these innumerable hamlets scattered over the countryside. The biblical text stems immediately from groups and individuals who possessed a high level of literacy as well as the support, both financial and institutional, necessary for carrying out the tasks of writing and preserving such extensive literature. Neither this literacy nor support was normally to be found in the villages, but only in cities or in communities, such as Qumran, dedicated to sectarian interests. In all likelihood, the Hebrew Bible therefore emerged out of primarily urban settings. Prior to the final compositional stage, traditions—stories, proverbs, songs, laws, and the like—circulated in a variety of settings, including the rural districts, above all in the oral mode.[2] To the extent that any such materials reached written form, they most certainly underwent modification, if not even full transformation, in the process. Thus in the Hebrew Bible we do not read the direct expressions of village life, but at most only the city-dwellers' perceptions of village life.

This situation pertains especially for the laws. Let us take the Book of the Covenant (BC) as an example. The laws recorded in Exodus 21–23 are commonly held to represent the legal traditions of Israel before the monarchy. Since Israelite urbanization began in full force only during Iron Age II, that is, during the time of the centralized state, a pre-monarchic origin would place these laws squarely in the social period when villages served as virtually the only context of human settlement in the land, apart from the city-states in the coastal region and certain inland areas. The fact that many of these laws are preoccupied with agricultural matters, as well as the sparse evidence of centralized powers in BC, appears in the view of many to reinforce this notion of its rural provenance or roots. Even if one stipulates that BC was recorded after the advent of statehood and by persons living in the city of Jerusalem, it seems to be assumed—sometimes tacitly but often explicitly—that the laws it contains derive from communities located outside the cities.

---

[2] Burke O. Long, the honoree of this volume, called early attention to the important contributions of anthropological field-work to our understanding of oral tradition in ancient Israel: "Recent Field Studies in Oral Literature and Their Bearing on OT Criticism," *VT* 26 (1976) 187–98; and "Recent Field Studies in Oral Literature and the Question of Sitz im Leben," *Semeia* 5 (1976) 35–49. See also the studies of Robert C. Culley, especially his *Oral Formulaic Language in the Biblical Psalms* (Near and Middle East Series 4; Toronto: Univ. of Toronto Press, 1967). For a recent discussion, see Susan Niditch, *Oral World and Written Word: Ancient Israelite Literature* (Library of Ancient Israel; Louisville: Westminster John Knox, 1996; London: SPCK, 1997).

Frankly, in my view the Deuteronomic laws are much more plausibly connected to cities than the BC laws are to villages and towns—certainly in their present form as a collected whole, but probably also as individual laws. How might the BC laws have been collected? The countryside contained many hundreds of tiny settlements. If we are to think of the BC laws as the laws of rural society, then we ought to be able to conceive of a plausible means whereby they became assembled. Yet it is hard to imagine that someone roamed over the land, asking villagers to recount their laws and recording them for the benefit of either the villagers themselves or others.

There is an intriguing analogy from nineteenth-century Germany— Jacob and Wilhelm Grimms' *Kinder- und Hausmärchen,* the collection of German fairy tales commonly held to be the world's (or just the West's?) most often translated and reprinted book second only to the Bible. There is a widespread notion concerning its origin, and I confess to sharing this view until only recently upon reading several current studies. According to the legendary account, the Brothers Grimm collected their fairy tales by painstakingly crisscrossing Germany, visiting out-of-the-way settlements and succeeding in getting the local peasants to recount their stories. In smoky cabins or in small outside gatherings of children and adults they heard storytellers, especially housewives, spin the tales that had existed only in oral form for generations and centuries, and Jacob and Wilhelm assiduously committed them to writing. Back in their homes, they collated the various renditions of each tale, producing eventually their classic of world literature in 1812–15.

Such a romantic legend is, however, "patently false."[3] Far from going out to find stories among the common folk, the two brothers largely heard the tales in their own setting. Rather than collecting them from unknown informants, they heard many of them from two groups of friends as well as other acquaintances. Their informants were not quaint, wizened specimens from another age, but generally younger persons in their teens, 20s, and 30s who were recalling stories from their own childhood. Instead of the image of illiterate, uncultured peasants, a scene with mainly middle- and upper-class, educated urbanites appears more appropriate. Furthermore, Jacob and Wilhelm searched through older written sources for tales that could be adjusted to conform to their notion of charming little narratives. The Grimm brothers did not intentionally deceive their readers con-

---

[3] Walter Scherf, "Jacob and Wilhelm Grimm: A Few Small Corrections to a Commonly Held Image," in *The Brothers Grimm and Folktale* (ed. James M. McGlathery; Urbana and Chicago: Univ. of Illinois Press, 1988) 187. For further discussion of the details of the Grimms' sources and methods, see other articles in this same volume, particularly Heinz Rölleke, "New Results of Research on Grimms' Fairy Tales," 101–11; and Linda Dégh, "What Did the Grimm Brothers Give to and Take from the Folk?" 66–90.

cerning their sources, though they left the impression that their folktales were to be found natively in rural, tradition-oriented settings. Scholars have only rather recently managed to cast doubt on their legendary activities through a careful analysis both of external records and indications and of internal comments made by the Grimms themselves.

Who in ancient Israel would have been motivated to assemble laws—whether in the legendary or the more probable manner of the Grimms—and then to write them down and preserve them? The villagers themselves, who hardly possessed literacy equal to such a task, had little reason to engage in such a painstaking process for their own benefit. Each community had its own legal customs, which were sufficient to get them through until some new conflict arose that required fresh adjudication by the villagers themselves. They had no need of, nor could have read, a written code of their laws, much less a compendium of laws from villages around the country.

Just as innumerable variations for most of the stories were identified by the Grimms, so also there could hardly have been full uniformity in the legal traditions of the multitudinous Israelite settlements, which had virtually no direct contact with any others than those closest at hand. What then do these BC laws represent? It strains credulity to propose that they reproduce or encapsulate rules that enjoyed widespread legal acceptance across the land. Who could have established for them such broad currency? With no central authority during the pre-state period, no legislative arm, no agreed-upon place to which the disparate villages might have sent representatives to form a grass-roots national assembly, these scattered communities had no means to settle upon a set of laws authoritative for all of them.[4] It is difficult to conceive of the hamlets in even just one region collaborating, whether out of necessity or desire, to compile such a legal code for themselves. Even during the later state period, the villages were largely independent and relatively isolated from each other, continuing their tightly knit, kinship-centered, tradition-oriented, subsistence-level existence. The state officials and the economic elite, centered largely in the cities, needed to employ strict measures if they hoped to extract anything from the villagers—taxes or tributes, military conscripts, labor gangs, resources and produce for an urban or national market. The people in the hamlets faced enough difficulties in surviving from one year to the next, and they had little use for those on the outside who sought to drain them of

---

[4] For all its suggestiveness and initial appeal, Martin Noth's famous hypothesis of a twelve-tribe amphictyony (*Das System der zwölf Stämme Israels* [BWANT 4/1; Stuttgart: W. Kohlhammer, 1930]) has for understandable reasons not survived more recent sociological and historical analysis. There is little chance that the land's population, as diverse and scattered as it was, could have organized itself into a quasi-political, ideologically driven confederacy prior to the existence of the conditions that prompted the rise of a state.

their meager holdings.[5] Similarly, there was no good reason for them to share their legal traditions with others, and they must certainly have been amused, if not suspicious, if a governmental authority or religious representative sought to record their laws.

Of one thing we can be sure: BC *in its present form* does not coincide with village law. We confront the text now as literature, the product of urbanites. Even if it reflects laws that are thought to be the result of legal traditions brought by rural persons who relocated into cities, we are still faced with questions of how, by whom, and for what purposes the legal norms of various villages became recorded in their new social contexts. To press further on the question of the relation between village law and the Book of the Covenant, we thus approach a double-blind situation: on the one hand, the paucity of information about village life in Israel; and on the other, the activity of city-dwelling elites and literate specialists in producing the text that worked its way down to us.

Village Society

In order to provide a context for our following discussion of village law, I will provide here only the barest sketch of the distribution and character of these settlements during Israel's history, disregarding many of the differences among various areas of the land. The differences constitute, in fact, part of the argument I am offering: that entirely too wide a range of small, disparate, often isolated settlements persisted throughout ancient Israel's history for us to suppose that their legal customs could have been captured in the Book of the Covenant, or even in all of Pentateuchal law. Much the same, of course, could be said of the relation of villages to legal texts found elsewhere in ancient Southwest Asian cultures. At the same time, we should not suppose that we can facilely characterize "village society," which itself was likely as varied as were the settlements. Nonetheless, a certain typification of these settings can provide a basis for assessing whether or not the rural laws might have survived the transition to written record.

In terms of sheer numbers the villages occupied a remarkable position in Israel's social history. Although the evidence is and will remain incomplete, it would appear that the vast majority of the region's population—probably between 70 and 95 percent, depending on the period—resided in these villages, scattered by the hundreds over the entire countryside. The occasional cities and towns were not so populous in size as to amount to a total census of inhabitants even close to that of the rural population. However, the power wielded by these urban centers was disproportionate to their numbers, a sit-

---

[5] For a description of attitudes in contemporary villages in the region on political and economic matters, see C. A. O. van Nieuwenhuijze, "The Near Eastern Village: A Profile," *The Middle East Journal* 16 (1961) 295–308.

uation quite common in cultures both ancient and modern, deriving in the main from the city's ability to act in concert in pressing its demands and interests onto those sectors of the population too diffuse to resist effectively or to exert a comparable set of influences. Even nomadic groups, less susceptible to urban controls, could bring villagers to their knees if that was their intent. Note the text in Ezek 38:11, speaking of Gog and his army:

> You will say, "I will go up against a land of unwalled villages (פרזות); I will go against the undisturbed people dwelling in safety, all of them living where there are no walls or bars or gates."

An old adage has it that the city taxes the village and the nomad raids it. Although too generalized and simplified to serve as a historical summary, this observation amply describes the vulnerability of villages—as well as their frequent antagonism toward and suspicion of outsiders, which as it happened was often enough justified. Defenseless and exposed, they could scarcely resist anything larger than a small raiding party.

Distribution of Villages

Archaeologists, particularly during recent decades, have conducted extensive surveys of the countryside on both sides of the Jordan River in an effort to find evidence of ancient settlements. The resulting picture indicates that villages in remarkable number were distributed throughout many regions of the land beginning early in the Iron I period and stretching down to the Greco-Roman period and beyond. To be sure, the process of sedentarization during the twelfth and eleventh centuries BCE has attracted the greatest attention due to modern interest in uncovering details about Israel's beginnings. But village life on the whole thrived unabated throughout the millennium even though individual villages disappeared and emerged with some frequency. To a great extent, these hamlets are the unseen and unsung actors in Israel's history.

The Iron I age saw a dramatic increase in the number of villages in the highland region, from ca. 30 villages in 1200 BCE to over 250 by the year 1000. Significant numbers have been identified in other regions of the country.[6] On average, there was an increase of approximately eight times

---

[6] According to recent counts, which in most cases have not yet been completed for the entirety of the respective territories and will eventually produce even higher numbers, 240 Iron I sites have been identified in the central highlands: 122 in the territory known by the tribal name of Ephraim, 96 in Manasseh, and 22 in Benjamin and Judah. This total number in the central hill country during Iron I had risen to 254 in a report by the end of 1992; see Israel Finkelstein, "The Emergence of Israel: A Phase in the Cyclic History of Canaan in the Third and Second Millennia BCE," in *From Nomadism to Monarchy: Archaeological and Historical Aspects of Early Israel* (ed. Israel Finkelstein and Nadav Na'aman; Jerusalem: Israel Exploration Society; Washington: Biblical Archaeology Society, 1994) 153–71. In addition, evidence of at least

the number of villages known from the end of the Late Bronze period. Moreover, roughly half of these villages were founded on sites where there had been no previous settlement. This relatively short period of only two centuries was thus witness to a major demographic shift that became decisive for the remainder of Israel's social history. While cities were later built in these same highland areas during Iron II, the proliferation of villages continued, although not at the same rate as had occurred in Iron I. In the traditional tribal territory of Ephraim alone, the number of villages nearly doubled in the course of Iron II, and at the same time their average size increased as well. Statistics for the distribution of village sites during Iron II and later periods are not yet as readily available as they are for Iron I, perhaps because archaeologists and historians have typically been much more intrigued by the processes of urbanization and statehood during this period. However, we can at least note that living in villages remained the option most exercised by Israelites throughout the people's entire history. War wreaked the greatest havoc on larger cities, while villages—though vastly less defensible—were as a group more likely to survive the invasion of foreign troops, such as occurred during the eighth and sixth centuries BCE. Passing armies could easily commandeer agricultural resources and compel villagers to join them as slaves or soldiers, and since a village could scarcely offer resistance there would be little reason to attack and destroy it. In this respect the formidably walled cities proved less resilient and more vulnerable than did the villages.

Settlements were normally not scattered indiscriminately over the landscape. Rather, several key factors affected the location of villages: permanent and reliable water supply, preferably within a distance of 1 km. but often further away;[7] habitable terrain; proximity to the means for subsistence,

---

another 68 villages from this period has emerged in the Galilee, upwards of 60 in the Jordan Valley, and some 73 in Transjordan (Finkelstein, "Emergence," 162, sets the number in Transjordan during Iron I at 218, as of 1992). The archaeological surveys on which these data are based are published in various reports; see especially the overviews and the bibliographies in Israel Finkelstein, *Archaeology of the Israelite Settlement* (Jerusalem: Israel Exploration Society, 1988); Lawrence E. Stager, "The Archaeology of the Family in Ancient Israel," *BASOR* 260 (1985) 1–35; and James A. Sauer, "Transjordan in the Bronze and Iron Ages: A Critique of Glueck's Synthesis," *BASOR* 263 (1986) 1–26. For historical, political, and social assessments in light of these findings, see Gösta Ahlström, *The History of Ancient Palestine* (Minneapolis: Fortress; Sheffield: Sheffield Academic Press, 1993); and Thomas E. Levy, ed., *The Archaeology of Society in the Holy Land* (New York: Facts on File, 1995).

[7] Finkelstein, *Archaeology*, 194–98. A number of village sites in the Ephraim area, for example, were 2 km. or more removed from water sources, especially in the highland areas with substantial rock formations. Cisterns as well as storage jars provided the inhabitants with the necessary means for procuring and maintaining a water supply.

usually pasturage or arable land; availability of materials suitable for building houses, making pottery, and meeting other common needs for implements and the like; and relative safety, probably less from military forces
than from marauding raiders. One or more of these factors might be sacri-
ficed if others proved more inviting. Quite clearly, the means for subsistence
ranked as being of chief importance, and it should come as no surprise that
villages situated themselves most frequently next to arable land. Yet one
finds settlements in all types of terrain, from the desert fringe to very rocky
regions. In periods when a centralized state and economy could dictate it, a
village might specialize in the production of one or the other commodity, depending especially upon what was conducive in its environmental context.
Villages were much less likely than were cities to be situated near the well-
traveled roads; one can speculate that the reason lay in either the need for
safety or the preference for isolation. Villagers sought a place where they
could subsist and survive, as a rule by their own hand. Notable exceptions
were the villages situated deliberately near larger cities in order to supply
these urban centers with needed agricultural and pastoral produce. Known
as the בנות ("daughters") of the cities, these outlying satellites represent either an accommodation of the typical village to the market potential provided by population centers, or a coercive move by the urban powerful in
order to satisfy the needs of those in the city.[8]

Villages presumably associated most compatibly and congenially with
other villages like themselves, however. Density figures alone are rather
revealing.[9] The average for all types of topography throughout the entire
central highlands of Israel by the latter part of Iron I was at least 1 village
per 18 sq. km. (7 sq. mi.); as more villages are discovered, this number will
rise even further. During Iron II density almost doubled, but then receded
somewhat throughout later periods before rising to its greatest level in the
Roman and Byzantine periods.[10] Considering only the Iron I ratio of 1:18

---

[8] Frank S. Frick (*The City in Ancient Israel* [SBLDS 36; Missoula, Mont.: Scholars
Press, 1977]) has appropriately emphasized that an antagonism did not necessarily
exist between city and countryside since the inhabitants of each needed the other
for survival. There was, nonetheless, a difference between them in interests and
powers; see my essay, "Political Rights and Powers in Monarchic Israel," *Semeia* 66
(1994) 93–117.

[9] In one study of the territory of Ephraim, Iron I villages in the central range occurred as frequently as one per ten sq. km. (3.9 sq. mi.), while in the western slopes
the density thinned to one village for every 34 sq. km. (13.3 sq. mi.). Finkelstein, *Archaeology*, 190.

[10] Stager, "Archaeology," 4–5. On the process of ruralization during the Persian
period, see Kenneth Hoglund, "The Achaemenid Context," in *Second Temple Studies*, vol. 1: *The Persian Period* (ed. Philip R. Davies; JSOTSup 117; Sheffield: Sheffield
Academic Press, 1991) 54–72.

sq. km., the distance between villages would average a mere 4 km. (2.5 mi.). Of course, villages tended to cluster in hospitable terrain, and roughly 2 km. or less between them was not uncommon. In other words, quite typically two or more villages would be within eyesight of each other or a rather short walking distance apart. Such physical proximity suggests the need for some shared strategies and structures in the social, political, and economic—and thus also legal—arenas if the villages in a given area were to coexist and thrive.

It should be noted, however, that villages were by no means exclusively located in isolation from larger settlements. As indicated, cities usually had villages around them to help supply their needs for food and other products. Even in the absence of a city, a given region often had at least one town that was more populous than the other settlements and to which the smaller hamlets were subordinated, even if in only informal ways. Such a situation would suggest a hierarchy of interests and power, which could variously constitute or enhance the cooperative strategies within a village or among contiguous villages of similar size. If life for the majority of Israelites was lived out in the context of small villages, they normally were impacted by the presence of larger settlements—if not in their immediate vicinity, then at a further distance away but nonetheless powerful and demanding.

Size and Population

The Israelite villages were generally small in size, on average only 0.75–1.5 acres (0.3–0.6 hectare) and very often not more than a cluster of just a few homes.[11] Settlements of 7–14 acres (3–6 hectares) qualify as regional towns, and larger than that would be a city (Megiddo: 25 acres; Jerusalem at the time of Josiah: 125 acres). On average, only about half of a village's total space was occupied by residences. Thus a settlement encompassing one acre, for example, contained roughly 20–30 houses, although individual villages could be more or less densely inhabited.

Calculating the population of settlements is fraught with difficulties, and several different methods have been proposed, each with inherent problems.[12] Best estimates indicate that village population typically comprised

---

[11] For the Iron I period in the territory of Ephraim, Finkelstein (*Archaeology*, 192) distinguishes among three sizes of villages: a large central village, covering at least 0.5–0.6 hectare (1.25–1.5 acres); a small village of some 0.3–0.4 hectare (0.75–1.0 acre); and a grouping of only a few houses (or tents?). For the area between Shechem and Ramallah, he indicates ("Emergence," 162–63) that 23% of the sites during Iron I were over 0.5 hectare (1.25 acres) compared to 66% in Iron II, and 50% of the sites during Iron I were only 0.1–0.2 hectare (0.25–0.5 acre) compared to 34% in Iron II. Cf. Stager, "Archaeology," 3.

[12] For a survey and critique of various methods of estimating the population of

75–150 people, but very frequently even less than 75. Sites with only a few houses clustered together were not uncommon; in fact, during times such as the Iron I period in the territory of Ephraim, virtually half of all the known sites were very small, embracing fewer than 50 souls each.[13] All villages taken together yield the following totals: ca. 21,000 sedentary Israelites living west of the Jordan about 1150 BCE, and ca. 51,000 at the close of the 11th century BCE.[14] During Iron II the total village population increased appreciably, as did the number and size of cities. One recent estimate[15] sets the total population in the eighth century at the time of the arrival of the Assyrians at about 460,000, of which 350,000 were in the North and 110,000 in the South. Of importance for our purposes, approximately 68% of the population in Cisjordanian Israel and 71% in Judah lived outside the larger settlements. All of these figures underscore the prevalence of village life throughout the country, but ironically not its dominance over the culture. We meet here a hidden world, all too frequently undervalued by students of antiquity.

Summarizing the social makeup, institutions, and traditions of so many tiny settlements disbursed over the landscape is a daunting and precarious enterprise. This very fact should caution us against assuming that the laws in a text such as the Book of the Covenant faithfully reflect the legal practices of Israelite village life. There were far too many villages, too little direct contact among them, too wide a territory, and too long a time period for us to assume that we can know them and their customs well. Any suggestions we make about village society must consequently be very general in scope and tentative in nature.

---

ancient Israel, see especially Yigal Shiloh, "The Population of Iron Age Palestine in the Light of a Sample Analysis of Urban Plans, Areas, and Population Density," *BASOR* 239 (1980) 25–35. The main methods are: reasoning from water resources or agricultural potential of the area; applying a formula based on roofed living space (usually one inhabitant per 10 sq. m. [108 sq. ft.] of an enclosed dwelling), or a family coefficient (usually four persons per home); or calculating on the basis of a density coefficient per square meter of the whole settlement in question, a figure reached in light of multiple factors including the number and size of houses, the amount of public space, and the nature of the settlement. According to Finkelstein (*Archaeology*, 331–32), a reasonable, conservative density coefficient is 25 inhabitants per 1000 sq. m. (100 people per acre). Shiloh ("Population") works with a higher number, 40–50 persons per 1000 sq. m. (160–200 people per acre).

[13] Finkelstein, *Archaeology*, 192–93.

[14] Ibid., 330–35.

[15] Magen Broshi and Israel Finkelstein, "The Population of Palestine in Iron Age II," *BASOR* 287 (1992) 47–60.

Identifying Laws

To determine the legal traditions operative within the villages of ancient Israel requires attention to the specific characteristics of their society, about which we have little direct information. Three types of sources are available, each presenting its own special difficulties: a) the texts of the Hebrew Bible, which must be critically interpreted because they stem not immediately from the villages themselves but from people in the cities who purport to be writing in part about non-urban life; b) the material culture, the mute and circumstantial evidence uncovered by archaeologists and studied by historians interested in the life-styles and events of antiquity; and c) comparative information from other cultures, stemming from anthropologists or historians but not necessarily or always bearing directly on circumstances prevalent in ancient Israel.

Twelve criteria strike me as fitting in the effort to identify the laws or principles in the biblical texts that most likely reflect the legal controls at work in some—though, as mentioned, quite likely not in all—Israelite villages:

1. Village laws reflect and promote the social customs and traditions of the community. Representing what is often called customary law, they are developed and transmitted in oral form.

2. Village laws recognize the social and political hierarchy basic to village life and kinship groups, especially the patriarchal structure and local leadership.

3. Village laws rarely involve any formal institutions beyond kinship, at most only an *ad hoc* deliberative gathering of village elders.

4. Village laws seek to ensure cooperation and eliminate discord among members of the community. They attempt, as needed, to resolve conflicts, to remedy losses and injuries, and to clarify liability.

5. Village laws are especially concerned with matters affecting the family, kinship groups, marriage, and sexuality.

6. Village laws do not contemplate the more complex, layered society found in cities or at the national level.

7. Village laws tend to be oriented toward life on the land, i.e. toward agricultural or pastoral existence.

8. Village laws are sensitive to the priorities and perils inherent in a subsistence economy.

9. Village laws are more likely than urban or national laws to be responsive to conditions of vulnerability among the lower classes, as in the case of persons who suffer from hardships, death of a provider, or natural catastrophe.

10. Village laws foster the interests of the given village and, usually, those of nearby or similar villages as well, especially those with which there may be kinship ties.

11. Village laws do not support the diversion of the community's produce or resources to cities or other parts of the country, except insofar as a direct benefit (e.g., trade or security) can come to the villagers as a result.

12. Village laws tend to exclude or give limited protection to outsiders.

Not all of these criteria will be evident in each law, of course. However, I find it rather difficult to imagine any given law in a village running directly counter to these criteria. Again, for all the diversity presumably prevailing among the villages spread across the land of ancient Israel, the kinds of circumstances or orientations reflected in these criteria seem to be fundamental, and they also allow each separate community substantial latitude to develop its own customs. Villages with laws deviating significantly from these norms were most likely to be located close to cities and thus under their influence, or to be in existence during those monarchic or imperial times when overlords, large landowners, tax collectors, military and labor recruiters, and others representing outside interests interfered in village affairs to a greater extent than the villagers would have desired. Absolute economic and political equality within a given village cannot be expected, but much less of an imbalance prevailed than in larger settlements.

Admittedly, a considerable amount of speculation has contributed to this list of criteria, and others might construct a list quite different from this—or refrain altogether from even trying. In my view, however, the enterprise is warranted for four fundamental reasons: a) many hundreds of villages existed throughout the country and throughout Israel's history and contained the vast majority of the population, which should be reason enough for the historian to pay them attention; b) despite the variety among them, they must have shared much in terms of their social structure and social values because of similarities in their cultural backgrounds, their means of livelihood, their coping with outside pressures, and their response to the natural environment; c) enough information has now become available, especially from archaeology and anthropology, to give us a reasonable sense of issues and priorities in small-scale communities of this type; and d) customary laws develop quite naturally in such social groups in order to maintain order, resolve conflicts, and maximize the chances for survival. It therefore seems quite legitimate to inquire into the nature of village law, even in the absence of documents recording them explicitly. The above criteria do not spell out the content of the laws, but rather indicate their tendencies and their aversions.

The Book of the Covenant

The Book of the Covenant, or Covenant Code, serves as a convenient test-case for examining the relation between village law and Pentateuchal law. On the face of it, a number of the topics in Exodus 21–23 fit quite plausibly in a village context, especially the laws dealing with liability, restitution, marriage, violence, judicial procedure, and more. Other topics and specific laws, however, betray more of an urban or national agenda.

Laws having to do with slavery could hardly have been commonplace in villages, where subsistence needs were met only with considerable difficulty. To be sure, slaves in the ancient economy did not always denote luxury since persons could become enslaved through a variety of means, including capture, birth, or hardship. But in village contexts the average family did not have the means or the opportunity to acquire slaves; the greater danger was that these villagers would fall into debt and have no other recourse than to sell themselves into slavery. The impulse toward benign treatment of slaves and toward release of slaves after six years (Exod 21:2) conforms to the self-interests of villagers who could easily become indentured. Yet to have had teeth, the various laws detailing treatment (21:2–11, 20–21, 26–27, 32; 23:12) must have arisen in a context, such as a city, where slavery was an institution that could to some extent be regulated.

Exod 22:28 (Hebrew 22:27) contains an apodictic prohibition not to curse God or the leader of the people. This sudden reference to a "leader," when no other similar mention appears in these chapters, is startling, all the more so by being coupled in the same sentence with the warning against cursing God. The word for leader, נשׂיא, can well refer to a local or tribal leader, but just as easily to a king, which seems in this case especially likely because the person is identified as the "leader of your people." The close connection between the king and God occurs often in the Hebrew Bible, serving as an effective legitimization of the authority and standing of the monarch. Such an elevation of the distant royal house undercut the self-interests of those residing in the villages, who would not have thought to mandate such respect except as a self-protective measure.

Certain of the laws regarding judicial procedure reflect circumstances at an urban or national level. The perversion of justice for the poor (23:6) occurred more commonly in such contexts; villages may have had certain vulnerable individuals, but not whole classes of poor—unless essentially the whole village population qualified as being poor. Similarly, bribing those who sit in judgment (23:8) is certainly possible in village contexts, but a group of elders hearing a case against a person who is a neighbor and perhaps even a relative is less likely to be turned through bribery than is a judge who can use the office for personal gain. Injunctions to give truthful witness (23:1–2, 7) can be expected in both village and urban settings.

Virtually all of the religious laws in the Book of the Covenant reflect the interests of a centralized cultic institution, such as existed in the capital city or other urban or even town centers. BC begins with (or is preceded by) the so-called altar law in Exod 20:22–26, which combines elements from both urban and rural culture. The first part prohibits making gods of silver or gold, a law that can realistically reflect only a culture in which discretionary wealth was available; rhetorically, of course, villagers might also have proscribed such use of silver or gold, but possessing no such resources themselves they would scarcely have ordained such restrictions for their own cultic practices. The law continues, however, with an injunction to build altars only of earth or of undressed stone. With such a practice we seem to be in the village context, but it is also possible that this law in its present form reflects a reactionary or re-pristinizing impulse of priests at a central sanctuary who either sought to stop changes in cultic practices or aimed to cater to villagers coming to the city.

The other religious laws found in Exodus 21–23 seem to stem from the urban cult. The effort to prohibit sacrifices to other gods (22:20 [Hebrew 22:19]) expresses the interest in stamping out the pluralism of deities worshiped across the land, above all in the villages outside the reach of the central priesthood. Requirements for sacrificing the first-fruits (22:29–30 [Hebrew 22:28–29]) originated quite plausibly in the village contexts where the fertility of animals and crops was of immediate concern, but these laws have the flavor of commands to bring the hard-won harvest from the countryside into the cities. Similarly, the celebration of the three annual festivals (23:14–19) springs, we can imagine, from rural rites, especially the two timed for the harvest periods, but again these formulations suggest that the produce be brought to the central sanctuaries and offered as sacrifices there.

Most of the other laws present in the Book of the Covenant reflect conditions and norms conceivable in villages, although they are often formulated in a manner suggestive of urban or national interests as well. Issues of marriage and sexuality functioned as defining social indicators in villages, and controls arose to keep the lines clearly drawn. Remarkably, though, BC contains only the slightest references to marriage. One case focuses on marriage involving slaves (21:2–11), a social phenomenon reflecting a wealthier economy than villages typically managed; a slight hint of the vulnerability in such a marriage is expressed by this law, suggesting perhaps the viewpoint of the underclass, although the slave owner benefits as well if the male slave chooses to remain with his enslaved family. The only other marriage law (22:16–17 [Hebrew 15–16]) deals with the seduction of an unengaged virgin daughter; a bride-price is to be paid, and the man is to marry the woman unless her father forbids it. A prohibition against bestiality (22:19 [Hebrew 22:18]) is the sole law governing sexuality. For all the importance that marriage and family must have played in village society, the paucity of BC laws controlling their diverse aspects is a curiosity. Did the drafters of BC not understand the nuances of kinship laws within the villages, or was there too much variety from place to place to allow for a reasonable representation in this literature?

Laws touching directly on the primary means of livelihood in the villages, however, do occur, but again without much breadth of topic. Cultivation of fields figures as an issue of liability in the cases of a crop being destroyed due to negligence, either from grazing livestock or from fire

(22:5–6 [Hebrew 22:4–5]). The only other situation envisions not a case of legal conflict but rather a means for providing for the poor by letting the land lie fallow in the seventh year (23:10–11); as mentioned above regarding 23:6, this text with its acknowledgment of a class of poor people points to a stratified society, and the law may in fact issue from an urban group that seeks to use an agricultural practice as a means of offering relief to the poor, even though villagers as a whole were often not far from the poverty level themselves. Most of the laws regarding work animals and cattle (21:28–36; 22:1,3b–4 [Hebrew 21:37, 22:2b–3]) treat problems of liability or theft. Two other provisions, however, seem on the surface to speak of compassion and consideration: returning a donkey that has gone astray and helping up a donkey that has fallen under its burden (23:4–5); in both instances, however, property issues are also at stake. Work animals were certainly seen and used in towns and cities, so these laws may not be unique to rural contexts.

The legal constraints in BC against theft stem plausibly from villages; certainly, at least, some such provisions are to be expected there. However, these specific laws do not quite match the rural conditions where only 50–150 people are clustered in a community, everyone knowing well what others possess. It would be hard to get away with stealing animals (22:1, 3b–4 [Hebrew 21:37; 22:2b–3]), and breaking and entering is only slightly more thinkable among neighbors (22:2–3a [Hebrew 22:1–2a]). Either these laws were designed to specify punishments that would affect primarily only outsiders coming to the village, or they point to urban contexts where such theft stands a better chance of success. Liability for property held for another person (22:7–8, 10–15 [Hebrew 22:6–7, 9–14]) could also apply in both contexts; when animals are the property in question, the village is the most likely setting. On the other hand, if this property belongs in fact to a large landowner who has lent it to a tenant farmer, then these laws betray less a village ethos than a class division.

The legal terms for dealing with violence—murder, kidnapping, bodily injury (21:12–19, 22–25)—are quite conceivable as sanctions in village dealings. Specifying a place to which a manslaughterer could flee the blood-avenger suggests a national or, perhaps, territorial strategy that isolated villages could scarcely develop alone. All of these rules can also function in urban contexts.

Finally, the laws providing for the protection of the vulnerable—strangers, widows, orphans, and the poor (22:21–27 [Hebrew 22:20–26]; 23:9)—mirror the vulnerability of the village population itself. Such compassionate concern would be consistent with the people's values, although the text itself has the ring of rhetoric and exhortation, not of enforceable laws. Money-lending and the taking of collateral point to the presence of wealthier persons, such as were to be found in cities or large estates. Nonetheless, the interests of villagers who were exposed to such oppression and exploitation are discernible in these laws.

Conclusion

There is not much in the Book of the Covenant that can be traced unequiv-ocally to the villages of ancient Israel. As a whole, this text is a literary artifact and does not necessarily bear resemblance to any actual legal for-mulations or practices of the period. Just because it takes the form of direc-tives, restraints, prohibitions, and sanctions does not mean that we have in it a record of living laws, nor even of a promulgated code. To assume, as has traditionally been done by modern interpreters, that any of these state-ments reproduce legal controls actually at work in one or another social context of ancient Israel goes beyond the evidence we possess—and is just that: an assumption on our part.

The best we can manage in testing for correspondence between the text and social norms of the period is to apply a principle of plausibility, based on a mixture of textual, material, and comparative indications. On these terms, internal indications point toward an urban provenance for Exodus 21–23. The institution of slavery, the presence of both wealth and poverty, houses large enough to be burglarized while the residents sleep, a judge who can be bribed, a leader who should no more be reviled than should God, a formalized cult to which sacrifices are expected to be brought—all such phenomena are scarcely imaginable in villages averaging 50–150 in-habitants, most of them agriculturalists or pastoralists barely surviving in a subsistence economy. On the other hand, however, some vestiges of cus-toms and values conceivable in such villages can perhaps be detected in our text: some theft controls, two marriage or sexuality customs, liability specifications, instructions on treatment of work animals, sanctions against violence, guidelines for religious veneration using simple materi-als and the fruits of rural production, and concern for the vulnerable, both slaves and poor. Yet in no case are these topics treated fully enough to count as adequate protections or provisions for the ordering of life in the villages. The writers of Exodus 21–23 have at most incorporated highly se-lected legal traditions that *may* have been operative in *certain* villages. Of course, there were also agriculturalists living in or just outside of the cities who could have served as a source for these notions of the laws of the land. The villagers did not produce this text, not even something amounting to a first draft. Too many indications of city interests and too few of the villag-ers' must lead us to conclude that the Book of the Covenant, from its first appearance onward as a literary document, was a product of the city.

For what reason is it even important to consider the terms of village life when Israel's most notable cultural remnants—the texts, the monumental buildings and fortifications, the impact on history—stem from cities? Two compelling grounds suggest themselves. First, a social history seeking to appreciate the terms of living faced by the majority of the population, those who do not count among the powerful and influential, can round out our picture of that culture. Although our efforts at historical recovery are severely hampered because of the inadequacy of the sources, we should attempt to identify conditions and perspectives different from those dominating the relatively few cities of Israel—or at least question whether urban viewpoints coincide with the interests and customs of those living elsewhere. Second, this larger socio-historical picture can provide insight into the agenda of the writers of our texts, which were produced by, and in all likelihood mainly for, persons situated in the cities. The agricultural and pastoral economy depended on the work of all the villagers across the land, but as long as the persons at the center were able to control the economic and political systems, which a monarchic structure facilitated, it was not a high priority for them to cater overmuch to the interests of these villagers.

Both of these reasons should affect the way we think about the texts and culture of ancient Israel. Specifically, we can expect the legal literature to retain not much more than occasional traces of village practices and values, mediated always through the experiences and self-interests of urban, literate, largely upper-class or privileged groups. Nonetheless, the villagers themselves had to find order for their own social existence, which necessitated legal norms and structures for them to deal with disruptions and conflict. Contrary to conventional assumptions by modern interpreters, these villagers would have found little benefit in contributing to the production of the biblical legal texts, neither the Book of the Covenant nor any other Pentateuchal collection. Their primary interests lay not in texts but in their own traditions and in survival in the face of often extraordinary political, economic, and environmental odds.

Chapter 13

The Biblical Prohibition of the Mourning Rites of Shaving and Laceration: Several Proposals

Saul M. Olyan
Brown University

The biblical proscriptions of shaving and laceration rites have long baffled scholars, and continue to elicit new explanatory proposals.[1] Shaving and laceration rites are prohibited for priests in Lev 21:5, and for all Israelites in both Lev 19:27–28 and Deut 14:1. Of the many mourning rites[2] witnessed

---

[1] E.g., B. B. Schmidt, *Israel's Beneficent Dead* (1994; Winona Lake, Ind.: Eisenbrauns, 1996) 166–178 for a recent attempt at a solution. (On Schmidt's proposal, see my discussion in n. 13, ahead.) The most common explanation in the literature for the proscription of these rites associates them with alleged Canaanite practice supposedly abhorrent to Yhwh (e.g., B. Levine, *Leviticus* [JPSTC; Philadelphia: Jewish Publication Society, 1989] 143 and E. S. Gerstenberger, *Das dritte Buch Mose: Leviticus* [ATD 6; Göttingen: Vandenhoeck & Ruprecht, 1993] 252, 285, who cites the Canaanite theory with some hesitation). Yet as Schmidt, C. Carmichael (*The Spirit of Biblical Law* [Athens and London: Univ. of Georgia Press, 1996] 129–30) and others have pointed out, these mourning practices are frequently represented as legitimate Israelite rites except in the three texts in question. Yhwh even orders shaving for mourners in certain texts (Isa 22:12; Amos 8:10). Thus, the Canaanite theory fails to explain the evidence cogently.

[2] That these are rites associated with mourning can be shown from comparison with other biblical texts representing mourning practices (e.g., Jer 16:6; 41:5) as well as extra-biblical materials (e.g., KTU 1.5 VI 11–25). An association with mourning is also suggested by the mention of the dead in two of the three texts in question (Lev 19:28; Deut 14:1) and the general mourning context of Lev 21:1–6. See further Schmidt's helpful discussion (ibid., 167–171), and the comments of M. Noth, *Das dritte Buch Mose: Leviticus* (ATD 6; Göttingen: Vandenhoeck & Ruprecht, 1962) 123,

in the biblical text, only laceration and shaving are banned in any source, and their interdiction is attested only in the Holiness Source and Deuteronomy. In contrast to their treatment in Holiness and Deuteronomistic materials, laceration and shaving are represented as perfectly legitimate mourning rites in non-H and non-D texts, as others have shown convincingly.[3] Therefore, we must ask why they are proscribed in Holiness and Deuteronomistic texts and nowhere else. I will begin this paper by reviewing briefly the three texts in question, and go on to ask what—if anything—distinguishes shaving and laceration from other mourning rites. What, in other words, might have motivated Holiness and Deuteronomistic circles to prohibit these gestures of mourning while tolerating or accepting other mourning markers? After proposing what I believe distinguishes shaving and laceration among rites of mourning, I will go on to consider why they are proscribed for priests in Lev 21:5, and for all Israel in Lev 19:27–28 and Deut 14:1. As others have argued, the priestly ban likely antedates the interdiction for all Israel, and I will propose an explanation for the broadening of the prohibition. I offer this essay as a tribute to Burke O. Long, a colleague, mentor and friend for well over a decade now, whose honest daring, consistent rigor, and refreshing insight have long been an inspiration to me.

The three texts of central interest read as follows:

לא יקרחה קרחה בראשם ופאת זקנם לא יגלחו ובבשרם לא ישרטו שרטת:

They shall not shave a bald spot on their head(s), nor shall they shave the corner of their beard(s), nor shall they incise an incision in their flesh. (Lev 21:5)

לא תקפו פאת ראשכם ולא תשחית את פאת זקנך: ושרט לנפש לא תתנו בבשרכם וכתבת קעקע לא תתנו בכם אני יהוה:

You shall not round off the corner of your head(s), nor shall you destroy the corner of your beard(s). You shall not set an incision for the dead in your flesh, nor shall you impose the writing of a tattoo on yourselves. I am Yhwh. (Lev 19:27–28)

בנים אתם ליהוה אלהיכם לא תתגדדו ולא תשימו קרחה בין עיניכם למת:

Children shall you be to Yhwh your god. You shall not lacerate yourselves, nor shall you set a bald spot between your eyes for the dead. (Deut 14:1)

Lev 21:5 prohibits priests from shaving a bald spot on the head, shaving the corner (?) of the beard, and incising an incision in the flesh. Shaving a bald spot on the head is a well-attested mourning rite (e.g., Isa 22:12;

134–35; Gerstenberger, *Leviticus*, 252; and Levine, *Leviticus*, 143, among many others. G. J. Botterweck is, however, not convinced that Lev 21:5 describes mourning rites ("גלח," *TDOT* 3.7, 16).

[3] See citations in n. 1.

Jer 16:6; Amos 8:10), as is manipulation (including shaving) of beard hair (e.g., Isa 15:2; Jer 41:5; Ezra 9:3). Incising an incision, a form of laceration, is explicitly associated with the dead elsewhere—Lev 19:28, one of the three texts under consideration here—and another idiom for laceration (*Hitpael* of גדד) is closely associated with mourning in a variety of biblical texts.[4] In addition to proscribing incisions for the dead in language similar to that of Lev 21:5, Lev 19:27–28 forbids Israelites to "round off" (נקף) the corner of the head (?), "destroy" the corner of the beard, and tattoo the flesh. Rounding off the corner of the head, though obscure to us as a gesture, seems to refer to some form of shaving or hair cutting. Destroying the corner of the beard is probably the same act as shaving the corner of the beard mentioned in Lev 21:5. Tattooing the flesh must differ from incising an incision, though both appear to involve cutting the flesh.[5] Finally, Deut 14:1 forbids Israelites to lacerate themselves (*Hitpael* גדד) or set a bald spot between the eyes for the dead.[6] The pairing of laceration and shaving as mourning gestures is not restricted to these three texts alone; there are several other texts in which the two acts are represented as legitimate mourning rites (e.g., Jer 16:6, 41:5). But these three texts prohibit them.

What was it about laceration and shaving that led Holiness circles to ban them for priests, and later, Holiness and Deuteronomistic circles to proscribe them for all Israelites? In order to address this question, we must consider laceration and shaving as components of a larger complex of mourning rites that include sitting on the ground, moving back and forth (נוד), tearing one's garment, strewing ashes or dirt on one's head, wearing sackcloth, fasting, weeping, covering the upper lip, singing dirges and avoiding the sanctuary sphere. These mourning rites function to create and mark a distinct ritual status for the mourner, who is polluted through corpse contact and remains separated from quotidian life—including the cult—for a set period of time, generally seven days.[7] The rites that separate

---

[4] Laceration is most commonly expressed using the *Hitpael* of the verb גדד, as in Deut 14:1; 1 Kgs 18:28; Jer 16:6; 41:5; 47:5; Mic 4:14. In almost all of these examples, a mourning context for the act of laceration is clear. In contrast, the nouns שׂרט and שׂרטת and verbal forms of the root שׂרט occur only in Lev 21:5; 19:28 and Zech 12:3, and only in the former two passages do the noun and its verbal reflexes relate to mourning.

[5] The word קעקע, usually translated "tattoo," occurs only in Lev 19:28. On this, see further N. Tur-Sinai, "כתבת קעקע," *Encyclopedyah Miqra'it* 4.378–80.

[6] The location of the bald spot in Deut 14:1 is unusual. Most texts mentioning the shaving of a bald spot as a mourning rite locate it on the head, presumably where there is normally hair (e.g., Lev 21:5; Isa 15:2; Jer 48:37; Ezek 7:18; 29:18; Amos 8:10). On this, see Botterweck, "גלח," 7.

[7] Though most biblical texts bear witness to a seven-day mourning period,

the mourner from others and mark the mourner's distinct ritual status are often contrasted in biblical texts with a corresponding set of rites that are associated with a normal, clean ritual state and participation in the cult. We might call this second set of rites, rites of rejoicing. Some of these rites serve to move the mourner back to the normal, clean ritual state from the separation characteristic of mourning. These rites include rising from the ground, washing, wearing regular or festal clothes, anointing, dancing, eating and drinking.[8]

A number of biblical texts suggest the possibility of rapid reversal from a state of rejoicing to a state of mourning, and vice versa. In Amos 8:10, the Day of Yhwh is described. At that ominous time, Israel's joyous festivals will be transformed while in process: "I will turn (והפכתי) your pilgrimage festivals into mourning, and all your songs into dirges. I will put sackcloth on every loin, a bald spot on every head . . ." Ps 30:12 is similar in its description of a rapid transformation, here of mourning to rejoicing: "You turned (הפכת) my lament into dancing, you removed my sackcloth and girded me with joy . . ."[9] David's mourning for the first son of Bathsheba ends rapidly through a series of reversals in 2 Sam 12:20: He rises from the ground, washes, anoints himself, and changes his clothes, before going off to the sanctuary to worship and home to dine. When one considers most of the rites that characterize the activity of the mourner, it is clear that they are easily reversible: The one who sits on the ground rises; the one covered with ashes or dirt bathes; the one fasting eats. The same observation applies to the rites that separate the mourner from the rest of the community: Sackcloth replaces normal attire; the upper lip is covered; dirges replace joyful songs. Yet shaving and laceration do not fit this pattern.

Unlike other mourning rites that separate and mark the mourner, laceration and shaving are not easily reversible. Laceration of all types causes bleeding and scabbing that might last for weeks; it may even leave permanent scars. Shaving is at best only gradually reversible over an extended period of time.[10] Thus, shaving and laceration stand out as distinct because

---

mourning of one day (2 Sam 1:12) and thirty days (Num 20:29; Deut 34:8, cf. Deut 21:13) are attested.

[8] The most interesting study of these contrasting sets of rites is G. A. Anderson, *A Time to Mourn, A Time to Dance: The Expression of Grief and Joy in Israelite Religion* (University Park: Pennsylvania State Univ. Press, 1991), whose influence on my formulation above is obvious.

[9] The verb הפך is sometimes used in other contexts to express rapid change or transformation. See, e.g., Exod 7:17, 20; Ps 78:44; 105:29 (the Nile's waters are turned into blood); Ps 66:6 (Yhwh turned the Sea of Reeds into dry ground); Ps 114:8 (Yhwh brought forth water from the rock).

[10] We see this in 2 Sam 10:5, the case of David's humiliated emissaries to the Ammonite court. The men, beards half-shaven and genitals exposed in a mockery

they are not easily or rapidly reversible.[11] But there is more to say about the distinct character of laceration and shaving as mourning gestures. Unlike mourning rites that can be reversed at will, which last only as long as the mourner remains separated from the community, the physical evidence of laceration and shaving outlast the standard, seven-day mourning period.[12] At the end of seven days, sackcloth is removed and normal, quotidian clothing is donned; fasting ceases and eating and drinking begins. But the shaved head or the head with a bald spot remains after seven days, a conspicuous marker of mourning among non-mourners, as are lacerated arms or other body parts. Thus, the carefully constructed boundaries that separate the mourner from others are obscured by the continued presence of shaved head or lacerated body parts; these blur the social and ritual distinction between the mourner and others, a distinction made and marked by mourning rites.[13]

Now that the distinct character of shaving and laceration as rites of mourning has been established, I shall go on to consider what might have motivated their proscription for priests in Lev 21:5, and for all Israelites in Lev 19:27–29 and Deut 14:1. Priests find their primary locus in the sanctuary, where they present Yhwh's offerings at the altar and attend to other, specialized tasks. According to Lev 21:16–23 (H), priests with physical defects (מומים) such as blindness and lameness may not appear before Yhwh with offerings, nor may a blemished high priest approach the curtain at the entry of the holy of holies; to do so, says the text, would profane Yhwh's holy sanctuaries which Yhwh sanctifies (לא יחלל את מקדשי כי אני יהוה מקדשם).

---

of mourning rites, are ordered not to return immediately to Jerusalem, but to wait at Jericho until their beards have sprouted. The exposure of their nakedness was without doubt quickly remedied, but nothing could be done immediately about their half-shaven beards.

[11] In a footnote, Schmidt anticipates me by noting in passing the irreversibility of laceration and shaving's long-lasting effects, but he does not develop these observations (*Beneficent Dead,* 178).

[12] I am not the first to make this observation. See Schmidt, ibid., 178 and n. 178.

[13] Though he notes in passing the long-lasting effects of laceration and shaving, and observes that they outlast the mourning period, Schmidt, ibid., 178, argues that shaving and laceration are distinct because they "offer an *unparalleled* identification of the living with the dead and an *unprecedented* reminder of death's intrusion upon the world of the living. Moreover, the irreversibility of the markings embodies death's inevitability and its ever-present threat." I prefer to argue that their distinction resides not in any special kind of identification they might foster, but in their lack of easy reversibility and in the fact that they outlast the mourning period. We cannot know that shaving or laceration fostered any greater identification with the dead in this culture than did strewing ashes on the head or sitting on the ground weeping. Yet we can establish that the effects of laceration and shaving go beyond seven days.

Blemished priests may remain in the sanctuary and continue to eat holy foods as long as they do not approach Yhwh's primary loci (altar and holy of holies). It is clear from Lev 21:16–23 that Yhwh does not want to see physical defects on those who approach him *directly*, though he tolerates blemishes on those who do not (e.g., priests who do not serve at the altar). Yhwh's rejection of blemished priests who approach him directly helps us to understand the prohibition of shaving and laceration for priests in mourning in Lev 21:5. Just as Yhwh does not wish to see blemishes on the priests who approach him, so he does not wish to see permanent or long-lasting mourning markers such as a bald spot or lacerated arms on them.[14] The justification for the proscription of shaving and laceration in Lev 21:5 is remarkably similar to that offered in Lev 21:23 regarding blemished priests. Lev 21:23 states that the blemished priest shall not approach the altar or curtain because of his defect, that he not profane (חלל) Yhwh's holy sanctuaries which Yhwh sanctifies. Lev 21:6 exhorts the priests to be holy and not profane (חלל) the name of their god, "for the offerings of Yhwh, the food of their god, they bring near . . ." Thus, each passage justifies its particular restriction based on holiness, and the danger of its profanation, either by a blemished priest approaching the altar or by a priest with a permanent or long-lasting mourning marker doing so.[15]

But why is Yhwh offended by the presence of a priest at his altar with a permanent or long-lasting mourning marker? I believe that these tokens of mourning on priests at the altar offend Yhwh because they bring the symbolism of death and mourning directly into his presence. Yhwh, the holy god, has an aversion to death, the polluter and threat to holiness par excellence.[16] He cannot tolerate its presence in his sanctuary. Yet the lacerated or shaved priest brings death to Yhwh's altar. The distinction between mour-

---

[14] These, however, might be permitted to non-priests who enter the sanctuary and perhaps even to priests who do not approach Yhwh directly. Lev 21:6, which justifies the restrictions of 21:5, speaks specifically of priests *who present Yhwh's offerings*; it says nothing of the status of other priests who might not approach Yhwh directly, and nothing of worshipers.

[15] J. Tigay compares Lev 21:5–6 and 21:23, noting the similarity of the justification in each (*Deuteronomy* [JPSTC; Philadelphia: Jewish Publication Society, 1996] 136).

[16] Death is a most threatening polluter that must be carefully circumscribed, and all who have had contact with a corpse, a tomb, or bones must undertake elaborate purification procedures to become clean. According to Num 19:13, 20, whoever does not undertake the proper purification rites pollutes Yhwh's sanctuary even without entering it. A polluted sanctuary would result in Yhwh's departure from his earthly abode (Deut 23:15; Ezek 43:9). Some scholars have argued that all sources of pollution are related to death in some way, though this thesis remains unproven. For this, see, e.g., J. Milgrom, *Leviticus 1–16* (AB 3; New York: Doubleday, 1991) 46 and E. Feldman, *Biblical and Post-Biblical Defilement and Mourning: Law as Theology* (New York: KTAV/Yeshiva Univ. Press, 1977) passim.

ner and non-mourner, between the realm of death and that of cult, so carefully maintained under normal circumstances, is challenged by the presence of a priest at the altar marked as a mourner. The priest who returns to the sanctuary from a period of mourning is certainly no longer a polluter, and does not threaten the sanctuary with defilement per se. But if he continues to bear the markings of the mourner, he confronts Yhwh nonetheless with death's distinct tokens, which threaten to profane Yhwh's holy name according to Lev 21:6. Like the blemished priest who confronts Yhwh with unwanted physical imperfection, the shaved or lacerated priest who brings death to the altar, even without the pollution normally associated with it, is unwelcome before Yhwh the holy god. Thus, it is the distinct *symbolic* association of laceration and shaving with death that explains their proscription for priests who approach the deity directly. They signal death and its associated pollution, and also function to create the distinct ritual state of mourning, and these have no place in the cultic sphere.[17]

Not surprisingly, other mourning rites that are easily reversible and do not outlast the mourning period do not offend Yhwh. Several texts, including Lev 21:1–5, speak of priestly mourning both directly and indirectly. Though Lev 21:1–4 forbids the priest to have corpse contact with all but the closest of kin and 21:5 prohibits two types of shaving and incising an incision, they say nothing of other mourning rites. Yet other texts provide some insight into the mourning rites performed by priests. Ezek 24:16–17 suggests that for a priest such as Ezekiel, expected mourning behavior would include actions such as weeping, the unbinding of the hair, the removal of shoes and the covering of the upper lip.[18] Lev 10:6 may be read to

---

[17] Tigay, *Deuteronomy*, 136, argues that the mourning markers in question are "comparable" to blemishes (מומים), and therefore profaning to holiness. I am not certain what he means by "comparable" (i.e., that they are indeed blemishes, or that they have blemish-like associations). Though it is possible that these mourning markers were constructed as blemishes by the ancients, it is not clear that this was so, nor is it clear that they were even associated with blemishes. Blemishes are offensive to Yhwh; they are imperfections revolting to him (e.g., the sacrificial animal with a blemish is called an "abomination" [תועבה] in Deut 14:3). They are, however, not death-related, at least not in any clear and convincing way. Because the mourning rites in question are death-related and not obviously associated with blemishes in any text (e.g., they do not appear in any list of blemishes), I prefer to categorize them differently from blemishes, though the presence of either in the priest appearing before Yhwh would result in profanation.

[18] The text describes a symbolic act of the prophet, Ezekiel's refraining from performing these actions at the death of his wife. The perplexed reaction of his audience suggests that they expected Ezekiel to perform these acts of mourning. On this, see further the discussion of M. Greenberg, *Ezekiel 21–37* (AB 22a; New York: Doubleday, 1997) 509–510. Greenberg claims, incorrectly in my view, that "self-

suggest that the unbinding of hair and the tearing of garments are normally permitted for priests.[19] Thus, several texts suggest that priests may perform mourning rites that are easily reversible, and leave no physical trace beyond the mourning period. These would not offend the deity or threaten the holiness of his name because they would no longer be in evidence when a priest leaves his mourning state to resume his normal cultic duties. The boundaries between the realm of death and the cult would therefore be unchallenged; there would be no erosion of the social and ritual distinction between mourner and non-mourner, no death markers where they do not belong.

It remains to explain the prohibition of laceration and shaving for all Israelites in Lev 19:27–28 and Deut 14:1. If the proscription originally applied to priests approaching Yhwh's altar, how did it come to be generalized for all Israel in the Holiness Source and Deuteronomy?[20] The first thing to be noted is the parallel generalization of holiness to all Israel in both H and D. In the Holiness Source and in Deuteronomy, in contrast to other biblical materials such as the Priestly Writing, holiness is a quality shared by Israelites. Lev 19:2 addresses Israel as follows: "You shall be holy, for I, Yhwh, your god, am holy." Similarly, Deut 14:2 describes Israel as "a holy people to Yhwh" their god.[21] Lev 19:2 heads a series of laws in Leviticus 19, including the ban on shaving and laceration in 19:27–28; though it does not say so explicitly, the text gives the impression that obedience to these laws

wounding" mourning rites (i.e., laceration and shaving) were illegitimate in Israel (citing Lev 19:27–28; Deut 14:1–2), though texts such as Jer 16:6; 41:5 suggest otherwise. The evidence for their illegitimacy is restricted to H and D.

[19] Lev 21:10 prohibits the high priest from all corpse contact, and the mourning rites of unbinding hair and tearing garments. Given the restrictions on priests in Lev 21:1–5, 21:10 implies that the mourning actions forbidden to the high priest are permitted to priests, since 21:5 says nothing about mourning rites other than shaving and laceration, and explicitly permits corpse contact for next of kin, in contrast to 21:10 on the high priest. In contrast to these texts, Ezek 44:20 states that priests may neither shave their heads nor unbind their hair.

[20] As others have argued, it seems very likely that a restriction imposed on a single group (the priesthood) has been generalized to all Israelites. To argue the opposite thesis would, as Schmidt has pointed out, produce "unnecessary redundancy" (*Beneficent Dead*, 171). See also K. Elliger, *Leviticus* (HAT 4; Tübingen: J. C. B. Mohr/Paul Siebeck, 1966) 289, who believes that Lev 19:27–28 may represent a "democratization" of what was originally a rule restricting priests alone, and M. Fishbane, *Biblical Interpretation in Ancient Israel* (Oxford: Clarendon, 1985) 122.

[21] Note also Exod 19:6 (D), where Israel is said to have the potential to become a "holy people" (גוי קדוש). It is clear that H texts both call upon Israel to be holy (e.g., Lev 19:2) and assume Israel's holy state (e.g., Lev 20:8). On this, see further my argument in *Rites and Rank: Hierarchy in Biblical Representations of Cult* (Princeton: Princeton Univ. Press, 2000) 121, 174 n. 3.

is a component part of being holy. Deut 14:2 makes the connection between holiness and the avoidance of laceration and shaving for the dead more explicitly: Israelites should not shave a bald spot between the eyes for the dead or lacerate themselves *because* they are a holy people to Yhwh their god (כי עם קדוש אתה ליהוה אלהיך). Deut 14:2 and, less explicitly, Lev 19:2 may suggest that shaving and laceration as mourning rites are a threat to holiness. They are markers of death, and death's presence, even symbolically, can profane holiness, as Lev 21:6 suggests. Therefore, the ban on the mourning rites of shaving and laceration for all Israel may find its explanation in the generalization of holiness to the people as a whole.[22] Once the people are conceived as holy, their holiness must be protected from profanation caused by participation in mourning rites that outlast the circumscribed mourning period. Only these, apparently, are constructed as profaning to the people's holiness, and are therefore proscribed. Other mourning rites, easily reversible, are not prohibited to the holy people even though they have death associations. It is not easy to explain this, but it could be that even for the holy people, confronting and processing death is permitted as long as death remains restricted to its bounded realm. And restricting death to its circumscribed bailiwick means prohibiting mourning gestures that outlast the mourning period. This would be similar to the allowance to priests in Lev 21:1–5 to mourn within strict limits and even pollute themselves for close kin. Upon emerging from their mourning period, they bring no evidence of death with them when they reenter the realm of non-mourners and that of the cult.

---

[22] Similarly, Tigay, *Deuteronomy*, 136–37.

Chapter 14

Clan Sagas As a Source in
Settlement Traditions

Alexander Rofé
Hebrew University of Jerusalem

Students of ancient Israel long ago realized the complexity of the biblical accounts of the conquest of Canaan. *Inter alia,* they recognized the existence of distinct patterns in the depiction of this major event: Besides the dominant pattern of a national conquest—one people, a united army, and a single leader—there is a tribal model, expressed, for instance, in the story of the conquest of Laish (Judges 18).[1] In this article, I shall attempt to demonstrate the existence of yet another ancient model, found frequently among the settlement and conquest stories: the model of the clan enterprise, in which a hero, at the head of his clan, settles the land or conquers a place therein, as one well-integrated component of the larger complex of family episodes. This model, too, evidently comprises "divergent traditions," and scholars of the Bible and ancient Israel have already noted the atypical character of these traditions as well, wherever they encountered them.[2] However, it seems to me that scholars have never addressed all of these traditions together, as one category. Such a comprehensive study has the advantage of allowing each passage to shed light on the others. Align-

---

This article was translated by Simeon Chavel.

[1] Abraham Malamat, "The Danite-Migration and the Pan-Israelite Exodus-Conquest: A Biblical Narrative Pattern," *Biblica* 51 (1970) 1–16; idem, "The Proto-History of Israel—A Study in Method," in *"The Word of the Lord Shall Go Forth": Essays in Honor of D. N. Freedman* (ed. C. L. Meyers and M. O'Connor; Winona Lake, Ind.: Eisenbrauns, 1983) 303–313, esp. 307.

[2] See, for example, the following commentaries: John Skinner, *Genesis* (ICC; Edinburgh: Clark, 1903) 507; George B. Gray, *Numbers* (ICC; Edinburgh: Clark, 1903) 437–441.

ing all of the passages will bring the historical perspective embedded in them into sharper relief and clarify the literary genre to which they all belong. On this basis, it will be possible to suggest general conclusions regarding the source of these traditions, their reliability, and their value for today's historian.

1. Genesis 48:22

ואני נתתי לך שכם אחד על אחיך, אשר לקחתי מיד האמרי בחרבי ובקשתי:

על here means "in addition to, more than." Compare Num 28:10, על עולת התמיד ונסכה, so v. 24, with v. 31: מלבד עולת התמיד ומנחתו תעשו. על אחיך, then, represents the short form for the fuller phrase, על (אשר ל)אחיך, "more than to your brothers." Jacob bequeaths to Joseph a double portion, as the firstborn's share (cf. Deut 21:17; similarly, Joseph obtains a double portion in Gen 48:5–6). The word שכם, "Shechem," contains a word-play: the city of Shechem and a mountain-slope (as in the Hebrew idiom, the כתף, "shoulder," of the mountain). The city Shechem, Tel Balatah, situated on the lowest edge of the slope of Mt. Ebal, constitutes the extra portion Jacob bequeathed to Joseph. Therefore the verse is to be translated as follows:

> And now, [says Jacob to Joseph] I assign to you Shechem, one mountain more than to your brothers, which I wrested from the Amorites with my sword and bow.[3]

This brief verse contradicts all that is known of Jacob's history. Jacob did not conquer Shechem; rather, Simeon and Levi did—unbeknownst to Jacob at the outset and regretted bitterly by him afterwards (Genesis 34, esp. v. 30). Jacob then left the land, not to return, and sojourned in Egypt, where he declared his last will and testament to his sons and died (Genesis 46–50). Against this background, what value can the special inheritance Jacob leaves to Joseph in Egypt have? Clearly, then, the passage in Gen 48:22 operates under a different assumption: Jacob, by his own valor, conquered Shechem, just as he had conquered other parts of the land, and now, still in Canaan and prior to his death, he leaves his estate to his sons and bestows Shechem, as an extra portion, upon his favorite. Jacob conquers and settles the land—this constitutes an alternative tradition about the nation's patriarch.

2. Joshua 17:1b

למכיר בכור מנשה אבי הגלעד, כי הוא היה איש מלחמה, ויהי לו הגלעד והבשן:

For Machir, the first-born of Manasseh and father of Gilead, since he was a valiant warrior, he possessed the Gilead and the Bashan.

---

[3] Translations generally follow NJPS, but have been adapted to the author's understanding.

אבי הגלעד, "the father of Gilead," means the founder of the settlement in the Gilead; cf. 1 Chr 2:24, אשחור אבי תקוע, "Ashhur the father of Tekoa"; v. 42, "Meshah his first-born, who was the father of Ziph"; and many others. The continuation, כי הוא היה איש מלחמה, "since he was a valiant warrior," explains how Machir founded the Israelite settlement in the Gilead: Through his strength as a warrior he took the Gilead and the Bashan.

Again we stand in wonder. Who is this Machir? According to Gen 50:23, Machir was born in Egypt, where he married and begot children, all during the lifetime of Joseph, prior to the enslavement. Here, by contrast, he appears as a conqueror of Canaan. Josh 17:1b, then, knows neither the enslavement in Egypt nor the exodus therefrom. Moreover, Numbers 21 and Deuteronomy 2–3 claim Moses as the conqueror of the entire Transjordan. What room is there for the warrior Machir in a story about the division of the land, when the land has already been conquered? Rather, the note concerning Machir in Josh 17:1b contradicts the mainstream story of the conquest of the land. It contains a divergent tradition about Machir, the son of Manasseh and grandson of Joseph, who captured a territory by the force of his weapons and founded there a settlement: "the father of the Gilead."

3. Numbers 32:39, 41–42

וילכו בני מכיר בן מנשה גלעדה וילכדה, ויורש את האמרי אשר בה: . . . ויאיר בן מנשה הלך וילכד את חותיהם, ויקרא אתהן חות יאיר: ונבח הלך וילכד את קנת ואת בנותיה, ויקרא לה נבח בשמו:

The descendants of Machir son of Manasseh went to Gilead and captured it, and he dispossessed the Amorites who were there . . . Yair son of Manasseh went and captured their tent-villages, which he renamed Havvoth-yair, the tent-villages of Yair. And Nobah went and captured Kenath and its dependencies, renaming it Nobah after himself.

וילכו . . . וילכדה (קרי: וילכדוה) . . . ויורש, "they went . . . and captured it . . . he dispossessed"—the transition from plural to singular is not smooth and will be explained further on. וילכד את חותיהם, "he captured their tent-villages"—whose villages? The possessive pronoun has no antecedent and thus no referent. Therefore read: חות הם, "the villages of Ham." The name Ham belongs to this area according to Gen 14:5.

These verses occur at the end of the story of the allotment of the land of Ya'azer and the Gilead to the tribes of Gad and Reuben (Num 32:1–38). The tribe of Manasseh only makes its appearance in v. 33, where the sole mention of ממלכת עוג מלך הבשן, "the kingdom of Og, king of the Bashan," in the chapter occurs. Furthermore, the main part of the chapter, through v. 38, discusses the land already taken, which the tribes of Gad and Reuben now wish to settle; by contrast, vv. 39, 41–42 relate a string of new conquests: Machir in the Gilead, Yair in the tent-villages of Ham, Nobah in Kenath.

Between these two perspectives a clear clash emerges—the conquest of Transjordan and its settlement under the leadership of Moses (Num 21:21–22:1; 32:33; Deut 2:24–3:22; Josh 12:1–6; 13:8–33) and a conquest spear-headed by clan leaders in independent operations. Verse 40 constitutes a clear attempt at bridging this gap: ויתן משה את הגלעד למכיר בן מנשה וישב בה, "so Moses gave Gilead to Machir son of Manasseh and he settled there." By this harmonization, the independent operations now appear as though Moses commissioned them.[4] Similarly, the plural form in v. 39, וילכו בני מכיר, "the descendants of Machir went," which is followed by the singular ויורש, "he dispossessed," marks an attempt to harmonize the report concerning Machir with the settlement story of the tribes of Gad (vv. 34–36) and Reuben (vv. 37–38). Originally, behind vv. 39, 41–42 stood an independent tradition about the settlement of three conquerors from the tribe of Manasseh. The report in v. 39 concerning Machir complements well the mention of Machir in Josh 17:1b, discussed above; and the report concerning the tent-villages of Yair resembles, in a number of respects, that given about Yair in Judg 10:3–5:

ויקם אחריו יאיר הגלעדי, וישפט את־ישראל עשרים ושתים שנה: ויהי־לו שלשים בנים, רכבים על־שלשים עירים, ושלשים עירים להם. להם יקראו חות יאיר עד היום הזה, אשר בארץ הגלעד: וימת יאיר ויקבר בקמון:

After him arose Yair the Gileadite, and he led Israel for twenty-two years. He had thirty sons, who rode on thirty burros and owned thirty boroughs; these are called Havvoth-yair, the tent-villages of Yair, to this day, which are in the land of the Gilead. Then Yair died and was buried at Kamon.

The conception reflected here presents Yair as one of the "minor judges." But if we ignore the regular formulaic elements . . . ויקם . . . . וישפט . . . וימת . . . ויקבר, "arose . . . led . . . died . . . was buried at . . . ," what remains constitutes none other than a clan saga: Yair had thirty sons and thirty tent-villages, with each son inheriting one village.[5] Indeed, similar information exists in 1 Chr 2:21–23:

Afterward Hezron cohabited with the daughter of Machir father of Gilead—he had married her when he was sixty years old–and she bore him Segub; and Segub begot Yair; he had twenty-three cities in the land of Gilead. But Geshur and Aram took from them Havvoth-yair, the tent-villages of Yair . . .

---

[4] Cf. already Abraham Kuenen, *An Historico-critical Inquiry into the Origin and Composition of the Hexateuch* (trans. Philip H. Wicksteed; London: MacMillan, 1886) 44, 47.

[5] Among the "Minor Judges," Tola son of Puah (Judg 10:1–2) and Elon the Zebulunite (Judg 12:11–12) also appear as clan leaders in the genealogies. See, in Hebrew, S. Skulsky, "The Minor Judges," *Beth Mikra* 13 (1967/8) 75–99, esp. 97. In my opinion, the original tradition probably described most of them as "great people," heads of clans.

4. *Joshua 15:14–19*

וירש משם כלב את־שלושה בני הענק ... ויעל משם אל־ישבי דבר ... ויאמר כלב, אשר־
יכה את־קרית־ספר ולכדה ונתתי לו את־עכסה בתי לאשה: וילכדה עתניאל בן קנז,
אחי כלב, ויתן לו את עכסה בתו לאשה: ויהי בבואה ותסיתהו לשאול מאת אביה
שדה ...

Caleb dislodged from there the three Anakites . . . from there he marched
against the inhabitants of Debir . . . and Caleb announced, 'I will give my
daughter Achsah in marriage to the man who attacks and captures Kiriath-
sepher.' His kinsman Othniel the Kenizzite captured it; and Caleb gave him
his daughter Achsah in marriage. When she came [to him], she induced
him to ask her father for some property . . .

According to Josh 10:36–39 and the summary there, vv. 40-42, and similarly according to 11:21–22, Joshua, at the head of the entire Israelite
people, conquered both Hebron and Debir and cleared them of the
Anakites. Joshua 15 presents a different tradition: Caleb, at the head of his
clan, conquered Hebron, and Othniel his kinsman vanquished Debir. Josh
14:6–15 offers another attempt to harmonize variant stories, in relating
how Caleb's deeds had Joshua's authorization. Yet a fundamental contradiction persists: Did the conquest of Hebron and Debir take place prior to
the apportioning of the land (Joshua 10; 11) or afterwards (Joshua 14; 15)? It
is likely that originally there stood here an independent clan saga concerning Caleb's taking of Hebron and Othniel's defeat of Debir.

The passage in Judg 1:10–15 represents another reworking of this tradition, surprising in its direction:

וילך יהודה אל־הכנעני היושב בחברון ... ויכו את־ששי ואת־אחימן ואת־תלמי: וילך
משם אל־יושבי דביר ... ויאמר כלב, אשר־יכה את־קרית־ספר ולכדה וכו'

Judah marched against the Canaanites who dwelt in Hebron, and they defeated Sheshai, Ahiman, and Talmai . . . from there he marched against the
inhabitants of Debir . . . and Caleb announced, 'To the man who attacks and
captures Kiriath-sepher . . .'

And in v. 20:

ויתנו לכלב את־חברון כאשר דבר משה, ויורש משם את־שלשה בני הענק:

They gave Hebron to Caleb, as Moses had promised; and he drove the three
Anakites out of there.

In vv. 10–12, the subject switches with no warning: first the tribe of Judah, then Caleb. Verse 20, however, still treats Caleb as the original subject.
Since the entire chapter tells of the conquest of the land in a tribal framework—Judah, Simeon, Benjamin, the house of Joseph, etc.—there is no reason to doubt that editorial activity caused the unevenness in the story of
the conquest of Hebron and Debir: A clan story regarding Caleb has found
itself reworked into the tribal framework of Judah.

5. 1 Chronicles 7:20–24

ובני אפרים שותלח, וברד בנו, ותחת בנו . . . ועזר ואלעד, והרגום אנשי־גת הנולדים
בארץ, כי ירדו לקחת את מקניהם: ויתאבל אפרים אביהם ימים רבים, ויבאו אחיו
לנחמו: ויבא אל־אשתו, ותהר ותלד בן, ויקרא את שמו בריעה, כי ברעה היתה
בביתו: ובתו שארה, ותבן את־בית־חורון התחתון ואת־העליון ואת אזן שארה:

The sons of Ephraim: Shutelah, his son Bered, his son Tahath . . . also Ezer
and Elead. The men of Gath, born in the land, killed them because they had
gone down to take their cattle. And Ephraim their father mourned many
days, and his brothers came to comfort him. He cohabited with his wife,
who conceived and bore a son; and he named him Beriah, because it occurred when there was misfortune in the house. His daughter was Sheerah,
who built both Lower and Upper Beth-horon and Uzzen-sheerah.

This story, too, conflicts with the story of the descent to Egypt and the
conquest of Canaan in the time of Joshua. Ephraim here does not live in
Egypt, but rather in Canaan, in the southern part of the Ephraimite hills.
His sons engage in cattle-rustling in the area of Gath (in the area of modern
Ramle?). The people of Gath therefore kill them. Ephraim mourns, and his
kinsmen come to console him. His daughter Sheerah builds three cities in
the Ephraimite hills. Every detail here clashes with the portrayal in Genesis 37–Exodus 15. The rabbinic sages sensed this conflict and smoothed it
over by positing a premature Ephraimite attempt to flee Egypt; the mission
failed, and the bones of the Ephraimites were still hanging in the land of
the Philistines even in the time of Moses.[6] But even the Sages could not
properly situate the information regarding Ephraim who lived in Canaan,
in the hills, and his daughter who built three cities. At its root, this information constitutes a unique, divergent tradition about Ephraim and his first
children, the founders of settlements in the portion of the tribe that bears
their name.[7]

*   *   *

If we attempt to describe the common ground between the five reports
discussed here, we can summarize by saying that all of them contradict the

---

[6] *B. Sanh.* 92b alludes to the saga of "the Ephraimites who calculated the termi-
nus of the enslavement erroneously"; *Mekhilta de-Rabbi Yishmael* (ed. H. S. Horovitz
and I. A. Rabin; repr., Jerusalem: Bamberger & Wahrman, 1960), Beshalach, on
Exod 13:17; 15:14, relates the tradition in detail; *Exod. Rab.* 20:11 relates it at length.

[7] See Gershon Galil, 'The Chronicler's Genealogies of Ephraim," *BN* 56 (1991)
11–14. He estimated that the list in 1 Chr 7:20–24 contains harmonistic editorial activity that strives to accommodate the list to the dominant story of the descent to
and exodus from Egypt: The names have been doubled in a symmetrical-concentric
manner in order to extend the number of generations and to indicate that the
"grieving" Ephraim was not Ephraim son of Joseph. See also: N. Na'aman, "Sources
and Redaction in the Chronicler's Genealogies of Asher and Ephraim," *JSOT* 49
(1991) 99–111, and the additional bibliography there.

predominant narrative of Israel's beginnings. They do not know of the patriarchs' status as sojourners in Canaan, of the descent to Egypt and the subjugation there, or of the conquest of both sides of the Jordan by Moses and Joshua. They portray settlement and conquest in the generation of the patriarchs or immediately following. They speak of campaigns led by clan heads with their followers, campaigns entwined in family circumstances such as inheritance (Gen 48:22), birthright (Josh 17:1b), marriage, marriage price, and dowry (Josh 15:14–19), progeny (Num 32:41 + Judg 10:4), loss of children, mourning, and consolation (1 Chr 7:20–24). These reports lay out a complete family life-cycle, which justifies categorizing them as clan sagas of conquest. As for their outlook, they are very earthly, with no mention at all of God's intervention on behalf of the heroes. Moreover, not faith, but rather the desire to excel and win the leader's daughter, Achsah, impels Othniel's deeds. It is not prayer that assists Machir in his conquests, but rather his character as "a valiant warrior." There is even glorification of brute strength, of human valor: Jacob boasts that he vanquished Shechem "with my sword and bow."

This spirit, which glorifies human valor, did not sit well with later generations. The Mekhilta interpreted Gen 48:22, "with my sword and bow" as "with my prayer and supplication," which bears the exact opposite of the original sense![8] And long before the Mekhilta, the author of one of the Psalms denounces this mundane attitude towards the conquest of the land:

אתה ידך גוים הורשת ותטעם   תרע לאמים ותשלחם:
כי לא בחרבם ירשו ארץ   וזרועם לא הושיעה למו
כי ימינך וזרועך ואור פניך   כי רציתם:

> With Your hand You planted them, displacing nations;
>   You shattered peoples, and drove them out.
> It was not by their sword that they took the land,
>   Their arm did not give them victory,
> But Your right hand, Your arm, Your goodwill,
>   For You favored them (Ps 44:3–4).

And an historian from pre-exilic times, the author of Joshua 24,[9] truly sounds as though he is arguing against Gen 48:22, for he says: ואשלח לפניכם את־הצרעה, ותגרש אותם מפניכם שני[ם עשר] מלכי האמרי, לא בחרבך ולא בקשתך, "I sent the hornet ahead of you, and it drove them out before you—the twelve Amorite kings—not by your sword or by your bow" (Josh 24:12 LXX). The two passages share three elements: Shechem (the locale of the congrega-

---

[8] See *Mek.* (n. 6, above), 92. See also *b. B. Bat.* 123a. On this issue I have benefited from a paper presented by Mr. Eliashiv Frankel to Prof. Menaham Kister, at the Hebrew University, 1997.

[9] Not a Deuteronomistic editor, but an older one. See A. Rofé, "Ephraimite versus Deuteronomistic History," *Storia e tradizioni di Israele—Scritti in onore di J. Alberto Soggin* (ed. Daniele Garrone and Felice Israel; Brescia: Paideia, 1991) 221–235.

tion in Joshua 24), the Amorite as an inclusive term for the inhabitants of Canaan, and "sword and bow" (specifically, with possessive pronominal singular suffix). Clearly, then, Joshua 24 rejects Gen 48:22, explicitly negating the version of a conquest based on human strength. "Deliverance is the Lord's," determined later generations who emphasized that God saved his loyal ones in response to their prayers.[10]

Hence, one can explain the rejection of these clan sagas from the predominant narrative of Israel's history. Their religious conception did not fit the faith of later generations, who preferred those historical depictions which, in the end, merited sanctification in the biblical corpus: the portrayals of the patriarchs as sojourners who received a divine promise, the depiction of their children as slaves redeemed by God through wonders and miracles, and the description of their children, in turn, who traversed the desert under divine guidance and conquered Canaan under His leadership—all of which evince the divine providence over Israel. These stories, then, came to dominate the history of Israelite beginnings, while pushing aside other, alternative traditions.[11] This group of rejected traditions, remaining only in scattered fragments, comprises the clan sagas we have seen.[12]

Naturally, the question arises concerning the value of these clan sagas as sources for the history of Israel's settlement in Canaan: To what extent and in what way need the contemporary historian employ them to build an historical description? It appears to me that the answer is not unequivocal, for one must take into account a number of considerations.

First, one cannot ignore the etiological character of the clan conquest sagas.[13] They attribute to the distant past the origins of present situations:

---

[10] See Isac L. Seeligmann, "Menschliches Heldentum und Göttliche Hilfe—Die doppelte Kausalität im alttestamentlichen Geschichtsdenken," *ThZ* (Basel) 19 (1963) 385–411, and in Hebrew translation in the collection of his articles, *Studies in Biblical Literature* (ed. Avi Hurvitz et al.; Jerusalem: Magnes, 1992) 61–81.

[11] Which undermines Kaufmann's sharp distinction between "the patriarchal layer and the tribal layer"; see, for example, in Hebrew, Yehezkel Kaufmann, *A History of the Religion of Israel* (Tel Aviv: Dvir, 1937–1956) 2.302–311.

[12] A parallel process—and yet how different—occurred with the Greeks. Hecataeus of Miletus, in the beginning of the fifth century BCE, wrote of the origins of Greece with the intention of making order among the genealogies and explaining the myths rationally. In both instances, a later historian incorporated the ancient sagas; in Israel, the faith directed the history, whereas in Greece it was the rationalistic critique. On Hecataeus, see L. Pearson, *Early Ionian Historians* (Oxford: Clarendon, 1939) 25–108; G de Sanctis, *Studi di storia della storiografia greca* (Firenze: Nuova Italia, 1951) 3–19.

[13] The movement and function of these sagas is evident, despite the absence of alleged etiological formulae; see the seminal study of our beloved jubilarian, B. O. Long, *The Problem of Etiological Narrative in the Old Testament* (BZAW 108; Berlin: Töpelmann, 1968).

Why did the tribe of Joseph deserve an additional territorial portion? Why does the populace of the northern Transjordan consist of the descendants of Machir? Why do three settlements in the southern part of the Ephraimite hills trace their lineage to the clan of She'erah? And one cannot comfortably rely on etiologies as historical sources: They infer backwards in time from the present, and in particular, facts which in and of themselves are correct they link incorrectly.[14] If, for example, we take account of the fact that the Song of Deborah mentions Machir alongside the tribes situated west of the Jordan river (Judg 5:14), it stands to reason that the descendants of Machir migrated to Transjordan at some later date during the period of the judges. This conclusion undermines the attractive story about Machir son of Manasseh, "a valiant warrior," who founded the settlement in the Gilead and the Bashan. The result: The literary category of the sagas of conquest cannot offer us reliable historical sources.

On the other hand, these clan sagas represent alternative sources, as we have seen; with time, they were marginalized from the dominant description of the history of Israel, which serves to prove their antiquity, even when embedded in late books such as Joshua and Chronicles. Moreover, they appear to reflect a pre-national and in some measure even pre-tribal allegiance. Whoever first told the story of Caleb's taking of Hebron did not express a tribal consciousness, and, *a fortiori*, a national one; he gave expression to the Calebite allegiance (cf. 1 Sam 25:3; 30:14) and to the memories preserved among this clan. We may infer, then, that clan settlement sagas generally stem from the days prior to the consolidation of tribal and national solidarity in Israel; their historical provenance belongs to the period between the settlement and the monarchy.[15]

---

[14] I have encountered some interesting instances of this phenomenon when people speak of events in Jewish and Israeli history; see also Siegfried Herrmann, *A History of Israel in Old Testament Times* (trans. John Bowden; 2d ed.; London: SCM, 1981) 97–98; Roland de Vaux, *The Early History of Israel* (trans. David Smith; London: Darton, Longman & Todd, 1978) 481–482; Manfred Weippert, *The Settlement of the Israelite Tribes in Palestine* (trans. J. D. Martin; SBT[2] 21; London: SCM, 1971) 136–144.

[15] Cf. A. Jolles, *Einfache Formen* (1930; repr., Tübingen: Niemeyer, 1965) 62–90. Jolles described the Icelandic Sögur as emerging similarly: within the clan, prior to communal solidarity, before the Christianization of Iceland. The trouble is that a reading of Sögur poems and the attending literature does not bear out Jolles's thesis: The poems assume the existence of a supra-clan authority among the inhabitants. Moshe Weinfeld suggested a typological comparison with the Greco-Roman world, in his articles, "The Pattern of Israelite Settlement in Canaan," *Cathedra* 44 (1987) 3–20 (in Hebrew); "The Promise to the Patriarchs and Its Realization—An Analysis of Foundation Stories," in *Society and Economy in the Eastern Mediterranean (c. 1500–1000 B.C.)* (ed. M. Heltzer and E. Lipinski; Orientalia Lovaniensia Analecta 23; Leuven: Peeters, 1988) 353–369. The author marshals a very rich set of parallels, but in my opinion one must distinguish between different types of traditions and

From this emerges the conclusion that conquest sagas, although they contain incorrect details regarding the actual deeds, nevertheless reflect social-historical reality. In the settlement period, the clan served as the defining unit for migration, military operations, and settlement. This unit included a number of families who preserved a consciousness of shared origins. All in all, the clan comprised several dozen men, including both sons and slaves. Probably, a significant portion of the taking of Canaan occurred within the framework of activity of the Israelite clans.[16]

Finally, the clan conquest sagas testify to the existence of a wide variety of sources regarding the settlement, of which only a meager element has survived in the Hebrew Bible. And from the literature, we may conclude generally about Israel's history that the settlement of Canaan occurred as a protracted process, drawn out over an extended period of time. In this process, Israel infiltrated the land slowly and gradually, in various waves, sometimes in the framework of tribes or groups of tribes, and sometimes in smaller frameworks of clans led by individual heroes, clan leaders who evolved into founders of settlements. The variegated nature of the sources, then, serves as evidence of the complexity of the process of Israelite settlement in Canaan.[17]

*   *   *

Alongside the clan sagas that describe the settlement of Canaan exists another type of patriarchal military story. This type appears partially in Genesis and partially in the apocryphal literature.

Genesis 14 relates how Abram the Hebrew came to rescue his nephew Lot from the four great kings, Chedorlaomer king of Elam and the kings who came with him, trounced the kings and chased them all the way

the various stages of their development. Moreover, Momigliano has already taught: "In the field of political, social, and religious history, the differences outweigh the analogies." See Arnaldo Momigliano, "Studi biblici e studi classici," in *La storiografia greca* (Torino: Einaudi, 1982) 341.

[16] For the definition of the units משפחה and בית־אב, see Y. Liver, "משפחה," *Encyclopedia Miqra'it* (Jerusalem: Bialik, 1968) 5.582–588, and the bibliography there. I assume that numbers like three hundred for the Abiezer clan (Judg 8:1–4), six hundred for the Danite clan (Judg 18:1), and אלף, thousand, as a synonym for clan (Judg 6:15; 1 Sam 23:23) reflect a later reality.

[17] Therefore, I tend to accept the model of Alt and Aharoni for the description of the process of Israelite settlement. I. Finkelstein, *The Archaeology of the Israelite Settlement* (Jerusalem: Israel Exploration Society, 1988) has provided this model with a novel development; see his historical conclusions. For the problem overall, see Antoon Schoors, "The Israelite Conquest: Textual Evidence in the Archaeological Argument," in *The Land of Israel: Cross-Roads of Civilizations* (ed. E. Lipinski; Orientalia Lovaniensia Analecta 19; Leuven: Peeters, 1985), 77–92.

"north of Damascus," and returned Lot and his property along with the captives taken from Sodom to their land. This account constitutes the sole depiction of Abram as a warrior. Genesis 34 recounts the annihilation of Shechem by Jacob's sons in retaliation for the abduction and rape of their sister Dinah. The Book of Jubilees tells of the war Jacob and his sons waged against the seven Amorite kings who had attacked the sons while they were tending their flocks in the wilderness of Shechem (*Jub.* 34:1–9). Jacob and his sons defeated the kings and exacted tribute from them, "and they became servants to him until the day he and his sons went down into Egypt" (34:9).[18] Similarly, *Jubilees* 37–38 tells of the war Jacob and his sons waged against Esau and his sons who had hired mercenaries against them: Aram, Moab, Ammon, Philistines, Horites, and Hittites. Jacob defeated Esau and killed him, and his sons crushed all their enemies. At the war's end, Jacob buried his brother in Adoraim, while the sons subdued Esau's sons at Mt. Seir (38:9–10), "and they paid Jacob a tax until the day Jacob descended to Egypt" (38:13). The same wars against seven Canaanite kings and against Esau and his sons are recounted in *T. Judah* 3–7; 9. Apparently there was a common source from which these apocryphal books, as well as medieval Jewish *midrashim*, derived their material.[19]

On the face of it, it appears that these four stories belong together with the sagas surveyed above. All portray the patriarchs as warriors, and the wars have a clan setting. Abram fights to save his nephew (Genesis 14); Simeon and Levi avenged the offense committed against their sister by Shechem (Genesis 34); the war in the hills of Ephraim takes place in response to the Amorite attack on the sons tending their flocks in the wilderness of Shechem (*Jubilees* 34); the conflict between Jacob and Esau is a sibling quarrel over the birthright, in which Esau's sons initiate and Jacob's descendants retaliate (*Jubilees* 37–38). The narrative motifs here also appear in the fragmentary sagas mentioned above.[20]

However, at root, one may differentiate well between the two groups of sources and establish which are early and which are late. The sagas presented above comprise stories of conquest, occupation, and foundation of settlements; they take the settlement activities of Israel in Canaan as their subject. Therefore, they also fundamentally contradict the story of the descent to Egypt and the exodus therefrom. Not so the second group of

---

[18] According to the translation of O. S. Wintermute, *OTP* 2.35–142.

[19] Cf. M. de Jonge, *The Testaments of the Twelve Patriarchs: A Commentary* (Leiden: Brill, 1985) 26, 184–186, and ad loc.

[20] Actually, Albright considered all of them to be sound sources for the history of the settlement in the Late Bronze Age; see William F. Albright, *From the Stone Age to Christianity* (2d ed.; Garden City, N.Y.: Doubleday, 1957) 277. In this direction, but with more detail and more caution, treads also Yochanan Muffs; see his essay, "Abraham the Noble Warrior," *JJS* 33 (1982) 81–107.

stories. Their background does not concern the Israelite occupation of the land, and the wars described in them present no organic continuity: Abraham does not establish an empire; Simeon and Levi do not settle Shechem; even the subjugation of the Amorites and Edomites lasts only "until Jacob's descent to Egypt." These wars have a sporadic nature. It appears, then, that the accounts of these wars do not stem from authentic tradition; they give expression to ideological interests. They articulate the desires of later generations projected backwards onto the figures of the patriarchs— portraying them as imperial conquerors; deriding the people of Shechem as impure and contaminating, unworthy of acceptance into Israel;[21] employing Edom and the other nations (Amos 9:12; cf. Isaiah 34) as a paradigm for Israel vanquishing its enemies. It is not easy to identify the historical provenance of these stories, for it may range from the united monarchy (Genesis 14?) to the days of the Hasmoneans (*Jubilees* 37–38).[22] In any case, it is difficult to assume that before the author of Jubilees stood ancient traditions. Jubilees reports that Jacob buried Esau in Adoraim (38:9). Information such as this stems from the Persian-Hellenistic period, by which time the Edomites had already "forgotten" their original territory to the east of the Arabah and considered the Hebron hills as their ancient legacy; therefore they "discovered" there the grave of Esau their patriarch!

In sum, we have discerned two types of clan sagas concerning the forefathers. One type consists of complete stories, quite long, in which the forefathers wage war against Israel's enemies: Abram against the four kings (Genesis 14), Simeon and Levi against Shechem (Genesis 34), Jacob and his sons against the Amorite kings (*Jubilees* 34; *T. Judah* 3–7), and against Esau and his sons (*Jubilees* 37–38; *T. Judah* 9). These are not stories of conquest and settlement, stories of the inheriting of Canaan. They serve to glorify the nation's patriarchs as warriors chalking up victories against the classic enemies of Israel. The exploits of Israel in the historical period have been projected back onto the patriarchal period. The deeds of the sons have be-

---

[21] See already Abraham Kuenen's discussion, "Dina und Sichem (Gen 34)," 1880, which was translated into German by K. Budde in Kuenen's *Gesammelte Abhandlungen zur biblischen Wissenschaft* (Freiburg i. B. und Leipzig: Mohr, 1894) 255–276.

[22] Concerning Genesis 14, scholars have also pointed out its resemblance to late narrative, such as the Book of Judith. See, for example, Weippert, *Settlement*, (n. 14, above), 93–101. On the Hasmonean background of the wars in the Book of Jubilees, see F. M. Abel, "Topographie des campagnes machabéennes: 17. Interpretation haggadique de ces opérations," *RB* 34 (1925) 208–211; S. Klein, "Palästinisches im Jubiläenbuch," *ZDPV* 57 (1934) 7–27.

come portents for the fathers.[23] These stories wish to say: Israelite and non-Israelite traits have timeless roots; so may our lot be!

The other type, dealt with first, includes brief fragments—solitary verses and half-verses. They deal with the dispossession of the inhabitants of Canaan and settling in their place. They also deal with the building of cities in Canaan. The main issue consists of settlement, not war. These passages do not conform to the dominant version of Israel's history; rather they contradict that version either implicitly or explicitly. They have survived as the remnants of ancient traditions, tied to a specific clan or locale, that predate typologically (and sometimes also chronologically) the creation of an Israelite national consciousness. These fragmentary reports teach us how rich and variegated the Israelite historical tradition was, and through them we learn how complicated and complex were the beginnings of Israel. A protracted and complicated process that extended over generations and fractured into dozens of events in different regions, in the end brought Israel to the occupation of its land.

---

[23] On Genesis 14 see Umberto Cassuto, *La questione della Genesi* (Firenze: Le Monnier, 1934) 370–374. For a Hebrew translation, see Umberto Cassuto, *The "Quaestio" of the Book of Genesis* (trans. M. E. Artom; Jerusalem: Magnes, 1990) 311–314.

Chapter 15

"The Mother of All . . ." Etiologies

Jack M. Sasson
Vanderbilt University

> . . . *they who know the most*
> *Must mourn the deepest o'er the fatal truth,*
> *The Tree of Knowledge is not that of Life.*
> Lord Byron, *Manfred*, I/1

It is a pleasure to offer this study, really a reading of a biblical text, to Burke Long, a friend for a full generation, and an admired colleague for almost twice that long. I was entranced by Burke's scholarship when, as I wrote a commentary on Ruth, I sought an inventive approach to the issue of etiologies.[1] I come back to the same need in this paper, but this time the subject is one of the most familiar of Hebrew narratives, telling us how the first woman got her name. The bibliography on this narrative is so immense, however, that I am hoping that Burke will overlook my slighting it. Luckily, he (and readers of this essay) will know a number of recent Genesis commentaries whose authors have fortunately not shirked their responsibility as I am about to do.[2]

---

[1] Burke O. Long, *The Problem of Etiological Narrative in the Old Testament* (BZAW 108; Berlin: Töpelmann, 1968).

[2] Particularly useful in writing this essay were the commentaries of Claus Westermann, *Genesis 1–11* (Minneapolis: Augsburg, 1984) 178–278, and of Gordon J. Wenham, *Genesis 1–15* (WBC 1; Waco, Tex.: Word Books, 1987) 41–91; the studies of Richard J. Clifford, *Creation Accounts in the Ancient Near East and in the Bible* (CBQMS 26; Washington, D.C.: The Catholic Biblical Assoc., 1994); James Barr, *The Garden of Eden and the Hope of Immortality* (Minneapolis: Fortress, 1993); Patrick D. Miller, *Genesis 1–11: Studies in Structure and Theme*(Sheffield: Sheffield Academic Press, 1978); Howard N. Wallace, *The Eden Narrative* (Atlanta: Scholars Press, 1985);

Setting the background might be helpful. The Hebrew narrator tells us what happened when the woman heard the snake's reassurance that the forbidden fruit would bring knowledge equal to God's rather than death (Gen 3:6): "She saw how good was the tree for eating and how delightful it was to the eyes, and that the tree was desirable for gaining wisdom, so she took from its fruit and ate. She also gave her man who was by her, and he ate."[3]

We observe in this verse a number of allusions, plotted around the senses. The verb רָאָה, "to see," is for the first time attributed to the human pair, anticipatively exploiting the snake's assurance that eyes will open upon partaking of the fruit. The woman is said to grasp the fruit, an act that surely reassured her about her survival since she had mistakenly imagined a ban against touching it (Gen 3:3; see below). There is also the mention of טוב, "good," here applied to the potential taste of the fruit, but again recalling a virtue attached to the knowledge the snake said was the couple's to have.

But most remarkable is the wholesale replay of qualities attached to the

and Richard J. Clifford and John J. Collins, *Creation in the Biblical Traditions* (CBQMS 24; Washington, D.C.: The Catholic Biblical Assoc., 1992). Terje Stordalen has written a massive thesis on all aspects of the narrative: *Echoes of Eden: Genesis 2–3 and Symbolism of the Eden Garden in Biblical Hebrew Literature* (CBET; Leuven: Peeters, forthcoming). I am beholden to a lively correspondence with him. I must not fail to mention Burke Long's good contribution, *The Problem of Etiological Narrative*, 53–54. See also diverse biblical dictionaries under such entries as "Tree of Knowledge"; "Tree of Life"; "Eden"; "Paradise"; "Adam and Eve"; etc.

Interesting for their tone, perspective, willingness to restate questions, even passion, are a number of essays in *A Feminist Companion to Genesis* (ed. Athalya Brenner; Sheffield: Sheffield Academic Press, 1993) and *The Feminist Companion to the Bible (Second Series)* (ed. Athalya Brenner; Sheffield: Sheffield Academic Press, 1998). Other essays that are worth consulting are those of Paul Kübel, "Zur Entstehung der Paradieserzählung," *BN* 65 (1992) 74–85; Dan E. Burns, "Dream Form in Genesis 2.4b–3.24: Asleep in the Garden," *JSOT* 37 (1987) 3–14; Joel Rosenberg, "The Garden Story Forward and Backward: The Non-narrative Dimension of Gen. 2–3," *Prooftexts* 1 (1981) 1–27; David Rutledge, "Faithful Reading: Poststructuralism and the Sacred," *BibInt* 4 (1996) 270–228.

I register here my gratitude to Edward Greenstein for an insightful reading of this paper.

[3] Ps 36:2–4 shares many words and sentiments with what we find in Gen 3:6, and may well be commenting on it (see also Prov 13:12):

> I feel within me what transgression tells the wicked
> not pondering the fear of God
> fooling himself to consider
> that his iniquity is beyond discovery or resentment.
> His words are heinous and deceitful
> and he ceased to improve though gaining wisdom (לְהַשְׂכִּיל לְהֵיטִיב).

tree that were once associated with the trees God planted in his garden. This is clear from a comparison of Gen 2:9 and 3:6:

Gen 2:9	Gen 3:6
ויצמח יהוה אלהים מן־האדמה כל־עץ נחמד למראה וטוב למאכל . . .	ותרא האשה כי טוב העץ למאכל וכי תאוה־הוא לעינים ונחמד העץ להשכיל . . .
Lord God made grow from the ground every tree that was appealing to the sight and good for eating . . .	When the woman saw how good was the tree for eating and how delightful it was to the eyes, and that the tree was desirable for gaining wisdom . . .[4]

The switches in vocabulary pertaining to the trees (נחמד is applied to sight in Gen 2:9, but to the gaining of wisdom in Gen 3:6), in the use of controlling verbs (God "makes trees grow," but the woman "sees," referring to perception and anticipation), and in the sequence of the senses (sight then taste in Gen 2:9, but taste then sight in Gen 3:6) are worth brief notice. But in giving us access to the woman's perceptions about the forbidden tree, the narrator reveals them to parallel God's own characterization of the flora in the garden. True, the woman is made to merge into one tree arboreal qualities that God had reserved for many. Also true, the woman once again (see her comment about touching the tree in Gen 3:3) was expanding eccentrically on traits assigned the tree when she thought it was "desirable for gaining wisdom," a quality strikingly absent from God's own expectations for them.[5] Nevertheless the implication of her meditation is far-reaching, for it makes it impossible to deny that, *even before she had taken one bite from any fruit,* the woman's capacity to reason was fairly sophisticated, potentially even a match for God's. In fact, nothing in later Genesis chapters gives evidence that eating from the forbidden tree improved on (or detracted from) the type of knowledge or quality of discernment that the woman was displaying just then.[6] This observation compromises the credibility of the regnant interpretation that would have the couple cross a forbidden threshold after partaking from the Tree of Knowledge of Good and Bad, forcing God to further deny them access to the Tree of Life. We therefore need to reinspect what the tale has to say about the evolution of the pair's perception of their condition and God's response to their acts.

---

[4] This statement is made up of two object clauses introduced by conjunctions (כי), and a third clause without the conjunction. It would not do, therefore, to homogenize by excising העץ from the third, as is frequently done on the basis of versions that have their own syntactic rules, for example the LXX or Vulgate.

[5] She might have imagined that the tree would "be desirable to open the eyes" or that it would "give her knowledge of good and bad," perceptions that she may have assimilated from the snake's reply in Gen 3:5.

[6] See also Edward L. Greenstein, "Deconstruction and Biblical Narrative," *Prooftexts* 9 (1989) 50.

Let us go back to the woman's response to the snake's initial (and timidly exploratory) inquiry. "We may eat from the fruits of any tree in the garden," the woman had said in reply, "but from the fruits of the tree at the center of the garden, God said, 'Do not eat from it; do not even touch it, lest you die'" (Gen 3:6). Commentators galore, from time immemorial, have struggled with the woman's understanding of God's warning. How did she learn of it? Why did she expand on the charge as originally addressed to the earthling alone (Gen 2:16–17)? Why did her mate standing by her side not correct her formulation? I cannot improve on the speculations that are rehearsed in practically every Genesis commentary and specialized study, and would not even polemicize against them; but if one holds (as I do) that literary resolutions cannot hinge on episodes or scenes that are not delivered by the text under inspection, then this sort of query must be left to dramatists or midrashists, for the Eden story itself offers few clues on such matters.

It also follows from the above principle that no literary evaluation (in contrast to documentary or tradition analysis) can be based on versions of the narrative that are no longer available to us. This observation is particularly relevant to the debate about the specific tree from which the woman plucked fruits. In Gen 3:6, the woman is clearly talking about partaking from the tree in the "center of the garden." That tree is certainly the Tree of Life, for, in harking back to Gen 2:9, we remember that "Lord God made grow from the ground every tree that was appealing to the sight and good for eating, with the Tree of Life in the center of the garden, and the Tree of Knowledge of Good and Bad."[7] Sensing the need to explain the discrepancy regarding which tree was first sampled, scholars have relied on proven

---

[7] Henceforth, for convenience we will call the latter the "Tree of Knowledge."

In both passages (Gen 2:9 and 3:3) the Tree of Life is distinguished not so much by its location as by a phrasing that syntactically detaches it from the other trees and from the Tree of Knowledge as well. Moreover, when the compound preposition בתוך is followed by a noun with a definite article, it almost always translates into "in the midst," "at the center," or the like. In contrast, notice how in Gen 3:8 the insertion of עץ between בתוך and הגן allows us to translate "The earthling and his wife . . . hid themselves *among* the trees of the garden" (hardly "in the tree of the garden"). Finally, it must be noted how senseless would have been a reply to the snake that read, "We may eat from the fruits of any tree in the garden, but from the fruits of a tree *among those* in the garden, God said, 'Do not eat from it; do not even touch it, lest you die'" (Gen 3:6).

While it is not of immediate interest to me what is implied by "good and bad" when associated with "knowledge," I agree with those who understand the phrase merismatically, that is, to refer to an all-encompassing knowledge that is especially God's. Wallace, *Eden Narrative*, 115–132 is particularly good in presenting the argument for this position, while Wenham, *Genesis 1–15,* gives the most accessible recent review of proposals.

tactics, proposing "original" settings for the story that depend on hypotheses such as the following:

- that there were no trees at all;
- that there was one tree (some say it was the "Tree of Life"; others suggest that it was the "Tree of Knowledge");
- that there was one tree, but over the lifetime of the tale it divided into two, each with its own attributes;
- that there were two trees (one more marginal than the other), with (or without) overlapping qualities.

All these proposals have merits, and some may even be correct in reconstructing the lost prototype for the story; but how could any scholar confirm their accuracy?[8]

So we are now in a quandary: Our inspection has revealed that woman—as logical, discerning, and discriminating as any mortal came to be—ate from a tree that, her false notion about its attribute notwithstanding, was never explicitly forbidden, neither to her nor to her mate. For this reason—and as the snake had predicted—God's death threat could not materialize.[9] Yet at their inquest the pair sheepishly conceded God's charge that they ate from a forbidden tree (3:11) and they were judged on the basis of that failure (3:17).[10] Moreover, after dispensing fates on those involved, God expels the pair from the garden, thinking, "With the earthling now like one of us in knowing good and bad, what if he should now stretch out his hand and also take from the Tree of Life and eat—he will live forever" (Gen 3:22). Centuries of exegesis (see Sirach 25:23: "In woman was sin's beginning, and because of her we all die"), especially Christian (see Romans 5:12–14), depended on these verses to conclude that the pair had indeed sampled from the Tree of Knowledge of Good and Bad (but hardly the

---

[8] The issue is replayed in practically every commentary. See also Kübel, "Zur Entstehung der Paradieserzählung," 74–85; Jacques Vermeylen, "Le récit du paradis et la question des origines du Pentateuque," *Bijdragen* 41 (1980) 230–250; A. J. Soggin, "Philological Linguistic Notes on the Second Chapter of Genesis," in his *Old Testament and Oriental Studies* (BibOr 29; Rome: Biblical Institute, 1975) 169–78.

[9] We should not weaken God's threat of Gen 2:17 ("but from the Tree of Knowledge of Good and Bad, you must not eat; for upon your eating from it, you must die") into such a flaccid rendering as ". . . you shall be doomed to die" (or the like).

[10] In Gen 3:12, the earthling does not challenge God's charge that the couple had eaten from the forbidden tree. The earthling's reaction was enigmatic from the beginning of the drama, for he did not correct the woman when he heard her spouting patently incorrect views about what was forbidden. Perhaps he had counted on his capacity to dissimulate or to persuade through excuse. At any rate, it is important to note that the two felt they had disobeyed once they ate, whether or not from the forbidden fruit.

"Tree of Wisdom"), thus burdening the whole of mankind in consequence of their "fall."[11]

To resolve our dilemma, we backtrack to the beginning of the episode, whether we locate it at Gen 2:4a ("These are formation accounts of heaven and earth, in their being created . . .") or at 2:4b ("When the Lord God made the earth and heaven . . .").[12] Generally, scholarship has attributed what is said about the pair in paradise to "J," and has recognized in it elements for a second creation narrative; the first, in Gen 1:1–2:4a, is attributed to "P." Yet just because the two accounts rehearse how diverse components of the universe originated, it may be too accommodating to classify both of them as "creation narratives." In fact, on such a justification many other passages in the Hebrew Bible will need to be so termed.[13] It is, however, possible to discriminate among narratives that contain such material in a number of ways. For example, we could contrast on the basis of vision (broad and inclusive—from heavens to grass—versus narrow and specific), types of creative act (command, birth, separation, combat, artisanship) and logic of progression (cause-and-effect sequence versus "haphazard" arrangement). But here I am most interested in contrasting the phraseology that reports on what did or did not exist when creation was launched.

It is observable that the backdrop for the creation of the earthling is given in negative phrasings, describing what had not yet come to be ("When any shrub of the field had yet to be on earth and when any grass of the field had yet to sprout . . ." [Gen 2:5]), rather than in positively-stated formulations (with many variations, for example, "When first God created the universe, earth was a hodge-podge, darkness was over the deep, and a

---

[11] Countering the "sin and fall" interpretation of this myth is particularly successful in feminist scholarship; see Carol Meyers, *Discovering Eve: Ancient Israelite Women in Context* (Oxford: Oxford Univ. Press, 1988) 72–138, and her chapter "Gender Role and Genesis 3.16 Revisited," reprinted in *Feminist Companion,* 118–141. A fine overview of feminist and structuralist inspections of the tale is given by Pamela Milne, "The Patriarchal Stamp of Scripture: The Implications of Structuralist Analyses for Feminist Hermeneutics," reprinted in *Feminist Companion,* 146–172; see also her "Eve and Adam: Is a Feminist Reading Possible?" *Bible Review* 4 (1988) 12–21. In "Rethinking the Interpretation of Genesis 2.4B–3.24," in *Feminist Companion,* 78–117, Lyn M. Bechtel finds in the story a model of human growth, from infancy through maturely accepting separation from authority.

[12] I think that the whole of Gen 2:4 serves both to conclude the previous narrative and to initiate the next one. A review of the issues is given by Terje Stordalen, "Genesis 2,4: Restudying a *locus classicus*," *ZAW* 104 (1992) 163–177.

[13] And in fact many biblical passages do get labeled as such, among them Pss 8, 33, 104, 139, 148; Job 38–41; and Prov 8, as well as diverse fragments from the prophets. Useful overviews on Mesopotamian creation legends can be found in

divine/mighty wind swept over the waters, God said . . ." [Gen 1:1–2]).[14]
This distinction between the two formulations must not be taken as evidence for differing levels of theological sophistication or conviction; rather,
the use of negative phrasing permits a sharper focus on a select number of
soon-to-be created objects, in our case the earthling. But what is initially
declared not yet to have existed is certain to be featured in the ensuing narrative. (Notice how earth, shrubs, and anxiety about rain are reinvoked in
the fate allotted the earthling, Gen 3:17–20.) The formation of any other objects (trees, animals, the woman) is limited to elements that serve the story
launched by the initial creation (the earthling's), rather than to exhibit the
fullness of the cosmos or to praise the greatness of the creator. (Notice how
nothing is said about sun, moon, sea-monsters, or the like in this particular
story.) This linkage of fates among a succession of created objects is what
makes Gen 2–3 such a rich storehouse for etiologies, that is, for explanations of how things came to be; so much so, that I would rather speak of
Gen 2–3 as an extended etiological narrative, reserving the phrase "creation narrative" for such texts as Gen 1:1–2:4, with its grand vista of a gen-
erated cosmos and its broad grouping of created objects (animate and
inanimate).[15]

The chain of densely-packed, interlocking episodes that we call (fittingly or not) the "Eden" or "Fall" narrative (Gen 2–3) gains its momen-
tum, then, from the negatively-stated assessment of an earth lacking the
potential (no vegetation, no rain) and lacking the mechanism (no earthling) for regeneration. The first to be created is the earthling, from soil
(עפר), and he acquires breathing ("God blew into his face/nostrils [באפיו]
living breath," Gen 2:7) in an act that is highly reminiscent of the ancient
Near Eastern "mouth-opening" rituals for quickening divine images. This
succession of what-was-not-yet and what-first-came-to-be will prove pro-
tean, and although there will be unpromising solutions (earthling working
in God's own garden), a satisfying explanation for hard toil as the lot of
humans will not come until Gen 3:17–19, where choice vocabulary from
the initial verses is replayed (reluctant vegetation; face/nostrils [זעת אפיך];
earthling reverting to soil).

The narrative's controlling etiology, however, is not launched until
God, realizing that it would not do for the earthling to be alone, proposes
for him an עזר כנגדו, "a helper, comparable to him" (or the like). The phrase

Gwendolyn Leick, *Sex and Eroticism in Mesopotamian Literature* (London: Routledge, 1994).

[14] See the Appendix, "What Has Not Yet Come to Be."

[15] For differing opinions on Gen 2–3, see Westermann, *Genesis 1–11,* 186–190,
and John van Seters, "The Story of Paradise," chapter 5 of his *Prologue to History:
The Yahwist As Historian in Genesis* (Louisville: Westminster/John Knox, 1992),
107–134.

is repeated at Gen 2:20, thus providing a frame for an anecdote of humorous potential. This helper was not to be selected from the same species as the human, since the earthling (like Tarzan before Jane's arrival) could have instilled the characteristics he sought in a helper simply by assigning a name to any of the animals (land or air) that God was busily creating for his inspection.[16] The experiment failed; for the earthling, having fixed the nature of all animals (the snake's too?) and, in effect, having determined the rapport they were to have among each other, could not yet imagine a shared destiny with any of the creatures parading before him. It is crucial to note that this particular etiology—how the earthling came to recognize what were the true role and lot of his mate—does not find completion until Gen 3:20, when the earthling arrives at a fitting name for the woman. At that point, he calls her "Eve," for (as he explains it), "it was she who was the mother of all the living."[17] This explanation for the woman's name (indeed, her lot) admits to a *gender* differentiation between the two, even as, implicitly, it establishes a sexual demarcation between them.[18] Within this narrative stretch (Gen 2:18–3:20), there will be ample room for a cento of etiologies. Among them is one that depends on God sculpting the woman from a rib (Gen 2:22–24). This one explains *etymologically* (actually *paronomastically*) how "woman (אשה)" was derived from "man (איש)." But it also delivers (as the narrator's aside) an *institutional* explication of how marriage was inaugurated among humans. There will soon also be a particularly sophisticated threefold etiology, which we will presently explore, when God imposes punishment on the three conspirators (Gen 3:14–19). This transformation of the woman from being a helper into becoming a mother ("Eve") could have occurred only after partaking from the "tree in the center of the garden," that is, from the Tree of Life and not from the Tree of Knowledge.

The text tells us that "the two of them were naked, the earthling and his

---

[16] This is the only occasion in the Hebrew Bible where נגד is construed with the comparative particle ־כ, making the precise nuance of the phrase עזר כנגדו a bone of contention. The notion here, I think, is that God wished the earthling to identify someone who could stand by him (see the usage of לנגדו in Josh 5:13), whose company he could share (see מנגדו in Ps 10:5), possibly also who could do the same work. To debate whether this phrase implied (an ideology about) dominance, equality, or subordination among the sexes would at this point in the story be incongruous narratologically (but obviously not homiletically) because the earthling never did select a helper from the available choices. Nevertheless, it could be pointed out that when Gen 2:18 is quoted in Tobit 8:6, it is to bless the union of mates (Tobiah and Sarah), who were deemed equal in all respects.

[17] The "true" etymology for the name "Eve" is not of immediate import to us.

[18] The terms זכר ונקבה, "male and female," do not occur here, as they do in Gen 1:27 where only a *sexual* differentiation is at stake.

wife; "ולא יתבששו" (Gen 2:25).[19] It is commonly suggested that nakedness here is a sign that the pair were like children, innocent and sexually immature.[20] The tense of יתבששו, a *Hitpolel* imperfect, is frequentive, factitive, and reflexive, hence meaning, "they did not shame/embarrass each other," underscoring the banality of nakedness to a pair for whom sexual distinction and the physiology of conception have not yet become at issue.[21] However, even in the Hebrew Bible (let alone in antiquity), nakedness is metaphoric for many other predicaments beside sexuality or shame (in Hebrew Scripture, never entailing guilt), such as poverty (as in the many references to the virtue of clothing the naked, immaterial of how they got that way), lack of protection (as when bereft of parents or husbands, e.g., Ezek 16:7), and loss of control of one's personal fate (as in the references to captivity, e.g., Deut 28:47; reversed, upon release, through clothing, e.g., 2 Chr. 28:14).[22] We might therefore imagine that as the snake was readying for its fateful discussion with the woman, the pair had as yet to be conscious of its auton-

---

[19] There may be an intentional play on this episode in Prov 12:23 ("A skillful man conceals what he knows [אדם ערום כסה דעת]").

[20] Quoting from David P. Wright, "Unclean and Clean," *ABD* 6.739:

> It can be argued that eating from the forbidden tree represents a person's (or persons') growing-up. Before eating the woman and man are like children: without wisdom or knowledge, sexually immature, unashamed of nakedness, immortal (i.e., as children who are not entirely cognizant of their mortality), and not responsible for or aware of sin. After eating the couple becomes wise and knowledgeable, sexually mature (in the J story only after the eating does the subject of reproduction come up, Gen 3:16, and naming the woman Eve "life," the "mother of all the living" occur, v 20), ashamed of their nakedness, mortal, and sinful. This suggests that the latent reason for the pair's expulsion from the garden is their acquisition of a mature, mortal, human nature.

This sentiment is widely shared among commentators and may, in fact, be informed by Hellenistic notions regarding nakedness as innocence, as in the striking example of adults communing in nakedness to emulate the (alleged) guilelessness of childhood in the *Gospel of Thomas* (21, 37).

[21] For this rendering, see my *"wᵉlōʾ yitbōšāšû* (Gen 2,25) and Its Implications," *Biblica* 66 (1985) 418–421. An approximate opinion is given by John Skinner, *Genesis* (ICC; Edinburgh: T. & T. Clark, 1910) 70 [notes], "The Hithpael (only here) probably expresses reciprocity ('ashamed before one another') . . ." See also the articles on the word בוש by H. Seebass in *TDOT*, 2.50–60, and in *Theological Lexicon of the Old Testament* (ed. Ernst Jenni and Claus Westermann; Peabody, Mass.: Hendrickson, 1997) 1.204–207.

[22] The same metaphoric usage is found in Mesopotamia; see Robert D. Biggs, "Nacktheit," *Reallexikon der Assyriologie* 9 (1998) 64–66. Interesting articles on nakedness are those of B. N. Wamback, "'Or tous deux étaient nus, l'homme et sa femme, mais ils n'avaient pas honte,'" in *Mélanges bibliques en hommage au R. P. Béda Rigaux* (ed. Albert Descamps and André de Halleux; Gembloux: Duculot, 1970)

omy or to know how to differentiate itself from the animals once offered as the earthling's potential companions.

Partaking from the Tree of Life brought radical changes in the pair's condition, but the reaction of those involved differed. For the pair, the immediate effect was a change in their perception of themselves. We are told that the "eyes of the two came to open," ‏ותפקחנה עיני שניהם‎ (Gen 3:7). In other citations, the verb ‏פקח‎ (in contrast to the ubiquitous ‏פתח‎) always applies to the senses (sight; but once [Isa 42:20] also hearing), and always implies an enhanced consciousness. Here, unlike other contexts (such as at Gen 21:19, Num 22:31, 2 Kings 6:17), this sharpening of insight is achieved without divine intercession. We might also note that the opening of the eyes as a sign of maturation occurs to newborns only among animals and not among human beings.

But the snake had been much more subtle in what it had predicted. "You will not die," it had exhorted, "for God knows that the moment you eat from it, your eyes will become open, and you will become like God (or gods) in knowing good and bad" (Gen 3:4–5). The snake was granting the recognition of a changed state not just to the pair but above all to God. Therefore, whether or not the pair ate from a forbidden tree—indeed, whether or not either of them thought that they had eaten from the forbidden tree—was not as much at issue as whether or not God, recognizing a change in the two, linked it to their disobedience. The reactions of those concerned tells us much about each side's response to the new situation.

The first reaction of the earthling and his woman was to create clothing of leaves and then to hide when they heard God's moving in his garden. In a scene reminiscent of Enkidu's passage from the animal to the human world (2nd tablet of the Old Babylonian Gilgamesh Epic), the donning of clothing (however flimsy) was a statement about the pair's sharpened perception of how remote they were from the other animals.[23] The change

---

553–556; J. Coppens, *La Connaissance du bien et du mal et le péché du paradis: Contribution à l'interprétation de Gen. II–III* (ALBO 11/3; Leuven: Nauwelaerts, 1948); Jonathan Z. Smith, "The Garments of Shame," *HR* 5 (1965) 217–237; Rosenberg, "Garden Story," 16.

For Mesopotamia, see Zainab Bahrani, "The Iconography of the Nude in Mesopotamia," *Source: Notes in the History of Art* 12/2 (1993) 12–19. As far as Mesopotamia is concerned, there is a noticeable discrepancy about nudity between art (many figures) and texts (rare mention); see the series of articles (by different authors) in *Reallexikon der Assyriologie* 9 (1998) 46–68.

[23] The first-millennium versions of Enkidu's discovery of his humanity differ from the Old Babylonian evocation of the event. Where the Old Babylonian has Enkidu learning about his new status from the *ḫarimtu* who treats him as a child once he emotionally bonds with her, the later versions are sharply psychological. After enjoying the *ḫarimtu*'s favors, Enkidu wishes to resume his feral life and only

must not be attributed to an increase of mental capacity due to eating any fruit, forbidden or not, but rather to sharpened notions about their own singularity. Moreover, if we continue to appreciate this particular scene through Mesopotamian lore, we may even recognize that the loss (and retrieval) of characteristic garments is also the loss (and retrieval) of divinity, as is eloquently conveyed in both the Sumerian and Akkadian versions of "Inanna/Ishtar's Descent to the Netherworld." We might therefore dare to imagine that the pair were making a statement about their own divinity, taking to heart the snake's advice that "you will become like God (or gods) in knowing good and bad" (Gen 3:5). In this sense, it may be ironic that when eventually God had them wear animal skins (Gen 3:21), outwardly the pair displayed some of the same feral forms as the animals from which they had thought to distance themselves. Perhaps God was delivering a lesson thereby.

But more telling was the earthling's need to lie about his state when God sought him out: "Having heard the sound of you in the garden, I became afraid, for I am naked, so I hid" (Gen 3:10). This lie was not due to an increase in knowledge (let alone wisdom), but directly resulted from a developing discernment that had been the earthling's before partaking from either tree. Thus, when empowered to name (and thus categorize) the animals in the process of selecting a mate, the earthling had already become perceptive enough to realize that none could be a fit helper.[24]

For God, however, the pair's furtive actions and the earthling's lie made the transgression so manifest that the matter did not require profound examination. He might have gone beyond his limited inquest (Gen 3:11–13), for example, by asking questions of the snake or by inspecting the trees themselves, for, as we know from other narratives such as the Tower of Babel (Gen 11:5–6) and especially the Sodom and Gomorrah affair (Gen 18:20–21), God does investigate before deciding on terrible reprisals. For

---

recognizes the order of animates to which he belongs when animals recoil from the human scent about him.

In the Sumerian Disputation between Sheep and Grain (see n. 11), this is what is said about primordial beings:

> The people of those distant days
> Knew not bread to eat,
> They knew not cloth to wear;
> They went about in the Land with naked limbs
> Eating grass with their mouths like sheep,
> And drinking water from the ditches.

[24] This point is well-argued by George W. Ramsey in "Is Name-Giving an Act of Domination in Genesis 2:23 and Elsewhere?" *CBQ* 50 (1988) 34. We now recognize that the earthling and the woman each displayed intricate reactions to choices. The great difference is that the earthling's motivation, unlike the woman's, is God-incited and was doomed to fail.

God, however, the dilemma was not that the pair had through trespass acquired more knowledge than they had previously (in fact they would always have the same amount of it), but that, having eaten from the Tree of Life, the two had already achieved an immortality that could make them as eternal as gods. This condition could not have been acceptable to God. Nor could it have helped God's disquiet about the pair to have them believe they had disobeyed yet had escaped death.

God's solution to this intolerable situation is carried through the linked etiologies of Gen 3:14–19, in which he institutes major changes in the fate or natural behavior of each of the protagonists. The program itself was two-fold. It was first a *paradigm* for the interdependence of nature: Cursed, the serpent is now to crawl, feeding on soil, and its brood is to be in deadly conflict with the woman's descendants. But if human beings will hence-forth kill snakes, snakes will feed on the putrefying flesh of their mortal en-emies. In this way, the fates of each and all lock in cyclical dependence. The program can also be read as a *parable* for the transfiguration of the immor-tality the pair had achieved through access to the Tree of Life.

God had said to the woman, "I will greatly increase your suffering dur-ing pregnancy: You will bear children in pain. Your desire will be for your man, and he will take control of you" (Gen 3:16). We notice two peculiari-ties to this terse verdict. God refrains from hectoring the woman, as he did the snake ("Because you have done this . . ."; Gen 3:14) and afterwards the earthling ("Because you listened to your woman's voice, eating from the tree about which I instructed you, 'Do not eat from it' . . ."; Gen 3:17). More tellingly, in contrast to the vocabulary for punishment imposed on the snake (Gen 3:14) and (indirectly) on the earthling (Gen 3:17), the verb אָרַר, "to curse," is not at all displayed when it concerns the woman. Rather, as penalty the woman is transformed, from being a potential "helper" to be-coming a host for human life, a vehicle for human permanence and eter-nity. How this miracle unfolded is told to us in a sequence inverted to focus on the woman's singular contribution in the metamorphosis. The earthling is to take charge of the woman's future (marriage, taking control from her parents). Instinctively, the woman will desire her mate.[25] But in becoming pregnant, the woman will experience the distension of her body and will periodically yield to uncomfortable functions. Birthgiving, at once myste-rious and natural, will always be painful to her. Acknowledging that this extraordinary process is singularly the woman's, the earthling finally finds a name that more precisely acknowledges his helper's exceptional contri-bution to their lives: חַוָּה, "Eve," forebear to us all (Gen 3:20).

With the immortality of the human *species* now affirmed, death must

---

[25] The narrative may be implying that desire is a drive for restoration into one unit, and may thus be alluding to Gen 2:24.

now be introduced as the destiny of *individuals*. The longest of God's sentences (Gen 3:17–19) is more diffuse than the others, for, as mentioned above, it tries to replay vocabulary from before the earthling's creation. The earthling will no longer work the well-watered garden God had himself planted in Eden. (But who will work it henceforth?) For him as for his species, life itself will henceforth be hard, for the earth that gave him body is itself cursed because of his action. Until earth reclaims him, he will work hard to earn any further contribution from her.

With his transformations completed, God admits: "With the earthling now like one of us in knowing good and bad, what if he should now stretch out his hand and also take from the Tree of Life and eat—he will live forever" (Gen 3:22). Notice how the construction of הֵן with the perfect (הָאָדָם הָיָה כְּאַחַד מִמֶּנּוּ) achieves a situation in which there is little temporal concern, hence not at all confirming the conventional renderings that suggest a response to a developing crisis.[26] Thus, when the RSV translates our passage "Behold, the man has become like one of us, knowing good and evil . . . ," the implication is that God is reacting to a new set of circumstances. Yet, as is usual in Hebrew, the immediate reason for God's apprehension is not stated in the sentence until וְעַתָּה, generally rendered, "and now." The syntax of Gen 3:22, therefore, locates God's alarm not in the pair having attained a knowledge equal to his own (it was potentially always the couple's), but in what could occur with the Tree of Life remaining within human reach. In fact, it is only after their transfiguration into "Adam" and "Eve," that is, into individuals capable of producing children, grandchildren, and descendants galore, that continued access to the Tree of Life becomes alarming; for with such access would come the certainty of populating the garden with prolific and knowing immortals.[27] From God's

---

[26] This is generally so in constructions where the particle is followed by a verb in the perfect, such as in Gen 4:14, 15:3, 19:34, 27:37, and 47:23. An excellent example occurs at Num 31:16. Moses scolds the army that had just won a victory against Midian: "You have spared every female, yet they were the very same to incite Israel into trespass against the Lord in the Peor matter (. . . הֵן הֵנָּה הָיוּ . . . . לִמְסָר־מַעַל בַּיהוה)."

Two articles have a different take on the Eden narrative. Nahum M. Waldman, "What Was the Actual Effect of the Tree of Knowledge?" *Jewish Bible Quarterly* 19 (1990–1991) 105–113, argues that partaking from the Tree of Knowledge had no effect on the pair other than to identify them as rebellious. He revives Calvin's notion that Gen 3:22 should be read as sarcasm. Allen S. Maller, "What About the Tree of Life?" *Dor le-Dor* 15 (1986/87) 270–271, writes a sermon in which Adam encourages Eve to eat from the Tree of Life to give himself seniority over her. But she eats from the other tree to promote her own fertility, choosing mortality along the way.

[27] Overpopulation and the risks it brought are well-known themes in Mesopotamian lore, whether the expansion occurred in heaven or on earth. On this topic one can still read profitably Anne D. Kilmer, "The Mesopotamian Concept of Over-

perspective, this was not at all an attractive prospect. And as he evicts the pair from his garden, the only tree God chooses to safeguard from the encroachment of individuals is the Tree of Life.[28]

*   *   *

This brief essay grew out of two disquieting observations when reading the "Eden" narrative: One, that the woman was capable of making a thoughtful decision about what is right for her and for her man before she partook of any fruit; two, that the fruit came from the tree at the center of the garden, hence the Tree of Life. I sought to solve the mystery of a pair who met death when tasting life, but in doing so became ancestors for humanity. I have found in their behavior misguided disobedience, but no fault; transformation, but no fall; immortality, but only for the human species; death, but only for individuals; and dependence, but no harmony, among God's creatures. Yet I am not insisting that Burke, or any other reader of this essay, give up a traditional interpretation that centers around partaking of the Tree of Knowledge. In truth, every interpretation of narratives leaks, especially of those that have stayed the centuries as sources for lessons and morals. I can only hope that Burke will find that my reading leaks just a tad less than those he has sampled elsewhere.

---

population and Its Solution as Reflected in Mythology," *Orientalia* 41 (1972) 160–177; William L. Moran, "The Creation of Man in Atrahasis I 192–248," *BASOR* 200 (1970) 48–56; and idem, "Atrahasis: The Babylonian Story of the Flood," *Biblica* 52 (1971) 51–71.

[28] In the Hebrew Bible, the Tree of Life (עץ החיים) and the Tree of Knowledge of Good and Bad (עץ הדעת טוב ורע) are found only in this narrative. A tree of life (עץ חיים) occurs as a metaphor for wisdom (so not at all as a "real" tree) only in Proverbs (3:18, 11:30, 3:12, 15:4). Neither tree is known from Near Eastern lore, although plants with magical powers (to rejuvenate, primarily) are featured in diverse narratives; see the commentaries, as well as the good chapter on this topic in Wallace, *Eden Narrative*, 101–141 (rehearsed in tighter form in "Tree of Knowledge and Tree of Life," *ABD* 6.656–660); and see J. Alberto Soggin, "עץ, tree," *Theological Lexicon of the Old Testament* 2.941–942.

Appendix

"What Has Not Yet Come to Be"

Non-existence as a prelude to creative acts is known elsewhere in Hebraic lore. In Prov 8:22–26, Wisdom is said to have pre-existed the creation of earth, water, mountains, and soil, and was with God as he created them (8:27–29). See discussion and bibliography in Jacques B. Doukhan, *The Genesis Creation Story: Its Literary Structure* (Berrien Springs, Mich.: Andrews Univ. Press, 1978) 105–114; Terje Stordalen, "Man, Soil, Garden: Basic Plot in Genesis 2–3 Reconsidered," *JSOT* 53 (1992) 3–26 (with bibliography on earlier literature). There is also an esoteric and highly literary sequencing of soon-to-become divine acts in 2 Esdras [= 4 Ezra] 6:1–5, but it cannot be treated as "creation narrative"; see Jacob M. Myers, *I and II Esdras* (AB 42; Garden City, N.Y.: Doubleday, 1974) 189–190.

In Mesopotamian literature, negative phraseology for acts of creation readily occurs, such as in the opening lines of the *Enuma Elish*. Most often, they are featured as a backdrop for spells and as an introduction for disputation texts. Among the former are an Akkadian incantation against a sty (see Benjamin R. Foster, *Before the Muses: An Anthology of Akkadian Literature* [Bethesda, Md.: CDL Press, 1996] 839 [¶IV.33d]) and a recounting of a Sumerian spell responsible for the multiplicity of languages (see William W. Hallo, ed., *The Context of Scripture* [Leiden: Brill, 1997] 1.547–548). Among the latter is the Akkadian "Debate between the Tamarisk and the Palm" (Foster, *Before the Muses*, 891 [¶IV.56]) and the particularly impressive Sumerian "Dispute between Sheep [laḫar] and Wheat [ašnan]" (Hallo, *Context*, 575–578). In such texts, any allusion to creation tends to be artificial and context dependent, since the primary motivation is to fulfill destinies for the disputants or to reverse through spells attacks that would otherwise be destructive; see the excellent article of H. L. V. Vanstiphout, "Lore, Learning, and Levity in the Sumerian Disputations: A Matter of Form or Substance?" in *Dispute Poems and Dialogues in the Ancient and Mediaeval Near East* (ed. G. J. Reinink and H. L. V. Vanstiphout; Orientalia Lovaniensia Analecta 42; Leuven: Department Oriëntalistiek, 1991) 23–46, and the brief discussion (with bibliography) in Clifford, *Creation Accounts*, 25–32. I should note that negative phraseology can be applied very strikingly in non-creation contexts, as when conjuring a pristine and "paradisiacal" Dilmun in the Sumerian "Enki and Ninhursanga" (Jean Bottéro and Samuel Noah Kramer, *Lorsque les dieux faisaient l'homme: Mythologie mésopotamienne* [Paris: Gallimard, 1989] 151–164). Piotr Michalowski treats a number of passages that play on what he calls "the semantic of negation," in "Negation as Description: The Metaphor of Everyday Life in Early Mesopotamian Literature," in *Velles Paraules: Ancient Near Eastern Studies in Honor of Miguel Civil* (ed. P. Michalowski; = Aula Orientalis

9/1–2 [1991]; Sabadell, Spain: Editorial AUSA, 1991) 131–136; reference courtesy G. Rubio.

Sequenced non-existence also occurs in proems for incantations on the (re)dedication of temples. A puzzling example was published by J. Van Dijk in "Existe-t-il un 'Poème de la Création' Sumérien," in *Kramer Anniversary Volume: Cuneiform Studies in Honor of Samuel Noah Kramer* (ed. B. Eichler et al.; AOAT 25; Neukirchen-Vluyn: Neukirchener, 1976) 125–133, with comments by Bendt Alster, "On the Earliest Sumerian Literary Tradition," *JCS* 28 (1976) 121–122. This brief Ur III text (NBC 11108 = 6N-T650) seems to be complete in one tablet (so not the first in a sequence of tablets) and describes what did not exist (for example, light) before earth and heaven were separated. Yet it also seems to end *in medias res*, making its goal difficult to pin down. But of most interest is the (unfortunately incomplete) bilingual that may well have served as proem to an incantation for the purification/reconstruction of a temple. (Translations in Alexander Heidel, *The Babylonian Genesis* [Chicago: Univ. of Chicago Press, 1951]) 62–3; and in Jean Bottéro and Samuel Noah Kramer, *Lorsque les dieux faisaient l'homme*, 497–502.) Often termed "Marduk, Creator" (or the like), this text opens abruptly on a series of statements about the non-existence of shrines and of materials for their construction: reed, timber, brick, brick-mold, homes, urban centers. Marduk, marshaling the gods into recognizing the pre-eminence of Babylon and its temple, creates humanity to do the heavy work. As elsewhere in Mesopotamian myths, the goddess Aruru is credited with making human fertility possible. We are then told of the creation of animals, of rivers, of reed (and the like), that is, of all heretofore non-existent material that humans will need for the building of temples. On this text, see further Van Seters, *Prologue*, 60, 122–125.

The phenomenon of negative creation phraseology is also known from Egyptian lore; see the excellent chapter, "The Challenge of the Nonexistent," in Erik Hornung's *Conceptions of God in Ancient Egypt: The One and the Many* (Ithaca: Cornell Univ. Press, 1971) 172–185 (citing previous literature, most notably Hermann Grapow's broad survey, "Die Welt vor der Schöpfung," *Zeitschrift für Ägyptische Sprache und altert(h)umskunde* 67 (1931) 34–38. For a contrary position, see Susanne Bickel, *La cosmogonie égyptienne avant le nouvel empire* (Fribourg: Editions Universitaires, 1994) 23–31 (reference courtesy J. Baines).

Chapter 16

W. F. Albright and His "Household": The Cases of C. H. Gordon, M. H. Pope, and F. M. Cross

Mark S. Smith
New York University

Among Burke Long's publications, one of the more recent has injected considerable insight and controversy into the field of biblical studies in the United States. Long's recent book, *Planting and Reaping Albright: Politics, Ideology, and Interpreting the Bible*,[1] places particular emphasis on ideological aspects of the Hopkins program and personnel of the "Albright school" in the United States. The work was perhaps something of a "bombshell" lobbed into the field, given how it had become accustomed to respectful treatments of Albright's thought and legacy,[2] not to mention the sometimes saccharine biography of Albright by L. G. Running and D. N. Freedman.[3] It is not merely the critical or neutral tone of the book that separates Long's work from other examinations of Albright's legacy. Instead, it is the interest taken in Albright's sociological impact on the biblical field in the United States that distinguishes Long's study. In Long's book the figure of Al-

---

[1] Burke O. Long, *Planting and Reaping Albright: Politics, Ideology, and Interpreting the Bible* (University Park, Pa.: Pennsylvania State Univ. Press, 1997).

[2] See *The Scholarship of William Foxwell Albright: An Appraisal* (ed. G. van Beek; HSS 33; Atlanta: Scholars Press, 1989); and the essays in *BA* 56/1 (1993). See also P. Machinist, "William Foxwell Albright: The Man and His Work," in *The Study of the Ancient Near East in the Twenty-First Century* (ed. J. S. Cooper and G. M. Schwartz; Winona Lake, Ind.: Eisenbrauns, 1996) 385–403 (with further bibliography).

[3] L. G. Running and D. N. Freedman, *William Foxwell Albright: A Twentieth-Century Genius* (New York: Morgan, 1975).

bright himself somewhat recedes,[4] as the story becomes dominated by his students' efforts to promote their teacher's comparative agenda in biblical and ancient Near Eastern studies.

Long's study may be located within a wider context of scholars attempting to come to grips with the history of these fields.[5] These works analyze the intellectual milieu of scholars of the ancient Near East (mostly working in the United States). One feature emerging from these studies is the influence of social context on scholarship. Long's book portrays a particularly energetic and learned, yet religiously motivated, "house" of scholars driven, further, by their sense of mission to replicate and advance Albright's agenda. Within this context Albright maintained a number of different relations with scholars his junior. Of course, many came to work directly with Albright and these were promoted by him. Others sojourned at Hopkins and received professional support from Albright. He was also on fine scholarly terms with many other scholars whose work was of interest to him. This piece addresses three paradigmatic figures in chronological order. The oldest is Cyrus Gordon, who sojourned at Hopkins in the mid-1930s following his feud with Ephraim Speiser of the University of Pennsylvania. The second, Marvin Pope, knew Albright, and his work directly benefited from Albright's advice, though he never studied formally with him. The third is Frank Cross, in many respects Albright's prize student at Hopkins in the post-war era. These three figures are paradigmatic not only because of their massive learning, but also because their relationships with Albright illustrate his influence in the field of biblical studies into the 1980s and beyond. By paying attention to their relationships with Albright, a deeper sense of the development of the field may emerge. Accordingly, this exercise follows the agenda in Long's book insofar as it touches on the sociology of knowledge in the biblical field.

Of course, writers treating such a subject are necessarily implicated in their work. I happily acknowledge my studies under Cross at Harvard in 1979–80 and with Pope at Yale in 1980–85. As for Gordon, I never studied with him. Apart from kibbitzing with him in the Knesset during lectures

---

[4] In this respect Long's article, "Mythic Trope in the Autobiography of William Foxwell Albright" (*BA* 56/1 [1993] 36–45), differs.

[5] See for example, the following very different studies: C. H. Gordon, *The Pennsylvania Tradition of Semitics* (SBL Centennial Publications; Atlanta: Scholars Press, 1986); B. Kuklick, *Puritans in Babylon: the Ancient Near East and American Intellectual Life, 1880–1930* (Princeton: Princeton Univ. Press, 1996); a history of American scholarship on the Near East for the period of 1650–1950, in preparation by B. R. Foster; and my forthcoming book, *Untold Stories: The Bible and Ugaritic Studies in the Twentieth Century* (Peabody, Mass.: Hendrickson, in press). Gordon has recently published his autobiography, entitled *A Scholar's Odyssey* (Biblical Scholarship in North America 20; Atlanta: Society of Biblical Literature, 2000).

delivered by the great Sumerologists T. Jacobsen and S. N. Kramer in April 1984,[6] I had no contact with him until I undertook this project. When I contacted him in the winter of 1998, he generously responded to my letters, and I have enjoyed our conversation by phone. As a result, I have been able to understand his story better. I have been greatly aided as well by correspondence with Frank Cross, who most generously answered my queries.[7] Sadly, Pope died before this research commenced. Indeed, this topic has perhaps been inspired by his death as well as by the death of his fellow student at Yale and friend, Jonas Greenfield, my teacher of Ugaritic and Israelite religion at the Hebrew University. Fortunately, it is possible to resurrect details of Pope's academic life thanks to the access to his correspondence granted by the Yale Divinity School Library; I am grateful as well for permission to cite this correspondence. I have been given permission also by Dropsie College (now the Center for Judaic Studies of the University of Pennsylvania) to cite the correspondence of Albright, Gordon, Speiser and others. Finally, the American Philosophical Society (henceforth APS) archives has provided access to Albright's correspondence (cited here within the restrictions of Fair Use laws). Thanks to all of these resources, what emerges is a picture of the development of these figures vis-à-vis Albright. Given our mutual interest in Albright and his household as well as our many years of friendship, I am very pleased to be invited to honor Burke Long.

1. Cyrus Herzl Gordon (1908–)

A native of Philadelphia, Gordon was born of immigrant parents. Following his arrival from Lithuania, his father became a doctor. Gordon first attended Gratz College, then pursued a B.A., M.A. and Ph.D. at the University of Pennsylvania (henceforth Penn), while he took courses under Max Leopold Margolis at the Dropsie College for Hebrew and Cognate Learning, also located in Philadelphia. After studying with Speiser at Penn, Gordon joined his teacher in the field in Iraq in the early 1930s. At Tell Billa in 1931, Speiser and Gordon read cuneiform copies of Nuzi texts

---

[6] See *Biblical Archaeology Today: Proceedings of the International Congress on Biblical Archaeology, Jerusalem, April 1984* (Jerusalem: Israel Exploration Society/The Israel Academy of Sciences and Humanities in cooperation with the American Schools of Oriental Research, 1985) 284–98.

[7] I received two letters from Cross, dated 7 December 1998 and 23 January 1999. For more information on Cross's background, see the preface to *Ancient Israelite Religion: Essays in Honor of Frank Moore Cross* (ed. P. D. Miller, Jr., P. D. Hanson and S. D. McBride; Philadelphia: Fortress, 1987) xi. See also *CBQ* 49, Supplement (1987) 52.

at night by the light of kerosene lamps.[8] In his 1986 book, *The Pennsylvania Tradition of Semitics,* Gordon recounts those days:

> Though I respected Speiser's gifts as a savant and teacher, he took a dislike to me and, while denying any prejudice or animosity, proved to be the most damaging professional enemy of my entire career. I left an instructorship at Penn to go into the field where I began to work with Speiser in 1931–32 at Billa and Gawra. In the evenings we read Chiera's published corpus of Nuzi tablets. Those sessions got me started in Nuzi studies. As far as I can tell, it was my following in his footsteps in Nuzi scholarship—including the biblical parallels—that kindled his ire against me. I always felt pleased when a student emulates me and walks in my footsteps, but Speiser was resentful and jealous. He wanted me to work on Aramaic incantations *instead.* I indeed kept working on those incantations, but not *instead* of Assyriology.
>
> I continued to look up to Speiser throughout most of 1931–32, until I made the mistake of asking his advice on a project that I wanted to undertake: a beginner's manual of Akkadian based exclusively on Hammurapi's laws. He forbade me to undertake it because "only a senior scholar should write an elementary textbook in any field." I still think his advice was wrong, but since I had sought his advice, I was loath to flout it. That was the last time I sought a superior's advice on any project I wished to undertake.[9]

Gordon proceeds to label Speiser "a bully," with "more than a touch of a Napoleonic complex." He adds: "He was skilled at kissing up and kicking down." Gordon balances his view, noting Speiser's capabilities as "a savant and teacher," "a remarkable linguist at all levels," "an accomplished scholar," and "an outstanding teacher."[10]

Unlike Gordon's assessment of Speiser, Speiser's view of Gordon was confined to personal communications. In a letter to Cyrus Adler dated 4 November 1931, Speiser wrote from Tell Billa:

> I am very fortunate to have this year a splendidly balanced and capable staff. Gordon is very willing and takes occasional rebuffs in a nice spirit. He is really growing up, though he will probably never lose the unfortunate knack of saying trite and commonplace things at the worst time imaginable.[11]

The season at Tell Billa clearly had a deleterious effect on their relationship. Gordon's account of Speiser's reaction reflects the norms of scholarly tradition that only a senior scholar should take on an elementary textbook. A

---

[8] "Interview with Cyrus H. Gordon, Center for Judaic Studies at the University of Pennsylvania, February 3, 1998" (a videotape taped and housed at Dropsie College, now the Center for Judaic Studies of the University of Pennsylvania).

[9] Gordon, *The Pennsylvania Tradition of Semitics,* 70–71. Gordon's italics. His sharper comments might be read against the background of his later efforts to secure a university post. See below.

[10] Ibid., 72.

[11] Dropsie College Adler files, Box 100, File Folder 16.

younger scholar was expected to begin with more focused specific studies and move progressively toward larger projects. Gordon would have nothing of this; he had his eye on bigger projects already at this early stage. After this dispute over his proposed grammar, Gordon published a catalogue of cylinder and stamp seals as well as studies of Nuzi texts and Aramaic incantations.

Speiser's criticism of Gordon did not end with the excavations, but dogged him through the 1930s. In a letter written to Albright in March of 1936, Speiser is critical of the "kind of rut in which Gordon seems to revel in wallowing." Here Speiser is refering to Gordon's series of studies on women in Nuzi texts, with its "meaningless transliterations . . . full of ridiculous errors." The norm for working on texts was a high level of careful and precise craftsmanship, a touch which Speiser felt was lacking in Gordon. Speiser continues with a general assessment:

> I feel that he is off on the wrong foot, following the line of least resistance instead of doing solid and honest work, modestly and with humility. He is much too young to attempt to cash in on a reputation that does not exist. I feel it is a pity, because he can do good work when not overimpressed wth himself.[12]

Clearly Speiser saw some good in Gordon's work, but here Speiser reiterates the old scholarly model of beginning with smaller and more careful projects that yield surer results. (At the same time we should bear in mind Speiser's critical cast; the same letter contains sharp criticism of Ginsberg's work as well.) Despite such criticism, it was clear that Gordon would not be controlled by the brilliant but difficult Speiser. Speiser's rejection of Gordon's plans for an Akkadian grammar led him to other projects. Indeed, had it not been for Speiser's early antipathy toward Gordon, he might have concentrated on Assyriology, Aramaic and biblical studies and as a result he might never have moved to Ugaritic.[13] The turn of the decade would find Speiser expressing a more sympathetic view of Gordon. In the summer of 1939 Speiser wrote to Albright: "I am sincerely happy that Gordon will be in Princeton next year and I hope from the bottom of my heart that this appointment will lead to something permanent."[14] Albright would report to Gordon in 1941 that "Speiser said that you gave a good

---

[12] Letter dated 15 March 1936, APS archives Albright Corresp. 1936–38.

[13] For Gordon's account of this story, see also his article, "Sixty Years in Ugaritology," in *Le Pays d'Ougarit autour de 1200 av. J. C.: Historie et archéologie: Actes du Colloque International, Paris, 28 juin–1er juillet 1993* (ed. M. Yon, M. Sznycer, P. Bordreuil; Ras Shamra-Ougarit 11; Paris: Éditions Recherche sur les Civilisations, 1995) 41–42. When I proposed this reading of his early history over the telephone in spring, 1999, Gordon found it plausible. On Gordon's move to Ugaritic, see below.

[14] Letter dated 7 June 1939 (APS archives Albright Corresp. 1938–40).

paper at Chicago."[15] However, such comments were too late to help Gordon; the damage was done. A decade of negative relations had hurt Gordon's efforts to find gainful employment.

In the wake of his teacher's rejection, Gordon found a supporter in Albright. Gordon's relationship with Albright developed over several years beginning in the early 1930s.[16] In 1931, while Gordon excavated with Albright at Beit Zur, Albright had pointed out to him the importance of Ugaritic for biblical studies. Gordon recalls that Albright told him: "Every student of the Old Testament would do well to work on Ugaritic."[17] Gordon would follow Albright's cue. According to Gordon, he began working on Ugaritic grammar in 1933 under the influence of H. L. Ginsberg's many fine translations and grammatical observations, well-known from his published work. According to his later recollection, Gordon first met Ginsberg in the early 1930s in Jerusalem at the American School of Oriental Research (later the Albright Institute).[19] In the foreword to his *Ugaritic Grammar,* Gordon recounts how he often consulted the best translations, in particular those of Ginsberg.[20] Gordon has long acknowledged his debt to Ginsberg's work. In a letter he acknowledged another influence on his work: "I formulated my *UG* [*Ugaritic Grammar*] on the principles of Semitic linguistics exclusively on what Max Margolis drummed into me."[20]

After his split with Speiser, Gordon moved to Hopkins as a post-doctoral fellow, thanks to Albright's support. There he sat in on Albright's Ugaritic course, and he also taught other students. Despite his knowledge of Speiser's feeling toward Gordon, Albright was clearly pleased with his learning and teaching. Asked by Theophile J. Meek in the summer of 1936 to recommend candidates for a post in Akkadian, Arabic and Hebrew at the University of Toronto, Albright first notes Gordon's bad blood with Speiser and some papers which were "a mistake." Then he comments:

> However, Gordon is a very competent Semitist, and knows all the important Semitic languages. His Hebrew is excellent, including the spoken language of the day . . . His Arabic is good, and he speaks both Syrian and Iraqi

---

[15] Letter dated 30 April 1941 (APS archives Albright Corresp. 1941).

[16] In "Interview with Cyrus H. Gordon," Gordon mentions that he first met Albright in Max Margolis's office at Dropsie.

[17] Quoted in Gordon, *The Pennsylvania Tradition of Semitics,* 54.

[18] So "Interview with Cyrus H. Gordon." So also Cyrus Gordon, personal communication via Constance Gordon by email to me, 18 October 1998.

[19] Gordon, *Ugaritic Grammar: The Present Status of the Linguistic Study of the Semitic Alphabetic Texts from Ras Shamra* (AnOr 20; Rome: Pontifical Biblical Institute, 1940).

[20] So Gordon's letter of 9 October 1998.

dialects very well, besides having a respectable knowledge of the classical tongue. He is entirely at home in Aramaic and Syriac, and is an excellent teacher.[21]

In a subsequent letter to Meek, Albright praised Gordon's research on the Nuzi material and the parallels it afforded with the patriarchal stories in Genesis.[22] Albright would be more direct in a letter written later that year to support Gordon's candidacy for a post at Cornell: "Speiser's opposition to him, which is quite without foundation, as I can assure you with absolute confidence, has done him a great deal of harm."[23]

This complex of relations set the stage for Gordon's work in Ugaritic. The year before the war broke out, Gordon proposed to Fr. Alfred Pohl that the Pontifical Biblical Institute Press publish a grammar of Ugaritic that he would undertake. When Albright learned of the project, he expressed his opposition; in Gordon's words:

> He was furious and informed me in no uncertain way that my plan was not only presumptuous but impossible: no one could do it in the foreseeable future. I realized then and there that Baltimore was no longer big enough for the two of us and I moved to Smith College in the fall of 1938.[24]

According to his account, Gordon wrote the grammar in the summer of 1939 in Uppsala and completed it during the 1939–40 academic year at Smith College.[25] Although the war started on September 3, 1939, this event did not prevent the completion of the project. Gordon used the Vatican's diplomatic pouch service, which Father Pohl placed at his disposal, and the book was published in 1940.

When *Ugaritic Grammar* appeared, it was generally well-received.[26] In his own review, Albright retracted his opposition, welcoming the publication of the work. Still, Albright's published remarks are qualified. In his review, Albright commented that such "a detailed grammatical treatment of the new Canaanite dialect seemed premature to many, including the reviewer. The author refused to be daunted by dissuasion." Albright further characterized the work as "collaborative" with Ginsberg, and ends a bit oddly: "we congratulate him [Gordon] and ourselves on the appearance of

---

[21] Letter dated 23 June 1936 (APS archives Albright Corresp. 1936–38).

[22] Letter written on 5 January 1937 (APS archives Albright Corresp. 1936–38).

[23] Letter written to Nathaniel Schmidt of Cornell University on 21 June 1937 (APS archives Albright Corresp. 1936–38).

[24] Gordon, *The Pennsylvania Tradition of Semitics,* 55. Gordon reiterated this story in a letter to me dated 9 October 1998.

[25] So Cyrus Gordon, personal communication via Constance Gordon by email to me, 18 October 1998. See also *Ugaritic Grammar,* vii.

[26] For example, see F. Rosenthal, review of *Ugaritic Grammar,* by Gordon, *Or* 11 (1942) 171–79.

the book!"[27] Later, in 1945, Albright referred to the work as "the excellent *Ugaritic Grammar* of a young scholar who began Ugaritic with me and continued working under Ginsberg's influence."[28] And in 1950 Albright would refer to the work as "invaluable."[29] Despite such public acclamation, privately Albright withheld his full approval, attributing the best of Gordon's grammar to Ginsberg's influence.[30] Despite Albright's misgivings, the appearance of this grammar marked a new level of synthesis in the area of Ugaritic studies.

Gordon's difficulties with both Speiser and Albright did not help his search for a university post. While Gordon is best known as a longtime professor first at Brandeis (1956–73) and then New York University (1973–89), it is not usually remembered that following his years at Hopkins and Smith College, he cast about for a position and struggled to make ends meet. In September of 1941 Gordon expressed his willingness to consider other means of support, including popular writing if necessary (though Gordon tells Albright that he had no intention of giving up ancient Near Eastern studies).[31] The war tided Gordon over during an academically fallow period thanks to his stint in the government. His first secure academic appointment came only after the war, a full decade after completing his doctorate. In 1946 Cyrus Gordon returned to his old academic home, Dropsie College, as Professor of Assyriology and Egyptology.[32]

---

[27] See Albright, review of *Ugaritic Grammar*, by Gordon, *JBL* 60 (1941) 434–48. This story is recounted also by M. Lubetski and C. Gottlieb, "'Forever Gordon': Portrait of a Master Scholar with a Global Perspective," *BA* 59 (1996) 7.

[28] Albright, "The Old Testament and Canaanite Language and Literature," *CBQ* 7 (1945) 13.

[29] Albright, review of *Ugaritic Handbook: Revised Grammar, Paradigms, Texts in Transliteration, Comprehensive Glossary,* by Gordon, *JBL* 69 (1950) 385.

[30] So Gordon's letter of 9 October 1998; and D. N. Freedman's letter to me of 24 October 1998. In Gordon's words, "Albright maliciously spread the rumor that I stole everything from Ginsberg." Cf. Gordon's wording in *Ugaritic Grammar,* 7. I have not come across such a sentiment in Albright's correspondence. Ginsberg and Gordon enjoyed friendly relations after the publication of *Ugaritic Grammar.* Several of Ginsberg's notes to Albright following this event speak well of Gordon (APS archives Albright Corresp. 1938–40), and at Gordon's request Ginsberg read his chapter on Ugaritic for his book *The Living Past* before publication (so Gordon's postcard to Albright postmarked 19 April 1941, in APS archives Albright Corresp. 1941). Ginsberg and Gordon worked together in the summer of 1946 in Martha's Vineyard (reported by Ginsberg to Albright in a letter dated 3 July 1946, APS archives Albright Corresp. July 1946). See also Ginsberg's praise of Gordon's work in "Interpreting Ugaritic Texts," *JAOS* 70 (1950) 156–60.

[31] So in a letter to Albright dated 22 September 1941 (APS archives Albright Corresp. 1941).

[32] So "Interview with Cyrus H. Gordon."

Gordon was an adventurer all his academic life, and it is no accident that *A Scholar's Odyssey* is the title for his autobiography. An Odysseus figure and a bit larger than life himself, Gordon traveled the Near East and Aegean not only by land and sea but also by new texts and scripts. Clearly, new texts, their scripts and their decipherment represented the arena for his ever-expanding horizons. (Accordingly, his book *Forgotten Scripts: Their Ongoing Discovery and Decipherment* reads in part like a record of Gordon's scholarly pursuits.[33]) New explorations following the trail of newly discovered texts would move him first from Akkadian and Aramaic to Ugaritic, later from Ugaritic to Linear A as well as the Phoenicians in South America, and still later to the texts from Ebla.[34] In the 1990s Gordon's new explorations would not cease as he entered yet a seventh decade of research. The final years of the millennium would witness his investigation into the possible relationship between the Ugaritic alphabet and twenty-two Chinese letters said to have phonetic readings.[35] In retrospect, Gordon's inauguration of a wider comparative agenda between the Aegean world and the Levant (an enterprise which his student M. Astour would dub "Hellenosemitica" in his own work) nowadays seems positively prophetic.[36] If in retrospect Gordon seemed to be pursuing specters with little methodological control, his work—whatever its flaws—was embraced by a number of scholars.[37] Since Gordon's initial work, the study of the eastern Mediterranean has emerged as a subject of special attention, thanks mostly

---

[33] Gordon, *Forgotten Scripts: Their Ongoing Discovery and Decipherment* (rev. and enlarged edition; New York: Basic Books, 1982).

[34] For Gordon's seminars on the Ebla texts, see *Newsletter for Ugaritic Studies* 31 (April, 1984) 13. He also published essays on Ebla, for example: "Echoes of Ebla," in *Essays on the Occasion of Seventieth Anniversary of the Dropsie University (1909–1979)* (ed. A. I. Katsh and L. Nemoy; Philadelphia: Dropsie University, 1979) 133–39; "West Semitic Factors in Eblaite," in *FUCUS: A Semitic/Afrasian Gathering in Remembrance of Albert Ehrman* (ed. Y. L. Arbeitman; Amsterdam Studies in the Theory and History of Linguistic Science, Series IV, Current Issues in Linguistic Theory 58; Amsterdam/Philadelphia: John Benjamins, 1988) 261–66. See also Gordon's description in *Forgotten Scripts*, 153–72.

[35] For example, Gordon, "Philology of the Ancient Near East: My Seventy Years in Semitic Linguistics," in *Built on Solid Rock: Studies in Honour of Ebbe Egede Knudsen on the Occasion of His 65th Birthday April 11th 1997* (ed. E. Wardini; Serie B: Skrifter 98; Oslo: Novus forlag: Instituttet for sammenlignende kulturforskning, 1997) 91–101.

[36] Gordon, "Homer and the Bible: The Origin and Character of East Mediterranean Literature," *HUCA* 26 (1955) 43–108. See also M. Astour, *Hellenosemitica: An Ethnic and Cultural Study in the West Semitic Impact on Mycenaean Greece* (Leiden: Brill, 1967).

[37] See E. Ullendorff, "Ugaritic Studies Within Their Semitic and Eastern Mediterranean Setting," *BJRL* 46 (1963) 242–44.

to the sophisticated combination of archaeological and textual evidence from both the classical world and the Levant.[38] Gordon did not have access to the important information produced by later archaeological discoveries, such as the Ulu Burun shipwreck;[39] nor did he have the benefit of doctoral-level training in classical literature. Gordon therefore deserves particular credit for investigating an area that enjoyed less credibility at the time. Given the agenda of "Hellenosemitica," it was perhaps only natural that in the late 1950s and early 1960s Gordon would use his knowledge of classical and Semitic languages to pursue the larger challenge involving the decipherment of Minoan Linear A.[40] Gordon extended his comparative agenda to include the arrival of Indo-Europeans into northern Mesopotamia as well as Europe, as a means to account for parallels between the West Se-

---

[38] On the Near Eastern side, see for example J. Muhly, "Homer and the Phoenicians: The Relations between Greece and the Near East in the Late Bronze and Early Iron Ages," *Berytus* 19 (1970) 19–64; O. Negbi, "Evidence for Early Phoenician Communities in the East Mediterranean Islands," *Levant* 14 (1982) 179–82; and E. Puech, "Présence phénicienne dans les îles à la fin du IIe. millénaire," *RB* 90 (1983) 365–95. On the classical side, see H. G. Niemeyer, "Die Phönizier im Mittelmeer im Zeitalter Homers," *Jahrbuch des Romisch-Germanischen Zentralmuseums Mainz* 31 (1984) 1–94; W. Burkert, *The Orientalizing Revolution: Near Eastern Influence on Greek Culture in the Early Archaic Age* (trans. W. Burkert and M. E. Pindar; Revealing Antiquity 5; Cambridge, Mass./London: Harvard Univ. Press, 1992); S. Morris, *Daidalos and the Origins of Greek Art* (Princeton: Princeton Univ. Press, 1992); and her article, "Greece and the Levant," *Journal of Mediterranean Archaeology* 3/1 (1990) 57–66. See also the wide-ranging studies by J. P. Brown: "Kothar, Kinyras, and Kytherea," *JSS* 10 (1965) 197–219; "The Mediterranean Vocabulary of the Vine," *VT* 19 (1969) 146–70; "The Sacrificial Critique in Greek and Hebrew (I)," *JSS* 24 (1979) 159–75; and *Israel and Hellas* (BZAW 231; Berlin/New York: de Gruyter, 1995). The relative rarity of second millennium West Semitic sources in Brown's studies perhaps points to a methodological difficulty.

[39] G. Bass, "A Bronze Age Shipwreck at Ulu Burun (Kas): 1984 Campaign," *AJA* 90 (1986) 269–96; idem, "Oldest Known Shipwreck Reveals Splendors of the Bronze Age," *National Geographic* 172/6 (1987) 693–733; G. Bass, C. Pulak, D. Collon, and J. Weinstein, "The Bronze Age Shipwreck at Ulu Burun: 1986 Campaign," *AJA* 93 (1989) 1–29.

[40] Gordon, "Notes on Linear A," *Antiquity* 31 (1957) 124–30; "Minoica," *JNES* 21 (1962) 207–10; "Eteocretan," *JNES* 21 (1962) 211–14; "The Dreros Bilingual," *JNES* 22 (1963) 76–79; and *Forgotten Scripts*, 131–44. Credit given to Gordon in this area varies. See G. A. Rendsburg, "Jan Best and Minoan Linear A," *Newsletter for Ugaritic Studies* 30 (October, 1983) 120; "'Someone Will Succeed in Deciphering Minoan': Cyrus Gordon and Minoan Linear A," *BA* 59/1 (1996) 36–43, esp. 42. In contrast, J. Chadwick's discussion of Linear A and other Mediterranean scripts does not mention Gordon's work; Chadwick, *Reading the Past: Linear B and Related Scripts* (Berkeley/Los Angeles: Univ. of California Press/British Museum, 1987).

mitic and Aegean worlds and beyond.[41] The jury remains out on the gains achieved by Gordon's investigations of Linear A, texts from Ebla or points beyond the Near Eastern and Aegean worlds.

Despite the long-term successes of "Hellenosemitica," Gordon's spirit of adventure, or at least the sorts of projects that it engendered early on, ran counter to the expectations of established scholarship. Gordon's early rejections first by Speiser and then later by Albright were predicated on a number of factors. Clearly, grand projects executed quickly by someone perceived as a relative neophyte in the fields in question sullied Gordon's work in the eyes of his mentors. Where most scholars might spend a decade or longer on a single subject or even project, Gordon moved by comparison with great dispatch, sometimes with results that clearly dismayed his teachers, but at other times with results that pleased them for their learning. The standard hierarchical model of mentor-student relations clearly suited Gordon only up to a certain point. As a result, Speiser did not aid Gordon in his academic advancement, and even Albright's letters cited above constitute a series of mixed signals. In a conversation with me, Gordon observed that a letter of recommendation hardly needs to recount the past troubles of a student, yet Albright regularly did just that. Perhaps Albright's letters of recommendation manifested his own mixed sense of Gordon by mentioning his troubles with Speiser. Finally, Gordon's background as a non-observant Jew made him non-kosher in Jewish circles but too Jewish in non-Jewish circles. Gordon thought that as a result Albright would not push very hard for his candidacy in most universities. And it is true that Gordon's appointments came from either Jewish institutions (Dropsie) or institutions with a significant Jewish presence (Brandeis and New York University), while non-Jewish scholars such as Pope and Cross would find their way into the halls of the Ivy League.

2. Marvin Hoyle Pope (1916–1997)

Born in Durham, North Carolina, a Methodist by upbringing, Pope began his academic life at Duke University (1934–39). Duke had long been part of his life. In 1955 Pope would recall: "As a lad I roamed what was to become

---

[41] Gordon, "Indo-European and Hebrew Epic," *Eretz-Israel* 5 (1958 = B. Mazar volume) *10–*15. For more recent work in a similar vein, see Gordon, "The Near Eastern Background of the Rigveda," in *Ancient Egyptian and Mediterranean Studies: In Memory of William A. Ward* (ed. L. H. Lesko; Providence, R.I.: Department of Egyptology, Brown University, 1998) 117–20. I wish to thank Gary Rendsburg for bringing the former reference to my attention. For Gordon's views on Phoenicians in South America, see below, in the final section of this essay.

Duke Forest and watched the University being built."[42] Pope's first university experience provided him with intimate links to W. F. Albright. Pope first studied Hebrew with William Stinespring in his first year on the Duke faculty in 1936–37, and Stinespring was none other than Albright's brother-in-law. Stinespring was also a friend of Albright's student, John Bright. Given that Stinespring had been a student of C. C. Torrey at Yale, it was perhaps quite natural for Pope to attend graduate school at Yale, but it was also quite natural that Pope would come to Albright's attention, given their academic interconnections as well as Pope's own later achievements.

When Pope arrived at Yale, his two main teachers were Albrecht Goetze and Julius Obermann. Like many other German scholars in the late 1930s, Goetze had departed for the United States, taking up the Laffan Chair of Assyriology and Babylonian literature at Yale University. In the war era Goetze was one of the major figures in the ancient Near Eastern field. A giant in Assyriology and Hittitology, Goetze attracted students both in America and from abroad. Besides teaching Ugaritic, he is perhaps best known in Ugaritic studies for his article on Ugaritic and Canaanite.[43] He also offered studies on Nikkal wa-Ib (KTU 1.24) and on a passage in the Baal Cycle.[44] Clearly Goetze's great strengths lay in Akkadian and Hittite, as Albright, Speiser and others readily acknowledged, but it was apparent that his knowledge of Akkadian overly influenced his analysis of Ugaritic grammar. Indeed, his 1938 debut at the American Oriental Society meeting, which treated the Ugaritic tenses somewhat along the lines of Akkadian, sullied his reputation in the area of West Semitics.[45]

Compared to Goetze, the Arabist Julian Obermann devoted more of his

---

[42] Pope's letter to Professor Russell Richey on 10 February 1955 (Yale Divinity School archive).

[43] Goetze, "Is Ugaritic a Canaanite Dialect?" *Language* 17 (1941) 127–38.

[44] For a listing of Goetze's contributions to Ugaritic studies, see A. Herdner, *Corpus des tablettes en cunéiformes alphabétiques découvertes à Ras Shamra-Ugarit de 1929 à 1939* (Mission de Ras Shamra 10; Paris: Imprimerie Nationale/Librairie Orientaliste Paul Geuthner, 1963) 309.

[45] This presentation was published as "The Tenses of Ugaritic," *JAOS* 58 (1938) 266–309. Z. Harris also criticized the piece in a letter to Albright dated 11 June 1937 after Goetze presented this paper to the American Oriental Society in Cleveland that year (APS archives Albright Corresp. 1936–38). Albright also voiced concerns to Goetze in a letter dated 7 July 1937 (APS archives Albright Corresp. 1936–38); he did accept Goetze's present *yaqattal for Ugaritic (so in a letter to Goetze dated 4 October 1940, APS archives Albright Corresp. 1938–40), but he was a bit put out that Goetze had not read up on all that he and others had written on the subject. In a letter to Albright dated 26 July 1938, Ginsberg entirely rejected Goetze's presentation (APS archives Albright Corresp. 1938–40).

energies to Ugaritic.[46] He authored many works on the subject, ranging from grammar to mythology. In the late 1930s, Obermann's initial forays into Ugaritic were privately not well received. In January of 1937 Albright described his and Ginsberg's reactions to a paper given by Obermann, probably the one given at the meeting of the Society of Biblical Literature held in the fall of 1936:

> It will take me a long time to get over the superlatively dreadful paper by Obermann. While my opinion of his work in his pre-Arabic field was previously very low, it has descended into the depths of Arallu. When he finished both Ginsberg and I were completely paralyzed; we had not dreamed that such a paper was possible.[47]

However, Obermann's work on Ugaritic steadily improved over the next decade. His 1946 piece on sentence negations in Ugaritic and his piece on Baal's conflict with Yamm in KTU 1.2 IV in the following year won some respect from the field.[48] His 1948 monograph, *Ugaritic Mythology,* reflected an early effort to provide a literary study of motifs in the texts.[49] This publication was met with a polite review by H. L. Ginsberg.[50] Obermann's larger contribution, as recognized by Ginsberg, involved his effort to study the larger motifs and type-scenes in the texts. Indeed, Obermann was clearly ahead of Albright and Ginsberg in addressing literary aspects of the Ugaritic mythological texts.

Goetze and Obermann together offered the first instruction in Ugaritic at Yale in 1939 to a single student, Marvin Pope. Each claiming Ugaritic as his own domain, the two Yale professors disagreed greatly over Ugaritic grammar, Goetze being influenced by Akkadian and Obermann by Arabic. Pope recalled that after initial class meetings with the two of them, Goetze and Obermann so vehemently disagreed that he later met with each of them separately.[51] As a result, Pope's way through Yale was not without its adventures, and Albright later congratulated Pope on receiving his doctorate, largely for having survived the conflicts between Goetze and

---

[46] For examples of Obermann's work, see the listing in Herdner, *Corpus des tablettes,* 321.

[47] Letter written to Theophile Meek on 5 January 1937 (APS archives Albright Corresp. 1936–38). Given the timing of this letter, I believe that the paper in question would have been Obermann's "The Historic Significance of Ugaritic Script," mentioned in *JBL* 56 (1937) iv.

[48] Obermann, "Sentence Negations in Ugaritic," *JBL* 65 (1946) 233–48; "How Baal Destroyed a Rival," *JAOS* 67 (1947) 195–208.

[49] Obermann, *Ugaritic Mythology: A Study of Its Leading Motifs* (New Haven: Yale Univ. Press, 1948).

[50] Ginsberg, review of *Ugaritic Mythology,* by Obermann, *JCS* 2 (1948) 141.

[51] Pope, personal communication.

Obermann.[52] Pope's doctoral studies were interrupted by his military service at a weather station in northern Australia, but in 1949 he completed his dissertation entitled "A Study of the Ugaritic Particles W, P and M, with an Excursus on B, L, and K." This thesis investigated a number of particles and their functions in both Ugaritic and Biblical Hebrew. Many of these particles' uses in biblical texts could be illuminated partially by comparing their usage in the Ugaritic texts. This dissertation exemplified the traditional model of research: a project of limited scope with solvable difficulties suited to the research of a gifted doctoral candidate. Furthermore, Pope would present his research in measured, indeed brief, articles that showed careful knowledge of the original texts and a penchant for solving grammatical problems. It was a fine start for a young, promising scholar trained in the comparative paradigm of biblical and Near Eastern studies, at this point the dominant model in the United States thanks to the leading programs, in particular those at Hopkins, Penn, Dropsie and Yale.

After teaching at Duke from 1947–49 while he finished his dissertation, Pope returned to Yale as Assistant Professor in 1949. Later he would be named Louis J. Rabinowitz Professor of Semitic Languages.[53] From Goetze he learned a masterful control of the linguistic details, and from Obermann he developed his interest in mythology. Pope went beyond what his professors taught him, breaking new ground on a number of topics, including deities and later devotion to the dead. In his 1955 book, *El in the Ugaritic Texts*, Pope combined a high level of philological work with great depth of religious knowledge in studying the traditions about El.[54] Moreover, he initiated a research program to devote a major study to each deity.[55] In his contribution to the 1965 *Wörterbuch der Mythologie*, he undertook just this task.[56] Thanks to their ongoing contacts, Albright watched Pope's progress. Pope's articles were read with great interest by Albright, as Pope's work fit very well the paradigm of scholarly advancement in this field. With short but sure first steps in philology and comparative research, Pope blossomed into a new and insightful commentator on Ugaritic myth and

---

[52] So Pope to me in conversation during the preparation of his collected essays; see *Probative Pontificating in Ugaritic and Biblical Literature: Collected Essays* (ed. M. S. Smith; UBL 10; Münster: Ugarit-Verlag, 1994) 1.

[53] Rabinowitz also supported the important Yale Judaica Series. On Rabinowitz, see W. F. Albright, "Louis Rabinowitz in Memoriam," *BASOR* 146 (1957) 2–3.

[54] Pope, *El in the Ugaritic Texts* (VTSup 2; Leiden: Brill, 1955).

[55] Ibid., vii.

[56] M. H. Pope and W. Röllig, "Syrien: Die Mythologie der Ugariter und Phönizier," in *Wörterbuch der Mythologie* (ed. H. W. Haussig; Stuttgart: Ernst Klett, 1965) 1.1.235–312. The two authors mostly split the articles and co-authored some. For a full listing of Pope's contributions, see Pope, *Probative Pontificating*, 380.

its relations to the Bible. While he was not entirely averse to the work of the "myth and ritual" school, Pope's work showed little of its influence, a good thing from Albright's perspective (as he privately complained of this line of research manifest in the work of T. H. Gaster and others). In Albright's eyes, Pope's careful philology did not suffer from the wild speculations of such an approach. Indeed, Albright was a fan of Pope's work on mythology. In a letter to Pope, Albright called *El in the Ugaritic Texts* "very well done,"[57] and later he approvingly cited Pope's comparison of the goddesses Anat and Kali.[58] Albright also took a great personal interest in Pope's Anchor Bible series commentary on the Book of Job.[59] Reading the manuscript of the commentary before publication, Albright called it in 1962 "certainly one of the best of the Anchor series."[60] Albright's respect for Pope is shown further by signing off his letters at this time with "William," an advance over "W. F. Albright" that shows up in their correspondence in the 1950s. By the time of the Job commentary, Pope's reputation in Albright's eyes was clearly sealed. Finally, it is perhaps not beyond the larger landscape of this discussion to note that Albright and Pope were both Methodists, which would only add to the comfort level in their relations.

In the 1970s Pope's work took a new turn, reflected in his learned commentary on the Song of Songs.[61] This commentary was especially celebrated for its imaginative and tireless pursuit of the divine background to the book's descriptions of the lovers and for the encyclopedic range of sources cited. In these and other works, Pope explored areas of research that most scholars overlooked or avoided. Without any hesitation, he addressed Ugaritic texts describing sex and death (whether in the human or divine realm), divine cannibalism and drunkenness. (The index of topics to the Song of Songs commentary reads in part like the table of contents to a sex manual.) At times Pope's imagination ran ahead of the available data, yet the field was enriched by his fertile mind. A few years before his death, Pope would see his collected essays appear under the papal title *Probative Pontificating in Ugaritic and Biblical Literature.*[62]

---

[57] Albright to Pope on 24 September 1955, letter in Yale Divinity School collection.

[58] Albright, *Yahweh and the Gods of Canaan: A Historical Analysis of Two Contrasting Faiths* (New York: Doubleday, 1968; repr., Winona Lake, Ind.: Eisenbrauns, 1994) 131. Note also D. Pardee, "The New Canaanite Myths and Legends," *BO* 37 (1980) 275. For the origins of this research in the 1950s, see Pope, *Probative Pontificating,* 2 n. 4.

[59] Pope, *Job* (AB 15; New York: Doubleday, 1965; rev. ed., 1973).

[60] Albright to Pope on 4 June 1962 and 23 March 1965, letters in Yale Divinity School collection.

[61] Pope, *Song of Songs* (AB 7C; New York: Doubleday, 1977).

[62] The introduction to this volume presents a retrospective look on my part at

Pope's career at Yale was enhanced by the company of major scholars of varied backgrounds, in particular F. Rosenthal, J. Goldin, W. W. Hallo, B. S. Childs and R. R. Wilson. Rosenthal, a vastly learned Old World scholar, managed by his massive knowledge and understated manner to over-whelm many of his students. First appointed at Yale to the Rabinowitz chair in Semitic Languages and later as Sterling Professor, Rosenthal pro-vided instruction in the entire range of Aramaic dialects, the field of Arabic, and Comparative Semitics.[63] Even the other faculty deferred to Rosenthal's great learning. On one occasion Rosenthal meant to ask us students if there was any question that he could answer for us, but the question came out as "Is there any question that I cannot answer?" One in-timidated student lunged forward and offered a hearty "no." Momentarily delayed by the students' laughter, Rosenthal smiled and moved on to the next point of grammar.

At Yale until his retirement in 1986, Pope showed students how to be-come scholars by his own example in class. He would pursue etymologies and information in the books and articles in the office, and his North Carolina wit and kindliness kept students at ease. The dissertations di-rected by Pope and read by Rosenthal tended to focus on topics involving Ugaritic with some Bible, mostly in the areas of religion and myth. In this period, Pope recognized the great amount of material available on deities, especially with the publication of *Ugaritica V,* and it was his plan to have some dissertations include the new *Ugaritica V* texts in the discussion of deities. From the 1960s through the mid-1980s numerous Yale dissertations were produced on deities. The late 1960s and onwards also witnessed many theses on grammatical topics.[64] With only a handful of students in most classes, Yale's program produced an ideal mentoring situation. Most of the classes with Pope and Rosenthal took place in their dusty offices in the Hall of Graduate Studies. In this phase these two greats were aided by the biblicists Brevard S. Childs and Robert R. Wilson, himself the student of all three in the early 1970s. Childs used to advise his students that they take Ugaritic. Indeed, contrary to a perception in the biblical field in the United States that Childs in his so-called "canonical approach" diminished the im-portance of extra-biblical languages,[65] Childs himself took Ugaritic and

---

Pope's work, with some recollections of Pope as a person (see esp. pp. 3–4, 12–14).

[63] On Rosenthal and the Rabinowitz chair, see W. F. Albright, "Louis Rabino-witz in Memoriam," *BASOR* 146 (1957) 2.

[64] See the list in Pope, *Probative Pontificating,* 385–86.

[65] So J. J. M. Roberts, "The Ancient Near Eastern Environment," in *The Hebrew Bible and Its Modern Interpreters* (ed. D. A. Knight and G. M. Tucker; Philadelphia: Fortress; Chico, Calif.: Scholars Press, 1985) 80.

Syriac with W. Baumgartner in Basel[66] and Akkadian with Goetze after he came to Yale, and throughout his career at Yale Childs insisted on having doctoral students take Ugaritic, Akkadian and other extra-biblical languages. Pope was only happy to accommodate the steady stream of students in the biblical field as well as his own doctoral candidates.

3. Frank Moore Cross, Jr. (1921–)

Cross was born in Marin County, California, where his father attended San Francisco Theological Seminary.[67] (Cross's first memory was getting caught stealing raisins from the seminary commissary; as he comments, "An appropriate memory for a Calvinist.") At the age of eight, Cross's family moved to Birmingham, Alabama. Three generations of the family were from southern Alabama, and following family tradition, Cross attended Maryville College (A.B., 1942), where his father was a trustee. Afterwards Cross went to McCormick Theological Seminary in Chicago (B.D., 1946). There he studied with G. Ernest Wright, a student of Albright prior to the war. Cross's distinguished career was heralded already prior to his doctoral studies when McCormick awarded him the Nettie F. McCormick Fellowship for an essay that he later published under the title, "The Tabernacle: A Study from an Archaeological and Historical Approach."[68] The judge for the contest was none other than Albright, who judged Cross's piece (submitted under the pseudonym, "Uncle Remus") superior to the two other entries ("John Doe" and "Conrado Carducci," themselves judged quite highly by Albright). Cross then attended Johns Hopkins, working with D. N. Freedman on two joint dissertations directed by Albright.[69] Following his doctoral training, Cross returned to McCormick, joining Wright on the faculty before leaving for Harvard to serve in the Divinity School Old Testament Chair in 1956. In 1958 Wright too left

---

[66] This information comes courtesy of B. S. Childs, letter to me dated 22 January 1999.

[67] The biographical material in this section derives from three letters from Cross to me, dated 27 November 1998, 7 December 1998 and 23 January 1999, in addition to sources cited below. I am very grateful to Professor Cross for providing this information.

[68] Cross, "The Tabernacle: A Study from an Archaeological and Historical Approach," *BA* 10 (1947) 45–68. So letters of Albright to Wright dated 21 and 28 January 1946 and Wright's response dated 15 February 1946 and Albright's official report dated 9 February 1946 (APS archives Albright Corresp. 1946).

[69] Cross and Freedman, *Early Hebrew Orthography: A Study of the Epigraphic Evidence* (AOS 36; New Haven: American Oriental Society, 1952); and *Studies in Ancient Yahwistic Poetry* (SBLDS 21; Missoula, Mont.: Scholars Press, 1975; sec. ed., The Biblical Resource series; Grand Rapids, Mich.: Eerdmans, 1997). For further bibliography of Cross and Freedman, see p. vii of the second edition of the latter

McCormick for Harvard, and replaced Cross in the Divinity School Old Testament Chair (Wright would later be named the Parkman Professor of Divinity). At that point Cross assumed the oldest chair in the biblical field in the United States, the Hancock Professorship of Hebrew and Other Oriental Languages, and chairmanship of the Department of Semitic Languages and History (later renamed Near Eastern Languages and Civilizations).[70] Wright served at Harvard until he died of a heart attack on August 29, 1974, at the age of sixty-four. Including their years as co-faculty at McCormick Theological Seminary, Cross and Wright were colleagues for over two decades.[71]

In 1960 Cross and Wright were joined at Harvard by two other students of Albright, the learned Semitist Thomas O. Lambdin and the expert in western peripheral Akkadian and West Semitics, W. L. Moran.[72] After his studies with W. F. Albright and Frank Blake at Hopkins, Lambdin joined the Hopkins faculty and later departed for Harvard. In 1966 Moran joined Cross and Lambdin at Harvard after a stint on the faculty of the Pontifical Biblical Institute in Rome.[73] An expert in the El-Amarna letters (in particular the correspondence from Byblos), Moran provided over two decades of training in Assyriology at Harvard and many publications showing, as nicely put by the editors of his festschrift, "a humane quality, a concern for

work. See their quoted remarks together on their early experience with Albright in Running and Freedman, *William Foxwell Albright: A Twentieth-Century Genius*, 209–11. Freedman started at Hopkins in 1945, following a stint in the church in Washington State; he was an undergraduate at Princeton.

[70] For a nice appreciation of Cross, see the preface to *Ancient Israelite Religion*, xi–xiii. The same volume contains a bibliography of Cross's publications on pp. 645–56.

[71] See F. M. Cross and G. E. Wright, "The Study of the Old Testament at Harvard," *Harvard Divinity Bulletin* 25 (1961) 14–19. On the doctoral program specifically, see pp. 17–20. For Cross on Wright, see the preface to *Magnalia Dei, the Mighty Acts of God: Essays on the Bible and Archaeology in Memory of G. Ernest Wright* (ed. F. M. Cross, W. E. Lemke and P. D. Miller, Jr.; Garden City, N.Y.: Doubleday, 1976). The information about Wright's death derives from the first (unpaginated) page of this volume.

[72] For nice appreciations of Lambdin, see J. Huehnergard, "Lambdin: Probably from the Root *lmd*, 'To Learn', D 'To Teach'," pp. ix–xii, and R. J. Clifford, "Thomas O. Lambdin," pp. xiii–xiv in *"Working with No Data": Semitic and Egyptian Studies Presented to Thomas O. Lambdin* (ed. D. M. Golomb; Winona Lake, Ind.: Eisenbrauns, 1987). The same volume contains a bibliography of Lambdin's publications on pp. 263–64.

[73] See "William L. Moran: An Appreciation," in *Lingering Over Words: Studies in Ancient Near Eastern Literature in Honor of William L. Moran* (ed. T. Abusch, J. Huehnergard and P. Steinkeller; HSS 37; Atlanta: Scholars Press, 1990) ix–x. The same volume contains a bibliography of Moran's publications on pp. xi–xviii.

broader issues that expresses the intellectual and vital excitement that he brings to a text."[74] Moran's training in Akkadian was rigorous, demanding, at some times hilarious and at other moments terrifying, as he asked his students to translate English sentences into Akkadian and to reproduce paradigms for weak verbs not yet studied in class. Lambdin's courses on Historical Grammar and Comparative Semitics were the linguistic hub of the Harvard doctoral program. In these courses the great structures shared by the Semitic languages came to life. (So did Lambdin's wonderfully droll sense of humor. He used to tell students that "Ugaritic is an undeciphered language."[75]) Together, Cross, Wright, Lambdin and Moran, all four gifted students of Albright and all professors at Harvard, would cover the range of biblical texts, related extra-biblical West Semitic texts and the archaeology of Syria-Palestine. And they would be aided by the luminary T. Jacobsen as well as others in the field. As a result, Albright's legacy was preserved and expanded at Harvard.

With the aid of his colleagues, Cross directed one hundred and six doctoral dissertations.[76] Whether in the basement of the Harvard Semitic Museum or in its newly renovated second-floor seminar room, Cross conveyed a dignified, deeply learned presence in his graduate seminars. Indeed, Cross was the epitome of the eminent, beloved, respected patriarch, a whole sensibility which Albright had earlier inspired in his own students.[77] Cross's own work, accomplished in so many areas ranging from Ugaritic and biblical studies to epigraphy and Dead Sea Scrolls, has held up as a model of scholarship for decades. Of all the fields, his greatest love has been epigraphy,[78] but it is perhaps his penetrating analysis in the area of Israelite religion that has brought him the greatest recognition. Cross continued and extended in new and powerful ways the old comparative agenda fostered by Albright, first in his 1973 book of essays, *Canaanite Myth and Hebrew Epic,* and later in the 1998 sequel, *From Epic to Canon.*[79] *Canaanite Myth and Hebrew Epic* massively extended the discussion of Israel's religion on a number of fronts. One major contribution was to illustrate the close relations of Ugaritic and Israelite conceptions of divinity.

---

[74] Ibid., x.

[75] I was reminded of this well-known quip of Lambdin by P. K. McCarter in a conversation on 22 November 1998.

[76] By Cross's count, in a letter to me dated 27 November 1998.

[77] So Long, *Planting and Reaping Albright,* 17–19.

[78] See an interview with Cross published in *Bible Review* 8/6 (December 1992) 52. A volume on epigraphy is in the works.

[79] The full references are: Cross, *Canaanite Myth and Hebrew Epic: Essays in the History of the Religion of Israel* (Cambridge, Mass./London: Harvard Univ. Press, 1973); *From Epic to Canon: History and Literature in Ancient Israel* (Baltimore/London: The Johns Hopkins Univ. Press, 1998).

These conceptions were shown to be more than a series of parallels. In addition, Cross's analysis represented the culmination of the field's research, indicating that Israelite religion belonged to the same larger West Semitic culture as the Ugaritic texts. Cross's work held wide respect and readership because of its detailed documentation and depth of synthesis, which drew not only on approaches deriving from his teachers, but also on the research of the best German and Scandinavian scholars.[80] Cross's synthesis ventured to mediate between the history-of-redemption and mythic frameworks by proposing a tension between the two in biblical literature while seeing the dominance of myth in Canaanite literature. Although others had raised the religious and cultural issues in a new way, it was both the depth of Cross's synthesis and analysis and his esteemed place in the Albrightian household—so dominant in the United States in the early 1970s—that moved this discussion into the mainstream of American biblical scholarship. As a result, the relationship of Israelite and Canaanite religion could no longer be posed in primarily oppositional terms.

Sometimes in scholarship, massive and deep syntheses by master figures build successfully on earlier work and thereby become the hallmark of a certain approach or the best-known treatment of a particular set of problems. In the wake of such figures, their lesser predecessors sometimes are forgotten. Among such scholars in biblical studies are Robertson Smith, Wellhausen and Cross. Their works continue to resonate not only because of their real intellectual achievements, but also because their like-minded colleagues and disciples disseminate the importance of their works. To illustrate, it is unlikely that Cross's 1998 volume, *From Epic to Canon,* will have the same impact as his 1973 book, *Canaanite Myth and Hebrew Epic,* not simply because the latter seemed so new and fresh at the time while the former follows in a similar vein, although Cross has augmented his studies by extending their intellectual horizons in comparative literature and sociology. It is also because the Albright household is hardly as dominant in American biblical studies in the 1990s, a shift reflected today in the Harvard program itself.

Cross, perhaps more than any other figure of the Albright household, advanced his mentor's academic vision. Cross was the ultimate product of the Hopkins academic system. Brought to Albright's attention by one of his leading pre-war students, Cross came to Hopkins already marked by achievement. The Hopkins "farm-system" later served Cross by providing him with his first academic post at McCormick and then by supporting him further by promoting his appointment at Harvard. In turn, Cross would recreate the Hopkins program at Harvard by aiding several other talented Hopkins students to join its professorial ranks. None of these de-

---

[80] For example, Cross, *Canaanite Myth and Hebrew Epic,* 79–90.

velopments diminishes Cross's inherent talent or achievements. On the contrary, his life at Hopkins and later at McCormick and Harvard helped Cross to develop, but these institutions also benefited greatly in turn. The "farm-system" produced by Cross and his colleagues at Harvard in the 1960s through the 1980s far outstripped—at least by numbers—the academic placements by Hopkins graduates from the 1930s through the 1950s. Finally, it might be argued that Cross's religious sensibilities conformed to the dominant religious sensibility of the Albright household, another aspect contributing to his advancement therein. For example, the arguments made for the high antiquity of covenant and law in earliest Israel by G. E. Mendenhall, J. Bright and Cross himself perhaps reflect a larger mainstream Protestant religious worldview that Albright himself participated in, and it is this religious paradigm that is brought out by Burke Long's research.[81] As this religious sensibility in American biblical scholarship has receded before the contributions made by professors of Bible deriving from other religious and non-religious backgrounds, this feature of the Albright household now seems more pronounced in retrospect.

IV. Crossing Paths

Given their many overlapping interests, it was perhaps inevitable that Gordon, Pope and Cross would engage in scholarly dialogue. The exchanges between Cross and Pope illustrate the discourse of two scholars working, at least on the philological and historical levels, within the same general agenda. Two examples will suffice to illustrate. In the 1970s Cross and Pope enjoyed friendly exchanges over Ugaritic, in particular over vocalizing Ugaritic words and over the interpretation of one text sometimes called "The Birth of the Beautiful Gods" (KTU 1.23). Cross had been trained by Albright to vocalize Ugaritic.[82] (Cross writes that "we struggled to vocalize, usually deeply wounding Albright's Semitic sensibilities."[83]) When Cross defended and practiced vocalization in *Canaanite Myth and Hebrew Epic* in 1973,[84] Pope took exception to the book's vocalizations of some Ugaritic words and stated his preference to avoid the potential "fudge factor," to cite Pope's expression.[85] Yet Pope conceded the value of

---

[81] See Long, "Mythic Trope in the Autobiography of William Foxwell Albright," 36–45. This is not to deny the importance of Albright's relations with Catholics and Jews, a point documented in some detail in M. S. Smith, *Untold Stories* (see n. 5), chapter two.

[82] See Running and Freedman, *William Foxwell Albright*, 209–11.

[83] Cross, letter to me dated 27 November 1998.

[84] See especially *Cross, Canaanite Myth and Hebrew Epic*, 21 n. 50.

[85] So Pope, "Notes on the Rephaim Texts," in *Essays on the Ancient Near East in Memory of Jacob Joel Finkelstein* (ed. M. de Jong Ellis; Memoirs of the Connecticut

vocalization, for it serves both a heuristic and a pedagogical purpose. More recently, Cross has offered a vocalized Ugaritic text with accent marks on words.[86]

Cross and Pope also sparred over the depiction of the god El.[87] Pope studied El in some detail in his 1955 monograph, *El in the Ugaritic Texts.* Pope covered the topics of El's many qualities, his abode, his marital situation and his diminished status in the pantheon. Pope also recognized El's patriarchal profile in the Ugaritic pantheon, as well as many first millennium reflexes of El in West Semitic religion, including in ancient Israel. In his 1973 *Canaanite Myth and Hebrew Epic,* Cross extended this basic point in studying the massive influence of El on the descriptions of Yahweh in the Bible (especially with regard to the descriptions of Yahweh in the heavenly council, the divine appearances in dreams to humans and the identification of Yahweh with El Shadday in Exodus 6:2–3). Indeed, these similarities led to Cross's conclusion that Yahweh was originally a title of El, a position that would elicit its own share of supporters and critics. Cross also questioned Pope's view of El as an ineffectual figure fallen from power (*deus otiosus*) and doubted Pope's portrait of El in KTU 1.23 as temporarily impotent. Instead, Cross saw El in this text as a virile patriarch, more than able in sexual matters.[88] In a 1979 *Ugarit-Forschungen* article punningly entitled "The Ups and Downs in El's Amours," Pope responded in greater

---

Academy of Arts & Sciences 19; Hamden, Conn.: Archon Books, 1997) 181–82 n. 90, republished in Pope, *Probative Pontificating,* 222 n. 90. For a more skeptical view of vocalization, see E. Ullendorff, "Grace in Ugaritic?" in *Ugarit and the Bible: Proceedings of the International Symposium on Ugarit and the Bible, Manchester, September 1992* (ed. G. J. Brooke, A. H. W. Curtis and J. F. Healey; UBL 11; Münster: Ugarit-Verlag, 1994) 359. For D. Pardee's well-placed criticisms of Ullendorff on this issue, see his review of the volume in *JAOS* 117 (1997) 377–78. For a good example of Pardee's own practice of vocalization, see his *Ugaritic and Hebrew Poetic Parallelism: A Trial Cut ('nt I and Proverbs 2)* (VTSup 39; Leiden: Brill, 1988) 1 n. 5. See also his remarks in "Further Studies in Ugaritic Epistolography," *AfO* 31 (1984) 228 n. 45.

[86] Cross, *From Epic to Canon,* 101. In a letter to me dated 7 December 1998, Cross writes about this particular accented version of vocalized Ugaritic:

My accentuation of Ugaritic is really to show what an accentual meter would look like. The pattern of accent follows a proposal for West Semitic: accent on antepenult if the penult and the ultima are short, on the penult if it is long or in a closed syllable, and on the ultima if it is long. Segholates are treated as monosyllabic nouns. Like all Proto reconstructions, it is tentative, especially in the light of the fact that Proto languages are based on the principle of parsimony, not fact.

[87] See F. M. Cross, "El," *TDOT* 1.242–61; *Canaanite Myth and Hebrew Epic,* 3–75; Pope, *El in the Ugaritic Texts;* "The Ups and Downs in El's Amours," *UF* 11 (1979 = C. F. A. Schaeffer Festschrift) 701–8, reprinted in Pope, *Probative Pontificating,* 29–39; and "The Status of El at Ugarit," *UF* 19 (1989) 219–29, reprinted in Pope, *Probative Pontificating,* 47–61.

[88] Cross, *Canaanite Myth and Hebrew Epic,* 24.

detail that the god suffered from an initial bout of impotence before being coaxed by the two females by magical means.[89] The issues argued by Cross and Pope illustrate the sorts of problems posed by Ugaritic as well as their own mastery of the language and texts, and their exchanges showed the congeniality and mutual respect of two major American scholars of Ugaritic in this period. El's positive traits as presented by Cross and Pope perhaps evoke a bit of their own character and personality. For Cross, El was a vigorous, respected patriarch. El as represented in Pope's writings was a kindly and beneficent figure. (Pope was also hardly reticent in discussing El's sexual life or his drunkenness.)

The story of Gordon's one major exchange with Cross was unfortunately different. In the 1960s Gordon would explore South American connections with the Semitic world.[90] He accepted claims for an authentic Phoenician presence in Brazil in part based on the so-called Parahyba inscription. Following Gordon's proclamation of the inscription's authenticity, Cross responded with a detailed examination of the inscription's putative background and letter-forms and declared it a fake.[91] Gordon's answer in turn hardly addressed Cross's specific observations about problems involving the inscription's letter-forms and instead depended more on rhetorical denunciations of "micrometry," "minute discrepancies," "hyperfinesse" and the like.[92] Gordon's response did little to obviate Cross's objections, and it left the impression of an adventurous modern Odysseus infatuated with the possibility of a new world to explore. In a sense Cross and Gordon replayed the drama that ended with Gordon's exit from Hopkins in the summer of 1938. With Gordon's claims about the inscription departing so markedly from the scholarly norm of careful observation, one of the most learned of the Albright household expressed the sorts of criticisms echoing from Gordon's academic life almost a half century earlier.

---

[89] See also Pope, *El in the Ugaritic Texts*, 37–42. The debate turns largely on the interpretation of the word *mmnnm*. For discussion and Cross's more recent view of *mmnnm*, see S. M. Olyan, *Asherah and the Cult of Yahweh in Israel* (HSM 34; Atlanta: Scholars Press, 1988) 42 n. 12. As indicated in his letter of 7 December 1998 to me, Cross may finish an article on this text, so I will refrain from citing his current view.

[90] Gordon, "The Authenticity of the Phoenician Text from Parahyba," *Or* 37 (1968) 75–80.

[91] Cross, "The Phoenician Inscription from Brazil: A Nineteenth Century Forgery," *Or* 37 (1968) 437–60. See Cross's further comments in his article, "Phoenicians in Brazil?" *BAR* 5 (1979) 36–43. Gordon's work on this inscription was attacked also by J. Friedrich, "Die Unechtheit des phönizischen Inschrift aus Parahyba," *Or* 37 (1968) 421–24, which was followed by Gordon's reply in his essay, "The Canaanite Text from Brazil," *Or* 37 (1968) 425–36.

[92] Gordon, "Reply to Professor Cross," *Or* 37 (1968) 461–63.

Gordon, Pope and Cross all worked extensively in the comparative agenda advanced by Albright, and all three devoted extensive periods of research to Ugaritic and biblical studies. All white men with access to major universities, they advanced according to the norms of research established in East Coast departments of ancient Near Eastern studies. They also departed from the consensus paradigm of scholarly research in differing manners. With their various talents and interests, all three largely worked out of Albright's comparative paradigm, and they were all aided by learned colleagues. Pope's Yale colleagues, Rosenthal, Hallo and Childs, came from vastly different academic backgrounds. Cross's colleagues at Harvard, Lambdin and Moran, largely derived from the Hopkins mold, yet they were also highly independent scholars, as was Jacobsen. In contrast, Gordon at Brandeis was more of a one-man show. His major colleague in the Brandeis program, G. D. Young, had been his student at Dropsie. Young would provide a great deal of the basic language teaching at Brandeis while Gordon pursued study of the newly discovered texts. Such an arrangement may seem reminiscent of the Hopkins program, where Albright dominated the scene while Frank Blake provided so much of the basic language instruction—Blake was not only Albright's colleague, he had been his teacher as well.

In temperament, Gordon clearly was the most adventurous; indeed, his life's work may appear to represent a paradigm of "explorer" as opposed to the "house-builder" model of scholarship represented by the solid and detailed work of Cross. Pope by comparison partook of both paradigms, careful in his philology yet more expansive in his cultural comparisons. This spectrum of approach likewise matches their proximity to the Albright household. If we may speak of Albright and his program as a household, Cross was clearly a most capable, eldest son destined to inherit. Pope was an accepted "in-law," who maintained ties to the Albrightians even as he developed his own agenda on deities, death and sex. While Pope's approach largely resonated with Albright's, it was his choice of topics—at least from the 1970s onwards—that distinguished him from the Albrightians. Gordon in some senses was the sojourner who left the Albright household in search of his academic identity without what he perceived to be the unfair judgments or limits placed upon him by any academic patriarch. It was not only some of Gordon's subjects, but also his speculative impulse that departed from the discipline customary in the house of Albright. In sum, the courses that the academic lives of Gordon, Pope and Cross took varied in part because of their backgrounds and in part because of the degree to which they conformed their research to the accepted paradigm of scholarly method and progression. Yet it is equally clear that Albright was no small factor in the development of these three scholars.

Chapter 17

Metaphor and Myth: Percy, Ricoeur and Frye

Hugh C. White
Rutgers University

Burke Long, in his insightful work, *Planting and Reaping Albright*, exhibits a strong interest in the relation of metaphor and myth to history. This essay, offered in honor of his retirement from teaching, explores some of the philosophical and semiotic dimensions of these themes.

Since the time of Aristotle, the most appealing feature of metaphor has often been seen as its capacity to add rhetorical vitality to speech: "Liveliness is specially conveyed by metaphor, and by the further power of surprising the hearer; because the hearer expected something different, his acquisition of the new idea impresses him all the more."[1] This led Aristotle to consider metaphor under the topic of rhetoric rather than dialectics where language was governed by literality and the canons of strict logic,[2]

---

[1] Aristotle, *Rhetoric* III, ch. 11, par. 1412a, l.15–25.

[2] Metaphor is related to dialectics, but in a very distant way through the enthymeme and the logic of probabilities. The enthymeme is a rhetorical device to be used in public discourse, often in the form of maxims that state commonly held opinions not containing their premises. It, like rhetoric in general, is designed to appeal to those who cannot follow the careful thought of systematic logic: "The duty of rhetoric is to deal with such matters as we deliberate upon without arts or systems to guide us, in the hearing of persons who cannot take in at a glance a complicated argument, or follow a long chain of reasoning" (*Rhetoric* I, ch. 2, par. 1357a, l. 1). The metaphor has a place within the maxim as a useful stylistic device. However, metaphor in general must take second place to literal language, and has no place in strict logic and higher dialectics. Elsewhere Aristotle notes: "We may add that if dialectical disputation must not employ metaphors, clearly metaphor and metaphorical expressions are precluded in definition: otherwise dialectic would involve metaphor" (*Posterior Analytics* II, ch. 13, par. 97b, ll. 39–43). He also comments: "It has already been pointed out that the enthymeme is a syllogism, and in what sense it is so. We have also noted the differences between it and the syllogism

doubtless because of the ambiguity entailed by a metaphor's double refer-ence.[3] This distinction between metaphorical language that has its place in the intersubjective realm of rhetoric, and dialectics as the mode of lan-guage for rational dialectics, has been firmly maintained by most philoso-phers from Aristotle's time until today.

This has had a number of unfortunate results. The philosophical dis-cussion of metaphor has focused almost entirely on the cognitive problem created by metaphorical ambiguity, as will be seen below especially in the work of Paul Ricoeur. The affective dimension of metaphor is correspond-ingly seen to be of limited philosophical interest. In the discipline of reli-gion, metaphor, which is of central importance in religious discourse, has also been viewed primarily through the eyes of this philosophical dichot-omy that privileges higher dialectics and is skeptical about its cognitive importance.[4] Systematic theology in the West and the rigorous negative logic of Buddhist Madhyamika philosophy in the East, both attempt to sub-ject as much of the play of religious metaphor as possible to analytic logic.

The purpose of this article is to place the traditional dichotomy be-tween the cognitive and affective dimensions of metaphor into question, and to propose a view of metaphor that is rooted both cognitively and af-fectively in intersubjectivity. This will be done by showing how the semio-tician/novelist Walker Percy's intersubjective understanding of metaphor contributes to and extends the global theory of metaphor represented by Janet Soskice, Northrop Frye, Derrida, and others, and undermines the central argument in Ricoeur's theory of metaphor that is dependent upon the traditional dichotomy between the affective and cognitive dimensions. It will then be shown how Percy's view clarifies and strengthens Frye's conception of the ecstatic metaphor that is a fundamental feature of reli-gious myth.

*   *   *

---

of dialectic" (*Rhetoric* II, ch. 22, par. 1395b, ll. 21–22). Metaphor as a stylistic device he considers under the general rubric of the enthymeme, and thus is clearly sepa-rated from the syllogism of dialectics strictly considered.

[3] *Posterior Analytics* II, ch. 13, par. 97b, ll. 39–43.

[4] Mary Gerhart and Allan Russell realized this problem of the derogation of metaphor to dialectics, but proposed to solve it by defining the experience of the "cognitive flash" as the source of both religious/metaphorical insight and scientific truth (*Metaphoric Process: The Creation of Scientific and Religious Understanding* [for-ward by Paul Ricoeur; Fort Worth: Texas Christian Univ. Press, 1984]). While this brought metaphor close to the cognitive realm, it did so at the price of making met-aphor into a non-verbal experience. The tension that arises out of the intersub-jective communication event is here individualized, internalized and understood as primarily cognitive. The affective, intersubjective dimension is thus given no importance.

Walker Percy, who alternated writing novels with composing provocative essays on semiotics and the philosophy of language, has made a little-noted but potentially significant contribution to our understanding of metaphor in an article found in his popular book of essays, *The Message in the Bottle*.[5] The model for his understanding of the primal metaphor is provided by the experience of the deaf-mute, Helen Keller, who first became aware of the nature of names as her teacher, Ann Sullivan, wrote the word 'water' in her hand while pouring water over it. For Percy, this kind of "aboriginal naming act is . . . the most obscure and the most creative of metaphors" (78).[6] The effect of metaphor, for Percy, is not merely rhetorical, as it is for Aristotle, but has to do with the formation of subjectivity. Such a primal experience of metaphorical naming was, for Helen Keller, the experience of her breakthrough into the wonder of human consciousness and the distinctively human perception of "reality." In addition, metaphor is unique in its capacity to bring into consciousness previously private inarticulate experience and thus to create new language. For Percy, "Metaphor is the true maker of language" (79). Since it is language that accounts for the distinctively human way of knowing the world, metaphor in its capacity to create both human subjectivity and language is central to the uniquely human form of consciousness itself: "We do know, not as the angels know [unmediated] and not as dogs know [stimulus response] but as men, who must know one thing through the mirror of another" (82).

Percy illustrates the way in which metaphor functions in this primary language-creating situation by referring to a childhood experience. When he was out in the southern woods with his father and a black guide, he saw an unusual bird and asked the guide what its name was. The guide said it was a "blue-dollar hawk." His father later corrected this "mistake," saying that the proper name was a "blue darter hawk." Young Percy, nevertheless, preferred the first "incorrect" name. Though the proper name described more accurately what the hawk *did*, the first offered a poetic metaphor that said for him what it *was*, i.e., it gave its ontological status (71).

He discusses this phenomenon under the topic, "Metaphor as Mistake." Metaphor, at this primary level, does not depend upon a comparison of some kind with another preexisting term, a fundamental feature of

---

[5] Walker Percy, "Metaphor As Mistake," in *The Message in the Bottle: How Queer Man Is, How Queer Language Is, and What One Has to Do With the Other* (New York: Farrar, Straus and Giroux, 1989) 64–82.

[6] For Percy, the experience of Helen Keller was not an exact duplication of the primary act of naming, because of her language acquisition until the age of 19 months, but only an example that "distilled the essential elements of the normal naming experience." He utilized work by psycholinguists on early childhood language acquisition to support his views (*Conversations with Walker Percy* [ed. Lewis A. Lawson and Victor A. Kramer; Jackson: Univ. Press of Mississippi, 1985] 132).

Aristotle's view, since such a metaphor lacks any logical connections to other contextual symbols. It thus seems closer to catachresis, conventionally understood as the misuse or strained use of a term, or the derivation of a false form of a word through folk etymology. Percy, thus, refers to this phenomenon as a "catachrestic metaphor" (76). Since the exclusion of metaphor from the realm of dialectics was due to the semantic ambiguity caused by metaphor's double reference, the type of catachresis that Percy describes presents a particular problem. It represents both rhetorical liveliness and unity of reference and thus does not fit smoothly into Aristotle's dichotomy between the rhetorical/figurative and dialectical/literal realms of speech.

It is precisely because it lacks any logical, contextual connections that a catachresis such as "blue-dollar hawk" is the purest form of metaphor for Percy. Such connections would, in his view, deprive the name of the mystery associated with its being, and reduce it to a functional description. A good conventional metaphor, he says, is at most only a "gentle analogy" that always requires us to make the connections ourselves (73).

But this connection is established not only between the metaphorical term and its referent. In making this connection we are also joined through an intersubjective act with the inner world of another person. The metaphor is offered by one to see if it can elicit a response from another: "For at the basis of the beautiful metaphor . . . there is always the hope that this secret apprehension of my own, which I cannot call knowing because I do not even know that I know it, has a chance of being validated by what you have said" (73). When the connection is made, the private apprehension is validated, and the experience is brought into the common world, broadening and enriching it. Only in this way does knowledge grow. Similarly, when Helen Keller discovered that "water" was a name of something, she was not only introduced to the word "water," but also to the subjectivity of her teacher, Ann Sullivan, who could confirm for her the meaning of this new symbol. Percy thus views the intersubjective, communication event as crucial for understanding metaphor, rather than the relation of the metaphor to its referent.

How does Percy's view relate to other more recent understandings of metaphor? The conclusions to which the various recent studies of metaphor lead depend to a large extent upon the type of metaphorical expression that is viewed as normative by the analyst. It is thus helpful to sketch the trajectory that is formed by the various types of metaphor. Related to the issue of metaphorical type is also the issue of reference. Some contend that metaphor can only set up a comparison (referring to the new in terms of the old), and others maintain that true metaphors use figurative terms to point to a single new referent—a single unified subject—that, while creating figurative tension, is not semantically dependent upon comparison.

The former can be easily paraphrased without cognitive loss, while the latter is indispensable to the message being conveyed. This difference correlates with a different perception of what is assumed to be the normative type of metaphor.

It should be kept in mind that all of these views define the problem of metaphor as cognitive and exclude a role for intersubjectivity in the production of meaning. They are thus operating within the basic categories established by Aristotle that separate the cognitive/dialectical from the rhetorical/emotive. The question of the relevance of Percy's view will thus appear when it is shown that the current discussion has not led to a satisfactory solution to the chronic problems of metaphor interpretation without including the dimension of intersubjectivity. It will then be possible to see how the intersubjective perspective of Percy may heal the breach between the cognitive and emotive while also resolving some of the perennial questions regarding metaphor.

At one end of this trajectory is the simple metaphor, or as Max Black calls it, the "trivial" metaphor.[7] Many of Aristotle's examples fall into this category; for example, the metaphorical transfer from genus to species: "This ship of mine stands there" (lying at anchor is a species of standing).[8] A metaphor such as this is trivial because it relies upon a rather unsubtle comparison, that can be easily reduced to a literal paraphrase. Black argues that a more philosophically interesting type of metaphor is the "interaction" metaphor. This type cannot be reduced to a literal meaning, but rather requires that two contrary meanings or subjects be kept simultaneously in mind: "The use of a 'subsidiary subject' to foster insight into a 'principal subject' is a distinctive intellectual operation . . . demanding simultaneous awareness of both subjects but not reducible to any comparison between the two."[9] For Black, to attempt to state an interaction metaphor in literal terms will result in a loss of cognitive content.

Beyond the interaction metaphor lie the catachresis and the dead metaphor. The catachresis uses a term figuratively to name the new without relying at all upon the semantic field originally associated with the chosen term, thereby creating a high degree of tension between the term and its referent. In the view of some, the tension is so great that the connection is completely broken, causing the figure to fall toward the end of this trajectory, the dead metaphor. For others, however, the catachresis surpasses other forms of metaphor by transcending comparison, and achieving a unified reference while maintaining a high degree of figurative tension.

---

[7] Max Black, *Models and Metaphors: Studies in Language and Philosophy* (Ithaca, N.Y.: Cornell Univ. Press, 1962) 45.

[8] Aristotle, *On Poetics*, Bk. 21.

[9] Max Black, *Models and Metaphors*, 46.

The signal of metaphorical death is the disappearance of the tension between the literal and figurative meanings so that the figurative meaning becomes the literal meaning.[10]

In a more recent work, the British theologian Janet Soskice uses Black's interaction metaphor as a prime example of metaphoricity. She too is not interested in the 'trivial' metaphor that can be understood as a comparison and is easily reduced to a paraphrase.[11] But she finds Black's two-subject theory of interpretation, in spite of his insistence that it cannot be understood as a comparison, to depend in the end, nevertheless, on some degree of comparison due to his reliance upon the concept of analogy to explain the relation between the two subjects (42). To the extent that it still relies on comparison, unity of reference would not be achieved and the simultaneity of the interaction would be diminished or eliminated.

She considers I. A. Richards' terms, "tenor" and "vehicle," less divisive of the basic unity of the interactive metaphor than Black's terms, "principal subject" and "subsidiary subject." The "tenor" can be equated with the "principal subject," and "vehicle," with the "subsidiary subject." Soskice's concern is to show that, together, "tenor" and "vehicle" refer to only a single subject: "It is only by seeing that a metaphor has one true subject which tenor and vehicle conjointly depict and illumine that a full, interactive, or interanimative, theory is possible" (47).

But exactly how does this single subject emerge from what appears to be the semantic tension of a split reference? To treat the problem of reference, Soskice follows the well-established path of distinguishing between meaning and reference on the one hand, and sense and denotation on the other. Meaning/reference are utterance-bound and contextual, whereas sense/denotation concern the dictionary definitions of terms and what they designate.

Where the reference of utterances is concerned, much looser rules apply than to the denotation of terms. An utterance may successfully refer even when the speaker is mistaken about the object of reference, e.g., a person may shout to a pedestrian, "Lookout for that car," and successfully warn her of an oncoming vehicle, when in fact it was a truck rather than a car that was approaching. The imprecision of the reference would not seriously undermine the meaning of the utterance. Thus, in the context of an utterance customary denotations of terms can be more easily violated by a metaphor without causing the breakdown of linguistic communication,

---

[10] For a complete discussion of the catachretical metaphor see Heinrich Lausberg, *Handbook of Literary Rhetoric: A Foundation for Literary Study* (trans. Matthew T. Bliss, Annemiek Jansen, David E. Orton; ed. David E. Orton and R. Dean Anderson; Leiden and Boston: Brill, 1998) par. 552.

[11] Janet Martin Soskice, *Metaphor and Religious Language* (1985; repr., Oxford: Clarendon, 1989) 26.

since reference is accomplished by the whole, unique utterance in its individual context and setting.[12]

In the case of the trivial or simple metaphor, the reference is usually clear and can be easily translated into another literal term or phrase, as when a baseball announcer refers to a baseball that has been dropped by a player as a "hot potato." Other more complex metaphors, however, are so unique in their reference that they may not be able to be translated at all into other terms.

Soskice cites a particularly imaginative metaphor from a novel by Virginia Wolf that depicts a character's grief with the image of a dark shaft in a way that cannot be reduced to even a subtle paraphrase: "The metaphor and its meaning (it is artificial to separate them) are the unique product of the whole and the excellence of a metaphor such as this one is not that it is a new description of a previously discerned human condition but that *this* subject, this particular mental state, is accessible only through the metaphor" (her emphasis).[13] This kind of metaphor thus produces a cognitive gain that would be lost in a paraphrase.

Such references produce a unique cognition that is unified and singular and does not have to involve semantic tension with a second subject. The plurality of the metaphorical utterance is at the level of sense (associative network of senses) rather than at the level of reference that is determined by the utterance context (88). The whole utterance, then, describes one single undivided referent in terms of the associative network of senses of another. It is only in this limited sense that you get "two ideas for one." This leads then to Soskice's definition of metaphor as "a speaking about one thing or state of affairs in terms which are suggestive of another" (53). It is in this sense (plurality at the level of sense; unity at the level of referent/subject) that she favors the interactive theory of metaphor.

The catachresis is a form of metaphor that lends itself particularly well to producing this kind of unified reference. The feature of catachresis that Soskice emphasizes is its capacity to extend language in order to fill lexical gaps (61). By joining together a complex of associated meanings, it can describe something so new and unique that it cannot be described in any other way. For this reason catachresis is also particularly useful in describing invisible (e.g., scientific models) or spiritual (e.g., God the Mother) realities that cannot be perceived or known independently of the catachresis. A

---

[12] This does not mean, however, that Soskice follows Donald Davidson's pragmatic view ("What Metaphors Mean," *Critical Inquiry* 5 [1978] 31–47) that metaphor is a phenomenon of language use with entirely no meaning-creating capacity (Soskice, *Metaphor*, 28). For a more thorough-going critique of Davidson's speech-act approach to metaphor, see Roger M. White, *The Structure of Metaphor: The Way the Language of Metaphor Works* (Oxford and Cambridge: Blackwell, 1996) 194.

[13] Soskice, *Metaphor*, 48.

genuinely unique reference, however, would result in immense semantic strains with the associated meanings, and raise the possibility of communicative failure, as happens occasionally especially in poetry.

In order to avoid the ambiguity that this view of reference seems to entail, Soskice goes on to argue that reference has its primary roots in concrete, contextually bound instances of discourse. Thus, reference is not the product of a fixed code, as is denotation, but of an utterance that is relative to its context, and anything but fixed. A metaphor that violates the fixed sense and denotations of one of its terms may thus still refer successfully and meaningfully, though the truth of the reference is always qualified. This is why she terms her position one of "critical realism."

It is in this fashion that metaphors may also generate new knowledge. This occurs not only through poetry, but also through various metaphors found in science. Thus, in Soskice's view, "metaphor has the added capacity to expand our lexicon, and in so doing, it expands the conceptual apparatus with which we work" (62). Soskice sees such creative metaphors that give rise to new and often unique cognitive insights as the normative form of metaphor.[14]

*   *   *

In light of the importance Soskice and others assign to the role of metaphor in the creation of new knowledge, and the centrality of the issue of unity of reference to that role, it is necessary now to address the most formidable argument against these views made by Paul Ricoeur, whose views on this issue stand in the Aristotelian tradition of metaphor theory.

These issues are brought into the open by the problem of catachresis that is central to the metaphor theories of both Soskice and Walker Percy.[15] The fundamental question here is whether or not catachresis is actually a species of metaphor, since it does not arise from comparison and thus prop-

---

[14] Soskice goes further to argue that not only does metaphor contribute to conceptual knowledge, but that our most fundamental conceptual systems are themselves deeply intertwined with metaphorical imagery: "In almost all areas of abstract thought (mathematics might be an exception but even that seems doubtful), the very frames within which we work are given by metaphors which function in structuring not only what sort of answers we get, but what kind of questions we ask" (ibid., 63). She thus aligns her position with the "strong metaphor theory" such as that of Vico (Marcel Danesi, *Vico, Metaphor, and the Origin of Language* [Advances in Semiotics; Bloomington and Indianapolis: Indiana Univ. Press, 1993]). A recent example of the strong metaphor theory being applied to the novel and biblical literature can be found in Kari Syreeni, "Metaphorical Appropriation: (Post)Modern Biblical Hermeneutic and the Theory of Metaphor," *Literature and Theology* 9:3 (1995) 321–337.

[15] Soskice, *Metaphor*, 61–64.

erly belongs outside of the category of figurative language.[16] Because of the lack of semantic connection between the catachretical term and its referent, the tension between the catachretical use and the term's established sense may decline and eventually disappear. This is why little distinction is often made by critics between catachresis and dead metaphors. The expression "foot of the mountain" is classified by some as a dead metaphor and by others as a catachresis. This is doubtless because the expression has become so lexicalized that the semantic tension associated with figurative meaning has disappeared for most language users.

This issue is an important one because it is a catachresis, such as light, that is the most common form of figurative language found in speculative, philosophical vocabulary.[17] These forms thus constitute the battle line between those who want to argue for the final dependence of speculative, philosophical thought on figurative language, and those who defend its independence. The value given catachresis in the trajectory of figurative language will determine not only how metaphor is understood, but also the relative importance of figurative language in relation to speculative thought.

It is in the debate between Paul Ricoeur and Jacques Derrida regarding metaphor and catachresis that these issues are drawn the most sharply. For Derrida, terms such as "light" are catachretical metaphors that occur in formative ways in the history of Greek philosophy.[18] Such a primordial metaphor as "light" in the thinking of someone such as Descartes (and others in the metaphysical tradition of Socrates and Plato) is so implicated in the very possibility of rational thought, that one cannot accord to the conceptual any type of priority: "Prior to every determined presence, to every representative idea, natural light constitutes the very ether of thought and of its proper discourse."[19] He seeks to show that the catachretical metaphor of natural light is inseparably intertwined with the very genesis of Descartes' mode of critical thought.[20]

---

[16] Figures and tropes may be categorized separately or tropes may be placed under the category of figures. See Lausberg, *Handbook,* 272 par. 601. I am following the latter practice.

[17] Lausberg, in his monumental study of figurative language, supports the view that catachresis is a primary source of language for speaking of the invisible dimensions of life (*Handbook,* 255 par. 562).

[18] Lausberg gives the support of classical rhetoric to Derrida's analysis. He observes that it is "plausible" that spiritual realities are referred to by means of catachretical metaphors (ibid.).

[19] Jacques Derrida, *Margins of Philosophy* (trans., with addnl. notes, by Alan Bass; Chicago: Univ. of Chicago Press, 1982), 226.

[20] See also Marcel Danesi, who presents Vico's argument that metaphor has enabled seeing externally, associated with the ancient Greek word *Ideein,* to become a

Derrida, thus, wants to "explode" the barrier between tropic and philosophical dialectic erected by Aristotle.[21] In his view, metaphors have been and continue to be indispensable to philosophy: "The constitution of the fundamental oppositions of the metaphorology (*physis/tekhne, physis/nomos,* sensible/intelligible . . .) has occurred by means of the history of a metaphorical language, or rather by means of 'tropic' movements which, no longer capable of being called by a philosophical name—i.e. metaphors—nevertheless, and for the same reason, do not make up a 'proper' language" (229).

Ricoeur, however, wants to create a clear line of demarcation between metaphorical and speculative discourse. The problem he finds with metaphorical language is its profound ambiguity. For him, the element of tension between the figurative and lexicalized uses is the most distinguishing characteristic of metaphor: "It is best put by saying that deviation in relation to the context is not only a signal that orients the interpretation, but a constitutive element of the metaphorical message."[22] He characterizes this tension or deviation as being a clash between sameness and difference that is governed by the logic of comparison or resemblance: "In metaphor, resemblance can be construed as the site of the clash between sameness and difference." This clash remains ambiguous within the terms of the metaphor, and it is the task of conceptual thought to purge this ambiguity from metaphor. Whereas in metaphor's similarity, "'the same' operates *in spite of* 'the different,'" in speculative thought "the conceptual structure of resemblance opposes and unites identity and difference," thereby eliminating the ambiguity (196; his emphasis).

Ricoeur maintains that the entire discussion of metaphor takes place within the framework of philosophical terms that must, itself, be fundamentally independent of metaphorical discourse: "The speculative fulfills the semantic exigencies put to it by the metaphorical only when it establishes a *break* marking the *irreducible difference* between the two modes of discourse" (301; my emphasis). Speculative discourse, furthermore, is philosophically prior to and more fundamental than the discourse of metaphor: "In the horizon opened up by the speculative, 'same' grounds 'similar' and not the inverse. . . . What affirms this? Speculative discourse does, by reversing the order of precedence of metaphorical discourse, which attains 'same' only as 'similar'" (ibid.).

---

type of seeing internally that is the basis of the modern "idea" (*Vico, Metaphor, and the Origin of Language,* 78).

[21] Derrida, *Margins,* 270.

[22] Paul Ricoeur, *The Rule of Metaphor: Multi-Disciplinary Studies of the Creation of Meaning in Language* (trans. Robert Czerny, Kathleen McLaughlin, and John Costello; Toronto: Univ. of Toronto Press, 1977) 184.

Ricoeur still wants to accord to living metaphor the role of introducing the "spark of imagination" into speculative thought, but it is the responsibility of speculative thought to purge it of all sensory content in order to produce abstract, unambiguous, speculative truth. This process of purging is called interpretation: "Interpretation is necessarily a rationalization that at its limit eliminates the experience that comes to language through the metaphorical process. Doubtless it is only in reductive interpretation that rationalization culminates in clearing away the symbolic base" (302). Here the distinction Aristotle made between the rhetorical metaphor which speaks in terms of ordinary sensory experience that can be understood by the man on the street, and serious dialectics reappears. It is the role of speculative thought to dampen this metaphorical spark and establish a "break" in order to produce an "irreducible difference" between these two modes of thought, even if the symbolic base is not always totally "cleared away." This lays the foundation for his view that the metaphorical and speculative modes of discourse exist in a dialectical relation based upon their irreducible difference (313).

Catachresis is, perhaps, the single largest obstacle to the success of Ricoeur's argument, since catachretical terms are ubiquitous within philosophical language. His solution to this problem, following the eighteenth-century French philosopher Fontanier, is to rule that catachresis is not a metaphor, or even a figurative expression. A figurative expression must both deviate from the simple, proper use of a term, and be freely, imaginatively chosen rather than forced (53). For a term to be freely chosen, there must be another "proper" expression available for which the figurative term is a substitution. If there is no other term, then Fontanier considers it a "forced" usage, i.e., only an "extension" of the established use (55). This makes the catachresis similar to the dead metaphor that functions as an established, "proper" term. In addition, by declaring the etymological resurrection of dead metaphors in philosophy to be illegitimate on historical grounds, Ricoeur can eliminate both of these troubling phenomena altogether from the realm of speculative thought (292).

There are a number of problems with Ricoeur's argument, the most basic of which is the exclusion of catachresis from the category of metaphor. By founding his argument regarding catachresis on Fontanier, Ricoeur has used an argument that is not supported by modern rhetoric. In Lausberg's comprehensive study of rhetorical language from the classical to the modern age, catachresis is clearly classified as a form of metaphor.[23] While Fontanier's and Ricoeur's view of catachresis as a forced usage that is required by the absence of a word (*inopia*) is common in ancient rhetoric (as

---

[23] See Lausberg for a discussion of catachresis as a type of metaphor (*Handbook*, 254 par. 562).

well as in Soskice), it has been substantially modified in the modern period, according to Lausberg: *Inopia,* which according to classical theory is required for a catachresis, has been replaced in modern linguistics by the principle of "vitality." As Lausberg says regarding the application of the principle of vitality to catachresis, "An actual expression which already exists can be displaced by a metaphor if it has for some reason (e.g., by homonymy) become 'weak' or if the metaphor has developed expansive power by virtue of its evocative content." This means that catachresis can be as "freely chosen" as any other type of metaphor in order to enhance the "vitality" of the expression, and Ricoeur's argument for the exclusion of catachresis from the realm of metaphor is no longer viable. When this occurs, however, the catachretical metaphor will not always be based on a comparison or even associated senses, but may arise from something such as a phonetic similarity or mishearing (255, par. 562).

In Percy's example of the "blue-dollar hawk," an example of catachretical mishearing, the break between the established meaning of "dollar" and the catachretical use in this expression could not be greater, and yet its figurative vitality makes Percy prefer this designation to the proper functional expression, "blue darter hawk."

Another example from modern vernacular would be the use of "cup-a-joe" to refer to a cup of coffee, the "joe" probably arising from the common initial letter shared by joe and java (another term for coffee derived metonymically from the place of origin of a type of coffee bean). Here playful alliteration would account for this catachresis rather than phonetic mishearing as in Percy's example. Again, the catachresis is not the result of *inopia,* but a preference for a more interesting expression.

One of Soskice's tests with regard to whether a metaphor is dead or not is the presence or absence of a recognizable "dissonance or tension . . . whereby the terms of the utterance used seem not strictly appropriate to the topic at hand," i.e., the "vitality" test.[24] If this test is applied to either of the above examples, then they would clearly pass as examples of figurative language, and thus as catachretical metaphors.

The catachresis, thus, in spite of the illogical semantic twisting that sometimes severs its connections with its lexicalized use, can still retain, in some cases, the important capacities of metaphor to embody figurative tension. What has become obvious from this discussion, however, is that catachresis may either draw upon the associated senses of the vehicle in the case of *inopia,* or may have no semantic connection between tenor and vehicle at all. Soskice seems aware of only the former possibility, whereas the latter actually makes possible a more complete realization of her criteria of vitality and unity of reference since there is a total semantic cleavage

---

[24] Soskice, *Metaphor,* 73.

between the original lexicalized use and the figurative use. No trace of positive semantic comparison survives in this type of catachresis even within the field of associated senses, though figurative tension from the negative inappropriateness remains. This makes this type of catachresis the best example of pure metaphoricity as Soskice understands it. It becomes equally obvious that the way in which you understand catachresis reflects the way in which you understand metaphor itself. For those who value the catachresis as metaphor, the most important values of metaphor are understood to be its capacity to name the new and to achieve a unified reference.[25]

Another problem stemming from Ricoeur's reliance upon Fontanier is the absence of any role for metaphor in the creation of new knowledge. On the one hand, Ricoeur wants to argue that metaphorical discourse can "bring to light new aspects of reality by means of semantic innovation." But, on the other, this semantic innovation requires a tension between the proper and figurative to operate, i.e., always a somewhat ambiguous contrast, not an entirely new meaning. Soskice uncovers the implication of this understanding when she observes that Ricoeur's interpretation of metaphoric denotation as mimetic redescription[26] "implies that there is some definite, preexisting thing . . . that the metaphor is about and simply redescribes." She goes on to argue that "the interesting thing about metaphor, or at least about some metaphors, is that they are used not to redescribe but to disclose for the first time. The metaphor has to be used because something new is being talked about."[27]

In Ricoeur's comparison view of metaphor, it is difficult to see how radically new knowledge could be expressed in metaphorical language. Not only is the metaphorical reference so ambiguous as not to qualify as knowledge, it is also finally the role of speculative thought to match concepts that have been purged of metaphorical ambiguity to pre-existing reality. This requires the operation of the conceptual to be fundamentally independent of the metaphorical: "The *necessity* of this discourse is not the extension of its possibility, inscribed in the dynamism of the metaphorical. Its necessity proceeds instead from the very structures of the mind, which it is the task of transcendental philosophy to articulate."[28]

Nevertheless, he concludes by seeing the speculative and the poetic in a dialectical relationship, each retaining its own independence, but continuously interacting. The metaphorical supplies an ambiguous "sketch," em-

---

[25] Metaphor is an important term in Freudian psychoanalysis, where it refers to similarity. This view is not inconsistent with Soskice's and Percy's emphasis upon catachresis; e.g., see Kaja Silverman, *The Subject of Semiotics* (New York: Oxford Univ. Press, 1983) 94, for an example of catachresis.

[26] Ricoeur, *Rule*, 245, 305.

[27] Soskice, *Metaphor*, 89.

[28] Ricoeur, *Rule*, 300.

bracing two referential fields at once, and must be reduced to conceptual and systematic form by speculative thought. Thus metaphorical discourse, though suggestive, remains one step removed from reality, and, in itself, cannot add to our cognitive knowledge of the world (299).

The dilemmas to which Ricoeur's thought led, however, are not totally solved by Soskice's view of metaphor. Soskice's effort to overcome the dual subjects of Black's view by confining the metaphoric tension to the associated senses is more philosophically deft than convincing, since the new field of associated senses brought together by metaphor would still achieve the capacity to refer only by the exclusion of some senses and the acceptance of others. While she is correct to emphasize that a unique unity may emerge around a single subject at the end of this process, it is difficult to see how the initial phase requiring the acceptance of some senses and the rejection of others completely escapes comparison with the literal. The catachresis of the second type, which Soskice does not recognize, eliminates this problem by preventing a field of associated senses that might unite tenor and vehicle from arising at all.

In apparent recognition of the state of affairs presented by the retention of the associated senses of the vehicle, Soskice argues, in opposition to Ricoeur, that "the alternative to the reference made by metaphor is not its (shattered) literal reference but no reference at all."[29] But when the literal reference is truly shattered, there are no associated senses, and the tension even at the level of sense is eliminated. Soskice's description thus seems to apply to the second type of catachresis more than the first.

If, however, you eliminate or greatly reduce the tension between the established senses and the metaphorical use, and pose the unique metaphor against the absence of any lexicalized reference, how can its meaning and reference be established at all within the terms of Soskice's argument? This would seem at best to produce extreme ambiguity, and at worst to make the innovative metaphor or radical catachresis incomprehensible.[30] Soskice might reply to this criticism by saying that the utterance context would make the meaning clear. However, if the semantic links to lexicalized uses are totally broken, the entire meaning of the utterance would then depend on the non-verbal context. While context is clearly the critical factor in explaining such a metaphorical utterance, a great deal more needs

---

[29] Soskice, *Metaphor*, 88–89.

[30] White makes a similar criticism of theories like that of Soskice, in *Structure of Metaphor* (see n. 12, above): "The Theory spins in a vacuum with nowhere to gain a foothold, and always ends by merely extolling the virtues of this special sense, without giving any substantial characterization of what this sense actually is" (165). White, however, is proposing a solution to the problem of metaphor, and completely ignores the problem that catachresis presents to his solution.

to be said about this context than Soskice has said.[31]

The problem of the bifurcation of language into emotive/rhetorical and dialectical spheres bequeathed by Aristotle has thus led to an impasse at the juncture of the catachretical metaphor. Soskice, while not bringing together the rhetorical and cognitive dimensions of metaphor, has pointed the way out of this impasse by showing the inadequacy of the comparison theory and emphasizing the unity of the metaphorical reference. She has also, however, indirectly illustrated the need for a new perspective to solve the problem of the semantic vacuum in which her metaphorical referent is left suspended.

*   *   *

It thus appears that the current discussion has led to an insoluble problem. The role that the catachretical metaphor has in naming the new, and especially naming those non-material dimensions of human experience that are centrally important to religion as well as science, give it a place of pivotal importance. Yet the understanding of catachresis developed by Soskice leaves the meaning of many such metaphors unexplainable. Neither is a solution offered to the bifurcation of the cognitive and emotive dimensions of metaphor originating with Aristotle. It is precisely at this point that the perspective of Walker Percy may provide some helpful insight by proposing an understanding of catachresis within the context of intersubjectivity.

Percy's understanding of metaphor is quite close to that of Soskice in many of its fundamentals. For Soskice as for Percy, the purest form of metaphor is the type that creates new meaning without reliance upon comparison or analogy. This is why Soskice argues that metaphor does not rely for its meaning upon some opposition to the literal. Rather, the fundamental opposition is reference vs. no reference. Similarly, Percy argues that the figurative phrase "blue-dollar hawk" does not require any prior, established functional meaning to qualify it to serve as a proper name for the bird. New meaning is created by the metaphorical articulation of an experience that lies dormant in unconscious bodily memory. Metaphor thus functions the most purely where its opposition is no reference at all, i.e., where the contrast is with a dormant, unacknowledged, barely conscious experience. Both argue that the meaning arises from the total context of the particular utterance rather than from an assumed system of synchronic semantics.

At this point, however, their perceptions diverge with regard to how they understand this context, and the way in which reference works. For

---

[31] Kari Syreeni, speaking more recently from a largely Ricoeurean viewpoint, has also criticized Soskice's effort to eliminate dualism from metaphor theory (Syreeni, "Metaphorical Appropriation" [see n. 14, above], 325).

Soskice the context of metaphor is one of language use by a fully developed, conscious subject engaged in an act of reference: "Words make no reference beyond that which *speakers* employ them to make in sentences."[32] I emphasize here Soskice's use of the term "speaker" to indicate that this is a given datum that she does not probe into more deeply.

Percy, in contrast, is interested in opening up the intersubjective process in which the speaker's human, semiotic consciousness emerges as a response to language. The speaker, as a language user, cannot be assumed to exist prior to a primal intersubjective language occurrence. In *Message in the Bottle* he argues that consciousness itself is a product of intersubjectivity: "The *I think* is only made possible by a prior mutuality: *we name*" (275).

The denotative capacity of language arises from something that happens[33] in a communicative act between two subjects that lifts a neural response to the symbolic level where it becomes fully conscious: "Denotation, the act of naming, requires the two, namer and hearer. My calling this thing a chair is another way of saying that it 'is' a chair for you and me . . . Every symbolic formulation, whether it be language, art, or even thought, requires a real or posited someone else for whom the symbol is intended as meaningful . . . Denotation is an exercise in intersubjectivity" (270–271). The capacity of a term to refer thus does not depend upon an unambiguous reference in the individual intellect. Rather it depends upon the term being recognized as a signifier by another. This takes place simultaneously with the awakening of awareness to an experience of the object of reference shared by both subjects.

In the environment of this kind of intersubjective language event, the grammar of the sentence does not yet have to come into play. Percy, following C. S. Peirce (but, finally, not adhering to Peirce), argues that the fundamental context is not the assertive act in which a speaker uses a sentence to establish a connection between the sign and its referent, but a signifying exchange between two subjects that can be as short as a single word. This does not mean that Percy is moving back from the syntagmatic to the semiotic (in Ricoeur's sense), but rather that he is seeing the primary context of a signifying expression, not as the grammatical system, but as a single intersubjective language occurrence consisting of *both* the speaker's utterance *and* its reception by a hearer.

This argument corresponds closely to what M. M. Bakhtin terms the "translinguistic" dimension of language. Bakhtin, like Percy, believes that one must begin to understand language by looking at concrete discourse between two subjects rather than at an abstract language system detached

---

[32] Soskice, *Metaphor*, 136.

[33] Percy considered this "something" a profound mystery (*Message in the Bottle*, 327).

from its living context. The fundamental unit of language is not the pho-neme or even morpheme, but the "word" understood as a concrete utter-ance of indeterminate length (from one word to a longer discourse) made to an addressee by a speaking subject having a specific position: "The word (or in general any sign) is interindividual. . . . The word cannot be assigned to a single speaker. The author (speaker) has his own inalienable right to the word, but the listener also has his rights, and those whose voices are heard in the word before the author comes upon it also have their rights (after all, there are no words that belong to no one)."[34] Language for Bakh-tin, in its primal sense, is always dialogical, i.e., a concrete written or oral statement by a speaker, that is responsive to and includes the total commu-nicative context.[35]

It is the necessity of this intersubjective context of signifying language occurrences that makes the experience of Helen Keller archetypal for Percy. It was not just that Helen Keller, herself, was able to link the letters of the word "water" with a referent through some kind of barely conscious neurological conditioning. In her dramatic breakthrough into language, she understood that the letters constituted a word with meaning that was shared by her teacher. With this insight she then became aware that *every-thing* had a name that she could learn and use to participate in this new shared world of meaning. Before, she was a "responding organism," but now, Percy says, she became a "semiotic creature."[36]

---

[34] M. M. Bakhtin, *Speech Genres and Other Late Essays* (trans. Vern W. McGee; ed. Caryl Emerson and M. Holquist; Univ. of Texas Press Slavic Series 8; Austin: Univ. of Texas Press, 1986) 121; Mikhail Bakhtin, *Problems of Dostoevsky's Poetics* (trans. R. W. Rotsel; Ann Arbor, Mich.: Ardis, 1973) 152. While Bakhtin only analyzes tropes within the context of his discussion of the monological nature of poetry, it is clear that his general observations regarding the dialogical nature of language apply to Percy's fundamental observations regarding the catachretical metaphor; see Gary Saul Morson and Caryl Emerson, *Mikhail Bakhtin: Creation of a Prosaics* (Stanford: Stanford Univ. Press, 1990) 325. See also Paul de Man, "Dialogue and Dialogism," *Poetics Today* 4:1 (1983) 99–107, and Mathew Roberts, "Poetics Hermeneutics Dia-logics: Bakhtin and Paul de Man," in *Rethinking Bakhtin: Extensions and Challenges* (ed. Gary Saul Morson and Caryl Emerson; Evanston, Ill.: Northwestern Univ. Press, 1989) 115–134.

[35] "Dialogical intercourse is the genuine sphere of the *life* of language" (*Prob-lems of Dostoevsky's Poetics,* 151).

[36] In Patrick Samway, ed., *A Thief of Peirce: The Letters of Kenneth Laine Ketner and Walker Percy* (Jackson: Univ. Press of Mississippi, 1995) 41, 42. The above-mentioned turn toward the intersubjective language event as the basis of metaphor is what separates Percy from the general philosophical approach. Earl R. Mac Cormac, when he gets to the basis of his cognitive level where metaphors structure knowledge, does not turn toward the intersubjective dimension to seek understanding of the origin of this primary level of language, but rather speculates about smaller "lin-

It is at this level that we can understand more clearly why Percy says that Helen Keller's utterance, "water," was "the most obscure and creative of metaphors."[37] The distinctive aspect of metaphor is not that it can suggest new meanings through a semantic process of comparison or analogy. Metaphor poses a new term in a language occurrence in such a way as to require the instantaneous understanding of a new referent by the receiver that opens up a shared world of communication. This is why Percy and Soskice both chose the catachretical type of metaphor as a centrally important form, since the catachresis, though making a reference, reduces or eliminates the positive dimension of comparison while preserving the highest degree of purely figurative tension, as Percy's "blue-dollar hawk" illustrates.[38]

This understanding of catachresis reveals that the tension at the base of metaphorical language is not the tension caused by an ambiguous double reference, but the tension at the root of denotation itself that makes every word involve a risk of communicative failure with another person and offers the immense satisfaction of communicative success.[39] The metaphor is profoundly important in language use because, by disturbing the fixed system of denotations, it reawakens these primal tensions, uncertainties,

---

guistic units" that might constitute a "natural language," or a language similar to the "machine language of a computer" (*A Cognitive Theory of Metaphor* [1985; repr., Cambridge, Mass.: MIT Press, 1990] 202). While he clearly has reservations about these possibilities, this is an example of the mechanistic dead end to which this line of reasoning, based as it is on an exclusively individualistic model of language use, can lead.

[37] See also Marcel Danesi's exposition of Vico's theory of the origin of language: "There is no 'universal grammar' in the human species; there is only the mind's capacity to organize metaphorically forged concepts into cognitive structures." Vico sees metaphor entering to effect the connections of pictographic images and their oral counterparts into words and concepts in the mind. This movement from initial iconic perceptions to first order terms and concepts is roughly parallel to Percy's move from the empirical, neural connections between the mind and objects of reference, to the semiotic denotation (*Vico, Metaphor, and the Origin of Language*, 79).

[38] Alan Singer explains how some of the metaphors in Joyce interrupt the contextual flow of the plot, and do not depend on the semantics of the context: "The metaphor of the bird surpasses the 'world' projected by setting and action, which ordinarily condition the identity of character" (*A Metaphorics of Fiction: Discontinuity and Discourse in the Modern Novel* [Tallahassee: Univ. Presses of Florida, 1983] 27, also 30).

[39] The metaphoric character of our most fundamental experiences of language has been explored by Jacques Lacan. See Alan Singer, who sees the applicability of Lacan's theory of post-Oedipal, metaphoric language to the interpretation of the avant-garde novel, in *A Metaphorics of Fiction*: "Lacan's psychoanalysis engenders something like a rhetorical analysis of psychic process insofar as metaphoric trope is the model of the Oedipal succession to language" (50).

and profound satisfactions at the foundation of every human semiotic expression, and thus returns both speaker and hearer to the primal roots of the experience of language itself. Here the cognitive and emotional, the literal and rhetorical, cannot be separated, and Aristotle's bifurcation cannot be sustained. It is clear as well that the problem of referential instability in the unique metaphor at the cognitive level is overcome by the intersubjective context in which it is received and understood by a subject who, somewhat mysteriously, responds to the previously unconscious common experience brought to awareness by the metaphor. A catachretical metaphor thus reenacts, better than other metaphorical forms, this primal event of human language at its most fundamental level where language creates the distinctively human, semiotic consciousness in the very same instance that it also makes a reference that is not dependent upon a prior, literal meaning to communicate. Since it was understanding how the link was established between language and meaning in the consciousness of the speaker or interpreter that was the focus of Percy's concern, he saw the "mistake" of the catachretical metaphor as best preserving the clue as to how this occurred.[40]

When Percy comes to consider the issue of the "fit" between the signifier and its object of reference, he stresses the interconnection between the denotative act and the epistemological event. The relating of a word to its object of reference is represented as a "pairing" of symbol with thing. Following Cassirer on this point, Percy states: "It is the pairing or formulation itself . . . which comprises the act of knowing."[41] One thus does not consciously know the object, somehow, prior to or apart from the act of symbolization. The connection between the subject and the referent, however, does not begin with the sign, but is empirically based upon a physical, neural response of an organism to this potential referent in its environment, before it becomes a fully conscious, semiotic occurrence (270). While the empirical, neural connection is not yet a denotation, there is no radical epistemological gap as Descartes envisioned between the knower and the referent in the primal situation. It is then the role of the primal metaphor to lift that neural response into consciousness.

---

[40] Percy, *Message in the Bottle*, 42. In Percy's lively and informal correspondence with the Peircean philosopher Ken Ketner, he expressed this interest in the connection of intersubjectivity to language in a typically graphic way while discussing the possibility of escaping the Cartesian split: "What I would like to do is, instead of explaining away mind, exorcizing the Cartesian ghost in the machinery, rather to give the utterer his proper place in the semiotic. If you can't altogether exorcize the ghost, you can at least see how he's hooked up to the machinery" (in Samway, *A Thief of Peirce*, 42).

[41] Percy, *Message in the Bottle*, 273.

But how then can one be sure of the truth of this knowledge? Here he argues, similarly to Soskice, that every act of recognition is "only an approximation, a cast of one thing toward another toward the end of a fit" (273). The adequacy of the "fit" can only be determined by subsequent experience. But the empirical measure of this "fit" would only be possible after the primary symbolization had made the object knowable.[42] It can never be viewed as anything more than an approximation, however, since it is always colored by the intersubjective relation within which the act of symbolization occurs.[43] The intersubjective nature of the knowing act, however, based on shared experience, offers at least a modicum of otherness to the primary symbolization of the object of reference.

Rather than attempting to argue, in some qualified sense, for the truth of the object of reference, however, Percy, following Marcel and Buber, would rather speak of the authenticity or inauthenticity of the intersubjective relation which serves as the basis of the epistemological act. He does not develop this intriguing possibility, however, in his semiotic writings.[44]

---

[42] Soskice similarly argues, in explaining the centrality of models and metaphors to scientific theory making, that "the metaphorical predicates which a model generates can, prior to definitive knowledge, be seen as denoting candidates for real existence and enable one to say that the employment of metaphorical theory terms, while not exhaustively descriptive, may be 'partially denoting' or reality depicting" (*Metaphor,* 13).

[43] Mac Cormac similarly speaks of metaphorical truth as an approximation: "I assert that all metaphors are true *to a degree*; that is, through their novel juxtaposition of referents they express insights that are proper assertions" (*Cognitive Theory of Metaphor,* 208; emphasis added). He resists allowing metaphors to be viewed as relativistic, however, by showing how both the coherence and correspondence theories of truth are necessary for their operation: "Metaphoric suggestions presume an integral semantic and cognitive connection with the ordinary world" (225). While he shows the deductive logic by which the correspondence and coherence theories of truth connect metaphors to the larger semantic universe and the natural world, he does not explain what can bring the knowing subject to a metaphorical leap that may transform the epistemological basis of his knowledge.

[44] Percy, *Message in the Bottle,* 272. This argument for the referential capacity of metaphor is consistent with the argument by Black for the centrality of metaphor in scientific model building. Black, in presenting this argument, points back to the original Aristotelian problem:

> Certainly there is some similarity between the use of a model and the use of metaphor—perhaps we should say, of a sustained and systematic metaphor. And the crucial question about the autonomy of the method of models is paralleled by an ancient dispute about the translatability of metaphors. Those who see a model as a mere crutch are like those who consider metaphor a mere decoration or ornament. But there are powerful and irreplaceable uses of metaphor not adequately described by the old formula of 'saying one thing and meaning another.' (*Models and Metaphors* [see n. 7, above], 236)

Percy, by showing that the fundamental tension that gives rise to metaphors is not the tension stemming from dual reference, or dual signification, but the tension that arises between speaker and hearer from the naming of the new, suggests a way beyond the difficulties connected with the comparison view of metaphor represented by Ricoeur. When denotation is understood in this kind of intersubjective context it also becomes impossible to separate the rhetorical/emotive factor from the cognitive. In addition, by illuminating the intersubjective dimensions of metaphorical communication he shows how the referential instability implicit in Soskice's position can be overcome.

*   *   *

Percy did not relate his understanding of metaphor to the larger phenomena of literature and myth. The literary critic Northrop Frye, however, has developed an understanding of metaphor and its linkage with myth on the basis of assumptions about the nature of language that are quite similar to those of Percy. By examining Frye's views from Percy's semiotic perspective it will be possible to make some of Frye's often elusive concepts more clear and precise while connecting Percy's view of metaphor to the larger world of myth and literature.

Frye attempts, as Percy had done, to understand metaphor in terms of its role in the shaping of subjectivity. As a literary critic rather than a semiotician, Frye's views arise out of existential analysis and literary insight rather than language theory. Nevertheless there are some interesting points of convergence with Percy's semiotics. Percy's argument for the metaphorical character of Helen Keller's experience of language in her awakening to human subjectivity is paralleled by Frye's global view of language as metaphor. Just as Helen Keller's consciousness was awakened by the metaphorical event of naming water, Frye argues that consciousness is formed when language as a whole, functioning as a metaphor, enables it to extend outside of itself to unite with what it is conscious of.[45]

Most of his analyses of metaphor, however, deal with the existing subject. Here he is not interested in the classical problem of ambiguity, but with a metaphor's subjective effect. Frye, along with many other critics, sees the form of metaphor as a statement: "A typical metaphor takes the form of the statement 'A is B,' examples being found in Jacob's prophecy of the twelve tribes of Israel in Genesis 49, 'Joseph is a fruitful bough . . .'" (7). While this example is clearly a "trivial" type of metaphor that could be easily paraphrased, Frye is not interested in its semantic dimension, but rather in its effect on the subject. He sees in every metaphor an erosion of the bar-

---

[45] Northrop Frye, *Myth and Metaphor: Selected Essays 1974–1988* (ed. Robert D. Denham; 1990; repr., Charlottesville, N.C.: Univ. Press of Virginia, 1996) 114.

rier between subject and object on both the existential and semantic levels. To call Joseph a bough or a man a blockhead when it is obvious that, in proper usage, they are not, blurs the established distinction between the subject and object in a way that has an existential effect on both the giver and receiver of the metaphor. The metaphor "not merely identifies one thing with another in words, but something of ourselves with both: something of what we may tentatively call existential metaphor."[46]

Although Frye is not speaking here of the primal consciousness-creating situation, what transpires here might be understood in terms of the primal situation that Percy describes. Whereas for Percy the denotation of an object by means of a previously meaningless sound (mediated by another subject) establishes unformed consciousness as a subject, in subsequent metaphors this arrangement would be placed at risk. The metaphorical vehicle loosens or breaks its established semantic ties, and risks becoming a meaningless sound as it refers to a different object for the first time. This would have an effect upon subjectivity that has been formed by language. Frye can thus say that the metaphor has an "existential" effect on both the speaker and recipient because, in Percy's terms, it breaks down the relation between the word and its referent by which the subject acceded to its position as subject in relation to another subject. When the metaphor is understood, the subject reenters community with the recipient, though the subjectivity of both would have been altered, however incrementally, by this new communicative relation.

By ignoring the cognitive/semantic comparison that might be made between, e.g., Jacob and a fruitful bough, and emphasizing only the "existential" effect of unifying the metaphor with its referent, he is also treating this metaphor as if it were a catachresis. It is only a catachresis (of the second type) that totally dispenses with cognitive comparison, and relies entirely on the intersubjective context, as Percy has described it, to link the metaphor and its referent. One might say then that Frye is viewing all metaphors in terms quite similar to the subjective problematic of catachresis that Percy has brought to light. The primary difference is that Frye does not espouse the triadic/intersubjective perspective of Percy. Nevertheless, fundamental aspects of Frye's concept can be clarified by Percy's understanding of catachresis as the primal form of metaphor.

---

[46] Idem, *Words with Power: Being a Second Study of the Bible and Literature* (New York: Harcourt Brace Jovanovich, 1990) 75, 76. As noted above, Lacan, building on Freud, also is concerned with the effect of figurative language upon the formation of the subject, although for him it takes the form of the unconscious displacement and deflection of the primary processes. Frye instead focuses on the conscious effect metaphor has on the formation of the subject's identity. These two approaches are not necessarily in conflict.

It is identity-changing metaphors that seem to be the prototype for Frye's view. While ordinary metaphors may have a subjective effect, they do not substantially change the identity of the user. Frye, however, points to certain religious and literary metaphors that do entail an identity transformation. Acts of identification involving the fundamental effacement or transformation of the subject constitute the deepest religious experiences for Frye: "What a man's religion is may be gathered from what he wants to identify himself with . . ." (except for wholly self-interested ideas).[47] Here he supplements the existential concept with Heidegger's view of ecstasy, which he interprets linguistically as a metaphor of *standing outside* oneself.[48] Instead of blurring the denotative subject/object relation of a lexical term, however, this type of metaphor blurs the established boundaries of the identity of the subjective self as it metaphorically names the experience of being "outside" itself. The same "A is B" format is present, but the "A" now is the subject itself in its primary identity, and "B" is the new object/state with which it is identifying.

The religious identity transformation appears in a variety of forms, from the shaman's ecstatic experience of possession (81) to the Hindu mystic's declaration, "Thou art that."[49] Another example of this would be the ritual initiation in archaic tribal societies where the initiate abandons a childhood identity and is given a new identity, usually through the ritual enactment of some form of death/resurrection metaphor that integrates the youth into the world of adult myth.

These metaphors of ecstasy and identity transformation can be seen from the viewpoint of Percy's metaphor theory as recapitulating the subject's first entry into language at a secondary level by bringing about a transformation of the identity that was formed within that initial intersubjective context, and integrating the subject into a new community of meaning that bestows a new self-identity. Frye describes this general process as "the transfiguring of consciousness as it merges with articulated meaning" (115).

Such identity-transforming metaphors are located in the context of religious myth. Myth begins for Frye with the naming of the gods. For instance, the Roman god of the sea, Neptune, Frye terms a "prefabricated metaphor, i.e., it unites a personality and a natural object, and is the entering wedge of that union between subjective and objective worlds that all creative activity depends on" (16). From the name of the god develops a cult that honors the name, and a story that depicts his/her character and activities, i.e., the myth (115). As the gods are portrayed by poets who are

---

[47] Frye, *Myth and Metaphor*, 21.
[48] Frye, *Words with Power*, 82.
[49] Frye, *Myth and Metaphor*, 106.

in ecstatic states of inspiration, the myth emerges as the articulation of a new sacred reality that casts the existing world into the shadows of the profane. It rises above the profane temporal world as a timeless world of eternal presence that gathers both past and future into itself. Frye observes that just as metaphor abolishes space in its fusion of the metaphor and its referent, the myth abolishes time by creating what appears at each moment to be an unchanging world of presence (118). The modes of this presence may be different, however. The ancient creation myths reactualize the past in ritual, whereas the prophetic/apocalyptic myth makes the future present in faith ("the substance of the 'hoped for'") and hope (99).

The center of myth, however, is the blurring of the subject/object distinction in the ecstatic metaphor which he calls "directly experienced metaphor." In this metaphorical self-transformation the meaning of metaphor is extended into life. Frye regards these experiences as moments of "simultaneously grasped aspects of a *mythos* or continuous narrative" (17). Or you might say that the ecstatic metaphor is the inner synchronic form and meaning of the diachronic mythical story.

The myth generally provides not only a model of self-transformation, but also a visionary model for the life of the community to become or return to. By implicitly exposing the flaws and thus lack of ultimacy of the existing humanly constructed order, the fictional visionary model in its perfection becomes the "touchstone of reality." The present world is thereby defamiliarized and renewed as it is elevated into a new reality by its visionary metaphorical transformation in the myth.

In literature, Frye points out, we find a similar process at work: "Literary metaphor, which is purely hypothetical, grows out of an existential type of metaphor . . . where a subject does identify himself with something not himself . . ." (226). A frequent metaphor in literature that embodies this identification process is the journey (212–26).

A related literary expression that Frye classes as metaphor concerns the experience of altered identity seen in the testimony of writers and poets that their work is not a product only of their own subjectivity: Montaigne says, "I have no more made my book than my book has made me." Mallarmé even more dramatically asserts that his vision has developed, "through what used to be me." Frye finds in all these expressions a metaphorical "renunciation of egocentric or subjective identity."[50]

Utilizing Percy's views, one can thus say that literature and myth offer a secondary recapitulation, on a larger temporal or cosmic scale, of what has occurred at the foundations of language when the new world of signification was first opened to consciousness. By metaphorically defamiliar-

---

[50] Frye, *Words with Power*, 81.

izing the present world, literature and myth can bring about a renewal or re-formation of self-identity.

*   *   *

In conclusion, we have seen that the separation of the cognitive and affective dimensions of metaphor leads either to the subordination of ambiguous "metaphoric meaning" to dialectics, or to a view of the metaphorical referent as so singular and ambiguous as to make it impossible to explain how it could have any meaning at all. When, however, we view metaphorical tension as being not primarily tension between two verbal subjects nor between previously incongruent senses, but as intersubjective tension that arises from the fundamental uncertainty of linking any signifier to its referent in dialogue, it then becomes possible to see the problem of metaphor in a new light that brings about the resolution of these traditional problems. At the point of the primal communicative act, the affective and cognitive are inseparable. The primal word/metaphor (Percy) introduces language to consciousness, thereby simultaneously opening up both the intellectual, cognitive wonder of signification, and the transforming, emotional experience of human subjectivity as intersubjectivity (Percy, Bakhtin). It is this experience that metaphor reawakens, especially through its extended forms in poetry, myth and literature (Frye). Because of the catachretical way in which language functions in the formation of human consciousness, catachresis also plays a central role in philosophical discourse and scientific models (Soskice, Black, Lausberg). Rather than continuing to belabor the cognitive problem of metaphorical ambiguity, the challenge for both religion and philosophy is to understand more completely the intersubjective matrix of language that is concealed beneath this "mistake" of the catachretical metaphor.

Chapter 18

"The History of Saul's Rise": Saulide State Propaganda in 1 Samuel 1–14

Marsha White
Somerville, Massachusetts

Ever since Martin Noth set forth the theory that Deuteronomy–Kings is a coherent history, i.e. the work of a single historian,[1] the idea of a Deuteronomistic History comprising Deuteronomy–Kings has exercised considerable sway over the field of biblical studies. Modifications of his theory have since been made; a double redaction theory positing a historian of Josiah's reign and an editor or editors during the Exile is widely accepted in this country.[2] The basic tenet of this theory is that a historian of the late seventh century BCE brought together disparate narrative and legal sources for the first time and wrote a coherent history of Israel and Judah extending from Moses' farewell speech to the author's time, which was somehow and at some time fitted with the Priestly Tetrateuch.[3]

---

[1] Martin Noth, *Überlieferungsgeschichtliche Studien: Die sammelnden und bearbeitenden Geschichtswerke im alten Testament* (Tübingen: Max Niemeyer, 1943). ET: *The Deuteronomistic History* (JSOTSup 15; Sheffield: JSOT Press, 1981).

[2] The classic statement of this view is by Frank Moore Cross, Jr. ("The Themes of the Book of Kings and the Structure of the Deuteronomistic History," in *Canaanite Myth and Hebrew Epic* [Cambridge, Mass.: Harvard Univ. Press, 1973] 274–89). Cross's theory was developed by Richard D. Nelson (*The Double Redaction of the Deuteronomistic History* [JSOTSup 18; Sheffield: JSOT Press, 1981]) and Richard Elliott Friedman (*The Exile and Biblical Narrative: The Formation of the Deuteronomistic and Priestly Works* [HSM 22; Chico, Calif.: Scholars Press, 1981]), and was refined by Steven L. McKenzie (*The Trouble with Kings: The Composition of the Book of Kings in the Deuteronomistic History* [VTSup 42; Leiden: Brill, 1991]).

[3] The assumption of a strict bifurcation between a Priestly "Tetrateuch" (Genesis–Numbers) and a "Deuteronomistic History" consisting of Deuteronomy–Kings has recently been questioned, although a full treatment of the problem is beyond the scope of this study. Joseph Blenkinsopp has summarized the evidence for

According to the theory, the Deuteronomists' sources included the "Deuteronomic Lawcode" (Deuteronomy 12–26), the "Ark Narrative" (1 Samuel 4–6), the "History of David's Rise" (1 Samuel 15–2 Samuel 8), and "Solomon's Succession Narrative" (2 Samuel 9–20, 1 Kings 1–2), among others.[4] Many scholars regard a loose "Saul Cycle" (popular legends behind 1 Sam 9:1–10:16; 11:1–15; 13:2–14:48) as a source used by the Deuteronomists,[5] based on the assumption that Israelite history-writing began no earlier than David or Solomon, and possibly as late as the Deuteronomists.[6] That is, the post-Noth assumption that Israelite historiography began no earlier

---

Deuteronomistic passages in Genesis, Exodus, and Numbers in *The Pentateuch: An Introduction to the First Five Books of the Bible* (New York: Doubleday, 1992) 33–37, 50–51, 122–26, 186–94, 206–209; and Richard Elliott Friedman has found evidence of J as Solomon's historian from Genesis 2 to 1 Kings 2 (*The Hidden Book in the Bible: The Discovery of the First Prose Masterpiece* [San Francisco: Harper, 1998] 3–56). This study is part of a larger argument for a seventh–sixth century BCE Deuteronomistic editing of a tenth-century Solomonic comprehensive history extending from the origins of the world (Gen 2:4b–3:24) to the climax of Solomon's reign (1 Kgs 10:23–25). I agree with Friedman that Solomon's historian was the one who brought together disparate sources to form the first comprehensive history. However, I think that one of those sources was a continuous royal history of Saul's rise, David's rise, David's suppression of two revolts, and Solomon's succession (1 Sam 1:1–2 Sam 20:26; 1 Kgs 1:1–2:46) that their historians had composed to secure their thrones. That is, first Saul's historian composed a document that formed the foundation of 1 Sam 1:1–14:48 (see below), to which David's historian added the "History of David's Rise" (1 Sam 10:8; 13:7b–15a; 14:49–2 Sam 8:18; see below), to which the same historian appended a "Revolt Narrative" (2 Sam 9:1–13; 13:1–20:26), to which Solomon's historian added the "Succession Narrative" (2 Sam 10:1–12:31; 1 Kgs 1:1–2:46).

[4] For a review of the scholarship on the Samuel sources, see P. Kyle McCarter Jr., *I Samuel: A New Translation With Introduction, Notes & Commentary* (AB 8; Garden City, N.Y.: Doubleday, 1980) 12–30; and idem, *II Samuel: A New Translation With Introduction, Notes and Commentary* (AB 9; Garden City, N.Y.: Doubleday, 1984) 4–16.

[5] McCarter, *I Samuel*, 26–27.

[6] Gerhard von Rad's position that Israelite historiography began with the late tenth-century "Solomonic Enlightenment" was generally accepted a generation ago ("The Beginnings of Historical Writing in Ancient Israel" [1944], in *The Problem of the Hexateuch and Other Essays* [trans. E. W. Dicken; London: Oliver and Boyd, 1966] 166–204). McCarter then made a strong argument for dating the "History of David's Rise" to David's reign ("The Apology of David," *JBL* 99 [1980] 489–504), based on its character as royal apologetic literature. In reaction to generalized early dating, John Van Seters argued for the beginnings of Israelite historiography in the sixth century BCE (*In Search of History: Historiography in the Ancient World and the Origins of Biblical History* [New Haven: Yale Univ. Press, 1983]; *Prologue to History: The Yahwist as Historian in Genesis* [Louisville, Ky.: Westminster/ John Knox, 1992]; *The Life of Moses: The Yahwist as Historian in Exodus–Numbers* [Louisville, Ky.: Westminster/John Knox, 1994]).

than David has precluded consideration of a possible coherent Saul history, and has relegated the above-mentioned Saul texts to the character of a "loose cycle" of "popular legends."

The question considered herein is the nature of the Saul source: its literary coherence or lack thereof, its popular or royal origins, its purpose, and its date. In anticipation of the conclusion, I hope to demonstrate that the Saul source was a fixed document (written or oral or both) that was composed by Saul's historian(s) in defense of his kingship. Forming the basis of what eventually became 1 Samuel 1–14, the Saul history was an *apologia* for Saul's kingship in the form of an account of the Elides' sin and judgment juxtaposed with Saul's piety and divinely ordained rise to the throne. It accounted for both Saul's unprecedented assumption of kingship and his slaughter of the Elide priesthood (cf. 1 Samuel 22). Incorporating the preexisting "Ark Narrative" (1 Samuel 4–6), Saul's history told the story of the Elide demise and Saul's rise in seven coherent and interlocking scenes. The addition of the "History of David's Rise" and later interpolation of Deuteronomistic commentary created a new text with profoundly altered meaning.

In looking for a possible Saul source, the obvious place to begin is the chapters concerning Saul and the inauguration of the monarchy (1 Samuel 7–14). The classic "two-source theory," as formulated by Wellhausen and his followers, postulated two coherent narrative sources that had been conflated: an early "pro-monarchic source" (1 Sam 9:1–10:16; 11:1–11, 15; 13:2–7a; 13:15b–14:48) and a later "anti-monarchic source" (1 Sam 7:2–8:22; 10:17–27a; 12:1–25).[7] The theory was later discredited, largely due to the equation with the J and E sources made by some of its advocates at a time when J and E were believed by most to be confined to the Pentateuch.[8] It was further undermined by Noth's widely-accepted identification of the "anti-monarchic source" with the Deuteronomist, which in turn gave force to his belief that the "pro-monarchic source" consisted of discrete traditions that were not brought together until the Deuteronomist wrote his history.

The influence of these criticisms and of Noth's historiographic analysis has obscured the coherence of the so-called "pro-monarchic" source. Shorn of the so-called "anti-monarchic" passages together with two anti-Saul

---

[7] For reviews of scholarship, see F. Langlamet, "Les récits de l'institution de la royauté (I Sam VII–XII): De Wellhausen aux travaux récents," *RB* 77 (1970) 161–200, and Bruce C. Birch, *The Rise of the Israelite Monarchy: The Growth and Development of I Samuel 7–15* (SBLDS 27; Missoula, Mont.: Scholars Press, 1976) 1–10.

[8] Those who advanced an equation between the "pro-monarchic" and "anti-monarchic" sources of 1 Samuel 7–14 and the Pentateuchal sources J and E included Karl Budde, *Die Bücher Richter und Samuel, Ihre Quellen und ihr Aufbau* (Tübingen: J. C. B. Mohr, 1890); and Otto Eissfeldt, "Noch einmal: Text-, Stil- und Literarkritik in den Samuelisbüchern," *Orientalistische Literaturzeitung* 31 (1928) col. 801–12; idem, *Die Komposition der Samuelisbücher* (Leipzig: J. C. Hinrichs, 1931).

and pro-David passages (1 Sam 10:8; 13:7b–15a),[9] a pro-Saul story line emerges that coheres and moves logically from segment to segment. It consists of the following three "scenes":

1. Saul is introduced. His apparently random search for his father's lost donkeys providentially leads him to the priest and prophet Samuel. As priest, Samuel seats Saul at the head of the sacrificial table, gives him the specially consecrated portion, and alludes to his future kingship over Israel. Then, as prophet, Samuel anoints Saul נגיד, "king-elect," charging him with the future muster of all Israel and deliverance of them from all their enemies.[10] The exact fulfillment of an elaborate threefold sign, the third aspect of which is Saul's seizure by the spirit of Yahweh, confirms the secret

---

[9] See below.

[10] Reading the LXX of 1 Sam 10:1:

> Then, taking a vial of oil Samuel poured it over his head, kissed him, and said, 'Has not Yahweh anointed you crown prince over his people Israel? It is you who will muster the people of Yahweh! It is you who will deliver them from the grip of their enemies all around! And this will be the sign for you that Yahweh has anointed you crown prince over his estate: . . .'

McCarter rightly points out that the "MT has lost everything between הלוא ["has not"] and כי ["that"] owing to haplography triggered by the repeated sequence (משחך יהוה לנגיד) ["Yahweh has anointed you crown prince"]" (*I Samuel*, 171).

All pre-Deuteronomistic uses of נגיד should be translated "crown prince," "designated successor," "future king." The following is a complete list: Saul in 1 Sam 9:16, 10:1 (LXX, twice) (Saul's History); David in 1 Sam 13:14 ("History of David's Rise"); and Solomon in 1 Kgs 1:35 ("Solomon's Succession Narrative"). Because Saul was the first king and therefore lacked the prerequisite designation as crown prince by his father, he is designated נגיד, "crown prince," by Yahweh through Samuel (1 Sam 9:16, 10:1 [LXX]) before he is actually made king by the army (1 Sam 11:15). David's history then employs the same prophet to reject Saul's kingship and appoint David as נגיד, "future king," at the beginning of the history (1 Sam 13:14), whereas he does not actually assume the kingship over Judah until 2 Sam 2:4 and over Israel until 2 Sam 5:3. In both cases, their appointments are secret or private and precede their public accessions to the throne. Because Solomon's father was on the throne but the succession was either in doubt or going to Adonijah, Solomon's history takes pains to demonstrate that David did indeed designate Solomon in a ritual and formal manner, even if the designation was obtained through trickery (cf. Isaac's blessing of Jacob, Genesis 27).

The Deuteronomistic passages containing נגיד show a semantic shift, translatable as "divinely ordained ruler." These are: the Deuteronomistic expansion of Abigail's speech to David (1 Sam 25:28–31; see 25:30b), of the kingship treaty that David made with the elders of Israel at Hebron (2 Sam 5:1–2; see 5:2b), of David's retort to Michal (2 Sam 6:21a), and of Nathan's oracle to David (2 Sam 7:8–16; see 7:8b); the Deuteronomistic prophecy to Jeroboam through Ahijah (1 Kgs 14:1–18; see 14:7b) and to Baasha through Jehu son of Hanani (1 Kgs 16:1–4; see 16:2a); and the Deuteronomistic phrase modifying "Hezekiah" (2 Kgs 20:5a [contrast its absence from the

appointment, and Samuel tells Saul to act when he sees fit (1 Sam 9:1–8; 9:10–10:7, 9–10, 13–16[11]).

2. Nahash the Ammonite's cruel oppression of Jabesh-gilead for harboring the escaped Gadites and Reubenites rouses Saul's dormant vocation as musterer and deliverer of Israel. Seized by Yahweh's spirit, he musters all Israel and delivers the city from the Ammonite enemy. As a result of his divinely inspired military success, the army makes him king (1 Sam 10:27b [4QSam[a]]–11:11, 15[12]).

---

parallel passage in Isa 38:5]). According to the Josianic Deuteronomist, David was the divinely ordained ruler and dynastic founder par excellence and the model for all subsequent rulers and founders of dynasties, both Israelite and Judahite.

[11] For a discussion of 1 Sam 9:9, see McCarter, *I Samuel*, 169, 177. 1 Sam 10:8 leads into the interpolated anti-Saul and pro-David passage of 1 Sam 13:7b–15a, and so was introduced by the same author (see below).

The etiology of the proverb about Saul among the prophets (1 Sam 10:11–12) is secondary. There is a repetitive resumption that marks the interpolation: ויכל מהתנבות, "when he had finished prophesying" (1 Sam 10:13a), repeats ויתנבא בתוכם, "and he prophesied in their midst" (1 Sam 10:10bB), after which the original narrative resumes with ויבא הביתה, "and he went home" (1 Sam 10:13b; conjectural emendation by McCarter, *I Samuel*, 172, following Wellhausen). Without the interpolation the narrative reads, ויתנבא בתוכם ויבא הביתה, "and he prophesied in their midst and went home." The secondary character of the etiology is clear because it bears no relation to Saul's appointment to future kingship, around which the rest of the scene is tightly structured.

[12] 4QSam[a] includes a lengthy introduction to the scene that provides the necessary background to Nahash's attack on Jabesh-gilead, and is supported by Josephus. The text as reconstructed by McCarter reads:

[ונ]חש מלך בני עמון הוא לחץ את בני גד ואת בני ראובן בחזקה ונקר להם כו[ל עי]ן ימין ונתן אי[ן
מושי]ע ל[י]שראל ולוא נשאר איש בבני ישראל עשר בע[בר הירד]ר אש[ר ל]וא נ[קר לו נח[ש מלך]
בני [ע]מון כול עין ימין ו[ה]ן שבעת אלפים איש [נצלו מיד] בני עמון ויבאו אל יבש גלעד ויהי כמו
חדש

> Now Nahash, the king of the Ammonites, had been oppressing the Gadites and the Reubenites grievously, gouging out the right eye of each of them and allowing Israel no deliverer. No men of the Israelites who were across the Jordan remained whose right eye Nahash, king of the Ammonites, had not gouged out, but seven thousand men had escaped from the Ammonites and entered into Jabesh-Gilead. About a month later . . .

The last phrase, כמו חדש, "about a month later," also appears in the LXX, which supports the 4QSam[a] reading. See T. Eves, "One Ammonite Invasion or Two? I Sam 10:27–11:2 in the Light of 4QSam[a]," *WTJ* 44 (1982) 306–26, and Frank M. Cross, "The Ammonite Oppression of the Tribes of Gad and Reuben: Missing Verses from I Samuel 11 Found in 4QSamuel[a]," in *History, Historiography and Interpretation: Studies in Biblical and Cuneiform Literatures* (ed. H. Tadmor and M. Weinfeld; 1983; Jerusalem: Magnes, 1986) 148–58. McCarter rightly includes this introduction in his text (*I Samuel*, 199–200).

I omit ואחר שמואל, "and after Samuel" (1 Sam 11:7), on the basis of Samuel's

3. Jonathan incites the Philistine enemy by killing their prefect at Gibeah.[13] Saul musters the army, but most hide or flee when they see the overwhelming Philistine force. Jonathan begins the Battle of Michmash by single-handedly killing the men of a Philistine outpost. With the spread of the battle into the Ephraimite hills, Saul imposes an oath on the army prohibiting the eating of any food until sundown and Yahweh's victory. Jonathan unknowingly violates the oath when he finds some honey. After the victory, the army's hunger drives them to eat the meat of the captured animals with the blood, but Saul stops them and improvises an altar for their proper sacrifices. When Saul's use of the lot exposes Jonathan's sin, Saul is ready to have him put to death in accordance with the oath. He is stopped by the army, who call attention to Yahweh's deliverance through Jonathan and act as a *deus ex machina*[14] (1 Sam 13:2–7a, 15b–20; 13:22–14:46[15]).

---

absence from military action otherwise in this scene. All the subsequent verbs describing Saul's actions in 1 Sam 11:8–11 are in the singular, leaving no room for shared military leadership. See Henry Preserved Smith, *A Critical and Exegetical Commentary on the Books of Samuel* (Edinburgh: T. & T. Clark, 1899) 78; McCarter, *I Samuel*, 203; and Ralph Klein, *I Samuel* (WBC 10; Waco, Tex.: Word Books, 1983) 104. Also, the reference to Judah at 1 Sam 11:8 is anachronistic, since Judah did not become a separate entity until its secession from Israel under David.

Saul's amnesty to the worthless men and Samuel's exhortation to the people to "renew" (ונחדש) the kingship at 1 Sam 11:12–14 is a later interpolation, probably Deuteronomistic, that harmonizes the original inauguration of Saul (1 Sam 11:15) with Dtr's alternative and pejorative inauguration (1 Sam 10:17–27a). See Julius Wellhausen, *Prolegomena to the History of Ancient Israel* (Cleveland: World Publishing, 1957 [German original: 1878]) 250; Smith, *Samuel*, 80; and Klein, *I Samuel*, 104. See below for a discussion of the Deuteronomistic additions to 1 Samuel 7–12.

[13] Reading גבעה, "Gibeah," for גבע, "Geba," with McCarter, *I Samuel*, 225.

[14] Cf. the sudden appearance of the ram in the thicket on Mount Moriah, which saves Abraham from having to sacrifice Isaac in obedience to Yahweh's command (Gen 22:13).

[15] At 1 Sam 13:1, the Deuteronomist supplied a regnal formula for Saul that fits him into the history of kings. The obvious problems with this passage are treated in the commentaries, and are beyond the scope of this paper. See below for a discussion of Yahweh's rejection of Saul's kingship as mediated by Samuel (1 Sam 10:8; 13:7b–15a).

1 Sam 13:21, the specification of the prices that the Philistines charged the Israelites for the repair of their farm implements, is most likely a later interpolation, since it interrupts the narrative and has no function in the story line. It was probably added by the Priestly writer, given P's interest in precision as exhibited in Priestly passages throughout the Bible. P's presence elsewhere in the "Deuteronomistic History" can be seen in, e.g., Joshua 18–19 (Blenkinsopp, *Pentateuch*, 237–38).

At 1 Sam 14:24a I accept the emendation, וידור שאול נדר ביום ההוא ויאל שאול את העם, "Saul vowed a vow on that day and adjured the army," that was proposed by Kosterman, adopted by Budde, and advanced by Smith (Smith, *Samuel*, 114–15,

The final scene demonstrates Saul's piety in the context of battle, which is necessary for Israelite victory in Yahweh's war.[16] He imposes an oath of fasting on the army, stops them from sinning by eating the meat with the blood, and is prepared to sacrifice his beloved son in accordance with his oath.[17] Only Saul's piety is complete, as opposed to the partial piety of both

117–18). Both the MT and the LXX for 1 Sam 14:23b–24a are problematic. The MT reads ויאיש־ישראל נגש, "the men of Israel were distressed," which employs the same verb that described their state of mind before the battle when they saw the massed Philistine troops and realized that they were in trouble (1 Sam 13:6a). It is unlikely that they still felt distressed immediately after their overwhelming victory (1 Sam 14:20–23a). The LXX, on the other hand, reads "And all the troops, about 10,000 men, were with Saul; and the battle spread into the hill country of Ephraim. Now Saul committed a grievous error that day." This reading is to be adopted up to and including "into the hill country of Ephraim" because it provides the context of continued fighting that explains the need for Saul's imposition of an oath of fasting on the army. However, the description of this oath as a "grievous error" is difficult because the imposition of an oath of fasting during Yahweh's war would normally be considered an act of piety, making it clear that the victory belongs to Yahweh alone.

Smith's argument for the emendation is based on the narrative context, which consists of a decisive Israelite victory at Michmash (1 Sam 14:20–23a) followed by scattered fighting in the Ephraimite hills (1 Sam 14:23bA [LXX]) that Saul determines to end through the imposition of a pious curse on anyone who eats before evening and before he has avenged his (i.e. Yahweh's) enemies (1 Sam 14:24b). Since the emendation is conjectural, the MT and LXX variants must be explained, which Smith and his predecessors failed to do. Neither variant (MT: ויאיש ישראל נגש, "the men of Israel were distressed"; LXX: "Now Saul committed a grievous error that day") can be accounted for by aural or visual scribal errors. It appears that both were created deliberately to make Saul look bad, although independently of each other, which can only be explained by the text's subsequent history. When David's historian added the "History of David's Rise" to Saul's history (see below), he framed the originally pro-Saul account of the Battle of Michmash (1 Sam 13:15b–14:46) with two scenes of Yahweh revoking Saul's kingship based on his disobedience (1 Sam 13:7b–15a; 15:1–35). The framing of the original story of Saul's piety and success in battle by his disobedience and Yahweh's rejection of his kingship caused the framed account to take on a pejorative cast. The framing was thus an intentional strategy by David's historian that created a new text in which no sooner was Saul made king (1 Sam 11:15) and the Philistines massed for battle (1 Sam 13:2–7a; 1 Sam 12:1–25 and 13:1 are later Deuteronomistic interpolations) than his kingship was rejected (1 Sam 13:7b–15a). The originally pro-Saul battle account was then vulnerable to textual alterations, such as the MT and LXX variants, that significantly changed its meaning.

[16] See the theory of "holy war" proposed by Gerhard von Rad in his *Holy War in Ancient Israel* (trans. Marva J. Dawn from *Der Heilige Krieg im alten Israel*, 1958; Grand Rapids, Mich.: Eerdmans, 1991), 41–51.

[17] For a comparison to Saul's willingness to sacrifice his son in obedience to Yahweh, see Abraham's test in the Akedah (Genesis 22). In each case the obedience

the army and Jonathan. The army observes the fast and fights bravely, but pounces on the spoil and neglects proper sacrificial procedure. Jonathan kills both the Philistine prefect at Gibeah and the men of a Philistine outpost through Yahweh's inspiration, but he unwittingly breaks Saul's oath. Saul, on the other hand, rectifies or is prepared to rectify both the army's and Jonathan's trespasses, at any cost to himself.

Finally, a conclusion (1 Sam 14:47-48) summarizes Saul's conquests of the surrounding nations and his powerful deliverance of Israel from all their enemies, which fulfills his commission (1 Sam 9:16; 10:1 [LXX]). This summary brings the history to a close, and asserts the benefit of his kingship to the nation.

The story line in these three scenes is continuous and consistent. It tells of Saul's divine appointment to future military kingship (the first scene); his initial military success while gripped by Yahweh's spirit, after which the army makes him king (the second scene); and his decisive victory as military king[18] over the Philistines in accordance with his divine appointment, popular election, and perfect piety (the third scene).[19] Since the narrative argues for both the divine and popular election of Saul as king and

---

of the hero is the point and not the sacrifice itself, as is clear by the prevention of what would have been disastrous events by arbitrary outside forces.

[18] The parenthetical description of Saul's position at the time of Jonathan's attack on the Philistine outpost (1 Sam 14:2–3a) indicates his established military leadership over all Israel. It reads: "Saul was sitting enthroned on the outskirts of Geba under the pomegranate tree which was at the threshing floor, and with him were about six hundred men, and Ahijah the son of Ahitub the brother of Ichabod the son of Phinehas the son of Eli, the priest of Yahweh at Shiloh who was bearing the Ark" (translation based on McCarter's reconstructed text [*I Samuel*, 235] and reading אָרוֹן, "the Ark," for אֵפוֹד, "the ephod," with Karel van der Toorn and Cees Houtman ["David and the Ark," *JBL* 113 (1994) 209–31]). His position sitting under the pomegranate tree on the threshing floor implies sacral leadership, and the presence of the Shilonite priest descended from Eli and bearing the Ark implies Saul's sole leadership. In other words, this authorial aside shows that the scene presumes the previous scene in which Saul came to the attention of all Israel and was made king.

[19] Baruch Halpern (*The Constitution of the Monarchy in Israel* [HSM 25; Chico, Calif.: Scholars Press, 1981] 51–148) and Diana Edelman ("Saul's Rescue of Jabesh-Gilead [I Sam 11:1–11]: Sorting Story from History," *ZAW* 96 [1984] 198–99; *King Saul in the Historiography of Judah* [JSOTSup 121; Sheffield: Sheffield Academic Press, 1991] 30–32) have argued for a three-part kingship installation ceremony common to Israel and the ancient Near East, consisting of designation, testing, and coronation, and modeled on the Ugaritic Baal vs. Yamm myth, among other myths. Edelman sees this ceremony reflected in 1 Sam 9:1–11:15, where יְחִי הַמֶּלֶךְ, "long live the king" (1 Sam 10:24), is the designation and וּנְחַדֵּשׁ means "let us inaugurate" (1 Sam 11:14). This analysis is problematic, however. First, it confuses myth with ritual; mythic texts are not necessarily accompanied by ritual actions. Second, even if

for the complete success of his military kingship, we expect the story to have a beginning and an ending. We are not disappointed: Saul is introduced in 1 Sam 9:1–2 and his charge to deliver Israel from all their enemies, which is the focus of the investiture (1 Sam 9:1–10:16), is cited as completely fulfilled in the conclusion (1 Sam 14:47–48).

It would appear, then, that there was a fixed narrative Saul source or "document" (written or oral or both), as opposed to a loose collection of fluid popular legends, and that this "document" consisted of at least the above-mentioned scenes in that order. The alternative to a fixed document is an extensive Deuteronomistic re-writing of a collection of legends that transformed them into the present narrative of 1 Sam 9:1–14:48.[20] However, the Deuteronomistic additions do not link and harmonize otherwise disparate stories, but rather introduce contradictions and difficulties into a perfectly unified story.[21]

In addition, there is no identifiable Deuteronomistic rhetoric in the pro-Saul narrative, whereas the Deuteronomistic passages are saturated with Deuteronomistic vocabulary.[22] Rather, the pro-Saul narrative is characterized by terse prose and is free of the Deuteronomistic advocacy of fidelity to Yahweh alone combined with threats of punishment to those who

---

1 Sam 10:17–27a, a Deuteronomistic interpolation, is excluded from the three-part installation pattern, Saul's defeat of the Ammonites (1 Sam 10:27b [4QSam[a]]–11:11) is not a test of his personal abilities. His latent and God-given vocation as Israel's musterer and deliverer (cf. 1 Sam 10:1 [LXX]) is roused when he hears the news from Jabesh-gilead, and he defeats the Ammonites by Yahweh's inspiration.

[20] For such an argument, see Steven L. McKenzie, "Cette Royauté Qui Fait Problème" (trans. Jean-Daniel Macchi), in *Israël Construit Son Histoire: L'historio-graphie Deutéronomiste à la lumière des Recherches Récentes* (ed. Albert de Pury, Thomas Römer, and Jean-Daniel Macchi; Le Monde de la Bible 34; Genève: Labor et Fides, 1995) 267–95.

[21] These additions are 1 Sam 7:2–8:22; 10:17–27a; 11:12–14; 12:1–25; and 13:1. (See Wellhausen, *Prolegomena*, 245–56, and Noth *Deuteronomistic History*, 47–52, for the classic identification of these passages as Deuteronomistic.) The most obvious difficulty is the presence of a second and pejorative inauguration account (1 Sam 10:17–27a). This account is both redundant with the preexisting divine designation (1 Sam 9:1–10:16) and popular election (1 Sam 11:15), and presents the new king in a bad light. The choice by lot implies guilt, since in all other texts where someone is taken by lot, that person is guilty of an offense: cf. Achan (Joshua 7), Jonah (1:7), and Jonathan (1 Sam 14:37–44). See McCarter, *I Samuel*, 195–96. Also, Saul's hiding among the baggage hardly augurs well for the courage needed by a warrior-king.

[22] Contra McKenzie, "Cette Royauté," 267–95. Examples of Deuteronomistic phrases in the Deuteronomistic passages are: וַיַּעַזְבֻנִי וַיַּעַבְדוּ אֱלֹהִים אֲחֵרִים, "forsaking Me and worshiping other gods" (1 Sam 8:8; cf. 1 Sam 7:3); עֲזַבְנוּ אֶת־יהוה וַנַּעֲבֹד אֶת־הַבְּעָלִים וְאֶת־הָעַשְׁתָּרוֹת, "we have forsaken Yahweh and worshiped the Baalim and the Ashtaroth" (1 Sam 12:10; cf. I Sam 7:3–4); תֹּהוּ, "worthless things" (1 Sam 12:21); עֲבֹד אֶת יהוה, "to serve Yahweh" (1 Sam 7:3; 12:14, 20, 24); יְרָא אֶת יהוה, "to fear Yahweh"

worship foreign gods or worship at places other than the temple in Jerusalem.[23] That is, the terse narrative that is free of Deuteronomistic language and ideology is also characterized by a pro-Saul stance, whereas the Deuteronomistic passages are either anti-Saul (1 Sam 10:17–27a) or anti-kingship (1 Sam 7:2–8:22; 12:1–25). The most reasonable explanation for this pattern is not that a Deuteronomist brought together originally independent positive stories about Saul's kingship and placed them in a remarkably logical order. Rather, a coherent positive history of Saul preexisted negative Deuteronomistic commentary on Saul and the kingship.

There is more involved, however, than a preexisting history of Saul with Deuteronomistic editorial commentary. Disregarding two short and inconsequential additions (1 Sam 10:11–12; 13:21),[24] the text exhibits a three-way split between the coherent pro-Saul narrative delineated above, two anti-Saul and pro-David additions (1 Sam 10:8; 13:7b–15a), and the "anti-monarchic" passages recognized by Wellhausen and Noth. The issue in the pro-Saul narrative and anti-Saul/pro-David additions is who is to be king, with both assuming the institution of kingship.[25] Only in the "anti-monarchy" passages is the issue that of the validity, necessity, and benefit of kingship as an institution.[26]

The two anti-Saul/pro-David additions build on the pro-Saul narrative of the establishment of Saul's kingship, but oppose the choice of Saul in

---

(1 Sam 12:14, 24); בכל לבב, "with all the heart" (1 Sam 7:3; 12:20, 24); סור, "to turn away" in the sense of apostasy (1 Sam 12:21); סור מאחרי יהוה, "to turn away from Yahweh" (1 Sam 12:20); and מיום העלתי אתם ממצרים ועד היום הזה, "ever since I brought them out of Egypt to this day" (1 Sam 8:8). See Samuel R. Driver, *An Introduction to the Literature of the Old Testament* (1898; Gloucester: Peter Smith, 1972) 99–102, and Moshe Weinfeld, *Deuteronomy and the Deuteronomic School* (1972; Winona Lake, Ind.: Eisenbrauns, 1992) 320–65, for lists of Deuteronomistic vocabulary.

[23] Samuel conducts a sacrifice at a במה, "shrine" (1 Sam 9:12–25), and Saul is lauded for building a מזבח, "altar," that is the first of many altars (1 Sam 14:31–35). Neither figure is castigated for these very un-Deuteronomistic actions, which indicates pre-Deuteronomistic authorship of both scenes.

[24] See above, nn. 11 and 15.

[25] See 1 Sam 10:1 (LXX), as noted above. The text emphasizes the choice of Saul over all other candidates for the kingship in its repeated use of "and you," preceding the phrases "will muster the people of Yahweh" and "will save them from the grip of their enemies round about" (McCarter, *I Samuel*, 171).

[26] It is difficult to imagine that such self-conscious doubts about the viability of kingship could have arisen at any time during the monarchy, even at its inception (*contra* Frank Cross, *Canaanite Myth and Hebrew Epic*, 219–29). Dynastic kingship was too broadly assumed throughout the ancient Near East for the institution to be questioned. Also, any royal scribe so writing would surely lose his job. Rather, the questioning of kingship along with the location of the assembly at Mizpah (1 Sam 7:5–11; 10:17), the seat of the Judean government immediately after the destruction

favor of David.[27] The attitude of anti-Saul and pro-David while assuming the necessity and validity of dynastic kingship is characteristic only of the "History of David's Rise" (1 Sam 10:8; 13:7b–15a; 14:49–2 Sam 8:15), which was composed to legitimate David's usurpation of the throne and his assassination of the Saulides.[28] The primary anti-Saul passage (1 Sam 13:7b–15a) combines Yahweh's rejection of Saul's kingship with an allusion to the choice of David (1 Sam 13:14), similar to the rejection of Saul and allusion to the choice of David in 1 Samuel 15 (see especially 1 Sam 15:28).[29]

These two rejection scenes clearly serve the interests of the "History of David's Rise," which is to be dated to David's reign.[30] The first rejection scene (1 Sam 10:8; 13:7b–15a) is interpolated into Saul's history and functions as a "hook" that ties the appended Davidic history onto the preexisting Saul history. In both rejection scenes, together with the rest of

---

of Jerusalem (2 Kgs 25:22–25), identify the author as a Deuteronomist writing early in the exile (P. Kyle McCarter Jr., "The Books of Samuel," in *The History of Israel's Traditions: The Heritage of Martin Noth,* [ed. Steven L. McKenzie and M. Patrick Graham; JSOTSup 182; Sheffield: Sheffield Academic Press, 1994] 278–80; Steven L. McKenzie, "Cette Royauté," 292–95; idem, "Mizpah of Benjamin and the Date of the Deuteronomistic History," in *"Lasset uns Brücken bauen . . .": Collected Communications to the XVth Congress of the International Organization for the Study of the Old Testament, Cambridge 1995* [ed. Klaus-Dietrich Schunck and Matthias Augustin; BEATAJ 42; Frankfurt: Peter Lang, 1998] 149–55). The writer apparently doubted the benefit of the institution after looking back on a long history of kings that led both nations to destruction and exile.

[27] Samuel's stern command to Saul at 1 Sam 10:8 to go to Gilgal and wait there seven days for him to come and sacrifice carries an abrupt shift in tone from the preceding appointment to kingship and bestowal of God's blessing (Wellhausen, *Prolegomena,* 258). The command sets up the rejection of Saul's kingship that follows in 1 Sam 13:7b–15a.

[28] See McCarter, "The Apology of David," *JBL* 99 (1980) 489–504; James C. VanderKam, "Davidic Complicity in the Deaths of Abner and Eshbaal: A Historical and Redactional Study," *JBL* 99 (1980) 521–39; Keith Whitelam, "The Defence of David," *JSOT* 29 (1984) 61–87; and Marc Zvi Brettler, *The Creation of History in Ancient Israel* (London/New York: Routledge, 1995) 91–111.

[29] See J. Groenbaeck, *Die Geschichte vom Aufstieg Davids (1. Sam. 15–2. Sam. 5): Tradition und Komposition* (ATDan 10; Copenhagen: Munksgaard, 1971) 25–29, 37–76, 261–62, and Tryggve Mettinger, *King and Messiah: The Civil and Sacral Legitimation of the Israelite Kings* (Coniectanea Biblica, OT Series 8; Lund: Gleerup, 1976) 33–35, for the argument that the "History of David's Rise" begins with the rejection of Saul's kingship (1 Samuel 15) and not the anointing of David (1 Samuel 16).

[30] McCarter ("The Apology of David," 493–504) argues convincingly that the multiple charges that David's history seeks to refute only make sense during David's reign, when his kingship was insecure and he needed the support of state propaganda.

David's history, the characters of Saul and Samuel are assumed. Also, the story of Saul at the beginning of David's history picks up where it left off at the end of Saul's history. This literary structure requires not only the pre-existence of the Saul history, but its use as the foundation for the Davidic history.

The "History of David's Rise," then, never existed as an independent composition, i.e., as one of the purportedly autonomous sources used by the Deuteronomist. Rather, it was composed as an extended update of Saul's story and introduction of David, and was created to be attached to Saul's history. The purpose of David's history, as attached to Saul's history, was both to draw on the establishment of kingship (1 Sam 9:1–10:16; 10:27b [4QSam^a]–11:11, 15) and to overturn the choice of the dynasty. David's history accomplished these aims by framing Saul's overwhelming success against the Philistines (1 Sam 13:15b–14:46) with Yahweh's rejection of his kingship (1 Sam 13:7b–15a; 15:1–35) and by the sheer bulk of the anti-Saul and pro-David story, which ends with Saul's ignominious death at the hands of the Philistines (1 Samuel 31) in contrast to David's defeat of the Philistines together with all Israel's enemies (2 Sam 8:1–15; cf. Saul in 1 Sam 14:47–48).

Other considerations also dictate that the Davidic history was composed in response to the Saul history; in particular, Davidic passages that answer directly to passages in Saul's history. These include:

1. The location of Saul's rejection at Gilgal in 1 Sam 13:7b-15a, which is geographically awkward.[31] The Davidic history was primarily appended to Saul's history, but also attached by means of this interpolation. According to the resulting larger Davidic history, no sooner is Saul appointed future king (1 Sam 9:1-10:16) and inaugurated (1 Sam 11:15) than Yahweh, speaking through Samuel, rejects his kingship in favor of David. At the stage of the addition of David's history to Saul's history, the Deuteronomistic interpolations had not yet entered the text. Therefore, in the larger Davidic history Saul's inauguration (1 Sam 11:15) was followed almost immediately by Yahweh's rejection of his kingship (1 Sam 13:7b-15a). The only text between Saul's inauguration and the rejection of his kingship was the mustering of Israel and the Philistines for battle at Geba and Michmash, respectively (1 Sam 13:2-7a).

Yahweh's rejection of Saul's kingship fittingly takes place at Gilgal, the shrine where Saul had been inaugurated in the pre-Deuteronomistic text (1 Sam 11:15). However, Saul's trip to Gilgal is exceedingly awkward both geographically and militarily, since it forces him to leave the army that he had just mustered at Geba in central Benjamin and travel alone to the Jor-

---

[31] Wellhausen, *Prolegomena*, 257.

dan River Valley. The awkwardness of Saul's trip shows its secondary character, but it also shows that the passage was interpolated for the purpose of placing the rejection of his kingship at the location of the institution of his kingship. The awkwardness of Saul's trip is what accounts for the corruption of the location of the Israelites from Geba to Gilgal (1 Sam 13:4), since their muster can only be at Geba opposite the Philistines at Michmash (1 Sam 13:16).

2. The pejorative question that Samuel puts to Saul regarding his inappropriate humility (1 Sam 15:17). This refers to Saul's genuinely humble protest at the time of his appointment (1 Sam 9:21), as indicated by the repetition of several words and phrases.[32]

3. The rejection of outstanding stature as a criterion for kingship in the case of Eliab (1 Sam 16:7). This is a reference to Saul's height as qualifying him for the office (1 Sam 9:2). Eliab poses as a "new Saul,"[33] and his rejection is a rejection of Saul "in effigy."[34]

4. The rushing of Yahweh's spirit on David from the time of his anointing onward (1 Sam 16:13). This charisma is presented as superior to Saul's temporary and episodic possession by the spirit (1 Sam 10:6a, 10b; 11:6).

5. David's anointing (1 Sam 16:1–13) as repeating Saul's anointing in several important respects. Both are mediated by Samuel, both are for the office of נגיד, "king-elect,"[35] both are conducted in private, and both are set at or shortly after a sacrificial meal.

Now, if the Davidic history was a royal *apologia* written during David's kingship to legitimize his usurpation of the Saulide throne and slaughter of the dynasts, and if it was composed in response to the preexisting Saul history and appended to it, then the Saul history must be dated earlier than the Davidic history. A pre-Davidic date of the Saul history is also required by the pro-Saul stance because Israelite historiography, in particular royal apologetic historiography, was by definition composed at the royal court. Only kings whose thrones were insecure had the need for such writing, and only they had access to the scribal resources to produce it. Since no Saulides ruled after Saul's son Ishbaal, the composition after Ishbaal's death of a document intending to defend Saul's kingship is highly unlikely. Even though Saulide partisans continued to exist for decades or even centuries outside the circles of power, their marginal status precluded the production and propagation of a literary history. Finally, the history advocates Jonathan as Saul's successor by its depiction of his divinely inspired deliverance of Israel (1 Sam 13:2–7a; 13:15b–14:23a). This promotion of Jonathan

---

[32] הלא, "is it not?," קטן, "small," and שבטי ישראל, "the tribes of Israel."

[33] Groenbaeck, *Aufstieg*, 72.

[34] Mettinger, *King and Messiah*, 175.

[35] See n. 10, above, for the argument that in all pre-Deuteronomistic contexts נגיד means "crown prince," "designated one," "king-elect," "successor."

at the end of the history is best read as an attempt to establish the dynasty, and therefore must pre-date the deaths of Saul and Jonathan.

*   *   *

Having distinguished the pro-Saul narrative from the anti-Saul/pro-David and "anti-monarchy" additions in 1 Sam 9:1–14:48, we can return to the question of the scope and aim of Saul's history. Saul is introduced in 1 Sam 9:1–2, but Samuel appears as a figure already known to the audience when Saul first encounters him (1 Sam 9:14). This poses a problem for our presentation of Saul's history thus far, because prior audience familiarity with Samuel requires their knowledge of the narrative in 1 Sam 1:1-4:1a.

A common solution to this problem and other putative "discrepancies" in Saul's investiture (1 Sam 9:1–10:16) is the hypothesis that an early folk-tale of Saul's search for the donkeys was overlaid with Samuel and the appointment to kingship.[36] However, a commonplace search for missing donkeys undertaken by an ordinary farmer's son is hardly the stuff of folk-tales. The folktale-like aspect is precisely that the farmer's son is Saul, who almost certainly was king of Israel at the time of the story's first telling. It is Saul's transformation from farmer's son to king-elect of Israel that gives the investiture its folktale-like quality, similar to the metamorphosis of the common frog into the royal prince when kissed by the princess. That is, the author made use of a common folktale motif to enhance the drama of Saul's transformation. The folktale-like nature of the story does not, however, require an actual underlying folktale.[37]

The intrinsic connection between the mundane search, frequently undertaken by farmers wherever livestock is left unpenned, and its unexpected outcome is required by the keyword מצא, "to find."[38] מצא carries a

---

[36] See, e.g., Hans Wilhelm Hertzberg, *I and II Samuel: A Commentary* (London: SCM, 1964) 78–80; L. Schmidt, *Menschlicher Erfolg und Jahwes Initiative: Studien zu Tradition, Interpretation und Historie in Überlieferungen von Gideon, Saul und David* (WMANT 38; Neukirchen-Vluyn, 1970) 63–80; Bruce C. Birch, "The Development of the Tradition of the Anointing of Saul in 1 Sam 9:1–10:16," *JBL* 90 (1971), 56; Mettinger, *King and Messiah*, 64–79; McCarter, *I Samuel*, 186–88; and McKenzie, "Cette Royauté," 275–81.

[37] The comparison with the prophetic *legenda* as defined by Alexander Rofé does not work (McKenzie, "Cette Royauté," 277). The prophetic *legenda* are stories of prophets who solve life-and-death crises of their followers (Rofé, *The Prophetical Stories: The Narratives about the Prophets in the Hebrew Bible, Their Literary Types and History* [Jerusalem: Magnes, 1988] 13–40). Saul's search for his father's missing donkeys hardly qualifies as a life-and-death crisis; it is merely a clever device for bringing Saul to Samuel under the guise of a donkey search, so that the appointment to kingship can remain secret. Also, Saul is not a disciple of Samuel.

[38] I am borrowing the concept of the *Leitwort* (keyword) from Robert Alter, who

double meaning: "to find" in the sense of "to discover" a thing, and "to find" in the sense of "to encounter" a person. Saul could not "find" (i.e., discover) the missing donkeys (1 Sam 9:4), but instead he "finds" (i.e., encounters) first the girls who direct him to Samuel (1 Sam 9:11–13), then Samuel, who was expecting him and anoints him king-elect (1 Sam 9:14–10:1a [LXX]), and then the three groups of men whose exact fulfillment of Samuel's highly specific threefold sign confirms Saul's kingship (1 Sam 10:1b [LXX]–6, 9–10). Finally, Samuel tells Saul that Yahweh will bless whatever his new power "finds" (i.e., discovers) to do (1 Sam 10:7), and Saul's story to his uncle about "finding" the donkeys underscores the secrecy of his appointment (1 Sam 10:14, 16).

The mundane search for the donkeys that leads to the providential encounter with Samuel, as linked throughout by twelve iterations of מצא,[39] precludes an early donkey-search folktale overlaid with a later appointment to kingship, because the story is structured throughout by the double meaning of the word. The twelvefold iteration of מצא unites the ordinary search with its extraordinary outcome, so that it is not an old folktale overlaid with the appointment to kingship, but two levels of a unified story. In addition, the use of the number twelve, found throughout ancient and classic documents such as Gilgamesh, supports the argument for unity.[40]

The recognition of two levels of a unified investiture account also solves the problem of Samuel's multiple identities as איש אלהים, "man of God" (1 Sam 9:6, 8, 10), ראה, "seer" (1 Sam 9:11, 18, 19), priest (1 Sam 9:12–13, 19,

---

quotes Martin Buber: "'A *Leitwort* is a word or a word-root that recurs significantly in a text . . . : by following these repetitions, one is able to decipher or grasp a meaning of the text, or . . . the meaning will be revealed more strikingly'" (Alter, *The Art of Biblical Narrative* [New York: Basic Books, 1981] 93). I have taken the liberty of using Alter's own English translation instead of the German word that Buber coined and that Alter uses.

[39] 1 Sam 9:4 (twice), 8, 11, 13 (twice), 20; 10:2 (twice), 3, 7, 16. Note that the turning point, the finding of the donkeys, happens at the seventh iteration (1 Sam 9:20).

[40] Gilgamesh V: 329 (72 and 24 are multiples of 12); VII: 39, 252–58; IX: 142, 227–79; X: 169–74; XI: 64–68 (3600 is a multiple of 12), 139. Also, the fact that all extant copies of the epic reflect twelve tablets indicates a belief in twelve as a number signifying wholeness.

Israel's understanding that it had always been comprised of twelve tribes could also be cited as an example of twelve signifying wholeness. However, it is doubtful that this understanding had coalesced by Saul's time, since the only tribes mentioned in Saul's history are the central hill country tribes of Ephraim (1 Sam 1:1; 9:4) and Benjamin (1 Sam 4:12; 9:1, 16, 21; 10:2) and the transjordanian tribes of Gad and Reuben (1 Sam 10:27b [4QSam^a]). Also, when Saul dismembers the yoke of oxen in order to summon all Israel to rescue Jabesh-gilead, there is no reference to twelve pieces (1 Sam 11:7), in contrast to the twelve parts of the Levite's concubine (Judg 19:29) and Elisha's twelve yoke of oxen (1 Kgs 19:19).

22–24), and prophet (1 Sam 9:15–17, 20; 10:1 [LXX]–7, 9–10).[41] At the mundane level of Saul's search for the lost donkeys, Samuel is the "seer" or "man of God" (i.e., generic holy man) known to the servant and sought by Saul to help him. At the level of Saul's appointment to future kingship, however, Samuel is the mediating priest and prophet. It is not that man of God, seer, priest, and prophet are competing roles for a historical Samuel, indicating different and incompatible provenances. Rather, the narrative demands that Samuel fill all roles at the same time, but be recognized differently by the different characters and by the audience. Saul's family and servant, i.e., those closest to him, are aware only of the donkey search and its successful outcome due to the encounter with the man of God/seer. Saul is at first aware only of the seer's help, but Samuel's actions as priest and prophet gradually disclose his appointment to future kingship. As intermediary, Samuel is informed of the encounter and given his mission the day before. Finally, the audience, who are the subjects of King Saul, know kingship is imminent the moment Saul is introduced.

If the מצא keyword structures the investiture account (1 Sam 9:1–10:16) and creates the two levels of the ordinary and the extraordinary, then the narrative's other keyword, the sevenfold הגיד, "to tell,"[42] points to Saul's vocation as the etymologically-related נגיד, "king-elect," which occurs three times.[43] Throughout the ancient Near East the reigning king designated one of his sons, often but not always the eldest, as crown prince. It was this status, in Israel נגיד, "designated one," that legitimated the prince's accession to his father's throne upon the death of the king, since the dynasty was understood as established by God.[44]

However, in the case of Saul, the fact that his throne was newly-created meant that he lacked the prerequisite royal designation. In order to make up for this lack, Saul is given a designation by God, typically invoked by those who attempt to start new dynasties.[45] Again, we have another an-

---

[41] McCarter, *I Samuel*, 186.

[42] *Hiphil* of נגד; 1 Sam 9:6, 8, 18, 19; 10:15, 16 (twice).

[43] 1 Sam 9:16; 10:1 (LXX, twice). The wordplay is noted by Martin Buber ("Die Erzählung von Sauls Konigswahl," *VT* 6 [1956] 126, 142); McCarter (*I Samuel*, 176); Shemuel Shaviv ("נביא and נגיד in I Samuel ix 1 – x 16," *VT* 34 [1984] 108–12); Lyle M. Eslinger (*Kingship of God in Crisis: A Close Reading of I Samuel 1–12* [Bible and Literature Series 10; Decatur, Ga.: Almond, 1985] 293, 335); Peter Miscall (*I Samuel: A Literary Reading* [Bloomington: Indiana Univ. Press, 1986] 62); and Robert Polzin (*Samuel and the Deuteronomist, A Literary Study of the Deuteronomic History, Part Two: I Samuel* [San Francisco: Harper and Row, 1989] 98).

[44] See Mettinger, *King and Messiah*, 158–62, and Tomoo Ishida, *The Royal Dynasties in Ancient Israel: A Study on the Formation and Development of Royal-Dynastic Ideology* (BZAW 142; Berlin and New York: Walter de Gruyter, 1977).

[45] Cf. the "History of David's Rise," especially 1 Sam 13:14; 15:28; 16:1–13; and 2 Sam 7:1–17.

cient and classic number signifying wholeness, i.e. seven.[46] It is clear, then, from both the מצא keyword and the הגיד keyword that the investiture account is a unified narrative, and that it together with the subsequent pro-Saul narrative was created to legitimate Saul's unorthodox accession to the throne.

But the question remains whether the Saul history as delineated thus far is the entirety of the document. We should consider the possibility that it also includes 1 Samuel 1–3, based on the assumption that Samuel's priestly and prophetic offices exercised in the investiture require his special birth and dedication to Yahweh at the temple of Shiloh (1 Samuel 1), his priestly apprenticeship under Eli (1 Samuel 2), and his prophetic call (1 Samuel 3). The inclusion of these passages provides Samuel with the credentials necessary for anointing Saul future king, which explains in part why Saul does not appear until 1 Sam 9:2.

That the Saul history does indeed begin with 1 Samuel 1 is strongly suggested by the keyword of that narrative, שאל, meaning "to ask for" or "to request" in the *Qal* and "to grant" or "to dedicate" in the *Hiphil*. Variations of שאל verbs and nouns occur seven times in Samuel's birth narrative, culminating in Hannah's speech to Eli with הוא שאול ליהוה, "he is dedicated to Yahweh," which is also "he is Saul of Yahweh."[47] A frequent explanation of this keyword, which is a glaring feature of the Hebrew text and is particularly dense at the end of the chapter, is that an original birth narrative of Saul was adapted for Samuel when political considerations dictated the change.[48]

However, the narrative progression is clear and logical: The child that is asked for and dedicated to Yahweh at the temple (1 Samuel 1) stays there to mature as a priest under Eli's supervision (1 Samuel 2), and then is given the additional vocation of prophet (1 Samuel 3). The roles of priest and prophet are exactly those of Samuel in Saul's investiture account; they do not correspond in the least with Saul's function as warrior-king. A more likely explanation for the שאל keyword is that the narrative was composed deliberately to operate on two levels. The story of Hannah's piety and Samuel's birth is the plain meaning of the text, but overtone and suggestion created by the sevenfold iteration of שאל foreshadow Saul's appearance.

A unified story with a dual (or triple) purpose is indicated by the fact that the seven שאל words are integral to the birth narrative. After an

---

[46] Gilgamesh I: 20, 175; IV: 233; VI: 42–77, 50, 53, 99, 105; VII: 151; X: 61, 134, 230; XI: 60, 127–30, 142–55, 157, 206–35, 317. Note that the turning point of the epic, the death of Enkidu, occurs in Tablet VII.

[47] 1 Sam 1:17 (twice), 20, 27 (twice), 28 (twice).

[48] See Ivar Hylander, *Der literarische Samuel-Saul-Komplex (I Sam. 1–15) traditionsgeschichtlich untersucht* (Uppsala: Almquist & Wiksell, 1932) 11–39; McCarter, *I Samuel*, 65–66; and Brettler, *Creation of History*, 109.

introduction of the characters and of the conflict between Hannah and
Peninnah (1 Sam 1:1–7a), the story consists of two contexts for שאל that correspond to the two conjugations: Hannah's שאלה, "request," for a son and
its fulfillment (1 Sam 1:7b–20), followed by her "dedication" (שאל, *Hiphil*)
of him to Yahweh at Shiloh (1 Sam 1:21–28). The narrative does not merely
include allusions to Saul, indicating a buried Saul birth narrative, but is
structured throughout for the purpose of foreshadowing his appearance.

At the same time, Hannah's perfect piety in handing over her beloved
son anticipates that of Saul (cf. 1 Sam 14:36–45). As she hands over Samuel,
so is Saul prepared to sacrifice his son Jonathan. Since Hannah is a fictitious character whereas Saul is a historical figure, Hannah is a cipher for
Saul. The narrative also introduces Samuel, the priest and prophet who
will mediate Saul's appointment to kingship. Therefore, Samuel's birth
narrative was the original introduction to Saul's history.

Since the introduction (1 Sam 1:1–28; 2:11a[49]) features significant inter-
actions between Hannah and Eli (1 Sam 1:12–18, 25–28a) and mentions Eli's
sons (1 Sam 1:3b), Saul's history probably included the three subsequent
scenes concerning Eli and his sons. These are:

1. Eli's sons sin against Yahweh by habitually and forcefully seizing
Yahweh's sacrificial portion from the people. Eli does not stop them, so a
man of God arrives and announces Yahweh's judgment against the Elide
priesthood. Even though the priesthood had a divine charter dating from
the Egyptian captivity, the entire lineage is to be destroyed, except for one
survivor to serve at the altar. The confirming sign will be the deaths of
Hophni and Phinehas together (I Sam 2:11b–34; 3:1a[50]).

---

[49] After Hannah's speech to Eli (1 Sam 1:26–28a), the introduction concludes
with ותעזבהו שם ותשתחו ליהוה ותלך הרמתה, "Then she left him there, and worshiped
Yahweh, and returned to Ramah" (1 Sam 1:28b; 2:11a). This text follows McCarter's
reconstruction (*I Samuel*, 57–58, 78), minus the interpolated Song of Hannah (1 Sam
2:1–10). The envelope construction created by the family leaving their home in
Ramah and then returning home at the end defines the scene (1 Sam 1:1–2; 2:11a). It
was later disrupted by the inclusion of Hannah's Song, which appears in different
places in different textual witnesses. Also, the threefold summary of Hannah's actions defines the conclusion. For a discussion of the interpolation of Hannah's Song
and speculation regarding when it may have taken place, see Steven Weitzman's
*Song and Story in Biblical Narrative: The History of a Literary Convention in Ancient Is-
rael* (Bloomington: Indiana Univ. Press, 1997) 113–17.

[50] The MT text of the oracle against the Elides (1 Sam 2:27–34) is exceedingly cor-
rupt. For a good textual reconstruction, see McCarter, *I Samuel*, 87–89.

1 Sam 2:35–36 is a Josianic Deuteronomistic expansion of the oracle against the
Elides. The expansion shifts the object of judgment from the Elides to the village Levites, in favor of the royal Zadokite priests. The כהן נאמן, "faithful priest" (1 Sam
2:35a), is Zadok (Wellhausen, *Prolegomena*, 126), and the promise of a perpetual dy-

2. While serving as a priestly attendant under Eli, Samuel mediates a confirmation of the judgment oracle against the Elides. As a result of his willingness to mediate without regard for personal consequences, he is established as prophet of Yahweh to all Israel (1 Sam 3:1b–4:1a[51]).

3. The incorporated "Ark Narrative" concludes the account of Eli's neglect and his sons' sin (1 Sam 4:1b [LXX]–18a; 4:19–5:4; 5:6–6:14, 16[52]). Saul's

---

nasty (בית נאמן, "an enduring house," 1 Sam 2:35b) makes the best sense in the context of Josiah's centralizing reform (2 Kings 22–23). The nature of the addition as a *post facto* prophecy of Josiah's reform is clear from the prediction of the disenfranchisement of the Levitical priests (1 Sam 2:36; cf. 2 Kgs 23:8–9). Also, the phrase בית נאמן in the sense of "a perpetual dynasty" is a Deuteronomistic construct (cf. 1 Sam 25:28; 2 Sam 7:16; 1 Kgs 11:38; Cross, *Canaanite Myth*, 254). Finally, there is a seam between the sign of the original oracle (1 Sam 2:34) and the judgment against the Levites (1 Sam 2:35–36). If a confirming sign appears with a prophecy, it is almost always at the end of the prophecy and not in the middle (e.g. 1 Sam 10:1b [LXX]–7, 9–10; 2 Kgs 19:29–30; 2 Kgs 20:1–11).

Throughout this scene Samuel's perfect ministry before Yahweh and Eli (1 Sam 2:11b, 18–21, 26; 3:1a) is contrasted with Eli's sons' corruption (1 Sam 2:12–17, 22–25, 27–34), with the brief notices of Samuel's obedience framing the lengthier descriptions of Eli's sons' disobedience. The virtually identical language of 1 Sam 2:11b (והנער היה משרת את־יהוה את־פני עלי הכהן), "Now the servant was ministering to Yahweh in the presence of Eli the priest") and 1 Sam 3:1a (והנער שמואל משרת את־יהוה לפני עלי), "But the servant Samuel was ministering to Yahweh in the presence of Eli") argues for the former as the introduction of the scene and the latter as the conclusion, creating an envelope construction.

[51] For the conclusion of the scene in 1 Sam 4:1a, see McCarter, *I Samuel*, 94–101.

[52] 1 Sam 4:18b is a Deuteronomistic interpolation fitting Eli into the history of the judges (McCarter, *I Samuel*, 114–15).

The etiology regarding the Philistine cult practice of leaping over the threshold at the temple of Dagon (1 Sam 5:5 and אל־המפתן, "on the threshold," of 1 Sam 5:4) is an interpolation. The secondary status of the etiology is clear both from the physical awkwardness of the broken statue and from the etiological formula עד היום הזה, "until this day." The breaking-off of the head and hands onto the threshold is difficult because in most ancient Near Eastern temples the entrance and the niche for the statue were at opposite ends of the longitudinal axis. Since it would be a stretch for the body parts to break off and travel all the way to the threshold, it appears that the author of the etiology had to strain a bit to fit it into the narrative. The etiological formula also argues against originality, because it implies an appreciable lapse of time between Israel's first acquaintance with the Philistine cult practice and the story of its origins. The "Ark Narrative," however, was composed prior to David's suppression of the Philistines, when their cult practices would have been relatively new to Israel (Patrick D. Miller, Jr. and J. J. M. Roberts, *The Hand of the Lord: A Reassessment of the "Ark Narrative" of 1 Samuel* [Baltimore and London: The Johns Hopkins Univ. Press, 1977] 74).

The secondary status of 1 Sam 6:15, the Levitical handling of the Ark, is agreed upon by most commentators (e.g. Smith, *Samuel*, 46–47; Hertzberg, *I & II Samuel*,

history was an original composition in all scenes but this. Here the historian took a preexisting short story about the capture, captivity, and return of the Ark[53] and included it by means of interpolations in order to make a point about the effects of Elide leadership. The "Ark Narrative" originally told of a contest between Yahweh and Dagon, in which Israel's defeat by the Philistines and their capture of the Ark were merely pretexts for Yahweh to attack the Philistines from within. The strategy was deliberate, the plague was devastating, and Yahweh's victory was complete.[54] In other words, the original "Ark Narrative" was not about Israel's defeat due to Elide sin,[55] but Yahweh's powerful deliverance of an innocent Israel from their oppressors. However, the Saulide additions (1 Sam 4:1bA [LXX], 4b, 11b–18a, 19–22[56]), which incorporate the older story into the account of the Elides, turn Yahweh's victory into Israel's defeat and blame that defeat on

---

56, 60; Antony F. Campbell, *The Ark Narrative [1 Sam 4–6; 2 Sam 6]: A Form-critical and Traditio-historical Study* [SBLDS 16; Missoula, Mont.: Scholars Press, 1975] 168; and McCarter, *I Samuel*, 136). In 1 Sam 6:14, the cart carrying the Ark stops beside a great stone and the Beth-shemeshites split up the wood of the cart and offer the cows as a holocaust to Yahweh, implying that ordinary Beth-shemeshites handle the Ark and use the stone as an altar. In 1 Sam 6:15, however, the Levites take the Ark from the cart and put it on the stone while the Beth-shemeshites offer sacrifices elsewhere. Not only is the handling of the Ark switched from the lay Beth-shemeshites to the priestly Levites, but 1 Sam 6:15 contradicts 1 Sam 6:14 by having the Levites put the Ark on the stone while the Beth-shemeshites perform the sacrifices some place else.

1 Sam 6:17–18, the specification of the number and origin of the tumor and mice images, is a later interpolation, probably by P (cf. the interest in precision exhibited in 1 Sam 13:21).

The notice about the plague that prompts the people to transfer the Ark from Beth-shemesh, where it came to rest at the end of the "Ark Narrative" and in Saul's history (1 Sam 6:12–14, 16), to Kiriath-jearim, where David locates it (2 Samuel 6; Baale-judah = Kiriath-jearim, cf. 1 Chronicles 13), identifies 1 Sam 6:19–7:1 as a later interpolation.

[53] Consisting of 1 Sam 4:1bB (LXX)–4a, 5–11a; 5:1–4; 5:6–6:14, 16.

[54] Cf. the Trojan horse. Yahweh's devastation of the Philistines by means of plagues is explicitly compared to the decimation of the Egyptians by plagues in the Exodus (1 Sam 4:8; 6:6), which argues for the original "Ark Narrative" as a story of Yahweh's deliverance of an innocent Israel.

[55] *Contra* Miller and Roberts, *The Hand of the Lord*, 27–31, 60–66.

[56] The phrase וארון אלהים נלקח, "and the Ark of God was captured" (1 Sam 4:11a), is almost exactly repeated in כי נלקח ארון אלהים, "when the Ark of God was captured" (1 Sam 4:22b), after which the narrative of the Ark's captivity resumes (1 Sam 5:1). This "repetitive resumption" identifies all of 1 Sam 4:11b–22 as an interpolation. 1 Sam 4:1bA (LXX) and 4:4b were added to lead into the account of Hophni's and Phinehas's deaths in battle, the report of their deaths and the capture of the Ark to Eli, Eli's consequent death, and the death of his daughter-in-law in childbirth

the sins of the Elides. Most important, the deaths of Hophni and Phinehas together in battle (1 Sam 4:11b) fulfill the sign of the oracle against the Elides (1 Sam 2:34), which confirms that the judgment (1 Sam 2:30–33) will take place some time in the future.

*   *   *

Saul's history now emerges in its entirety. The Elides and Samuel are introduced and Saul is anticipated in Scene One (1 Sam 1:1–28; 2:11a); the sins of the Elides lead to the judgment against them and Samuel is established as priest of Yahweh in Scene Two (1 Sam 2:11b–34; 3:1a); the judgment against the Elides is confirmed and Samuel is established as Yahweh's prophet in Scene Three (1 Sam 3:1b–4:1a); the sign of the judgment against the Elides is fulfilled and Israel reaches its nadir under Elide leadership in Scene Four (1 Sam 4:1b [LXX]–18a; 4:19–5:4, 5:6–6:14, 16); Saul is introduced and is designated future king and deliverer by the priest and prophet Samuel in Scene Five (1 Sam 9:1–8; 9:10–10:7, 9–10, 13–16); Saul's divinely inspired military success leads to his popular election as king in Scene Six (1 Sam 10:27b [4QSamª]–11:11, 15); Saul's overwhelming success against the Philistines is linked to his perfect piety in Scene Seven (1 Sam 13:2–7a, 15b–20; 13:22–14:46); and Saul's complete military success in fulfillment of his commission is summarized in a conclusion (1 Sam 14:47–48).

The seven scenes thus break down into three groups, two of which consist of three scenes each: an introduction (Scene One), the demise of the Elides (Scenes Two, Three, and Four), and the rise of the Saulides (Scenes Five, Six, and Seven). The Elides fall morally and politically in the first half of the history, causing the abandonment of Israel to Philistine oppression. However, the return of the Ark signals a turnaround (1 Sam 6:1–14, 16), and the appearance of Saul heralds Israel's deliverance at the beginning of the second half of the history (1 Sam 9:1–2). The closeness of the wording between the introduction of Elkanah and his two wives (1 Sam 1:1–2) and the introduction of Kish and Saul (1 Sam 9:1–2) has long been noted.[57] The repetition at the introduction of Saul of a genealogical format that occurs elsewhere only at the start of Saul's history means that Saul's appearance marks a new beginning after the debacle caused by the Elides.

The stark contrast between the Elides, whose wickedness causes Israel's defeat to the Philistines, and the pious and brave Saulides, who deliver Israel from their enemies, in particular the Philistines, strongly suggests apologetic intent. The anti-Elide bias of Saul's history is best explained

---

(1 Sam 4:11b–18a, 19–22). For a definition of "repetitive resumption," see Michael A. Fishbane, *Biblical Interpretation in Ancient Israel* (Oxford: Clarendon, 1985) 85.

[57] E.g. McCarter, *I Samuel*, 172, and Lyle M. Eslinger, *Kingship of God* (see n. 43, above), 285, and references therein.

with reference to the report of his massacre of the Elide priesthood at Nob (1 Samuel 22).[58] Although the report's location within the anti-Saulide "History of David's Rise" casts doubt on its reliability, the exact coincidence of Saul's reputed massacre of all the Elides but one (1 Samuel 22) with the highly specific *post facto* prophecy of violent Elide extinction save a single survivor (1 Sam 2:30–33) confirms both the historicity of the massacre and Saul's agency. That is, because the anti-Saulide "History of David's Rise" and the pro-Saul history agree on the slaughter of all the Elides except for one survivor, the historicity of the event can be trusted. And Saul's agency is assured by the lengths to which his history goes to prove Elide culpability, to show that they deserved their violent end. Whatever the circumstances of the massacre, Saul's consolidation of his power entailed the slaughter of all the Elides except Abiathar (1 Sam 22:20), exactly as his history claims that the man of God prophesied to Eli several generations earlier (1 Sam 2:33).[59]

The two subjects of Saul's history, the demise of the Elides and the rise of the Saulides, suggest that Saul was faced with defending two controversial and potentially damaging events: his unprecedented assumption of the throne and his slaughter of the Elide priesthood. We can conclude, therefore, that Saul's history was an *apologia* composed by his historian(s) to defend him from the charges of illegal arrogation of power and massive bloodshed perpetrated on a chartered priesthood. Just as David needed to justify his usurpation of the Saulide throne and slaughter of the ruling family, so did Saul need to legitimize his unprecedented assumption of the throne and assassination of the Elides. The similarity of Saul's history to that of David suggests the title, "The History of Saul's Rise."

---

[58] There are two clues indicating that the Elides, who were formerly at Shiloh, later relocated to Nob. One is the description of Nob as "the city of the priests" (1 Sam 22:19), which suggests that Nob replaced Shiloh as the center for the Ark and its attendant priests. A second clue is the lineage of Ahimelech, chief priest of Nob, who is the son of Ahitub (1 Sam 22:11–12, 20). Presumably this is the same Ahitub who is the brother of Ichabod the son of Phinehas the son of Eli (1 Sam 14:3), which means that Ahimelech is Eli's great-grandson and his son Abiathar is Eli's great-great-grandson (Cross, *Canaanite Myth and Hebrew Epic*, 196, 213).

[59] The *post facto* prophecy, "one man shall I spare you at my altar to wear out his eyes and use up his strength" (1 Sam 2:33a), did not refer originally to Solomon's banishment of Abiathar (1 Kgs 2:27a); that connection was made later by Dtr (1 Kgs 2:27b).

Chapter 19

Unity and Diversity in the Book of Kings

Robert R. Wilson
Yale University

In recent years, students of the Hebrew Bible have been engaged in heated debates about the methods which are most appropriate for the literary, historical, and theological study of the text. Although there are many reasons for these debates, certainly one of the major causes is the feeling of an increasing number of scholars that traditional historical-critical approaches to the Bible are limited, inadequate, or simply irrelevant. So, for example, biblical theologians such as Brevard Childs and James Sanders have charged that traditional scholarly analyses of the biblical text often engage in obscure arguments over the literary history of the text and at the same time ignore the text's final or "canonical" shape, the text as it now stands, the text which was read by synagogue and church and therefore the text in which theological meaning actually resides.[1] Approaching the same set of problems from another direction, scholars such as Moshe Greenberg have not neglected the historical and cultural background of the text altogether but have pointed to the hypothetical character of much historical-critical work and have advocated a "holistic" reading that is based on the Hebrew text as we now have it rather than on a hypothetical reconstructed text.[2] A similar approach is being taken by literary critics such as Robert Alter and an increasing number of biblical scholars, who argue that the original setting of a text, its literary history, and even the intentions of its author(s) are all irrelevant to the text's interpretation. According to this argument, any reader who is "competent" can interpret a text. The interpreter does not

---

[1] Brevard S. Childs, *Introduction to the Old Testament as Scripture* (Philadelphia: Fortress, 1979); James A. Sanders, *Torah and Canon* (Philadelphia: Fortress, 1972).

[2] Moshe Greenberg, *Ezekiel 1–20: A New Translation with Introduction and Commentary* (AB 22; Garden City, N.Y.: Doubleday, 1983) 18–27.

need to have any special knowledge about the text or its history but needs only to be a sensitive reader of the text as it now stands.[3]

It is not surprising that these challenges have provoked responses from practitioners of the more traditional historical-critical methods, who not only feel that their own approach to the field is being challenged, but also suspect that the "gains" of modern scholarship are in danger of being lost. Over the past few years this debate over method has become increasingly acrimonious and shows no signs of being resolved in the near future. Certainly one of the reasons for this impasse is that there has been a tendency to carry on the debate at the level of generalities or to work with a specific text and then to project the results of that work onto the Bible as a whole, as if the whole of scripture shared a common set of literary characteristics. In the end, biblical literature is not likely to turn out to be so uniform. As a result, the debate might take a more productive turn if scholars were to try out different methods on different types of literature in an effort to build up a comprehensive collection of cases that would separate fruitful methods from unfruitful ones. Such an approach may not result in the discovery of a single method that can be applied to all types of biblical literature, but it may result in isolating a range of interpretive options.

An excellent beginning on this sort of investigation has already been made by Burke Long, who, like many of his scholarly generation, has been actively involved in these debates over method. Beginning his career as a form and tradition critic with a dissertation on etiology in the Hebrew Bible, he began to realize as he worked on the Book of Kings that traditional form-critical approaches to this book missed much of the richness of the biblical narrative.[4] As a result, as his two-volume treatment of Kings progressed, he increasingly lost interest in the editorial layers and formulas that went into the text's formation, and put more and more stress on reading the individual stories in the book as complete narratives.[5] By shifting the focus of his work in this way, he provided his readers with a new ap-

---

[3] A convenient collection of such literary readings may be found in Robert Alter and Frank Kermode, eds., *The Literary Guide to the Bible* (Cambridge: Harvard Univ. Press, 1987). For a survey of recent approaches to the interpretation of scripture, see John Barton, ed., *The Cambridge Companion to Biblical Interpretation* (Cambridge: Cambridge Univ. Press, 1998) 9–128.

[4] Burke O. Long, *The Problem of Etiological Narrative in the Old Testament* (BZAW 108; Berlin: Töpelmann, 1968); idem, *1 Kings: With an Introduction to Historical Literature* (FOTL 9; Grand Rapids, Mich.: Eerdmans, 1984); idem, *2 Kings* (FOTL 10; Grand Rapids, Mich.: Eerdmans, 1991).

[5] An autobiographical account of his own struggles with methodological issues can be found throughout Burke O. Long, *Planting and Reaping Albright: Politics, Ideology, and Interpreting the Bible* (University Park, Pa.: Pennsylvania State Univ. Press, 1997).

preciation of the literary skill of the biblical writers and gave new depth to some of the Bible's most familiar stories.

In appreciation for Burke Long's work on the individual stories in Kings, this essay will consider an issue which the format of his volumes did not allow him to take up: the problem of how to read the entire Book of Kings as a single literary unit.[6] At first glance this problem does not seem to be a major one, but a brief look at the history of the book's interpretation will serve to illustrate some of the difficulties.[7]

Before the rise of modern biblical scholarship, the Book of Kings was, of course, read as a single literary unit. There were, and are, excellent reasons for taking this approach. The book presents itself as a coherent history that traces the fortunes of Israel's kings from the end of David's reign to the exile of the last king of Judah, Zedekiah, following the Babylonian destruction of Jerusalem and the Temple. Events are presented more-or-less in chronological order, a chronological order that is often marked by the inclusion of specific or relative dates. This chronological organization gives the work a clear direction and suggests that it is to be read, like any chronicle, from beginning to end.

Now to say that pre-modern readers read Kings as a unified whole is not to say that they read it uncritically. Early on, both Christian and Jewish interpreters recognized the importance of a number of features of the text that would later play a role in historical-critical interpretations. Thus, for example, although Kings was read as a whole, it was not read in isolation. It was clearly recognized to be a continuation of the story of the monarchy that began in 1 Samuel with the story of the rise of kingship in Israel and was part of an even larger history that began with Joshua's account of Israel's entry into the land. Furthermore, early interpreters recognized that although Kings had literary cohesion, it was not, strictly speaking, the work of a single author. On chronological and linguistic grounds, Jewish tradition attributed the book to the prophet Jeremiah (*b. B. Bat.* 14b–15a), but it

---

[6] The format of the Forms of the Old Testament Literature series prevented authors from considering these larger literary problems. I have elsewhere discussed some of the problems involved in reading the Book of Kings as a whole in Robert R. Wilson, "The Former Prophets: Reading the Books of Kings," in *Old Testament Interpretation: Past, Present, and Future: Essays in Honor of Gene M. Tucker* (ed. James Luther Mays, David L. Petersen, and Kent Harold Richards; Nashville: Abingdon, 1995) 83–96.

[7] For surveys of the scholarly interpretation of Kings, see Ronald E. Clements, *One Hundred Years of Old Testament Interpretation* (Philadelphia: Westminster, 1976) 31–50; Richard D. Nelson, *The Double Redaction of the Deuteronomistic History* (JSOTSup 18; Sheffield: JSOT Press, 1981) 13–22; and Steven L. McKenzie, *The Trouble with Kings: The Composition of the Book of Kings in the Deuteronomistic History* (VTSup 42; Leiden: Brill, 1991) 1–19.

was clear even to ancient readers that the author or authors of Kings used a number of literary sources in compiling the work. The book itself mentions some of these sources and refers the reader to them for further information.[8] So, for example, there are references to the "Book of the Chronicles of Solomon" (1 Kgs 11:41), the "Books of the Chronicles of the Kings of Israel" (1 Kgs 14:19 and sixteen other references), and the "Books of the Chronicles of the Kings of Judah" (1 Kgs 14:29 and fourteen other references). Unfortunately, it is not precisely clear just what these books contained, but Kings seems to imply that they were sources for the writer of the book as well as deposits of additional information. The author obviously considered historical information to be important and encouraged the reader to acquire more of it, presumably as an aid to understanding the book as a whole.

Scholarly approaches to Kings began to change with the advent of critical biblical scholarship. Not long after Wellhausen suggested that the Pentateuch contained four distinct literary strands, scholars began to wonder if these same strands continued beyond the Pentateuch. To explore this hypothesis, they began to apply to Kings the same methods that they had used in the Pentateuch. They looked for "rough spots" in the text, differences in linguistic usage and vocabulary, gaps in literary continuity, breaks in logic, and narrative contradiction—all of which, when found, were taken to be evidence of editorial activity. In this way some scholars extended the classic Pentateuchal sources into Joshua, Judges, and, in some cases, into Kings.[9] Eventually most scholars abandoned the enterprise, but the literary observations that they had made remained. As a result, there was general agreement that Kings was composed of distinct literary layers which could be disentangled through diligent effort, even though those layers were not continuations of the Pentateuchal sources. The book was considered to be the product of editorial activity that combined previously existing material.

A major challenge to this atomistic approach was mounted by Martin Noth, who advocated a unified reading of Kings, but one that was solidly based on historical-critical principles.[10] Noth argued that the bulk of the present Book of Kings was written in the exilic period by a single author,

---

[8] For the purposes of this discussion, it does not matter whether or not these cited sources actually existed or could have easily been consulted by the text's original readers. Even if these references are fictitious, as some modern scholars have claimed, the fact remains that the text gives the unambiguous impression that it does not contain everything that had been written down concerning the monarchy.

[9] For an example of this sort of approach to Kings, see Immanuel Benzinger, *Jahvist und Elohist in den Königsbüchern* (Berlin: Kohlhammer, 1921).

[10] Martin Noth, *The Deuteronomistic History* (JSOTSup 15; Sheffield: JSOT Press, 1981 [German original 1943; 2nd German ed. 1957]).

who collected various historical sources and traditions and creatively wove them into a comprehensive history stretching from Israel's entry into Canaan in Joshua to the fall of Jerusalem in Kings. To this so-called Deuteronomistic History the author then prefixed an early form of the present Book of Deuteronomy and wrote a general introduction to the whole work, an introduction now found in the first four chapters of Deuteronomy. In Noth's view, then, the writer of Kings was a genuine author and not simply a compiler or editor, as earlier scholars had suggested. Furthermore, Noth thought that later editors may have made minor changes at a few spots in the History, but that these alterations did little to modify the cohesive literary work which the original exilic author had created. The original purpose of the entire work was not simply to present to future readers the basic facts of Israel's history but to provide a theological explanation first for the fall of Samaria and the dispersion of Northern Israel and second for the fall of Jerusalem, the destruction of the Temple, and the Babylonian exile. As Noth interpreted the Deuteronomistic Historian, these traumatic events were God's just punishment on the kings and the people, who had rejected the God of Israel, worshiped other gods, and failed to live according to the covenant laws contained in the Book of Deuteronomy. Noth saw this bleak message of hopeless doom throughout the History in the author's selection and organization of traditional material, but the History's theological message was most apparent to Noth in the speeches, prayers, and editorial comments which the author composed and inserted at crucial points in the History (Deuteronomy 1–4; Joshua 24; Judg 2:11–23; 1 Samuel 12; 1 Kgs 8:22–53; 2 Kgs 17:7–23). While Noth's argument for a unified reading of Kings within the context of the larger Deuteronomistic History was immediately persuasive for a large number of scholars, there were almost immediately several dissenting voices. Initial objections to Noth's thesis did not challenge his theory that the History was the unified work of a single author but rather claimed that Noth's analysis of the themes of the work was not sophisticated enough. Gerhard von Rad, for example, argued that while Noth's analysis of the Deuteronomistic theology of sin and punishment was largely correct, his picture of the History overlooked the note of hope that the writer inserted by stressing the inevitable fulfillment of God's prophetic word. In Kings this prophecy-fulfillment schema is seen frequently in the accounts of confrontations between various prophets and the Ephraimite kings. In these stories the prophet condemns the king for a particular sin and then predicts the end of the king's dynasty. When the king's dynasty does end, the Historian points out the fulfillment of the original prophecy (1 Kgs 14:7–11 and 1 Kgs 15:25–30 are typical examples).

However, for von Rad, even more important than these examples of prophecy and fulfillment is the prophetic promise given to David by Nathan in 2 Samuel 7. In this crucial oracle, David is promised that his dynasty will be an eternal one. Although later editors modified this promise somewhat to allow for the just punishment of sinful kings, von Rad felt that the Historian never rejected the idea that the Davidic line would be eternal. Von Rad therefore interpreted the last verses of 2 Kings, which describe the Babylonians' release of the imprisoned king Jehoiachin (2 Kgs 25:27–30), as an understated expression of the hope that God had in fact been faithful to the promise to David and that the Davidic line had not come to an end with the exile.[11]

Similar thematic objections to Noth's thesis were made by Hans Walter Wolff, who pointed out that Noth also overlooked the prominent references to repentance that appear in the history. The theme of repentance appears in a major way for the first time in the History in the writer's summary of the period of the Judges (Judg 2:11–23), where it is said that the people did what was evil in the sight of the Lord and rejected the Lord to worship other gods. God then sent oppressors against the people as punishment for their sins. However, when the oppression became too great, the people cried out to God, who took pity on them and sent a deliverer to relieve the oppression. Wolff points out that this motif of sin, punishment, repentance, and forgiveness appears elsewhere in the History. Repentance figures prominently in Kings in 1 Kgs 8:46–53, where Solomon prays that God will listen to the people's penitential prayers in exile. Thereafter, the call for the people's repentance appears periodically in Kings and is prominent in the Historian's theological reflection on the fall of the Northern Kingdom. In 2 Kgs 17:13–15, the Historian claims that the people had repeatedly been warned by the prophets to repent but that Israel had ignored the warning. According to Wolff, the Historian thus gave exilic Israel the hope that repentance would lead God to end their captivity.[12]

Although both von Rad and Wolff offered important supplements to Noth's analysis of the major themes of the Deuteronomistic History, they seem to have accepted his basic point that most of the History was the creation of a single author writing in the exile. In the end, their discussion of additional themes in the History simply strengthened Noth's thesis that Kings should be read as a whole book. A different tack has been taken by Frank Moore Cross, who has incorporated von Rad's and Wolff's observations into a comprehensive theory of the editing of Kings.[13] According to

---

[11] Gerhard von Rad, *Studies in Deuteronomy* (London: SCM, 1953 [German original 1948]) 74–91.

[12] Hans Walter Wolff, "The Kerygma of the Deuteronomic Historical Work," in *The Vitality of Old Testament Traditions* (ed. Walter Brueggemann and Hans Walter Wolff; 2nd ed.; Atlanta: John Knox, 1982) 83–100.

[13] Frank Moore Cross, *Canaanite Myth and Hebrew Epic: Essays in the History of the Religion of Israel* (Cambridge: Harvard Univ. Press, 1973) 274–289.

Cross, Noth was essentially correct in his analysis of the theme of sin and judgment in the History but erred in his dating of the material. Cross feels that the bulk of the history was produced in the time of Josiah. This preexilic edition of the work was unified by two great themes. The first theme was that the Northern Kingdom fell to the Assyrians because all of the Israelite kings "walked in the way of Jeroboam the son of Nebat who made Israel to sin." This theme is introduced in 1 Kgs 13:34, the evaluation of Jeroboam's establishment of the shrines and the cults at Dan and Bethel, and is repeated in the Historian's evaluation of each successive Israelite king. The theme reaches its climax in 2 Kings 17, where the historian explicitly traces the destruction of Samaria to the fact that Jeroboam enticed the people of Israel to desert God. In spite of numerous prophetic warnings, the people continued to walk in the way of Jeroboam until they were taken into exile in Assyria (2 Kgs 17:20–23).

According to Cross, the second great theme of the preexilic edition of Kings is that God is ultimately faithful to the promise of an eternal Davidic line. Cross points out that even when Judah's kings do not walk in the way of their father David, God nevertheless preserves the dynasty "for the sake of David my servant and for the sake of Jerusalem which I have chosen" (1 Kgs 11:12, 13, 32, 34, 36; 15:4; 2 Kgs 8:19; 19:34; 20:6). This second theme reaches its climax in the Historian's account of the reform of Josiah (2 Kgs 22:1–23:25). As predicted in 1 Kings 13, Josiah destroys the idolatrous sanctuary at Bethel, renews God's covenant in the land, and restores the old Davidic empire by reincorporating Ephraim into the nation of Israel.

According to Cross, the preexilic edition of the Deuteronomistic History had to be updated when Josiah's untimely death and the Babylonian captivity raised serious questions about the credibility of the Historian's claim of an eternal Davidic line. The editor responsible for the second, exilic edition of the History made few changes in the first edition but did attempt to explain the destruction of Jerusalem by claiming that the sins of Manasseh were so great that the evil that he did and that he caused the people to do had to be punished (2 Kgs 21:2–15). The editor also added the brief historical notes that now follow the first edition's account of Josiah's reign and may have also been responsible for adding the repentance motif that Wolff traced so successfully.

Since Cross propounded his theory of a two-staged editorial history for Kings, several scholars have examined his proposal in detail and have generally supported his original conclusions. For the purposes of this discussion of the impact of scholarly research on the problem of reading the Book of Kings as a whole, it is not necessary to review in detail the arguments of the scholars writing in reaction to Cross's proposal. However, it is important to note the kinds of evidence which these later studies brought to bear on the investigation. Rather than focusing primarily on the themes in

Kings as a clue to the unity or disunity of the text, as did Noth, von Rad, Wolff, and, to a certain extent, Cross himself, subsequent scholarship has paid increasing attention to editorial markers found in distinctive vocabulary and in the various formulas that signal the beginning and end of the book's regnal accounts. Thus, for example, Richard Nelson has reinforced Cross's thematic observations with a careful linguistic study of terms that he takes to be characteristic of each of the two editors of Kings, and has correlated the study of this vocabulary with a close examination of the formulas used in the editorial process. Changes in both of these items are thought to support Cross's argument for an original Josianic edition of Kings followed by an exilic edition.[14] Similar signs of editorial activity have been collected by Gary Knoppers, whose massive study of the question also vindicates the basic outlines of Cross's position.[15] Finally, Steven McKenzie has reexamined all of the evidence adduced in the debate and agreed that Cross was correct in positing a Josianic edition of Kings, but McKenzie feels that the exilic editorial expansions of this original edition were not as systematic as Cross suggested.[16]

Using the same types of evidence but reaching somewhat different conclusions, Iain Provan has focused on the formulas used to evaluate the reigns of the Judean kings and has noted in this material the importance of the removal or non-removal of the high places. He has then suggested that the disappearance of this motif with the account of Hezekiah's reign indicates an initial edition of Kings in or shortly after Hezekiah's time, with later editorial additions designed to bring the book up to date.[17] Similar conclusions, based on a careful analysis of the formulaic evidence, have been reached by Baruch Halpern and David Vanderhooft, who suggest an initial edition in Hezekiah's reign, with later editorial updates in the time of Josiah and in the exile.[18]

Taking a somewhat different approach from those scholars reacting to Cross's proposal, several German scholars have used linguistic and formulaic analysis to propose a three-redaction hypothesis that does not resemble the ones discussed above. According to this way of reconstructing the editorial history of Kings, the basic text of Kings was created about 580 BCE by a Deuteronomistic writer designated DtrG. Not long after this first edi-

---

[14] Nelson, *Double Redaction.*

[15] Gary Knoppers, *Two Nations Under God: The Deuteronomistic History of Solomon and the Dual Monarchies* (2 vols., HSM 52, 53; Atlanta: Scholars Press, 1993, 1994).

[16] McKenzie, *Trouble with Kings,* esp. 135–145.

[17] Iain W. Provan, *Hezekiah and the Books of Kings: A Contribution to the Debate About the Composition of the Deuteronomistic History* (BZAW 172; Berlin: de Gruyter, 1988).

[18] Baruch Halpern and David S. Vanderhooft, "The Editions of Kings in the 7th–6th Centuries B.C.E.," *HUCA* 62 (1991) 179–244.

tion, a second Deuteronomistic writer with particular interests in prophecy (DtrP) added to the book a number of passages dealing with this theme. Finally, about 560 BCE a third Deuteronomist with legal interests (DtrN) made further additions and gave the book its final form. Rather than seeing the additional editing confined to passages after the Kings accounts of Hezekiah or Josiah, as in the theories discussed above, the German proposals locate the editing throughout the book.[19]

Rather than try to adjudicate the various proposals that have been made concerning the editorial history of Kings, the remainder of this study will grant the argument that our present book is an edited text composed of several editorial layers and will concentrate on the question of how, if at all, this situation facilitates or hinders an overall reading of the book as a whole. As a background to dealing with this question, it will first be useful to say something about the nature of edited texts and then to simply describe the nature and extent of the evidence for editorial activity that scholars have introduced into the debate.

Given the frequency with which biblical scholars appeal to the notion of edited texts, there has been relatively little attention given to the question of how one recognizes an edited text and distinguishes it from texts that are the product of a single author. The usual practice among biblical scholars has been to look for certain clues that indicate editorial activity. Among these clues are features such as shifts in characteristic vocabulary or idiom, breaks in literary or logical continuity, or contradictions in content, although much work remains to be done on the question of whether or not these items are adequate markers. Unfortunately, critics who deal with modern literature, which is mostly not composite, have not often worried about the issue, but the few studies that have been done suggest that the issue of recognizing signs of editing is more complicated than biblical scholars have usually assumed.

In one of the few thorough discussions of this issue with respect to modern literature, Jerome McGann has suggested that editors work on a text for two basic reasons. First, editorial work on a text may simply involve the correction of errors. Editors correct the mistakes that the authors have made or that have been accidentally introduced in the process of publication. Second, editors may revise a text in order to improve its effectiveness or to sharpen its impact on the reader. The editor may delete material that is considered harmful to the argument or to the cohesion of the text. Changes may be made to take into account new material that is relevant to the text, to incorporate the second thoughts of the author, or to respond

---

[19] For an example of this approach, see Walter Dietrich, *Prophetie und Geschichte: eine redaktionsgeschichtliche Untersuchung zum deuteronomistischen Geschichtswerk* (FRLANT 108; Göttingen: Vandenhoeck & Ruprecht, 1972).

to changed conditions in the study of particular subject matter. In the case of editions after the first, the editor, or even the author, may make changes in response to criticisms or questions raised by the readers or hearers of the text, and when the editor is successful in doing this, then the editor's hand should not be visible at all. Even when the reader knows that editorial changes have been made, those changes should not be visible unless the reader is able to compare the most recent edition with previous ones.[20]

Our knowledge of editorial techniques in the ancient Near East is almost non-existent, but the few studies that have been done suggest that the goals of ancient editors were similar to those of their modern counterparts. For example, studies of Mesopotamian king lists indicate that some of them were periodically updated, and the Sumerian King List was enlarged at some point in its history by the addition of a list of antediluvian kings. In some instances these changes seem to have been motivated by historiographic interests, and in other cases the scribal editors seem to have been advancing a political argument. However, the important point to notice is that the editorial changes cannot be detected without comparing the edited list with one of its predecessors.[21] The same thing seems to have been true in the case of royal inscriptions, which were periodically updated to stress new or at least different accomplishments of the king. The editors employed a variety of techniques: abbreviation, paraphrase, deletion, interpolation, harmonization, or even complete rewriting. Again, the editorial changes cannot usually be detected without comparison with earlier texts. The same seems to have been true in the case of ancient Greek historians, who organized the historical material that they received by using formulaic, stylistic, and thematic devices to unify their works and give them a sense of purpose and direction.[22]

On the other hand, some ancient Near Eastern texts show clear marks of editorial activity. The twelfth tablet of the Gilgamesh epic is an obvious example. In this case the tablet contradicts events narrated earlier in the epic, and little effort has been made to resolve the contradictions.[23]

The little evidence that is available from the ancient Near East thus suggests that when ancient editors worked on a text in a systematic way, they

---

[20] Jerome J. McGann, *A Critique of Modern Textual Criticism* (Chicago: Univ. of Chicago Press, 1983).

[21] For a thorough discussion of the king lists, see Robert R. Wilson, *Genealogy and History in the Biblical World* (New Haven: Yale Univ. Press, 1977) 56–119.

[22] For a convenient discussion of the Near Eastern evidence, as well as some useful bibliography, see Long, *1 Kings,* 17–20.

[23] Jeffrey H. Tigay, *The Evolution of the Gilgamesh Epic* (Philadelphia: Univ. of Pennsylvania Press, 1982); see also his discussion in *Empirical Models for Biblical Criticism* (ed. Jeffrey H. Tigay; Philadelphia: Univ. of Pennsylvania Press, 1985) 21–95, 149–173.

left no tracks. Their interest was in the cohesiveness of the text and in tightening its structure and sharpening its purpose. This would seem to suggest that thorough-going editing is impossible to detect. What then is to be made of the texts that contain contradictory material and that lack a cohesive structure or sharp focus? That issue still remains to be resolved and must be the subject of further study. However, it is possible that such texts follow principles of composition that are still not yet fully understood or that the texts have not been thoroughly edited. In the latter case it may be that the editors worked on certain parts of the text but left the rest of the text alone.

Against this background of what edited texts might be expected to look like, let us examine the sorts of evidence that scholars have introduced into the discussion of the composition of Kings. In general, this evidence has been of three sorts: (1) evidence of linguistic consistency, (2) evidence of structural consistency, and (3) evidence of thematic consistency.

Scholars have often attempted to use linguistic criteria to disentangle one editorial layer in Kings from another. Certain editors are said to prefer certain words and idioms that are not used by other editors, and on these grounds the work of the various editors is distinguished. Of all of the criteria employed to separate editorial layers, this one seems to be the least satisfactory. Scholars simply cannot agree in their identification of those linguistic features that are distinctive. Furthermore, the isolation of distinctive terminology is almost impossible in a book where all of the hypothetical editors are thought to be members of the same party or school. If the editors of the Deuteronomistic History were in fact all members of a Deuteronomistic movement of some sort and were all involved in carrying Deuteronomistic traditions, then it is to be expected that they would employ language that is characteristic of that tradition. The chances of a particular editor employing a radically different vocabulary are almost zero. Certainly their writing would not exhibit enough linguistic distinctiveness to permit vocabulary or idiom to be used to separate one editorial layer from another unless the items in question could be linked to separate geographical locations or time periods. Finally, it is necessary to assume that writers in any culture are quite likely to vary their linguistic usage somewhat in the course of their work. They are seldom rigidly consistent, and for this reason it is risky to use variation in the employment of language as a tool for distinguishing the work of a particular editor.

The second set of arguments that scholars have introduced into the discussion of the unity or disunity of Kings has to do with the book's structural features, particularly the formulas that are used to introduce and conclude each regnal account and those that are used to evaluate individual kings. There are three of these features that are worth noting.

First, Kings is clearly unified by the chronological notes that appear in connection with the account of each king's reign and with the reports of certain important events, such as the destruction of the Temple. Most of these notes have roughly the same form and help to give the book a coherent structure. They would fit well into Noth's theory that Kings is the work of a single author, although it is not possible to determine at what point in the growth of the book they may have been added to the present text. They could be the work of the original author, or they could just as easily be the work of later editors. In either case they clearly define the genre of Kings as historiographic literature of some sort, regardless of the historical accuracy of the material the book contains. We will return to this point below.

Second, various attempts have been made to separate editorial layers in Kings by analyzing the formulas that are used to evaluate the kings of Ephraim and Judah. Nelson has argued that most of the formulas exhibit too much variation for them to be used to distinguish particular editorial layers except in the case of the formulas that evaluate the kings of Judah who reigned after Josiah. These formulas at the end of Kings show a striking regularity, which Nelson interprets as support for Cross's theory of a Josianic and an exilic edition of the book. However, Nelson's argument may be overstated a bit. In fact, the formulas evaluating the northern kings are quite regular. All of them are said to have done evil in the sight of the Lord and to have walked in the ways of Jeroboam and in the sin which he made Israel to sin. The wording does vary a bit, but in each case the point is the same. All of the northern kings are part of a single "dynasty" or line of evil kings, who not only inherited the founder's deadly characteristics but caused the people to sin as well. This structural feature seems to be part of a consistent explanation that the fall of the north was due in the first instance to the sins of Jeroboam and in the second instance to the cumulative sins of all of the northern kings and the people. Both dimensions of this explanation appear in their clearest form in 2 Kings 17, the writer's theological reflection on the exile. However, it is not clear when this feature became part of the History. It is probably no earlier than the fall of Samaria, although it could of course be part of the final redaction of the book.

The formulas dealing with the southern kings show more variation, particularly in the language that they employ, but there are some interesting patterns. Many of the kings following David receive positive evaluations, although those closely connected with the north are evaluated negatively. Contrary to what might be expected on the basis of Cross's analysis, not all of the good kings are explicitly compared with David. Rather, good kings whose fathers were also good are said to have walked in the way of their father, while those kings whose fathers were evil are said to have walked in the way of their father David. As Provan has noted, until the time of Hezekiah all of the good kings are said not to have re-

moved the high places. On the other hand, the evaluation formula for Hezekiah is expanded to include an explicit description of his removal of the
high places. Such a note is lacking in the formulas of later Judahite kings,
including Josiah, although the narratives of Josiah's reforms do describe
his destruction of high places in both the south and the north. The point at
which the evaluation formulas for the southern kings change in a significant way thus parallels the point at which the evaluation formulas for the
northern kings end. This leaves open the possibility that at one time there
was a version of the history that traced the royal lines of the north and the
south as far as Hezekiah, as Provan, Halpern, Vanderhooft, and others
have suggested. In the north, all of the kings were the spiritual descendants of Jeroboam, who set up the shrines at Dan and Bethel and thus
caused Israel to sin and ultimately to be destroyed. In the south, in contrast, the kings did not act in a way to destroy the people, and in fact Hezekiah removed the high places and acted in accordance with God's law, thus
saving the people during the Assyrian invasion of 701.

The third structural feature of Kings that requires comment is the so-
called prophecy and fulfillment motif. Von Rad places great stress on this
motif as a unifying element in the History, but it is important to note that in
its most common form it extends only as far as the account of Jehu's revolution in the north. In this part of the History, it provides a unifying element
in the Historian's account of the northern kings by demonstrating the principle that sin on the part of an individual king inevitably leads to the destruction of that king's dynasty. In each case, a prophet addresses only the
king involved and does not concern himself with the people. When the
prophet's word is fulfilled and the king's dynasty comes to an end, the Historian duly notes its fulfillment. Examples of prophecy and fulfillment that
fall outside of the period from Jeroboam to Jehu do not fit this pattern and
do not seem to be part of the basic structure of the book. They may be a part
of individual prophetic stories or, as in the case of 1 Kings 13, they may deal
with something other than the king.

In the accounts of the southern kings, the parallel to the prophecy-
fulfillment motif is the motif of the promise to David that he will always retain a fief in Jerusalem. Although Cross highlights this motif as one of the
unifying themes of the History as a whole, in fact it appears only until the
time of Jehoram, who is the last evil king of whom it is said that for the sake
of David God did not destroy Judah (2 Kgs 8:19). The motif drops out of the
history after this point, and the later references cited by Cross (2 Kgs 19:34;
20:6) deal with God's fidelity to the city of Jerusalem and not with God's fidelity to the Davidic dynasty. It is therefore difficult to sustain the argument that the motif of preserving the Judahite dynasty "for the sake of
David" was a unifying motif of a Josianic edition of Kings. However, the
use of the motif in the evaluations of the southern kings through Jehoram

does provide an interesting contrast to the point being made by the prophecy-fulfillment notices. Up to the time of Jehu, northern kings who do evil are punished by the destruction of their dynasties. In contrast, in the south, during the same period, evil Judahite kings are not punished in the same way. Their dynasty is continued for the sake of David. Thus the prophecy-fulfillment motif and the promises-to-David motif can be said to provide structural unity to the parallel histories of the northern and southern kingdoms but not to the book of Kings as a whole, and it is possible that both motifs once played this role in a Hezekian edition of the book. However, it is equally possible that these structural features were originally part of a pre-deuteronomistic narrative of some sort.

The final collection of evidence on the unity or disunity of Kings has to do with thematic consistency in the book. Over the course of the debate on the book's editorial history, scholars have pointed to three clusters of themes thought to be useful in distinguishing the various editorial layers. The first of these is God's fidelity to the promises to David, a theme which is carried primarily by the formulaic language that we have already discussed. Two other themes can be treated more briefly. The first of these is the collection of themes concerned with explaining the destruction of Samaria and later the destruction of Jerusalem. It is in this collection that the greatest thematic inconsistencies are to be found. For the north, the explanation is complex but consistent. Samaria fell because of the sins of Jeroboam and his spiritual descendants, all of whom made Israel to sin. In the south, however, the explanations are more varied and are not easily harmonized with a history that seems to be leading up to an account of the reign of Josiah, the ideal king. On the one hand, Kings implies that Jerusalem fell because of the evils which the people had committed, although the text is never too clear on the specifics of those evils. On the other hand, the fall of Jerusalem is clearly traced to the sins of Manasseh (2 Kings 21). These two explanations are finally integrated in the same way that they are in the explanation for the fall of Samaria. Part of Manasseh's sin was that he caused the people to sin. However, in the case of Judah the literary integration of these two explanations is not as smooth as it is in 2 Kings 17. In opposition to both of these explanations is the curious notion that the exile was due to the fact that Hezekiah showed the messengers of the king of Babylon all of the Judahite royal treasures (2 Kgs 20:16–19).

The second theme that does seem to unify the History is the notion that repentance can reverse a threatened judgment or cause God to end just punishment. This theme, which has been analyzed by Wolff, appears in a number of different forms. On the one hand, it can apply to individuals, such as David or Josiah, whose repentance is rewarded with mitigated punishment. On the other hand, it may apply to the people as a whole and have the function of providing hope to the exiles from Judah. It is probable that these different uses of the repentance theme do not come from the same editorial level of the History, although much additional research will need to be done in order to resolve this issue.

Against this survey of scholarly evidence designed to demonstrate the unity or disunity of Kings, we may return to our original question of whether or not the book can be easily read as a whole literary work. Much more research would be required in order to give a fully satisfying answer to this question, but the discussion up to this point does suggest some general conclusions. As one might expect on the basis of the work of literary critics who have studied edited texts and on the basis of the few existing studies of ancient Near Eastern editorial techniques, much of the editorial work that may have gone into the composition of Kings has been carefully hidden to the point that scholars have a hard time agreeing on whether or not the signs of the editors' work exist at all. As a result, little of the literary evidence that scholars have adduced to demonstrate editorial layers in Kings has the effect of impeding a holistic reading of the book. This would certainly be true in the case of the arguments based on distinctive vocabulary, even if they were persuasive. Such vocabulary, unless it were very unusual, would not likely register on the average reader.

Many of the structural features in the book fall into the same category. As we have already noted, the chronological notes in the book definitely help to unify it and also provide the reader with clues about the literary genre into which the authors intend the book to fall. It is to be read as history, albeit a selective history and one that may not share modern standards of historiography.

The evaluation formulas are also unifying features of the book, although they may work in different ways in different parts of the narrative. They seem to be most tightly structured in the section of the book that deals with the parallel histories of the northern and southern kingdoms, and indeed, because of the small quantity of narrative material dealing with Judah before Hezekiah, the formulaic introductions, conclusions, and evaluations attached to each king sometimes carry the bulk of the historical reporting. In this portion of Kings the evaluation formulas serve to contrast the fates of the northern and southern dynasties and to give a theological explanation for that contrast. After the fall of Samaria, the function of the evaluation formulas is less clear, but it is important to note that they are still included, even though their form may change. Their presence alone gives the impression of literary unity. The same is true of the change-of-reign formulas and the death and burial notices. The small differences which scholars have detected in these formulas may well point to editorial activity, but these differences in and of themselves do not give the text a feeling of disunity. However, the same cannot be said of the prophecy-fulfillment formulas, which are quite localized and are a structural motif primarily in the long account of prophetic opposition to the dynasty of Omri. After the fall of Samaria, both the formulas and narratives focusing on prophets cease to play a major role in Kings. This suggests that the formulas and the prophetic stories themselves may have been part of an underlying narrative used by the writer(s) of Kings and should not be considered a unifying structural feature in the book as a whole.

Under the heading of thematic evidence for unity and disunity in Kings, the situation is considerably more uncertain, for in fact none of the major themes treated above seem to run consistently through the entire book. References to God's fidelity to the divine promises to David can be found up to the Hezekiah narratives, but after that point the text contains no indication that the Davidic line will be preserved, unless one wants to read such a claim into the last verses of the book. Similarly, the book provides no consistent explanation for the fall of Jerusalem and the exile, but different explanations are offered in different parts of the narrative. This is in sharp contrast to the explanations offered in 2 Kings 17 for the fall of Samaria. Finally, it seems wide of the mark to suggest that Kings is unified by the theme of repentance leading to a reversal of judgment. This motif may operate in the case of certain individuals, although even here the evidence is mixed. Josiah "repents" and reforms worship in Israel, but he still dies an untimely death. Even more important, the repentance of the people and the king in Josiah's time can do nothing to prevent the fall of Jerusalem and the exile.

All of this suggests that while many of the structural features of Kings are in the end unifying features, the overall themes of the book are not so clear. When a reader looks for such unifying themes, the book may appear disorganized in terms of its contents and interests. For example, the first part of Kings seems primarily interested in the successful opposition of prophets to the dynasty of Omri, while the story of Judah from 2 Kings 12 to the fall of Jerusalem seems to be interested in the reform of Temple worship and in the political relationships between Judah, Assyria, Babylon, and Egypt.

However, in spite of this impression of disunity in the contents of the book, Kings in fact contains two overall themes that have not previously been analyzed in detail. The first of these themes links together two theological claims: the claim that the worship of God in Jerusalem is the only legitimate form of Israelite worship, and the claim that treaties with foreign powers should be avoided on the grounds that such treaties are likely to lead to apostate worship. This theme is, of course, thoroughly Deuteronomic and appears often in the Book of Deuteronomy in the form of an injunction to avoid contact with the inhabitants of the land, who might entice Israel to worship foreign gods (Deut 7:1–6, for example). This composite theme runs throughout the Book of Kings and is first introduced in the chapters dealing with Solomon. Solomon is, of course, credited with establishing legitimate worship in the Temple, but he is ultimately condemned for making alliances with foreign nations and cementing those alliances through marriages to foreign women. These political relationships lead to heterodox worship in Jerusalem, and the result is a judgment on Solomon in the form of the loss of most of his kingdom (1 Kings 11). The history of the northern kingdom follows much the same pattern. Jeroboam was originally installed as the legitimate king over the northern tribes, but he also lured the people to worship at sites other than Jerusalem. Later his descendants repeated Solomon's error of making foreign alliances through marriage, and by so doing they introduced the worship of Baal into the royal court. The working out of the judgment against the dynasty of Omri for these violations of Deuteronomic law makes up most of the narrative of the history of the northern kingdom. While the narrative focus remains on the north, the formulaic evaluations of the southern kings keep alive the same two motifs, pointing out which kings allowed worship at the high places and which kings made foreign alliances. In the Hezekiah narratives, the king is praised for restoring unity of worship in Israel, but his flirtation with making treaties with the Assyrians is met with the strong object lesson of the Assyrian invasion of 701. Toward the end of his life the meeting with the Babylonian ambassadors is blamed, however improbably, for the eventual capture of Jerusalem by the Babylonians.

A second theme that runs throughout the book is the idea that repentance may postpone judgment but cannot eliminate it. The notion of the inevitability of judgment runs throughout many of the stories in the book, beginning with the account of Solomon's reign. He is condemned for allowing apostate worship, but the actual judgment falls on his son. The same is true of many of the northern kings, who are condemned by a prophet and told that their dynasties will come to an end, but who themselves are not punished directly. Even relatively good kings cannot turn back a promised judgment. Jehu is portrayed positively in the narrative for eliminating Baal worship in Israel, but he too is condemned for Jeroboam's sins, even though the judgment falls on the fourth generation of his line. Similarly, Hezekiah is said to have committed the sin that led to the exile, even though he himself did not experience any sort of punishment. Even Josiah, who repented and who caused the people to repent, was not able to avoid the judgment on Jerusalem, although he did not live to see it. Huldah's oracle of judgment is given before the reform, and the reform itself can do nothing to change it.

However, calling attention to these themes that help to unify the book does not lessen the feeling of disunity that is achieved by the multiple and contradictory explanations for the fall of Jerusalem and the exile. In this instance, at least, the traces of editorial activity are visible and lead to difficulties in reading Kings as a long explanation for the exile. Still, even this feature of Kings must be set in the context of the overall genre of the book. It is important to remember that Kings presents itself as historiography. By leaving their fingerprints on the exilic edition(s) of Kings, the editors may have provided a model for dealing with history and the ever-changing social and cultural situation in which Israel found itself. As the book now stands, it is a testimony to the affirmation that Israel reinterpreted its own history as it had new experiences, and it viewed its history in new ways when older interpretations no longer seemed adequate. The apparent contradictions in the text, then, may simply be an indication that history writing in Israel was not static but a continually developing, living art.

Chapter 20

Poetry Creates Historiography

Yair Zakovitch
Hebrew University of Jerusalem

The complex relations between biblical narrative (or historiography) and biblical poetry become apparent when we read the Hebrew Bible with a heightened sensitivity to intertextuality.[1] Connections between narrative and poetry may be found in various forms. In some cases, two versions of a tradition—one prose and one poetic—are located next to one another (e.g. Exod 14–15; Judg 4–5); alternatively, poetic elements may become incorporated into historiographic contexts (e.g. Gen 4:23–24, Num 21:17–18; 1 Sam 2:1–10; Jonah 2:2–10). Prophets interpreted—and midrashized—historiographic pieces, as in Jer 49:15 (Obad 2), which interprets verses in the Jacob cycle (Gen 27:42; 25:43; 25:34),[2] or Mal 2:11–12, which uses various elements from Genesis 38 in order to convey its objection to foreign women.[3] We also find prose titles added to psalms, thereby "revealing" the circumstances in which the poems were created, and so granting them an additional dimension.[4] Historical psalms (e.g. Ps 78:1–5) retell biblical history, making their own selection from biblical historiography and reshaping the events so

---

[1] For intertextuality within biblical literature, see e.g. D. N. Fewell (ed.), *Reading Between Texts: Intertextuality and the Hebrew Bible* (Louisville, Ky.: Westminster/John Knox, 1992).

[2] See Y. Zakovitch, *An Introduction to Inner-Biblical Interpretation* (Hebrew; Even Yehuda: Rekhes Hotsa'ah le-Or, Proyektim Hinukhiyim, 1992) 78.

[3] See A. Shinan and Y. Zakovitch, *The Story of Judah and Tamar: Genesis 38 in the Bible, the Old Versions and the Ancient Jewish Literature* (Hebrew; Jerusalem: The Hebrew University of Jerusalem, 1992) 230–31.

[4] See e.g. E. Slomovic, "Toward an Understanding of the Formation of Historical Titles in the Book of Psalms," *ZAW* 91 (1979) 350–80.

that they fit the psalmist's message.[5] The types of connections between historiography and poetry are indeed many.[6]

In this paper I will deal with a very specific phenomenon, a subcategory within this group: cases where the elaboration of historiographic traditions—and the creation of new ones—was inspired by the connections the author created between a historiographic tradition and a biblical poem or prophecy. Evidence of this type of elaboration may already be found within the borders of the biblical canon. That said, I will be discussing examples from many different canons. In many ways, any canon is a random collection of literature, with different religious groups holding to different canons. What is an extra-biblical book for one group may thus be found in the Scriptures of another congregation. Even more: A book that is in one canon may appear—but in a different version—also in others.

An examination of texts from the multiplicity of canons leads us to conclude that there is no actual difference between the types of interpretation/elaboration in the Hebrew Bible and those revealed in extra-biblical literature. The examples of historiographical elaborations caused by biblical poetry that will be presented here are gathered from different sources: extra-biblical compositions, textual witnesses, and even secondary elements such as additions and interpolations to biblical narratives.

I

I begin with cases where the source for elaborating the historiographic tradition is a poem that is, one way or another, related to it.

1. The historical Psalm 105 adds a detail to the life story of Joseph which has no basis in Genesis 39: "His feet were subjected to fetters; an iron collar was put on his neck" (Ps 105:18).[7] Genesis 39 tells us indeed that Joseph's master put him in prison, "So Joseph's master had him put in prison, where the king's prisoners were confined" (v. 20), but the dramatic presentation of Joseph being fettered seems to be the psalmist's own interpretative elaboration of the prison scene. In Joseph's "autobiographical report" in the *Testament of Joseph*, the information from the psalm is already incor-

---

[5] See e.g. Y. Zakovitch, "'He Did Choose the Tribe of Judah . . . He Chose David His Servant'—Ps 78: Sources, Meaning and Message," in *David King of Israel Alive and Enduring?* (Hebrew; Jerusalem: Simor, 1997) 117–202.

[6] I do not discuss here the impact biblical poetry (including prophecy) had on extra-biblical characters and their biographies, the most important example of which is of course the "biblical biography" of Jesus in the New Testament, which is related—overtly and covertly—to many biblical poems and prophecies.

[7] All quotations from the Hebrew Bible follow *Tanakh, the Holy Scriptures: The New JPS Translation According to the Traditional Hebrew Text* (Philadelphia: Jewish Publication Society, 1988).

porated into the central narrative: "They sold me into slavery; the Lord of all set me free. I was in bonds and he loosened me" (1:5–6).[8]

2. In the *Testaments of the Twelve Patriarchs*, the speakers, Jacob's sons, often incorporate elements from the blessing of their father (Genesis 49) into their biography. The example of Jacob's blessing of Zebulun will suffice: "Zebulun shall dwell by the seashore; he shall be a haven for ships and his flank shall rest on Sidon" (Gen. 49:13). In his testament, Zebulun presents himself as a culture-hero, the pioneer sailor: "I was the first to make a boat to sail on the sea, because the Lord gave me understanding and wisdom concerning it" (6:1). The whole chapter is actually dedicated to Zebulun's sailing and shipping career.[9]

3. Disagreements between the prose report of the battle against Sisera in Judges 4 and its poetic partner in chapter 5 are well-recognized.

a. The poem bestows a mythological atmosphere on the battlefield scene: "The stars fought from heaven, from their courses they fought against Sisera" (v. 20). In *Biblical Antiquities* the two biblical accounts are integrated into one paraphrastic composition, so that we are not surprised to find the echoes of Judg 5:20 in the narrative: "And when Deborah and the people and Barak went down to meet the enemies, immediately the Lord disturbed the movement of his stars. And he said to them, 'Hurry and go . . .' And when these words had been said, the stars went forth as had been commanded them and burned up their enemies. . . ." (31:2).[10]

b. Sisera's mother, a queen-mother type not mentioned in Judges 4, plays a decisive role in Judg 5:28–30. Encouraged by her ladies-in-waiting, this mother waits expectantly for her son's victorious return with the spoils of war—including many young women—while he has already been killed by a woman. Pseudo-Philo skillfully uses the mother's words, "they must be dividing the spoil they have found: a damsel or two for each man" (Judg 5:30), in order to avoid a possible problem for readers of Judges 4. In that chapter, Sisera's humiliating death by a woman may be understood as the punishment for Barak, who insisted that Deborah accompany him to the battlefield, "'If you will go with me, I will go; if not, I will not go.' 'Very well, I will go with you,' she answered. 'However, there will be no glory for you in the course you are taking, for then the Lord will deliver Sisera into the hands of a woman'" (vv. 8–9). Pseudo-Philo incorporates the idea from chapter 5—Sisera's mother's eager anticipation of the plundered women—

---

[8] H. C. Kee in *OTP* 1.773–828. For a similar tradition, see Josephus *Ant.* 2.60.

[9] For similar elaborations in *Testaments of the Twelve Patriarchs*, based on Jacob's blessings in Genesis, see e.g. Issachar (Gen 49:14 and *T. Issachar* 3:5); Gad (Gen 49:19 and *T. Gad* 1:2–3); Naphtali (Gen 49:21 and *T. Naphtali* 2:1).

[10] The translation of Pseudo-Philo follows D. J. Harrington in *OTP* 2.297–377. For a similar impact of the poetry on the prose, see Josephus, *Ant.* 5.205.

into Sisera's own speech before he attacks Israel, thereby supplying Sisera's pride as the reason for his deliverance into Yael's hands: "'I am going down to attack Israel with my mighty arm, and I will divide their spoils among my servants, and I will take for myself beautiful women as concubines.' And on account of this the Lord said about him that the arm of a weak woman would attack him . . . and even he would fall into the hands of a woman" (31:1).

4. With Gen 4:13–15 we find a narrative elaboration within the same chapter as the poem which inspired it. In his poem, Lamech praises himself as he speaks to his wives: "Adah and Zillah, hear my voice; O wives of Lamech, give ear to my speech. I have slain a man for wounding me, and a lad for bruising me. If Cain is avenged sevenfold, then Lamech seventy-sevenfold" (Gen 4:23–24). The words, "If Cain is avenged sevenfold" are interpreted in the story that precedes the poem. When Cain expresses his anxiety, ". . . anyone who meets me may kill me" (4:14), God resounds, "I promise, if anyone kills Cain, sevenfold vengeance shall be taken on him" (v. 15). Verses 13–15 were added in order to make sense of the otherwise unclear poem. Their secondary nature is clear from the interruption they present to the natural continuity of the narrative, between the beginning of the etiological explanation of the name "the land of Nod [= wandering]," and its end, between the words, "You shall become a ceaseless wanderer (נע ונד) on earth" (v. 12), and v. 16: "and Cain left the presence of the Lord and settled in the land of Nod (נוד) east of Eden."

5. One of the briefest historiographic traditions in the Bible was created in order to solve a mystery in a neighboring poem: The single verse telling about the judge Shamgar—"After him came Shamgar son of Anath, who slew six hundred Philistines with an oxgoad. He too was a champion of Israel" (Judg 3:31)—has become dislocated, breaking, as it does, the intended continuity between the story of Ehud (chap. 3) and the beginning of chap. 4: "The Israelites again did what was offensive to the Lord—Ehud now being dead" (v. 1).

The Shamgar tradition is a midrashic interpolation created in order to identify the previously unknown Shamgar who is mentioned in Deborah's poem: "In the days of Shamgar son of Anath, in the days of Jael, caravans ceased, and wayfarers went by roundabout paths" (Judg 5:6). As with Jael, the wife of Heber the Kenite (4:17; 5:24), Shamgar of the poem is not an Israelite:[11] his name testifies to a Hurrian origin.[12] The short story about his heroic deed was created under the influence of a similar salvation tradition

---

[11] See C. F. Burney, *The Book of Judges: With Introduction and Notes* (London: Rivingtons, 1918) 113.

[12] See B. Maisler, "Shamgar ben Anath," *PEQ* (1934) 192–4.

about Shammah son of Age (2 Sam 23:11–12)[13] who overcame the Philistines. Typical of secondary additions in the Bible, this tradition became
misplaced.[14] In some Septuagint manuscripts, the story of Shamgar follows the Samson cycle (after 16:31), because Shamgar, like Samson, fought
the Philistines, and especially because his victory with no real weapon in
his hand recalls Samson's killing of a thousand Philistines with the jaw-
bone of an ass (15:15). We may even speculate that the Shamgar tradition
was created after the Deuteronomistic redaction of the book of Judges,
since the Shamgar story lacks the common redactory formulas, and because
his victory is not attributed to God.

II

In the next series of examples, an historiographic narrative was elaborated
using a poem which was not previously related to it.

6. Enumerating the transgressions of Israel, the prophet Amos says,
"For three transgressions of Israel, for four, I will not revoke it: Because
they have sold for silver those whose cause was just, and the needy for a
pair of sandals" (2:6). Among the early interpreters of Amos were those
who wished to understand the general statement of Amos 2:6 as related to
a specific individual. They identified the poor victim with Joseph, the only
biblical character sold for silver: "when Midianite traders passed by, they
pulled Joseph up out of the pit. They sold Joseph for twenty pieces of silver
to the Ishmaelites, who brought Joseph to Egypt" (Gen 37:28).

In his testament, Zebulun speaks of the sale of Joseph: "'I had no share
in the price received for Joseph, my children. But Simeon, Gad, and our
other brothers accepted the money, bought shoes for themselves, their
wives, and their children. "We will not use the money for eating, which is
the price of our brother's blood, but we will trample it underfoot in response to his having said he would rule over us. Let us see what comes of
his dreams"'" (3:1–6).[15] The reason Simeon is blamed for accepting the
money is that he is the brother whom Joseph arrests when his brothers
came to buy food in Egypt (Gen 42:24). Joseph's motive for singling out
Simeon is now supplied by Zebulun's testament. Regarding the other two

---

[13] See P. Haupt, "Die Schlacht von Taanach" *BZAW* 27 (1914) 199–200; Maisler,
"Shamgar ben Anath," 192–4.

[14] See e.g. the different locations of the addition concerning the healing of Hezekiah in the different versions of the story (2 Kgs 20:7; Isa 38:21–22 and 1QIsaᵃ) and
see Y. Zakovitch, "Assimilation in Biblical Narrative," in *Empirical Models for Biblical
Criticism* (ed. J. Tigay; Philadelphia: Univ. of Pennsylvania Press, 1985) 181–5.

[15] See also *Targum Jonathan* to Genesis 37. According to *Pirqe de-Rabbi Eliezer* 38,
all brothers get shoes for the sale; see L. Ginzberg, *The Legends of the Jews* (New York:
Jewish Publication Society, 1947) 5.330 n. 51.

brothers, they are the firstborn of Bilhah and Zilpah, Jacob's concubines. Concerning these women's sons, "Joseph brought bad reports . . . to their father" (Gen 37:2), so that it is quite natural for them to seek revenge.

The three brothers use the sandals they buy for a measure-for-measure punishment: The pretentious Joseph wished to rise above his brothers, so they put him (i.e. the shoes purchased with the silver they received for selling him) under their feet.

7. The prophet Zephaniah threatens the ruling class of Judah: "I will also punish on that day everyone who steps over the threshold, who fill their master's palace with lawlessness and fraud" (1:9). What does the prophet mean regarding the "stepping over the threshold"? Is it a crime, a foreign custom that penetrated Jerusalem's cult, like the transgression mentioned in the previous verse: "I will punish the officials and the king's sons, and all who don a foreign vestment" (v. 8)? Another possibility is that stepping over the floor is a legitimate custom, but the prophet expresses disgust with his people who do not hesitate to tread underfoot social justice, to "fill their master's palace with lawlessness and fraud," and yet they are very keen on observing religious customs.

1 Sam 5:1–5, the story of the miracle of the Ark of God performed in the house of the Philistine god Dagon, is the only other evidence for the custom of not treading on the threshold. This etiological narrative even makes this specific event the reason for its creation: "That is why, to this day, the priests of Dagon and all who enter the temple of Dagon do not tread on the threshold of Dagon in Ashdod" (v 5). It is not surprising then, that interpreters of Zephaniah understood Zeph 1:9 as related to a foreign custom. *Targum Jonathan* to the Prophets even added words to Zeph 1:9 which make overt the relationship between the two texts: ". . . who step over the threshold [who follow the customs of the Philistines = המהלכין בנימוסא דפלישתאי], who feel the house of their master . . ."

What is important to us is the impact Zephaniah had on Samuel. In one of the textual witnesses, the Septuagint, a few words were added at the very end of v. 5: ὅτι ὑπερβαίνοντες ὑπερβαίνουσιν, "but step over it." The Hebrew behind these words should be reconstructed as כי דלג ידלגו.[16]

8. The next example allows us to follow closely the process of elaboration. There are two editions of the next tradition in the Bible: one in Kings (which is the original), and one in Chronicles (the elaborated one). The poem that initiated the addition was written after the book of Kings reached its final form and before the book of Chronicles was created.

In 2 Kgs 14:7 we read about King Amaziah: "He defeated ten thousand Edomites in the Valley of Salt and he captured Sela (the rock) in battle and renamed it Joktheel . . ." The elaborated edition of Chronicles reads: "Ama-

---

[16] See also *Midrash Shemuel* 17.

ziah took courage and, leading his army, he marched to the Valley of Salt. He slew ten thousand men of Seir; another ten thousand the men of Judah captured alive and brought to the top of Sela. They threw them down from the top of Sela and every one of them was burst open" (2 Chr 25:11–12). The source for Amaziah's cruel vengeance, throwing Edomites from the top of Sela, is the exilic psalm in which the psalmist identifies Edom and Babylon, since Edom was already a symbol for Israel's worst enemies: "Remember, O Lord, against the Edomites the day of Jerusalem's fall; how they cried, 'Strip her, strip her to her very foundations!' Fair Babylon, you predator, a blessing on him who repays you in kind what you have inflicted on us; a blessing on him who seizes your babies and dashes them against the rocks [= sela]" (Ps 137:7–9).[17]

III

In the previous section we dealt with elaborations of existing traditions caused by poems which were artificially associated with the narratives. In this, last, section, I will discuss stories whose very creation resulted from midrashic interpretations of poems which were unrelated to the protagonists and their life stories.

9. One of the Greek additions to the book of Daniel tells about the courageous Daniel who proves to the king that neither Bel nor the Dragon were gods. The writer—who wished to strengthen the image of Daniel as the actively belligerent monotheist—a potential martyr who did not hesitate to risk his own life for the sake of truth and the glory of God—used two verses from Jeremiah 51 as the springboard for his creation: "Nebuchadnezzar King of Babylon devoured me . . . he swallowed me like a dragon, he filled his belly with my dainties . . ." (v. 34); "And I will deal with Bel in Babylon, and make him disgorge what he has swallowed . . ." (v. 44).[18]

The two scenes of the addition tell indeed about the gods' eating habits. Though Bel doesn't eat, everybody, including the king, believes that he does because of the cunning of his priests (vv. 1–22). The dragon, on the other hand, does eat, but his stupidity is such that Daniel can kill him with the dish he prepares for this purpose (vv. 23–26). The narrator switched the narrative order of the Dragon and Bel from that in Jeremiah 51 out of a desire to create literary gradation: The challenge to prove that Bel, a mere image, is not a god is easier than killing the enormous and infamously

---

[17] For another elaboration of a biblical narrative, we may look at the relation between Genesis 34, based on a poem, and Jacob's words to Simeon and Levi in Gen 49:5–7; see Y. Zakovitch, "Assimilation in Biblical Narrative," 185–92.

[18] See C. H. Ball, "The Additions to Daniel," in *Apocrypha of the Speaker's Commentary* (ed. H. Wace; London: J. Murray, 1888) 346.

voracious dragon. Daniel indeed fills the dragon's belly, though with a lethal mixture: "Then Daniel took pitch, fat, and hair, and he brewed them together and made patties and fed them to the dragon. The dragon swallowed them and burst open" (v. 27). The prophecy is thus materialized in the narrative.

10. The mourner's call to God to look on Zion's terrible calamity in Lam 2:20—hungry mothers eating their newborn children and the murder of priests and prophets, God's servants, in his Temple—served the Chronicler in creating a narrative about the sin of King Joash, who sent his messengers to kill a priest—a prophet in the Temple's court (2 Chr 24:20–22).

Lam 2:20	2 Chr 24:20–22
See, O Lord, and behold, to whom You have done this! Alas, women eat their own fruit, their new-born babes! Alas, *priest* and *prophet* are slain in the Sanctuary of the Lord!	Then the spirit of God enveloped Zechariah son of Jehoiada the *priest;* he stood above the people and said to them, "Thus God said: 'Why do you transgress the commandments of the Lord when you cannot succeed? Since you have forsaken the Lord, he has forsaken you.'" They conspired against him and pelted him with stones in the court of the House of the Lord by order of the king. King Joash disregarded the loyalty that his father Jehoiada had shown to him, and killed his son. As he was dying, he said: "*May the Lord see* and require it."

The Chronicler needed to create a martyrdom story in order to justify the death of the king by two conspirators: "His courtiers formed a conspiracy against Joash and assassinated him at Bet-Milo that leads down to Silla" (2 Kgs 13:21). According to the Chronicler's concept of retribution, a terrible sin must precede such a disgraceful death and justify it, as a measure-for-measure punishment. In Chronicles, the king's death follows the story of Zechariah's murder and is overtly related to it: ". . . his courtiers plotted against him because of the murder of the son of Jehoiada the priest, and they killed him in bed" (2 Chr 24:25).[19] The attribution of such a crime to the king—the killing of a prophet—conforms to the Chronicler's interest in martyrology (see 2 Chr 16:7–10; 25:15–16). This view, characteristic of the time, is expressed also by Nehemiah: "They killed your prophets who admonished them to turn them back to you" (9:26).[20]

---

[19] For the Chronicler's concept of retribution, see e.g. S. Japhet, *The Ideology of the Book of Chronicles and Its Place in Biblical Thought* (Frankfurt am Main: P. Lang, 1989) 150–57.

[20] See A. Rofé, *The Prophetical Stories* (Jerusalem: Magnes, 1988) 197–213.

A by-product of the Chronicler's martyrdom tradition is the covert name-derivation of Zechariah (זכריה): "King Joash disregarded (ולא זכר) the loyalty that his father Jehoiada had shown to him . . ." (v. 22). The Chronicler does not miss an opportunity to create name-derivations (mostly covert ones), of which there are many examples.[21] The Zechariah episode, based on Lam 2:20, interprets the words of the lament: While the poetic verse intends that both calamities—parental cannibalism and the brutal death of priests and prophets in Jerusalem's Temple—occurred during the destruction of Jerusalem by the Babylonians, for the Chronicler the future cannibalism of children will be Jerusalem's punishment for killing a priest and a prophet—or a priest who is a prophet—Zechariah, son of Jehoiada, in the Temple.

The Gospels also correlate the destruction of the Temple (but the second one) to the killing of prophets (including Zechariah): "That upon you may fall the quiet of all the righteous blood shed on earth, from the blood of righteous Abel to the blood of Zechariah, the son of Berechiah,[22] whom you murdered between the temple and the altar. . . . O Jerusalem, you that killed the prophets, and stoned them, which are sent unto you . . . Behold, your house is left unto you desolate" (Matt 23:35–37; see also Luke 11:50–51).[23]

The rabbis, sensitive readers of the biblical text, exposed the relationship between our two biblical texts and used Chronicles for interpreting the verse in Lamentations:

> The story of Doeg ben Joseph whom his father left to his mother when he was a young child: Every year his mother would measure him by handbreadths and would give his [extra] weight in gold to the sanctuary. And when Jerusalem was surrounded, she slaughtered him and ate him, and concerning her Jeremiah lamented: "See O Lord, and behold, to whom You have done this! Alas, women eat their own fruit, their newborn babes!"

[21] See M. Friedländer, *Die Veränderlichkeit des Namen in dem Stammenlisten des Bücher der Chronik* (Berlin, 1903).

[22] Changing the father's name from Jehoiada to Berechiah can be explained as a midrashic identification between Zechariah of the story and the prophet "Zechariah son of Berechiah son of Iddo" (Zech 1:1). It is worth mentioning that the family line of the prophet as mentioned in Zech 1:1 is already derived from a midrashic identification between him and another Zechariah. In other references to the prophet Zechariah the name Berechiah does not appear, and Iddo is the prophet's father (Ezra 5:1; 6:14). It seems that the words "son of Berechiah" at the title of the book of Zechariah are a secondary element, added in order to identify him with Zechariah son of Jeberechiah (Isa 8:2); see e.g. S. H. Blank, "The Death of Zechariah in Rabbinic Literature," *HUCA* 12–13 (1937–1938) 327–350.

[23] These verses in Matthew and Luke may testify that the writers of the Gospels knew the same collection of Hebrew Scripture which we know: from Genesis to Chronicles.

(Lam 2:20). Whereupon the Holy Spirit replied: "'Alas, priest and prophet are slain in the sanctuary of the Lord' (Lam 2:20)—this is Zechariah ben Jehoiada." (*Sifra, beHukotai* 6:3)

*   *   *

In this paper we have seen how texts serve as building blocks for the elaboration of other texts, and even for the creation of new ones. Sometimes the elaboration is motivated by the need to bring two parallel (and even neighboring) traditions, one prose and one poetic, into agreement. In other cases, the linguistic association with an otherwise unrelated poem may stimulate the elaboration. We also find cases when the historiographer's ideology necessitates the creation of a new piece of narrative, the materials for which he collects from a well-known biblical poem.

The elaboration—or the new story—may appear either in an extra-biblical composition, in one of the textual witnesses, or even within the biblical text. The phenomenon is the same, but its expressions are reflected in a variety of literary contexts created over many centuries. Realizing that the same phenomenon which finds overt expression in extra-biblical compositions finds covert expression within the Bible should encourage further study of extra-biblical literature and its modes of interpretation, knowledge which will assist us in discovering parallel modes of interpretation and literary creativity within the biblical corpus.[24]

---

[24] See Zakovitch, *Introduction to Inner-Biblical Interpretation* (n. 2, above), 131–5.

Brown Judaic Studies

Brown Studies on Jews and Their Societies

Brown Studies in Religion

2004. 08. 09B   59.95 (5.04)